THE SOCIAL CHILD

THE SOCIAL CHILD

edited by

Anne Campbell
Durham University, UK

Steven Muncer
Teesside University, UK

Psychology Press
a member of the Taylor & Francis group

Copyright © 1998 by Psychology Press Ltd.
a member of the Taylor & Francis group

Psychology Press Ltd., Publishers
27 Church Road
Hove
East Sussex, BN3 2FA
UK

British Library Cataloguing in Publication Data
A catalogue record for this book is available from the British Library.

   ISBN 0-86377-822-4 (hbk)
   ISBN 0-86377-823-2 (pbk)

Typeset by Acorn Bookwork, Salisbury, Wiltshire
Printed and bound in the United Kingdom by
Biddles Ltd, Guildford and King's Lynn

To Jamie, children everywhere
and their fathers and mothers who bore them

Contents

List of contributors

Anne Campbell, Psychology Department, University of Durham, South Road, Durham DH1 3LE, UK.

Charles Crook, Department of Human Sciences, Loughborough University, Loughborough, Leicester LE11 3TU, UK.

Helen Demetriou, Institute of Psychiatry, De Crespigny Park, Denmark Hill, London SE5 8AF, UK.

Nicholas Emler, Department of Experimental Psychology, University of Oxford, South Parks Road, Oxford OX1 3UD, UK.

David P. Farrington, Institute of Criminology, Cambridge University, 7 West Road, Cambridge CB3 9DT, UK.

Willard W. Hartup, Institute of Child Development, University of Minnesota, 51 East River Road, Minneapolis MN 55455-0345, USA.

Dale F. Hay, Department of Social and Political Sciences, Cambridge University, Free School Lane, Cambridge CB2 3RQ, UK.

Gustav Jahoda, Department of Psychology, University of Strathclyde, Turnbull Building, 155 George Street, Glasgow G1 1RD, UK.

Peter Kutnick, Faculty of Education, Downshire House, Roehampton Institute, Roehampton Lane, London SW15 4HT, UK.

Kevin MacDonald, Psychology Department, California State University, Long Beach, California 90840-0901, USA.

Iain Manson, Faculty of Education, Downshire House, Roehampton Institute, Roehampton Lane, London SW15 4HT, UK.

Harry McGurk, Director, Australian Institute of Family Studies, 300 Queen Street, Melbourne 3000, Australia.

Mark Meerum Terwogt, Developmental Psychology, Free University of Amsterdam, Van der Boechorstraat 1, 1081 BT Amsterdam, The Netherlands.

Steven Muncer, Psychology Department, School of Social Sciences, University of Teesside, Middlesbrough, Cleveland TS1 3BA, UK.

David C. Rowe, School of Family and Consumer Resources, Division of Family Studies, University of Arizona, Tucson, Arizona 85721, USA.

John Shotter, Department of Communication, University of New Hampshire, Durham, New Hampshire 03824-3586, USA.

Hedy Stegge, Developmental Psychology, Free University of Amsterdam, Van der Boechorstraat 1, 1081 BT Amsterdam, The Netherlands.

Grace Soriano, Australian Institute of Family Studies, 300 Queen Street, Melbourne 3000, Australia.

Acknowledgements

We would like to thank the Society for Research in Child Development which granted permission for Dr Hartup's presidential address, to the biennial meeting, April 1995, Indiana, USA: "The company they keep: Friendships and their developmental significance" to be reproduced in this volume.

We would also like to thank *American Scientist* for giving us permission to use Professor Kagan's table and Professor Dasen for giving permission for his figure to be used, both in Professor Jahoda's chapter "Cultural influences on development".

Theories

1 Something happened: Fission and fusion in developmental psychology

Anne Campbell
University of Durham, Durham, UK

Steven Muncer
University of Teesside, Middlesbrough, UK

Once, about thirty years ago, social developmentalists saw the child as the end-point of a multistage process. Like a tiny Russian doll, the child was at the centre of an increasingly larger set of forces each one constraining the form and the scope of the one that it contained. The layers of influence could be unpacked beginning with the biggest doll of all culture. Culture was the reservoir of socially transmitted values and meanings. It might place a superordinate value on individualism and competition or on social cohesion and co-operation. It might emphasise the essential distinction between the sexes or minimise them. It also contained and directed its own internal organisation so that social structure (gender, class, ethnic, and age relations) varied from one culture to another. Within these structural niches, lived families composed of two parents whose overall orientation to socialisation was derived from their class position (via structural or subcultural influences) and orchestrated the style of child rearing that they adopted. This style might be authoritarian or permissive, neglectful or child-centred, involving or excluding extended family members. Within the family, the mother–child dyad was the principal unit for the transmission of social standards and styles of behaviour. Because this model placed the mother at the nearest point of influence to the child, she was held accountable for almost every child dysfunction. Bad mothers made bad children and mothers shouldered the blame for the deleterious effects of their too-zealous or too-lax toilet training, too much or too little discipline, cold or suffocating relationships, or maternal employment. (They rarely received much praise for children who turned out well.) In the very centre of these nested influences was the infant. Rousseauesque innocent, asocial egocentrist, or unprogrammed information-processing system—however his/her original nature was viewed, the infant was shaped by the forces of culture, social structure, parenting style, and mother–child interactions into his/her final adult form.

Then something happened. Or rather, a lot of things happened. Some were sociological—the divorce rate rose and with it single motherhood, Western women entered the work force in equal numbers to men, state communism collapsed and unfettered capitalism ascended, electronic media grew explosively so that children spent as much time watching television and playing video games as they spent in school. Some were methodological—broad studies of child-rearing styles gave way to micro-analysis of mother–child interactions, closer examination and redesigning of Piagetian tasks revealed that we had grossly underestimated the competence of the child, behavioural genetics techniques increased in sophistication, there was a disenchantment with etic laboratory studies and a focus on emic analyses which emphasised the social construction of play, mother–child relations, and even childhood itself. Some were ideological—feminists rejected essentialism and argued that gender was a socially constructed and variable concept, fathers demanded that they be admitted to the arena of child development, biologists argued that we ignore the impact of genetics at our peril and their opponents that little of psychological significance was "in our genes". Above all, there was a splitting and reforming of (sub)disciplinary alliances—evolutionary psychologists accused social psychologists of biophobia, anthropology was accused of grossly exaggerating (and even inventing) cultural diversity, and cognitivism (the dominant paradigm in the 1970s and 1980s) was attacked as reductionist and asocial.

In fact, these happenings were not as independent as we have suggested. Academics could be lined up more or less across a divide. On one hand were those who emphasised complexity, diversity, and constructionism. In general, they estimated genetic effects to be insignificant, cultural diversity to be marked, liberal social change to be beneficial, cognitivism to be individualistic, and meaning to be central to social life. On the other hand were those who emphasised singularity and determinism. In general, they estimated genetic effects to be strong, cultural diversity to be trivial, liberal social change to be the triumph of hope over experience, and the study of the individual to be central to understanding aggregate and societal levels of behaviour. This typology, like all others, is a gross oversimplification (as we hope to demonstrate) but it may give those readers whose academic career began later, a sense of what they missed. It was the kind of bifurcation of orientation that led to predictable exam questions of the kind "Is nurture more important than nature?", "What are the dangers of the experimental method?" and "Can we hope to understand children's development without an understanding of how they themselves experience childhood?". What we will do in this chapter is to offer a very personal description of the unfolding of some of the recent events that led to strange and unpredictable alliances and enmities in developmental psychology.

THE BIG BANG

In the telling of any story, beginnings have to be arbitrarily selected because history is continuous and events rarely unfold as linearly and neatly as we would wish. But we can begin when Sandra Scarr (1992) became president of the Society for Research in Child Development and gave a revolutionary presidential address entitled, with deceptive innocence, "Developmental theories for the 1990s". Prior to this time, there had been a fair bit of guerrilla warfare and sniping between environmentalists and geneticists despite attempts at diplomatic reconciliation. Plomin and Daniels (1987) from the latter camp, for example, made much of the new and important role for environmentalists revealed by behaviour genetic studies, whereas Cole and Cole (1989), for the former camp, were at pains to acknowledge that biological influences could not be ignored. Scarr summarised a number of behaviour genetic studies that demonstrated that genetic effects typically account for nearly half of the population variance on psychometric tests of personality and intelligence. Although noting that this left nearly half of the variance unexplained, she emphasised that these same studies had given clear signposts about where *not* to look. Environmental variance can be partitioned into shared and unshared components. Shared environment is that which is common to siblings within a family. It includes social class, geographical location, home resources (with its number of books, hours of permitted television watching, foods served, and so on) and, most importantly, parents. Studies showed that shared environment contributes almost nothing to twin similarity once the effect of shared genes is removed. Or to put it another way, children who are adopted resemble their biological mother more closely than their adoptive mother. Her conclusion was that parents' role is to sustain and protect their children as their genetically influenced traits developed. She noted that abuse and neglect, as examples of extreme environments, were likely to traumatically disrupt the normal epigenetic process but at the same time, the provision of enriched environmental choice for the child (access to sports, arts, and cultural experiences) would have the paradoxical effect of increasing genetic variance by allowing the genes a broader canvas on which to paint their own unique colour scheme.

This message provoked something of a response from those who had spent much of their lives examining how parenting styles affected children's temperaments and how such interventions as Headstart could improve long-term developmental outcomes. Baumrind (1993), for example, replied that Scarr seemed to be condoning half-hearted parenting by suggesting that parents' treatment of their children was immaterial and that Scarr was ignoring the massive discrepancies in the "average expectable environments" of children of different social classes and cultures. She and others took genetic studies to task for confounding their variables by ignoring selective placement of adoptees and monozygotic twins' physical similarity (see Rowe, Chapter 3). The thrust of the geneticists' reply was that if any serious confounding was going on it was in environmentalists' studies: By assuming that any parent–child resemblance arose because of a one-way causal connection between parental behaviour and child outcome, they ignored the fact that children's genotypes are given by these same parents. Hence, resemblance might occur directly because of shared genes or indirectly through passive gene effects—parents provide environments that are congenial to them and which (because their children share their genes) are also congenial to their children's developmental trajectory. (As a crude example, parents who love reading have many books. They transmit "enjoy reading" genes to their children so that they also like to read. They also have homes filled with books which encourages their child's love of reading.) What developmentalists should be doing, they countered, was to examine gene–environment relationships—of which passive effects are only one type. What about "reactive" gene–environment relationships? These could be correlated (aggressive children provoke counter-aggression from parents) or interactive (aggressive children provoke parental attempts at understanding and control which decreases the child's levels of aggression). What about "active" effects? As children develop they seek out friends, activities, and interests that are congenial to their own genotypic predisposition. The environmentalists replied that the behavioural geneticists' project was fatally flawed because they focused exclusively on similarity of personality or intelligence between parent–child pairs (Hoffman, 1991). What if parenting style worked not to make children like parents but different to them? If a mother, discontent with her own dependence, actually seeks to and succeeds in fostering in her child a strong sense of independence and autonomy, this will appear as a low correlation between parent and child and suggest that socialisation has been ineffective when in fact it has been totally successful from the parents' viewpoint. Besides the fact that parents may not socialise for similarity, they may also not socialise for personality but rather for behaviour and attitudes. Parents may be more concerned that a child grows up with good manners and an attitude of respect for others than that the child, like her parents, grows up to be low on neuroticism and high on extroversion. There were, however, a few areas of consensus. Both camps seemed to agree (for different reasons) that the way forward was the study of differences between children in the same family and both camps wanted to retain the family as a major force in children's development (also for different reasons).

Others began to doubt whether parents were as important as we (raised in Western nuclear families) have supposed. Assembled in this camp were a diverse assortment of researchers from evolutionary theory, cultural anthropology, and social psychology. They varied widely in the reasons for their scepticism about the socialising influence of the family.

MY ENEMY'S ENEMY: CULTURE AND EVOLUTION

Evolutionary theory has been something of a growth industry in the social sciences—widening its empire from biology to include neuropsychology, linguistics, medicine, and sociology. Predicated on Darwin's thesis of natural and sexual selection as an explanation of human behaviour, it takes the position that contemporary human morphology (and this includes the architecture of the mind and brain) is the result of evolutionary forces at work in the environment of evolutionary adaptation (about 200,000 years ago). Predispositions that were beneficial then have been retained so that babies are now born with the capacity and readiness to acquire language, to form attachments, to orient to and discriminate faces at an early age, to enjoy play as a means of honing skills they will later need, and a host of other things. If parents enter the picture, they do so primarily as protectors and nurturers of offspring whose altriciality has required a high degree of parental investment in each individual infant. Aside from this, parenting is most often discussed in terms of the sexual selection strategies that precede it and occasionally in terms of how early experience of a particular family structure affect the offspring's later choice of sexual strategy. (Draper and Harpending, 1982, for example, note that father-absent children may as a result of facultative expectation later pursue a similar "Cad" strategy of multiple sexual partners and short-term investment in children, rather than a "Dad" strategy of monogamous commitment.) In short, parents are seen as necessary carers of infants whose life course will be principally affected by adaptations that are common to all mankind and evolved in the Pleistocene. When evolutionary theorists use the term "innate" (and they rarely do) to describe such preadaptations, they mean not that the behaviour is unaffected by the environment but that the competence or ability expresses itself across a wide spectrum of different environments.

Now, at first blush, it might seem that evolutionary psychologists would make natural allies for behavioural geneticists. Both are relatively indifferent to "shared" environment in the form of differences between families in how they treat their children. More obviously, both are interested in the genetic bases of human behaviour. Or are they? Natural selection requires genetic variability. The hingepin of evolutionary psychology is the notion of inclusive fitness which sifts out those phenotypes (and their underlying genotypes) who reproduce less successfully than their rivals. Evolutionary psychologists are happy to acknowledge this process for the environment of evolutionary adaptation. But many are less happy to recognise that process as continuing today.

One motivation for such a view is ideological: Sociobiology (from whose ashes evolutionary psychology rose) had been tainted by an apparent association with a host of politically unacceptable views such as "determinism", "reductionism", "eugenics", and "scientific racism". Evolutionary psychologists wanted to put as much space as possible between themselves and such views. They were engaged in the study of natural selection and this entailed an attempt to recreate human prehistory by the use of archaeological data, primatology, cultural anthropology, and contemporary human universals. They rejected any interest in current genotypic variability. Others rejected human variability from a more theoretical position. They argued that the environment that humans have created has now ceased to select between viable and nonviable forms in the way it once did and thus that traditional forces of selection are at an end. Pre-term and disabled infants now survive where once they would have died, once-lethal childhood infectious diseases can be prevented by large-scale immunisation and the availability of contraception and abortion has severed the connection between sex and reproduction. These latter technologies have altered the historical connection between male status and reproductive success—successful men in the West have fewer rather than more children. Natural selection no longer selects—we do. Hence, genetic differences between individuals are of little relevance. However the most popular position was best articulated by Tooby and Cosmides (1990) whose argument hinges on the concept of "fixation". Any genetic adaptation that confers a significant advantage to its bearers will eventually become universal because non-bearers cannot compete. The adaptive trait "goes to fixation" and accounts for why all humans (barring genetic accident or environmental trauma) have two eyes, one bi-hemispheric brain, one heart, and so on. The proper subject matter for evolutionary psychology is human universals as they present prima-facie evidence of adaptedness by virtue of having gone to fixation. (Fixation means no population variance on the trait. No population variance means that it cannot be studied by behaviour genetics whose methods hinge upon the partitioning of variance.) Personality traits and IQ show variance and this is taken as evidence that the possession of high or low intelligence or extroversion cannot confer any systematic advantage for, if it had, we would all have them in the same quantity. These traits continue to show variance because they are, from the point of view of evolution, epiphenomenal and irrelevant to the process of natural selection.

Not everyone agreed and MacDonald (Chapter 2) was a dissenting voice. One counter-argument broadly argues that variability between humans is a positive benefit in an unpredictably changing environment. Sensation-seeking may not be very adaptive right now when most Westerners have to sit in an office for five days a week but one day it might come in handy—after a nuclear war, sensation-seekers might be critical in forging new civilisations while the more conservative among us starved to death in bunkers too frightened to go outside. Even without science fiction futures, it is clear that some traits will do better than others in particular environments. Athletic ability is useful for a male in a hunter-gatherer community but not especially useful for an account executive. Where a trait confers no immediate disadvantage, it will be retained because population genetic variability is a useful bulwark against an unknown future. Distributions along trait dimensions may also vary with sex. MacDonald and Campbell (Chapters 2 and 13) both consider how different traits which were associated with reproductive success in men and women might have been compounded over evolutionary time to produce average differences between boys and girls. Another view is that frequency-dependent selection maintains variability in traits. Psychopaths, who are characterised by a selfish exploitation of others and a corresponding absence of shame or remorse, can survive and flourish only if their density in the population remains low (Mealey, 1995). When too many psychopaths abound, they tend to meet the same sucker (or another psychopath) more than once and their exploitative strategy rebounds on them. So some traits are constrained by the social environment that they inhabit.

It was evolutionary psychology that expressed scepticism about the cultural diversity reported by cultural anthropologists. After all, to the extent that behaviour varied widely between cultures it seemed to suggest an absence of universality and hence a rather restricted scope for applying evolutionary theory. There were specific attacks on the reports of Mead (see Daly & Wilson, 1983) and a more general cynicism that anthropology rewarded findings of small difference while ignoring the major similarities between humans everywhere. As Tooby and Cosmides (1992, p. 92) put it:

> The best refutation of cultural relativity is the activity of anthropologists themselves, who could not understand or live within other human groups unless the inhabitants of those groups shared assumptions that were, in fact, very similar to those of the ethnographer. Like fish unaware of the existence

of water, interpretativists swim from culture to culture interpreting through universal human metaculture. Metaculture informs their every thought, but they have not yet noticed its existence.

Many evolutionary psychologists, however, took culture to be of central importance to their theoretical project and sought to bring it into the Darwinian empire. Evolutionary psychology, some argued, would never transcend mere sociobiology until it took into account the unique ability of our very social species to use language as an effective way of short-circuiting trial-and-error learning and as a way of transmitting meaning. The same words or gestures delivered in different cultures can have a different social force.

These co-evolutionary psychologists broadly fell under two headings. The first group emphasised culture as a distinct and (potentially) separate form of transmission working with memes rather than genes (Boyd & Richerson, 1985; Durham, 1991). Memes are packages of information that are transmitted not via sexual reproduction but via social interaction. A good meme survives, replicates, and inhabits the brains of its hosts because it is easy to acquire and memorable. The most extreme in this camp argued not only that natural selection of culture operates as a distinct track but that memes can often instruct behaviour that is antithetical to gene survival. (Dawkins, 1976, used the example of religion as a meme which has led to a fair amount of genocide.) Others more optimistically believed that culture would, in the long haul, favour behaviours that complemented or enhanced genetic survival via the operation of primary values (Durham, 1991). Primary values are innate evolved preferences that were called primary reinforcers in the days of behaviourism (e.g. food, warmth, sex)—behaviours that trigger dopaminergic reward systems in the brain. These values would prevent culture from complete arbitrariness because we would not endorse values and corresponding behaviours that would lead to our own destruction. Durham even argued for a reverse direction of causality whereby cultural practices would change gene pools. In a culture that employs animal husbandry and dairying, individuals whose tolerance for lactose did not extend past infancy would be less likely to survive. Hence, in the contemporary world, adult lactose absorption is higher in these cultures than in others.

In the second camp were those who saw culture as the aggregate manifestation of human genotypes. Lumsden (1988) argued that culture is the expression of and the selecting environment for traits. The distribution of many of these traits is universal but population differences can occur. An interbreeding group that must fiercely contest space and resources with a neighbouring group will develop a gene pool that favours bellicosity in males. These genotypes will be especially responsive to evaluative memes that favour aggression as a manly virtue. We can imagine "sticky" genes that pick up from the cultural pool those memes that are congenial to them. Although all these views are relatively recent and still hotly debated, they did forge an alliance between some segments of evolutionary psychology and those involved in the study of culture.

Cross-cultural psychologists have generally argued that there are no significant differences in the human genotype between different cultures or races. Babies everywhere are born with much the same distribution of abilities and traits but the specific course of their development depends on the activities, practices, and values of the culture they inhabit. As Jahoda (Chapter 4) points out, babies everywhere are able to discriminate the same set of articulated sounds but depending on the language community around them, they later lose the ability to discriminate those sounds that are irrelevant to their language. This kind of specialised and selective development can be easily imagined in the social sphere also. The degree to which there is cultural variation depends on whether we see glasses as half full or half empty. Women everywhere are the principal carers of infants and maintainers of the home. Although there is distribution overlap between the sexes, women in most cultures rate themselves as less aggressive and more nurturing than men (see Campbell, Chapter 13). Everywhere girls grow up to be women—but whether womanhood means gathering berries, working in an office, or staying at home all day depends on the culture. Culture then shapes the particular form of many universals.

It is when we come to the trickier issue of individual differences within a culture that things become more controversial. Behaviour genetics can reveal nothing directly about the impact of culture because, as Rowe (Chapter 3) notes, culture is a constant—at least for children inhabiting the same home and probably beyond that. Most children in Britain and the United States are exposed to television violence, frozen food, rock music, and so on. Therefore, cultural exposure cannot illuminate individual differences (within a culture) because it does not vary much between children. Yet individual differences exist. Perhaps there are "dosage" differences between children? Crook's Chapter 8 discusses the impact of television violence and certainly some children see more of it than others. But one problem is that, at the same level of viewing, some children show effects on their aggressive behaviour and some do not. Another problem is that we are left with the question of why some children choose to watch more of it than others. Here, there may be an avenue of connection both with behaviour genetics studies (for their answer will certainly be in terms of active gene–environment correlations) and with Lumsden's gene–culture co-evolution (where culture "sticks" differentially to different genotypes). It is doubtful that either of these two potential allies will, in fact, make congenial bedfellows for cross-cultural psychologists. Yet, a major challenge to cross-cultural psychology must be to embrace and explain individual differences between members of the same culture.

BEYOND THE FAMILY: WITH A LITTLE HELP FROM MY FRIENDS

The peer group has assumed enormous importance for researchers in the last decade as a result of a variety of sociological and epistemological changes. Ex-hippie parents who had believed that they would never "lose touch" had to acknowledge that a distinct social and cultural world of teenagers coexisted with their own. The 1980s were a time during which youth culture became commercial, lucrative, global, and self-conscious. Designer names were marketed directly to teenagers by international companies so that youth preferences were not only manipulated but universal. Teenagers became a distinct market and this focused attention on their "otherness". Younger children have been drawn in also by the kind of cross-modal marketing strategies described by Crook (Chapter 8). A trip to see a Hollywood film means the purchase of the accompanying books, videos, toys and T-shirts—with fashions changing so fast that adults can barely keep up with children's changing preferences. Parents realised that the door to this distinct world could be passed through only by their child and his peers—they were excluded and they wanted to know what was going on within.

It was a strange but genuine coincidence that just as Scarr was announcing that "good enough parenting" would do, the divorce rate was climbing in both Europe and the United States (see McGurk and Soriano, Chapter 5). Studies of divorce suggested that although neither the parents nor the children found it a positive experience, children had the additional burden of helplessness, an erroneous but profound feeling of responsibility, an apparently inexplicable change in social and economic circumstances, and a persistent nostalgia for what had been lost with little sense of better times to come. Jahoda (Chapter 4) questions whether there is anything universal or necessary about the nuclear family as a particular structure for raising children. Two cohabiting parents may not be required but the problem for the child is that he/she has developed a strong attachment to these particular individuals who have been there since his/her birth. The severing of one of these bonds is painful and it is often his/her peer group who remain constant through a time of difficult transition.

At the same time, studies in criminology had identified the peer group as a critical factor in the development of a delinquent lifestyle (e.g. Elliott, Huizing & Ageton, 1985; Raskin White, Padina, & LaGrange, 1987). Crime is rarely committed alone—most delinquency is group delinquency. Peers are critical in providing a supportive audience for the acts of daring that are so appealing to young men especially. Although some work suggested that delinquent friendships were less enduring and close than those of nondelinquents, contemporary thinking suggests that the identity of friends is more critical in predicting antisocial behaviour than the quality of the friendship (see Hartup, Chapter 6). Within criminology, however, a long-standing debate concerned the direction of causality. In the 1960s, during the heyday of subcultural theory, there had been wide consensus that a deviant peer group fostered and encouraged delinquency by according it value. Delinquent norms created delinquent behaviour. The norms were seen to arise as a reaction to failure in "straight" society either by creatively opposing middle class values, by rationalising avenues of illegitimate economic opportunity or by reaffirming traditional working class values such as short-term hedonism and exaggerated masculinity. Subcultural theorists, like cross-cultural psychologists, faced the problem of accounting for individual differences—why did some working class boys form delinquent peer groups whereas others redoubled their efforts to escape poverty through academic success or passively and noncriminally accepted their depressing economic future (Kornhauser, 1978)? Empirical findings that showed substantial stability over time for antisocial behaviour argued for another direction of causality: Birds of a feather flock together—bad boys find bad friends (Hirschi, 1969). But even when this became the dominant view, researchers concurred that delinquent careers were accelerated and amplified by the peer group. Researchers in drug abuse were rapidly reaching the same conclusions. The workings of the peer group became central to understanding and controlling antisocial behaviour. Peer programmes were initiated which tried to exploit adolescent relationships in the service of "re-norming" the group toward prosocial activities (Goldstein & Glick, 1994).

In psychology, there was a growing disenchantment with methods that seemed to have misled researchers about children's real abilities. The traditional technique of taking children out of the class and into a separate room where they were questioned about abstract and irrelevant problems ("Should Heinz steal the drug?", "Is it still a little girl now that her hair is cut short like a boy?") had highlighted the fact that the artificiality of quasi-laboratory settings failed to tap children's real abilities and behaviours. The formal wording and abstract problems lead to "incorrect" responses which were belied by children's performance in natural settings. Children's statements in interviews did not seem to correspond with their actual behaviour in real-life situations. Emler (Chapter 12) identifies this as a critical problem for cognitive approaches to moral development and proposes a radical reversal of traditional thinking about cause-and-effect relations which has placed moral reasoning in the driving seat of social behaviour. He suggests that children's understanding of the rhetorical forms by which actions can be warranted, rather than directing their behaviour, may be a discursive means by which children account for their own disapproved behaviour and control the antisocial behaviour of others. He places moral talk in the context of real social interactions, far away from the artificial abstract dilemmas presented in silent rooms by unknown experimenters. Other researchers also wanted to enter the hidden world that the children inhabited and to see how children's abilities were expressed in the social worlds that they created for themselves. Ethologists had been doing this for some time and had amassed considerable data on children's interactions in free play situations. The traditional etic approach (of experimental control and rigorous "operational definitions") was increasingly challenged by an emic approach (where children's own understandings and actions were of primary significance). To do this, researchers had to give up intervention and control and allow the peer group to express itself spontaneously. It was clear that children, for considerable periods of time every day, were engaged in a micro-community with its own structure, prohibitions, sanctions, rewards, and values. For example, while teachers tried to encourage integration between boys and girls in the classroom (see Kutnick and Manson, Chapter 7) and to reinforce gender-neutral or even cross-gendered play, children in the playground undermined the entire scheme by reverting to single-sex groups, teasing boys and girls who played together ("They're in l-o-v-e") and ridiculing as a sissy any boy who played "girls" games (Maccoby, 1990).

Another major spur to understanding the peer group came from the behaviour geneticists' revelations about the modest impact of parents. If parents do not shape their children, then who does? The peer group presented itself as a natural candidate. Harris (1995) was the first to formally spell out the theoretical link. Geneticists have found no effect of shared environment on the child's development, she argued, because they have effectively treated shared environment as meaning "shared postal address". But instead of looking at the parents' treatment of their children, we should look at the peer groups. In many societies, parents are the primary caregivers only up to the age of about four years when the child is sufficiently independent to join her peers. This group is the most important agent of socialisation because it forms the age cohort with which he/she will spend the rest of his/her life. Parents teach children how to act in the home but peers teach them how to act with their contemporaries and this is the knowledge that will fit them for life, long after they have left the parental home. Hence, two children who share a peer group should show substantially more similarity than two children taken from different peer groups in their play styles, preferred activities, and attitudes. Social identification theory (Hogg & Abrams, 1988) is introduced to elaborate between and within group differences. Groups strive to maximally differentiate themselves from other groups and this means exaggerating the differences between sex-segregated groups (see Campbell, Chapter 13) encouraging a good deal of animosity in the process ("Boys are rough and stupid"). At the same time, in-group processes encourage similarity and norm convergence and MacDonald (Chapter 2) points out how almost any minor similarity can be used as a means of cementing similarity ("Wow, we both like ice cream"). However, personal (as opposed to social) identity involves differentiation within the group so that children assume different roles (jocks, jokers, teacher's pet). An interesting question is the extent to which these two processes interact. Although we would expect groups to differ, do the roles assumed by members remain the same? And if they do, is a group A joker more similar to a group B joker than to a Group A jock? Are certain traits (e.g. an offbeat sense of humour) a prerequisite of role allocation or do these roles shape and direct the personality development of the child? Work in this area might go some way toward unifying the domains of behaviour genetics and social development already begun in Rowe's work on genetics and peer relations. But the debate will remain about directions of causal influence, interaction of variables, and final outcomes. As we shall see later, some researchers want to escape from this way of thinking.

WHERE IS THE "SOCIAL" IN THE SOCIAL CHILD?

Adult social behaviour, which most of us experience as an effortless stream, actually involves highly skilled behaviour. We understand turn-taking, accommodation to people and to settings, the rules that govern relationships and the tactical use of deception and concealment without apparent conscious awareness. As we watch children engaged in play and conversation, their behaviour already reveals astonishing sophistication. They anticipate and pre-empt, they joke and tease, they sanction and praise, they jockey for position and comfort one another, they play fight and real fight. The continuous flow of their behaviour reflects a moment-by-moment sensitivity to others and to themselves-as-seen-by-others, to their intended actions and to the unintended interpretations of them offered by others. When we look at behaviour as a stream of interpersonal actions between two children, we cannot help but wonder whether this can legitimately be frozen, categorised, measured, averaged, and used as an index of Child A's sociability or Child B's aggression. We move on now to consider interpersonal relationships, not as the meeting point of two unique constellations of intrapsychic traits, but as a fundamental competence that is common to us all. In the language of evolution, sociability is a "species typical" attribute. We have a profoundly social prehistory and it would be strange indeed if we had not evolved and retained qualities that make this possible. It is likely that one such quality is an ability to impute to others, with some degree of accuracy, beliefs and desires which explain their actions. The specificity of the deficits in this area associated with Asberger's syndrome and autism suggest that such an ability is domain-specific and domain-specificity is the hallmark of an evolutionary adaptation (see MacDonald, Chapter 2; Tooby & Cosmides, 1992).

Among those who have examined the belief–desire area there is a telling but important distinction of terminology. To call such an ability a "theory of mind" (Baron-Cohen, 1992) carries with it two distinct connotations. First, that it resides as a property within the individual child, and second, that it reflects the child's ability to abstract a theory from empirical information. The term "intersubjectivity", preferred by others (Hobson, 1990), carries different connotations for it highlights a situated interpersonal event and suggests less of a cognitive theory and more of an emotional and empathic response. This schism runs through a good deal of developmental research.

Since Piaget, there has been a strong tradition of examining age-related changes in competence. That competence is often measured by the child's success in solving problems. The role of the adult is to bring problems to the attention of the child so that the child through processes of assimilation and accommodation can elaborate their cognitive strategy. Theory of mind work has in a sense pursued this tradition by examining when children are able to impute correctly beliefs and desires to others under situations of increasing complexity (e.g. Does A know that B knows that A is lying?). As Meerum Terwogt and Stegge (Chapter 10) caution us, what children say in these hypothetical interview situations may reveal only their minimal competence. A "correct" answer clearly suggests competence but an incorrect answer may not *necessarily* reflect incompetence. The same problem they failed to answer correctly (*Question*: "Joe did not fall over but he is holding his leg and crying. Is he really hurt?" *Answer*: "Yes") may provoke a perfectly appropriate response in the playground later ("Get up—that wasn't a foul").

The main criticism of this approach, however, has been its tendency to view social competence as residing in the child rather than in the interaction: A social developmental theory that takes the "social" out of interactions between people and places it in the head of individual people fundamentally removes the very essence of what it seeks to study and turns social behaviour into a study of cognitive competence. Hay and Demetriou (Chapter 9) provide many examples of interpersonal sensitivity that predate the child's ability to develop a "theory" of the causes of other people's actions. Infants spontaneously use proto-declarative pointing to bring an object to their parent's attention although it is doubtful that they formally understand multiple perceptual perspectives or that gazing indicates attention or that their actions can alter the attentional state of others. When infants look to their mother's facial expression in a novel situation, this social referencing need not suggest a formal understanding that they can align their mood state with the attributed mood state of others. Rather, the child seems to be equipped with tools—imitation, turn-taking, responsiveness to other's distress, pointing—that are deployed appropriately within the stream of interpersonal activity that surrounds them. They emerge from the social nature of the infant and do not seem to depend on individual cognitive capabilities such as induction, inference, abstraction, and generalisation.

In line with this, new paradigm or social constructionist researchers see a particular interaction as an emergent property not reducible to the abilities of either of the two individuals who participate. An understanding of what is occurring comes from an appreciation of how meaning is given to and taken from actions as part of a particular situated interchange. The idea of unique nonreplicable events unfolding in the interpersonal space between people has an experiential appeal. Indeed, it is this resonance with personal experience that is invoked to stand in place of the theoretical detachment of traditional psychology. The key concepts here are meaning and what we will call the "space between people".

It is manifestly true that despite their concern with operationalising and objectifying social behaviour, traditional researchers also possess a normal human capacity to read meaning into children's activities. It is a tendency that in the past they have resisted. Pure behaviourism required that we record "Child shifts gaze from dog to mother" rather than "Child looks to mother for reassurance about the dog". It was resisted because meaning, like intention, was seen as located within the child and therefore as inscrutable. However, constructionists emphasise that as participants in the social community, researchers should exploit their native under-standing of meaning. The mother as a participant in the interaction understands that the child is seeking reassurance and we, observing as third parties, share her understanding. That is why we have no difficulty in decoding the social meaning of her next act which is to lean toward the child, pat the dog and say "Isn't he nice?". She is responding to an implicit request for assurance. In using the common currency of meaning, Shotter (Chapter 11) suggests we can avoid abstract theorising and in a practical way afford children developmental opportunities. The study of how language is used to create particular interpretations of situations and how such interpretations are (implicitly or explicitly) disputed and negotiated in talk has been the focus of much work in discursive and rhetorical social psychology (see Potter & Wetherell, 1987). What has emerged from some very dense and post-modern literary theorising is that, where discourse analysis is defined as the study of construction in relation to function, there is no ultimate arbiter of the "real" function or social meaning of an utterance. No one reading of the text is "privileged". Thus, where there is a dispute between the actor and the researcher about what was meant by a statement, there can be no appeal to the actor as the definitive judge of what he intended. Nor is the researcher entitled to act as psychoanalyst in divining and disputing what the actor really meant. Once a statement is made, it is no longer owned by the speaker or the listener. It has entered into the social space between people and is therefore public property. Now in analysing adults' speech and in the absence of any "true meaning" criterion, disputes about meaning can be handled by seeing which interpretation is most parsimonious and successful in informing interpretation of other things that the speaker has said. (In fact, it is rarely this easy because it is argued that change of construction signal changes in function and that functions of speech change within a given interaction. Hence, lacking any independent means of establishing change of function, change of construction stands as a proxy. This, in turn, eliminates parsimony as a criterion as consistency is not expected.) When we deal with children, meaning becomes even more problematic because of power asymmetries in the interaction. If the child's intended meaning is read as carrying a different meaning by the adult, it is that reading which will prevail. (Imagine a small child gazing through the window at the rain outside, shouting "water, water". His mother shouts from the other room "Say please if you want a drink".) Although constructivists may take this as an example of how meaning is social and interpersonally negotiated, it is nonetheless a real problem for those researchers who are more interested in what the child wants to say—rather than in the mother's power or the social process that is in operation between them. When interpretations of speech acts become more complex, so that even adults cannot agree—distinctions between real and feigned emotion, between sarcasm and sincerity, between naïvety and ingenuousness—whose meaning will prevail?

Putting the "social" back into the study of children's development, it is argued, also entails recognising the emergent or relational properties of interaction that are not decomposable into the minds of either of the two people involved. To those schooled in traditional "scientific" psychology this seems perilously close to mysticism. Shotter (Chapter 11), quoting Bakhtin, speaks of a "higher addressee" present in the interaction who evaluates and judges what occurs. Now, in one sense this strikes a chord in us. For when we speak we respond not just to what went before but to the entire situation as it now stands and to a kind of unseen listener who we imagine is nodding or shaking their heads at our statements. At a dinner party, we are often conscious of the impression we are making in relation to the current situation—of sounding pretentious or naïve, of appearing right wing or radical, of misinterpreting another's intended meaning, or offending someone. But such feelings do not have to be attributed to a metaphorical "other" if we accept that such evaluative judgements arise from the social knowledge that we possess and use to judge our ongoing performance. To say that interactions are situated, that actors have fleeting and changing goals, that we respond to the whole situation as well as to the preceding remark, that we attribute motives, beliefs, and desires to others and that we make judgements about the social and moral implications of our own and others' speech—does any of this mean that we need to invoke unseen beings or to deny the workings of mental processes in the heads of individuals? If we could perfectly know the history of A and B's relationship, how each of them viewed their own and the other's current aims and beliefs, how each of them judged and understood each action—*and* if this knowledge were available as it changed from moment to moment in the interaction, could we then relinquish terms such as "emergent" and "relational"? Can these terms, in short, be reduced to meaning a complete diachronic understanding of two individuals' dynamically changing goals and resources?

If the answer is no then, like physics, we face indeterminacy. Chaos theorists argue that a ball, starting from a uniform point, will never trace exactly the same descending trajectory twice. So, if our inability to predict a child's development is not measurement error and it is not a failure to include all the necessary components of a final explanation, then it is chance that plays a hand in one outcome rather than another. And chance is no stranger to other theoretical approaches. Behaviour geneticists identify as the largest single source of population variance, unshared environment. This includes random events and experiences that are unique to the individual and are independent of genes (gene-environment correlations are partitioned as genetic variation). It might, as Rowe (Chapter 3) notes, be a particular teacher who triggered your interest in maths, or a broken ankle that forever put you off athletic competition. More socially, it might be a fleeting interactional moment when you misread a playful push as a challenge to fight and acquired a reputation for hot temper that you could never shake off. In evolutionary theory, where so much attention has been paid to mate selection, a major factor is geographical propinquity—we can only marry those we meet and, in a peculiar sense, the college you attend might in the end determine the genes you leave behind. The peers who shape our social skills, preferences, and interests—who play a hand in whether our sensation-seeking tendencies lead us to drug abuse or mountain climbing—must be chosen from a cohort attending a certain school in a certain town at a certain time.

Perhaps God does play dice with a few parts of children's development.

REFERENCES

Baron-Cohen, S. (1992). The theory of mind hypothesis of autism: History and prospects of the idea. *The Psychologist, 5,* 9–12.

Baumrind, D. (1993). The average expectable environment is not good enough: A response to Scarr. *Child Development, 64,* 1299–1317.

Boyd, R. & Richerson, P. (1985). *Culture and the evolutionary process.* Chicago, IL: Chicago University Press.

Cole, M. & Cole, S. R. (1989). *The development of children.* New York: Scientific American Books.

Daly, M. & Wilson, M. (1983). *Sex, evolution and behavior.* Belmont, CA: Wadsworth.

Dawkins, R. (1976). *The selfish gene.* Oxford: Oxford University Press.

Draper, P. & Harpending, H. (1982). Father absence and reproductive strategy: An evolutionary perspective. *Journal of Anthropological Research, 38,* 255–273.

Durham, W. (1991). *Coevolutionary theory.* Stanford, CA: Stanford University Press.

Elliott, D., Huizinga, D., & Ageton. S. (1985). *Explaining delinquency and drug use.* Beverly Hills, CA: Sage.

Goldstein, A. & Glick, B. (1994). *The prosocial gang: Implementing aggression replacement training.* London: Sage.

Harris, J. R. (1995). Where is the child's environment? A group theory of socialisation. *Psychological Review, 102,* 458–489.

Hirschi, T. (1969). *The causes of delinquency.* Berkeley, CA: University of California Press.

Hobson, R. P. (1990). On acquiring knowledge about people and the capacity to pretend. *Psychological Review, 97,* 114–121.

Hoffman, L.W. (1991). The influence of the family environment on personality: Accounting for sibling differences. *Psychological Bulletin, 110,* 187–203.

Hogg, M. A. & Abrams, D. (1988). *Social identification.* London: Routledge.

Kornhauser, R. (1978). *Social sources of delinquency.* Chicago, IL: University of Chicago Press.

Lumsden, C. (1988). Psychological development: Epigenetic rules and gene-culture coevolution. In K. MacDonald (Ed.), *Sociobiological perspectives on human development* (pp. 234–265). New York: Springer.

Maccoby, E. E. (1990). Gender and relationships: A developmental account. *American Psychologist, 45,* 513–520.

Mealey, L. (1995). The sociobiology of sociopathy: An integrated evolutionary model. *Behavioral and Brain Sciences, 18,* 523–599.

Plomin, R. & Daniels, D. (1987). Why are children in the same family so different from one another? *Behavioral and Brain Sciences, 10,* 1–16.

Potter, J. & Wetherell, M. (1987). *Discourse and social psychology.* London: Sage.

Raskin White, H., Padina, R., & LaGrange, R. (1987). Longitudinal predictors of serious substance use and delinquency. *Criminology, 6,* 715–740.

Scarr, S. (1992). Developmental theories for the 1990s: Development and individual differences. *Child Development, 63,* 1–19.

Tooby, J. & Cosmides, L. (1990). On the universality of human nature and the uniqueness of the individual: The role of genetics and adaptation. *Journal of Personality, 58,* 17–67.

Tooby, J. & Cosmides, L. (1992). The psychological foundations of culture. In J. H. Barkow, L. Cosmides, & J. Tooby (Eds.), *The adapted mind: Evolutionary psychology and the generation of culture* (pp. 19–135). New York: Oxford University Press.

2 Evolution and development

Kevin MacDonald
California State University, Long Beach, USA

THEORETICAL BASICS

The thesis of this chapter is that evolutionary theory can make a major contribution to conceptualising children's social development. However, at the outset it is useful to begin with a few definitions and general ideas.

Evolutionists accept as a fundamental postulate that the process of natural selection over the course of evolutionary time has shaped every aspect of the human mind. Humans, like other animals, evolved a set of adaptations that functioned to solve particular adaptive problems occurring in the environment of evolutionary adaptedness (EEA)—the environment that humans evolved in and which presented the set of problems whose solutions constitute the set of human adaptations. Thus, for example, Bowlby (1969) proposed that a recurrent problem of our evolutionary past was that altricial human infants were helpless in the face of danger from predators. This problem was solved by the evolution of the human attachment system as a mechanism that reliably results in infants staying close to their mothers.

The general principle that natural selection sculpted the human mind, by itself, tells us little about the structure of the human mind and even less about development. Basic evolutionary logic, however, requires that at least some evolved systems be domain-specific (Cosmides & Tooby, 1987). Domain-specific mechanisms have two important characteristics: they evolved in order to solve a specific recurrent problem in the human EEA; the mechanisms are content-specific in the sense that they take in only a very delimited set of stimuli and, via a decision rule, produce only a limited set of outcomes which solve a highly discrete adaptive problem (Buss, 1995). Domain-specific psychological adaptations evolved in specific environments and responded to the recurrent properties of that environment. For example, the eye evolved to respond to the properties of light and the structure of surfaces as enduring and recurrent features of the environment, and children's cognitive abilities reflect adaptations to recurrent features of specific problem domains, including object construal, physical causality, motion, etc. (Gelman & Carey, 1991).

Within this perspective, then, domain-specific mechanisms are construed as species-typical universals that evolved to solve recurrent adaptive problems posed by recurrent features of the environment. However, there is every reason to suppose that domain-general mechanisms are also an important feature of human evolution. Domain-general mechanisms did not evolve to solve a specific recurrent problem in the human EEA, but rather can be utilised to solve a wide range of nonrecurrent problems. Moreover, domain-general devices would be able to take in a wide range of stimuli and produce a wide range of responses which could solve these nonrecurrent problems. Examples would be mechanisms of social learning (Boyd & Richerson, 1985, 1988) and the g factor of intelligence tests (MacDonald, 1991, 1997a,b). For example, whatever the precise nature of g at the level of proximal (neurophysiological) mechanisms, there is no reason whatever to suppose g is a domain-specific mechanism. Individuals with high intelligence perform better in complex, relatively unpredictable environments and succeed at a very wide range of tasks and occupations, so that there is no reason to construe the g factor as having evolved to solve a specific, highly circumscribed recurrent problem in the human EEA. Moreover, given the very wide range of test items involved in IQ tests and the very wide range of occupations that individuals of high IQ excel in, it is extremely unlikely that the underlying psychological mechanisms take in only a very delimited set of stimuli and produce only a limited set of outcomes which solve a highly discrete adaptive problem. From an adaptationist perspective, therefore, an essential feature of human intelligence is that intelligence facilitates the attainment of evolutionary goals (e.g. acquiring economic resources, obtaining mates, etc.), but that the nature of human intelligence is to be able to attain evolutionary goals in a very flexible manner by, for example, constructing novel solutions to nonrecurrent problems presented by an ever-changing and incredibly complex human environment. The activities that men engage in to attract mates or vanquish their adversaries may be very different now than in the remote past, but there is every reason to suppose that in both environments men, using domain-general abilities, were able to devise highly flexible strategies to attain their evolutionary goals.

Thus stated, however, an evolutionary approach must seem to be a weak theory in the sense that it makes no specific predictions about the contours of human development. In a sense this is true because it is inevitably an empirical question to ask what kind of species humans are. If humans evolved to be obligately monogamous like many bird species one would not expect to find important sex differences in behaviour resulting from males needing to compete with other males in order to obtain multiple mates. And if humans had evolved the haplo-diploid genetic system of the hymenopterans (ants, bees, and wasps), we might expect to find societies centred around sterile females co-operating to rear their sister's offspring.

Nevertheless, it is not really so hopeless as these considerations might suggest. The basic theorem of modern evolutionary biology might be phrased as "Thou shalt not construct a theory which implies that organisms are truly altruistic". A fundamental result of modern evolutionary logic is that true altruism can evolve only under very stringent conditions, and that even if it were to evolve it would tend to lose out in competition with nonaltruistic individuals within any group where it occurs (e.g. Alexander, 1987). (This is not to imply that human groups cannot impose altruism on their members, by, e.g. penalising nonaltruists in the interests of establishing cohesive groups (MacDonald, 1994; Wilson & Sober, 1994); however, this type of social regulation is not likely to be an aspect of children's evolved psychological adaptations.) The result is that an evolutionary perspective predicts that children's behaviour will be self-interested rather than truly self-sacrificing, and that children's moral reasoning, moral behaviour, and their relationships with parents and peers will reflect this generalisation.

Moreover, the enterprise of reconstructing the past can be accomplished in a principled manner. For example, there is considerable evidence that there are universal patterns of sexual dimorphism (e.g. sex differences in size) among humans that conform to patterns expected in a moderately polygynous species (Alexander, 1979). This in turn implies that an important aspect of human evolution is the development of sex-differentiated patterns of parental investment, with the implication that the human mind will reflect a human ancestral environment where females devoted more effort to parenting than males and males devoted more effort to mating than females.

This has very broad implications for the contours of children's development. At a conceptual level, organisms need to perform two very broad types of functions. They must approach the world and obtain resources related to adaptive functioning (e.g. food and mating opportunities) and they must have mechanisms for avoiding threats (e.g. predators, environmental dangers). Evolutionary theory predicts that in species with sex-differentiated patterns of parental investment, the sex with the lower level of parental investment (in this case, males) will pursue a more high-risk strategy compared to females, including being more inclined to have their behavioural approach and behavioural avoidance mechanisms balanced in favour of behavioural approach (e.g. being more prone to risk-taking, neophilia, and exploratory behaviour). This follows because the high investment sex (in this case, females) is expected to be able to mate relatively easily and is highly limited in the number of offspring she can rear (Buss & Schmitt, 1993; MacDonald, 1988; Symons, 1979; Trivers, 1972). However, mating is expected to be problematic for the low invest-ment sex, with the result that males must often compete with other males for access to females and there will be large differences among males in reproductive success.

Mating for males is thus expected to be much more of a high stakes enterprise, with much more to gain and much more to lose than is the case with females. Risk-taking directed at resource acquisition can therefore have very high payoffs for males compared to females, and, as a result, the evolutionary theory of sex makes predictions of sex-differentiated behaviour which go well beyond expected differences in mating strategies to encompass a wide range of behaviours that influence resource acquisi-tion. In terms of the following discussion, males in general are expected to be higher than females on behavioural approach systems (including sensation-seeking, risk-taking, and impulsivity) and lower on behavioural withdrawal systems (including caution and fear).

In addition, evolutionary theory predicts that in species with sex-differ-entiated patterns of parental investment, males, as the low investment sex, would gain more from aggression and social dominance—both of which are costly and dangerous—because engaging in these behaviours would be more likely to lead to increased mating opportunities. Females, on the other hand, are expected to adopt a more conservative strategy, benefiting less from aggression and social dominance. Females also benefit more from long-term mating relationships characterised by romantic involve-ment, trust, and empathy because these features of relationships are signals of a male's willingness to invest in the female and her children.

To conclude this introductory section, the foregoing implies that evolu-tionary biology constitutes a supra-paradigm for human development. A very common practice in textbooks in developmental psychology is to begin with several different theoretical approaches, including cognitive-developmental theory, social learning theory, biological and evolutionary approaches, and, perhaps, psychoanalysis (the latter, alas, not always included only for its historical interest). The relationships among these theories are typically not discussed, but it was not very long ago that it was common to argue that different theories constituted fundamentally incompatible world views and that scientists were forced to choose among them, ultimately for irrational reasons (e.g. Lerner & Kauffman, 1986; Overton, 1984).

An evolutionary perspective, however, begins with the proposition that all aspects of the phenotype are open to natural selection. The evolutionary perspective is highly compatible with the view that the phenotype is influenced not only by the highly dedicated, domain-specific mechanisms of development revealed by biological, cognitive-developmental, and information-processing research, but also by the domain-general mechanisms of social learning, developmental plasticity, and the *g* factor of intelligence tests. This does not imply that all aspects of the phenotype are genetically determined, but it does imply that one should not be looking for alternatives to evolutionary theory. Instead, one should attempt to understand how evolution has orchestrated a complex interplay among highly dedicated, domain-specific systems that evolved to solve particular adaptive problems in the EEA as well as domain-general processes such as social learning that facilitate adaptive behaviour even in the very novel set of environments that children and their parents confront in the contemporary world.

SEX DIFFERENCES IN SOME DOMAIN-SPECIFIC MECHANISMS

Discussions of adaptive systems among children inevitably raise the difficult question of specifying the adaptive niche of childhood and the relationship between adult systems and their precursors in children. From an evolutionary engineering standpoint, if a particular set of systems (e.g. those related to aggression) are important in adulthood then they must emerge full blown at some point during development. They need not, of course, develop at birth or during early childhood (e.g. the reproductive organs are not competent until adolescence). Nevertheless, there are at least three reasons to suppose that systems important in adulthood will often emerge much earlier at least in truncated form.

(1) Advanced animals are characterised by a prolonged period of plasticity in which learning takes place, typically during play (Fagen, 1981; MacDonald, 1988, 1993; Smith, 1982). Important behavioural systems are not genetically "hard-wired" units that suddenly emerge full blown in adulthood. There is a prolonged training period during which skills are honed and lessons learned. Thus the fact that boys are more aggressive than girls during nursery school quite possibly has nothing whatever to do with their obtaining more resources at this age which in turn leads to greater success as an adult. Nevertheless, the presence of this system allows the child to develop skills related to being effectively aggressive when it

really counts. Consistent with this, Pellegrini (1988) notes a shift in rough and tumble (r & t) play from a co-operative, playful style in younger children to a rougher style associated with dominance interactions and aggression in early adolescence.

(2) Secondly, evolved systems may be adaptive in childhood. In the following, I will discuss three biological systems that show sex differences during childhood. Two of these systems can be reasonably viewed as having an adaptive function during childhood (MacDonald, 1988, 1995). Thus, the behavioural approach systems are associated with curiosity, exploratory behaviour, creativity (see MacDonald, 1988, 1993), and holistic, synthetic thought processes (Tucker & Williamson, 1984). This trait is thus associated with interest in and responsiveness to the environment (whether social or nonsocial), and is thus presumably an important aspect of play (and certainly r & t play, see later) as a general Piagetian environment-engagement device. Evolutionary analyses of play emphasise the function of play as involving intrinsic motivators that facilitate interaction with the environment (e.g. Fagen, 1981; MacDonald, 1988, 1993; Smith, 1982). Similarly, systems underlying behavioural avoidance are functional, beginning early in life as systems that respond to external threats with behavioural inhibition and emotions such as fear and anxiety (Gray, 1982; Kagan, Reznick, & Snidman, 1987, 1989).

(3) Another reason for discussing evolved systems during childhood is that if a biological system is important in adulthood, then a nonfunctional version of the system may be present during earlier development because of what one might term the opportunistic nature of evolution itself. The evolutionary function of the human affectional system has been proposed to be that of producing close affectional relationships during adulthood in order to facilitate high-investment parenting (MacDonald, 1992). Given such a function, there would be no evolutionary necessity for the tendency for pair-bonding to develop out of relationships that occur during infancy. It is quite conceivable that intimate relationships, like reproductive competence, would develop *de novo* at puberty so that early affectional relationships would be irrelevant. However, natural selection appears to have opportunistically taken advantage of a pre-existing system involving maternal nurturance of the young, with the result that the tendency for affectional relationships in humans occurs at a very early age. Natural selection must work with what is available, and it is often much easier to modify existing systems rather than create a system *de novo*. In the absence of natural selection against such a trait occurring in childhood, the most efficient path for developing an adult trait may be to develop the trait (or a rudimentary

version of it) during childhood even if it has no adaptive function during childhood.

The purpose of the following is to show that the mean sex differences in three important personality systems related to the Five-Factor Model (FFM) of personality conform to the aforementioned evolutionary logic. Within this framework, the FFM is conceptualised as a set of universal human adaptations, and individual differences in these systems constitute a set of viable alternative strategies (see later). John, Caspi, Robins, Moffitt, & Stouthamer-Loeber (1994) have found the FFM factors replicate for children, and there are clear conceptual linkages between the FFM and early-developing temperament systems (see later). Whereas the FFM is derived from semantic information, the evolutionary perspective is strengthened by the following types of evidence. (1) Evidence for similar systems in animals that meet obvious adaptive needs. (2) Evidence for a structural basis for these systems in the brain. (3) Developmental evidence that recognisable precursors of the FFM exist during infancy or early childhood when there is little *a priori* reason to suppose that such dimensions of individual variation would answer to adult interests in describing individual variation. Here I will briefly summarise data related to the last type of evidence only. (See MacDonald, 1995, for details.)

Behavioural approach systems

Sex differences within the FFM factor space conform to evolutionary expectations. Particularly relevant are the dimensions of Dominance and Nurturance/Love which cover the same domain as Extroversion and Agreeableness on some FFM measures (Briggs, 1992; Trapnell & Wiggins, 1990). As Trapnell and Wiggins (1990) point out, the difference amounts to a rotational difference between two different ways of conceptualising the same interpersonal space. Nevertheless, an evolutionary perspective is better conceptualised with Dominance and Nurturance as the primary axes of interpersonal space, because the conceptualisation maximises theoretically important sex differences and is thus likely to have been the focus of natural selection. Men score significantly higher on the IAS-R-B5 DOM (Dominance) scale and significantly lower (by 0.88 standard deviations) on the IAS-R-B5 LOV (Love) scale (Trapnell & Wiggins, 1990). Theoretically expected sex differences are also pronounced on the Sensation Seeking Scale in studies performed in America, England, Scotland, Thailand, and Japan (Zuckerman, 1979, 1984, 1990, 1991). These scales tap variation in attraction to physically dangerous activities and lack of fear of physical harm, promiscuous sexual activity, disinhibition, and susceptibility to boredom.

Developmentally, there appears to be a pattern in which the most sexually differentiated aspects of behavioural approach are maximised during late childhood and early adulthood while the least sex-differentiated aspects of behavioural approach appear early in infancy and are highly associated with positive emotionality. However, boys are higher on behavioural approach even during infancy in cross cultural samples (see Rothbart, 1989, for a review), and sex differences in aggression (Eagly & Steffen, 1986), externalising psychiatric disorders (conduct disorder, oppositional/defiant disorder), risk-taking, and rough and tumble play (which is often associated with aggression) (DiPietro, 1981; Humphreys & Smith, 1987; MacDonald & Parke, 1986; O'Brien & Huston, 1985) can be seen beginning in early childhood. The social interactions of boys are also more characterised by dominance interactions and forceful, demanding interpersonal styles (Charlesworth & Dzur, 1987; Cowan & Avants, 1988; LaFreniére & Charlesworth, 1983; Leaper, 1991; Savin-Williams, 1987; Sheldon, 1990).

Conscientiousness and behavioural avoidance systems

The trait of Conscientiousness subsumes variation in the ability to defer gratification, persevere in unpleasant tasks, pay close attention to detail, and behave in a responsible, dependable manner. Widiger and Trull (1992) find that the psychiatric disorder most associated with conscientiousness is obsessive-compulsive disorder, a disorder which tends to co-occur with a variety of phobic states and other anxiety disorders (e.g. Marks, 1987; Öhman, 1993). The evolutionary theory of sex outlined earlier suggests that females would tend to adopt a more conservative strategy and thus be higher on measures of conscientiousness and more prone to anxiety disorders and behavioural inhibition.

Females are indeed significantly higher on IAS-R-B5 Conscientiousness (Trapnell & Wiggins, 1990). Females are also more prone to most anxiety disorders, including agoraphobia and panic disorder (e.g. Weissman, 1985; DSM IV). It is also noteworthy that girls report being more fearful and timid in uncertain situations than boys and are more cautious and take fewer risks than boys (Christopherson, 1989; Ginsburg & Miller, 1982). Girls are also more compliant than boys beginning in the toddler period and throughout childhood (Kochanska, Aksan, & Koenig, 1995; Minton, Kagan, & Levine 1971; Smith & Dagliesh, 1977), and girls are more prone to anxiety disorders (Weissman, 1985).

On the other hand, Attention Deficit Hyperactivity Disorder (ADHD) is overwhelmingly found among boys. ADHD is conceptualised by Tucker and Derryberry (1992) as involving a diffuse, extroverted attentional style which is the antithesis of the redundancy bias characteristic of the attentional style of obsessive-compulsive disorder. The characteristics of ADHD children clearly place them low on all of the typical descriptors of conscientiousness: undisciplined, unplanful, unreliable, noncompliant, disorderly, impulsive, incautious, nonpersistent in the face of difficulty, interested in immediate gratification, and lacking in neatness and tidiness (e.g. S. E. Shaywitz & B. E. Shaywitz, 1988).

Nurturance/love as an adaptation

As indicated earlier, the circumplex model of interpersonal descriptors (Kiesler, 1983; Trapnell & Wiggins, 1990; Wiggins, Trapnell, & Phillips, 1988) results in a highly sex-differentiated dimension of Nurturance/Love. Nurturance/Love is proposed to be a reward system that evolved to underlie adaptive relationships of intimacy and other long-term relationships, especially family relationships, involving reciprocity and transfer of resources to others (e.g. maternal and paternal investment in children). This trait is not considered as a temperament dimension of childhood, but individual differences in warmth and affection observable in early parent–child relationships, including secure attachments, are conceptually linked with this dimension later in life (MacDonald, 1992, 1997). Secure attachments and warm, affectionate parent–child relationships have been found to be associated with a high investment style of parenting characterised by later sexual maturation, stable pair-bonding, and warm, reciprocally rewarding, nonexploitative interpersonal relationships (Belsky, Steinberg, & Draper, 1991).

If the main evolutionary impetus for the development of the human affectional system is the need for high-investment parenting, females are expected to have a greater elaboration of mechanisms related to parental investment than males. Females, because of their very high, morphologically imposed investments in pregnancy and lactation are expected to be highly discriminating maters compared to males (e.g. Buss & Schmitt, 1993; Symons, 1979; Trivers, 1972). It was noted earlier that females score higher on the IAS-R-B5 LOV scale by a very robust 0.88 standard deviations (Trapnell & Wiggins, 1990). Moreover, IAS Nurturance is conceptualised as involving the tendency to provide aid for those needing help, including children and people who are ill (Wiggins & Broughton, 1985), and would therefore be expected to be associated with ideal child-nurturing behaviours. This dimension is strongly associated with measures of femininity, and is associated with warm, empathic personal relationships, and dependence (Wiggins & Broughton, 1985).

The tendency for females to be more strongly attracted to intimate relationships and pair-bonding has empirical support. Girls are more prone to engage in intimate, confiding relationships than boys throughout development (e.g. Berndt, 1986; Buhrmester & Furman, 1987). Females also tend, generally, to place greater emphasis on love and personal intimacy in sexual relationships (e.g. Buss & Schmitt, 1993; Hinde, 1984; Kenrick & Trost, 1989). Females are more empathic and desire higher intimacy in relationships (Lang-Takoc & Osterweil, 1992), and both sexes perceive friendships with women as closer, richer, more intimate, more empathic, and more therapeutic (Aukett, Ritchie, & Mill, 1988; Wright & Scanlon, 1991). Developmentally, sex differences related to intimacy peak during the reproductive years (Gutmann, 1977; Turner, 1981), a finding that is compatible with the present perspective that sex differences in intimacy are related to reproductive behaviour.

DO THE PHENOTYPIC CONTOURS OF HUMAN DEVELOPMENT MEET EVOLUTIONARY EXPECTATIONS?

Peer relationships

I noted earlier that an evolutionary perspective predicts that children's behaviour will be self-interested rather than self-sacrificing, and that their relationships with their peers will reflect this generalisation. Within this perspective, peer relationships may be viewed as a continuum ranging from high levels of commonality of interest to high levels of conflict of interest (see Table 2.1). Empirical research has focused on three points of this continuum. At one extreme is exploitation, defined as asymmetrical relationships in which one individual receives no benefit. Because the interests of the exploited child are compromised, such relationships are not voluntarily entered into, and the relationship is maximally prone to defection. Examples would be the bullying relationships studied by Smith (1991), and, in the following section, the relationship between aggression and peer rejection is considered in this framework.

At a second level are structured group settings in which there are limited resources. The empirical findings indicate that there is a tendency toward uneven access to resources among groups of children, a result highly compatible with the evolutionary expectation of conflict of interest among individuals regarding access to valued resources (Charlesworth, 1995). Paradigmatic of such group phenomena are relationships of dominance and subordination in naturally occurring groups of children. Unlike relationships of exploitation, relationships of dominance/subordination are voluntarily entered into and, indeed, dominance/subordination is a basic principle of social organisation among many species of animals. Dominance relationships are asymmetrical, with dominant children having priority of access to resources (Charlesworth & LaFreniére, 1983; Savin-

TABLE 2.1
Characteristics of focal types of peer relationships

	Friendship	Structured Group Relationships of Dominance and Subordination	Exploitation
Commonality of interest	High	Common interests can occur, but wide variation	Low
Degree of ability to choose other	High	Varies	High for exploiter None for exploited
Degree of control within relationship	High	Varies by dominance status	High for exploiter None for exploited
Symmetry of resource access	High	Low	Completely Asymmetrical
Reciprocity	High	Some, but unbalanced in favour of dominant	None
Phenotypic similarity	High	Not important	Not important
Likelihood of defection	Low	Relatively low for dominant; Relatively high for subordinate	High for exploited Low for exploiter

Williams, 1987). The evolutionary expectation that dominance/subordination, as a voluntary relationship, contains benefits for subordinate individuals is borne out in the animal literature (McGuire, 1974; Wilson, 1975), and Savin-Williams (1987) has noted that subordinate adolescent boys highly value membership in hierarchical peer groups. As indicated earlier, an evolutionary perspective predicts that boys' relationships are more likely to be characterised by dominance and subordination, and this is indeed the case.

On the other extreme of the continuum of commonality of interest are relationships of friendship (see also Hartup, Chapter 6). As is the case with relationships of dominance/subordination in naturally occurring groups of children, friendship is characterised by repeated interactions which are voluntarily entered into and from which neither party defects. However, unlike dominance/subordination, there is the implicit assumption that the individual can choose friends from a set of individuals who vary along a variety of dimensions. The choice of a friend is thus essentially a choice of a resource which, from the present perspective, is theoretically constrained by the requirement that the friendship satisfies the interests of both partners. As a result, it is expected that such relationships are more nearly symmetrical and based on reciprocity than are relationships based on dominance or exploitation.

The empirical research indicates that symmetry and reciprocity are central to friendship. Youniss (1986), taking an evolutionary perspective, summarises evidence that indeed children's positive social interactions tend to involve reciprocity. Infants exhibit toy sharing, turn-taking, and mutual imitation, and older children regard acts of symmetrical reciprocity as the hallmark of friendship. Friends share a variety of resources, help each other in times of emotional stress, and develop mutual dependence (Asher, 1990). Resources need not be exchanged immediately, but only over the long term. Friendship implies reciprocity, because, as Parker and Gottman (1989, p. 112) note: "If play is to be co-ordinated, it is simply not always possible to get one's own way. In service of the overall adventure, children must inhibit some actions [and] accept influence at times". Because reciprocity is lacking, children who always try to get their own way are thus not likely candidates for friends. This is presumably the reason why theorists since Piaget have emphasised the importance of peer interactions as influences on social cognition and perspective-taking: Becoming a successful social actor entails understanding others' interests.

Interestingly, Morgan and Sawyer (1967) found that friends prefer equality in division of rewards but would sometimes consent to unequal division. However, children who disliked each other insisted on absolute equality. LaFreniére (1996) and Hartup (1989) show that friends are more likely to engage in equitable exchanges and are more likely to co-operate rather than compete even in situations with limited resources (see also Rabbie, 1991, for similar data on adults). Nevertheless, Hartup makes the point that although reciprocity and equality are the hallmarks of friendship, one of the friends may be less favoured in the relationship and therefore be more willing to accept some imbalance in distributing rewards.

These findings are consistent with Charlesworth's (1996) findings: In a limited resource situation, there is a strong tendency for nonequal division of resources even among children who are friends, and this is the case cross-culturally. In such a situation one can conceptualise reciprocity as being achieved despite the lack of equal division of resources: The less favoured partner in the relationship must give up more in some tangible resource in order to maintain the relationship. For example, in the following section, sociometric popularity is conceptualised in terms of possessing a set of traits that are valued by peers. Thus, if a very popular child were friends with a somewhat less popular child, it is expected that the less popular child would have to allow the more popular child to obtain more tangible resources in a resource-competitive situation in order to maintain an overall reciprocity in the relationship.

A perhaps not so obvious result of this is that similarity is expected to be a basic feature of peer relations of friendship. From an evolutionary perspective, a child may be considered to be a concatenation of resource potentials for other children. If indeed reciprocity is the fundamental rule of peer relations, then a very likely outcome is simply a phenotypic matching process in which children aggregate on the basis of phenotypic similarity. Similarity ensures reciprocity because the resource value of a wide range of phenotypic attributes is matched within the dyad. Thus, if physical attractiveness is a resource, children of similar physical attractiveness are expected to be more likely to become friends because reciprocity in this resource attribute has been achieved. In addition, children's interests and abilities would be expected to be resources for other children who have similar interests and abilities: Sharing an interest (e.g. in baseball) provides both children with psychological rewards, so that reciprocity is maintained.

There is overwhelming evidence for the importance of similarity as a principle of assortment in children's friendships. In terms of the present theoretical perspective, the set of similar attributes constitutes a set of resources which are relevant to particular friendships. Humphreys and Smith (1987) found that children who engaged in rough and tumble (r & t) play tended to have similar rank in the dominance hierarchy, and Pellegrini (1988) found that this was the case not only for r & t, but also for engaging in games-with-rules and other types of social interactions (e.g. talking with a peer, comfort contact). Similarly among primates, co-operation and other types of association are much more likely among animals who are near to each other in the dominance hierarchy (Harcourt, 1992).

Cairns, Cairns, Neckerman, Gest, and Gariépy (1988) found that aggressive children formed groups with other aggressive children and were often nominated as best friends by other aggressive children. Panduit, the talking robot, used by Parker and Gottman (1985) to explore children's friendship formation, was rated much more likeable when it attempted to establish common ground with the child. Epstein (1989) found that similarity among friends occurs on a wide range of attitudes, behaviours, and interests, as well as personality and academic success. Moreover, the similarity of friends increases linearly with age (quite possibly because there tends to be a wider range of possible friends as one gets older), and closer friends tended to be more similar than casual friends (see also Brown, 1989). Cohen (1977) found that similarity was a prerequisite for friendship, not the consequence of friendship.

Interestingly, the subjective feeling of similarity is important to the friends themselves even when the similarities themselves seem trivial:

Parker and Gottman (1989, p. 110) state that: "it is not so much the nature of their similarities, as the presence of commonalities that interests these children. Indeed, children destined to become friends sometimes give the appearance of going to almost any length to find commonality, regardless of how frivolous (A: 'We both have chalk on our hands'; B: 'Right!')".

EVOLVED SYSTEMS INFLUENCING THE RESOURCE VALUE OF CHILDREN IN THE PEER GROUP

The aforementioned account has emphasised perceived interests in peer interactions but has not provided an evolutionary account of the specific resources sought in peer relationships. The following is an attempt to develop an evolutionary account of children's perceived interests in individual differences among their peers. The section will focus on the findings of research on peer sociometric status.

There are good theoretical reasons to suppose that humans will be greatly interested in the genetic and phenotypic diversity represented by individual differences among peers. For example, individual differences in personality may be viewed as an adaptive landscape in which "perceiving, attending to, and acting upon differences in others is crucial for solving problems of survival and reproduction" (Buss, 1991, p. 471). At a basic level, individual genetic and phenotypic variation constitutes the playing field on which the evolutionary game is played (MacDonald, 1991). Evolutionary theory implies that organisms will be keenly interested in genetic variation and its expression in a wide array of phenotypic traits. Phenotypic variation must therefore be seen as containing cues that influence how people evaluate each other, and different evaluations will be made depending on the putative role of the other person in their lives (Lusk, MacDonald, & Newman, in press). An evolutionary perspective suggests that children will be highly sensitive to the resource environment represented by individual diversity and mechanisms will evolve in order to take advantage of this diversity (MacDonald, 1991).

As conceptualised by Coie, Dodge, and Coppotelli (1982), sociometric status is established by a child's standing on two fairly independent dimensions of liking and disliking. Within this conceptualisation, the characteristics of popular children can be viewed as assets from the perspective of the social group, whereas the characteristics of rejected children constitute a set of liabilities. The assets are thus a set of resources for the child who possesses them as well as for the other children who value them. Similarly, the liabilities are attributes which not only fail to conform to the interests of other children, but are characteristics that children actively dislike. Individual differences in children can be viewed as a resource environment from the standpoint of other children, with popular children possessing a high net positive value of assets.

Regarding the characteristics of popular children, Coie, Dodge, and Kupersmidt (1990) find that positive social status at all ages of childhood is related to helpfulness, rule conformity, friendliness, and prosocial inter-action. Popular children become leaders and set norms for the group, and, especially as children get older, popular children tend to have high academic and athletic achievement. Popular children are also physically attractive (see Coie et al., 1982). Rejected social status, especially among boys, is related to aggression, hyperactivity, being off task in the classroom (inattention), and disruptiveness. In addition, Asher (1990) notes specific subgroups of rejected children, including mildly retarded and learning disabled children. Finally, Coie et al. (1990) describe evidence that neglected social status is associated with very low aggression as well as shyness and active social withdrawal.

These lists of attributes may be viewed as an empirically derived set of resources relevant to peer status. Several of the attributes of popular children can easily be seen as suggesting reciprocity and commonality of interest with peers. Thus, helpfulness, friendliness, and prosocial interac-tion are clearly attributes that suggest that popular children's peer relations are characterised not by attempts at exploitation but rather by reciprocity of positive social interactions. There is even the suggestion that the social status of popular children is achieved in part by maintaining a net resource outflow: Other children become indebted to them as a result of acts of friendliness, support, and helpfulness. Popular children are also characterised by highly heritable attributes such as athletic ability and physical attractiveness which appear to be valued in all cultures, suggesting natural selection for high valuation of these traits (Weisfeld & Billings, 1988). Within an evolutionary framework, athletic ability in males may be viewed as linked to success in warfare and hunting (Weisfeld & Billings, 1988), and physical attractiveness has been linked to physical symmetry which is itself linked to resistance to parasites (Gangestad, Thornhill, & Yeo, 1994). Intelligence and academic success are also resources that are related to achieving status within our own society and they are highly valued resources in mate choice around the world (Buss, 1994). For rejected children it is easy to see that their behaviour has a negative resource valuation by peers. Offensive aggression is an attempt to exploit others, whereas disruptiveness and inattention also conflict with other children's interests.

An evolutionary perspective proposes that at least some of the assets and liabilities important for sociometric status involve individual differences in evolved systems. Although extreme levels of behavioural approach are linked to peer rejection (including many children diagnosed as ADHD,

MacDonald, 1988, 1996, it is likely that moderate levels are actually a positive asset. Sociability and extroversion are genetically and phenotypically linked to the other behavioural approach systems emphasised here (Fulker, 1981), and presumably are linked with peer leadership and being at ease socially—traits linked to popularity. Controversial children would appear to be even higher on these externalising traits. Coie et al. (1990, p. 52) state that:

> Controversial children are the most socially active of all children. They are often engaged in active interaction with peers and are rarely observed in solitary activity. They talk frequently with peers and adults and make the peer group laugh with their humour. They are among the most aggressive of all children, and because of their disruptive activities, they are most often reprimanded by adult supervisors. They appear to be easily aroused to anger and yet are also seen as much more facilitative in groups than rejected children and are group leaders.

In terms of the present discussion, controversial children appear to be highly extroverted to the point where their behaviour, although attractive to some, is aversive to others. This fits well with the findings of Cairns et al. (1988) that aggressive children form social networks of friends but are also disliked by many children. Controversial children would thus appear to be intermediate on this dimension to popular children and the rejected/ hyperactive children.

Another personality dimension proposed as a resource for peer relations derives from the human affectional system described earlier. Children (especially girls) who are high on the human affectional system are expected to find intimate, affectionate relationships to be highly rewarding and eagerly seek out relationships, including peer relationships, in which this stimulation is available. Because the other person in such a relationship also finds this stimulation rewarding, the relationship is characterised by reciprocal positive affective exchanges. (See also LaFreniére's, 1996, discussion of attachment and reciprocity.) Friends are "intimate associates" and their relationship is characterised by reciprocity, commitment, co-operation and engaging in reciprocated prosocial support, intimacy and affection (Hartup, 1989).

In conformity with these expectations, I have already noted a sex-differentiated pattern in which girls are more strongly attracted to relationships, including peer relationships, characterised by warmth and intimacy. Moreover, Sroufe (1991; see also Sroufe & Fleeson, 1986) has found that securely attached children are more likely to have close friendships during early adolescence. Park and Waters (1989) found that pairs of securely attached children were more harmonious, less controlling, more responsive, and happier than secure–insecure pairs.

In addition to being a *sine qua non* of close friendship, warmth is undoubtedly an important positive asset in measures of liking in sociometric assessment. As described by Coie et al. (1990) popular children are friendly, helpful, supportive of peers, and engage in prosocial behaviour. Empathy, nurturance, and prosocial behaviour also appear to be traits linked to the human affectional system (see Digman, 1990; John, 1990; MacDonald, 1988).

Finally, children whose personalities are dominated by behavioural inhibition are clearly withdrawn and shy (Kagan et al., 1989)—exactly the characteristics of neglected children (Coie et al., 1990; Dodge, Murphy, & Buchsbaum, 1984). In terms of the present perspective, moderate levels of these traits are not resources for other children, either negatively or positively, but being behaviourally inhibited results in a lack of engagement with the wider peer group. Thus, whatever other resources such children may have are not available for other children, and the result is social neglect.

However, extremely withdrawn children can become rejected by the peer group (Rubin, LeMare, & Mills, 1990; see also Asher, Parkhurst, Hymel, & Williams, 1990). Asher et al. (1990) review data indicating that some extremely withdrawn children become victimised by the peer group, and that there is a subgroup of rejected children who are described as very shy and as likely to play alone. These data indicate that the characteristics of extremely socially withdrawn children are viewed not as neutral but as liabilities. Such victimised children are at the low end of the social status hierarchy and are thus viewed negatively by peers as children with whom they do not want to engage in positive relationships.

MORALITY AND ALTRUISM

An evolutionary approach also has implications for thinking about morality and altruism. As indicated earlier, an important strand of evolutionary thinking emphasises what one might term the individualistic/self-interested implications of evolutionary theory. Such a perspective is based on a fairly clear evolutionary logic, and much of the data in the area of morality and altruism can be interpreted in a manner that conforms to this logic.

Thus, Charlesworth (1996; see also Charlesworth & Dzur, 1987) has shown that self-interest emerges as an important factor in a paradigm involving co-operation and competition for a limited resource. Studies conducted within the social learning paradigm have also shown a large main effect for self-interest. Self-interest is typically apparent in the baseline condition and is still apparent after the treatment (see

MacDonald, 1988, pp. 242ff). Increases in helping or donating behaviour are often rather small even when they involve resources of little value and even in a laboratory situation where there is often a strong "pull" for donating behaviour. There is also a tendency for treatment effects to disappear over time.

Furthermore, the tendency to help other children is a function of the degree of expected reciprocity. For example, Kanfer, Stiflere, and Morris (1981) found that 3- to 6-year-old children would not continue a dull sorting task if the recipient of the reward for doing so was anonymous. Higher levels of work occurred if the recipient was a classmate, and even higher levels if the recipient was a friend.

The area of moral reasoning and its relation to behaviour is also highly compatible with an evolutionary perspective (see MacDonald 1988, pp. 246ff). Although children do indeed reason in a more abstract manner as they get older (and are therefore more effective than young children in rationalising their behaviour to themselves and others), there is little, if any, connection between moral reasoning and moral behaviour. Moreover, reasoning about moral issues changes depending on the possible costs and benefits to the reasoner. As Haan (1978, 1985) found, interpersonal reasoning focused on gaining resources through face-to-face encounters occurs in situations where there are high levels of costs and benefits resulting from this reasoning. On the other hand, formal Kohlbergian reasoning is more likely to occur "in pleasant situations where verbalisations could be cheaply produced" (Haan, 1978, p. 297).

Studies such as that of Gilligan (1982) also show the importance of self-deception in rationalising real-world moral dilemmas involving abortion. Evolutionists have shown considerable interest in deception and self-deception as mechanisms for furthering evolutionary goals (Trivers, 1985, 1991). As Trivers (1985, 1991) emphasises, the best deceivers are self-deceivers, and many of Gilligan's subjects rationalise abortions in situations where the father would not provide financial or emotional support for the child. However, rationalisations, in order to be psychologically effective, must be convincing to the rationaliser and this may require self-deception.

For example, Gilligan (1982) describes a subject's reasoning about whether she should seek an abortion. The subject realistically realises that having a baby will cut into her time and entail a lot of responsibility and she rejects her previous idea that having a baby would make her feel happy as "selfish". By counterfactually suggesting that having the baby would make her happy and then engaging in self-deception by providing a negative label such as "selfish" to this false idea, she is free to choose what in fact is a self-interested course of action and consider her course of action as moral or even altruistic. Other studies reviewed in MacDonald

(1988) indicate that people sometimes use advanced moral reasoning in a cynical (i.e. not involving self-deception) manner to deceive others and that people sometimes act in a selfish manner against their own moral reasoning.

Alexander (1979, 1987) has shown that the self-interested patterns of moral behaviour can be observed cross-culturally as well. This does not, of course imply that children do not co-operate with each other or that human relationships are necessarily exploitative. We have seen that reciprocity is an important aspect of children's peer relationships and that close friends are very co-operative and share valued resources. Even dominance relationships do not imply exploitation, and are actively sought by children.

Moreover, human cultures are able to provide intensive socialisation pressures that are at least somewhat successful at tipping the balance more in favour of altruism (see MacDonald, 1988, pp. 296ff, 1994). These intensive socialisation pressures are typically aimed at inculcating a very high level of within-group cohesion and altruism and are combined with hostility and exploitation of outgroups, as in the case of ancient Sparta and Nazi Germany.

Within the mainstream developmental literature, these findings are highly compatible with the findings of Sherif et al. (1961) that within-group cohesion is maximised in the context of hostility toward outgroups. Human moral behaviour is highly compartmentalised and there is every reason to believe that this is a feature of evolutionary design. Research on social identity processes has shown that the tendency to discriminate in favour of ingroups and against outgroups occurs even in so-called "minimal groups" (i.e. groups that are arbitrarily constituted and do not interact with each other) (Hogg & Abrams, 1987). These findings can be generalised across subjects of different ages, nationalities, and social classes, and a wide range of dependent variables (Bourhis, 1994), and anthropological evidence indicates the universality of the tendency to view one's own group as superior (Vine, 1987). Moreover, social identity processes occur very early in life, prior to explicit knowledge about the outgroup (see Campbell, Chapter 13). An evolutionary interpretation of these findings is also supported by results indicating that social identity processes occur among advanced animal species such as chimpanzees (Van der Dennen, 1991). Finally, the fact that social identity processes increase during times of resource competition and threat to the group (see Hogg & Abrams, 1987) is highly compatible with the idea that these processes involve facultative mechanisms triggered by between-group conflict. As emphasised by evolutionists such as Alexander (1979), external threat tends to reduce internal divisions and maximise percep-tions of common interest among group members. Such changes presumably reflect a species-wide facultative strategy of accepting higher levels of external authority and becoming more group oriented under conditions of external threat.

REPRODUCTIVE STRATEGIES: THE COHERENCE OF DEVELOPMENT

It was argued earlier that intelligence may be viewed as a domain-general information-processing device that evolved in order to more effectively attain evolutionary goals. However, the main message for developmentalists deriving from IQ research is the very substantial coherence of individual development on a very wide range of variables revealed by this research (e.g. Herrnstein & Murray, 1994; Rushton, 1988, 1995). Besides variables directly related to mental testing, such as school performance, these results indicate associations among IQ, poverty and welfare dependency, proneness to illegitimacy, child abuse, low birth weight, sexual behaviour, divorce (unstable pair-bonding), psychiatric diagnosis, rates of physical maturation, parent–child relationships, criminality, and even the likelihood of being classified as disabled. For all of these results, IQ is a better predictor of variables related to social functioning than is parental socioeconomic status. Moreover, the results indicate nonlinear trends at the lower end of the IQ distribution with a very strong upsurge in problem frequency in these populations. Similarly, although IQ is not considered in their analysis, Belsky et al. (1991) review data that support the general coherence of individual development, including especially the large intercorrelations among spousal harmony, parent–child relationship quality, children's interpersonal style, timing of puberty, sexual behaviour, and level of parental investment.

Traditional developmental research as well as evolutionary perspectives tend to compartmentalise humans into various domain-specific systems that (from an evolutionary perspective) evolved to solve particular adaptive problems. However, this research shows that there is also a very important central core of co-varying systems (many of them presumably domain-specific; see later) centred around at least one highly domain-general ability—the *g* factor of IQ tests. Although the associations among the various systems are not robust enough to preclude an important role for discrete evolved systems, such as the personality systems discussed earlier, the substantial coherence of individual development strongly suggests the importance of life history theory in conceptualising human development. Life history approaches to human development focus fundamentally on variation in reproductive strategies (e.g. Belsky et al., 1991; Chisholm, 1993, 1997; MacDonald, 1994, 1997a,b; Miller, 1994; Rushton,

1988, 1995), and within such perspectives parental investment is the critical variable.

Life history theory is highly compatible with the coherence of development because a reproductive strategy involves a co-ordinated organismic response to a central external ecological contingency that selects for optimum levels of partitioning mating effort and parenting effort, with the result that variables such as mortality rates, longevity, pair-bonding, age of first reproduction, period of pre-adult dependency, and levels of paternal and maternal investment evolve as a co-ordinated response to environmental pressures. The fundamental dimension of reproductive strategies may be construed as a dimension that ranges from a high-parental-investment/low-mating-effort strategy to a low-parental-investment/high-mating-effort strategy (e.g. Wilson 1975).

Within this perspective, a critical aspect of high levels of parental investment is the provision of optimal environments for children. If we accept the proposition that there was natural selection for high-investment parenting among humans (e.g. Fisher, 1992; Flinn & Low, 1986; Lancaster & Lancaster, 1987; Lovejoy, 1981; MacDonald, 1988), then it is reasonable to suppose that one result of this process is that high-investment parents provide certain types of high-quality environments for their children and that these environments contribute to the child's development. Parental investment clearly involves the provision of certain environments, and parents incur a considerable cost in providing these: Parental investment includes developing a strong affective relationship with the child, providing relatively high levels of verbal stimulation and parent–child play, and active parental involvement in monitoring virtually every aspect of the child's life (e.g. children's progress in school, children's peer relationships) (Belsky et al., 1991; MacDonald, 1988, 1992, 1993).

From a theoretical perspective the best evidence that the environments provided by high-investment parents must have benefits is the very clear evidence that they are costly to provide. Theoretically, it is difficult to conceive of a behaviour with clear costs remaining in a population without some overcompensating benefits. For example, if children do not benefit from paternal investment, it is difficult to conceptualise why males would provide such investment or females would seek it. Under these circumstances, males would be better off competing with other males for access to additional females than to invest in the offspring of one female, and, indeed, this is a common pattern in nature, especially among mammals (e.g. Kleiman, 1977, 1981).

Although the foregoing argues for the importance of children's environments, it is also consistent with evidence that high-investment parenting is itself genetically influenced. There is evidence for reasonably high heritability of all of the behaviours related to parental investment. Thus, measures of parents' and children's perceptions of parental control and especially parental warmth are genetically influenced, and parental stimulation and involvement (including measures of parental warmth and control) as measured by the Home Observation for Measurement of the Environment (HOME) and the Family Environment Scale (FES) also have a considerable genetic component (Plomin 1994). These measures of parental investment co-vary to a considerable degree with high IQ which is itself substantially heritable (Plomin, 1994; see also later). Interestingly, research with the HOME also supports the coherence of development: There is a substantial co-variation among the HOME subscales of emotional and verbal responsivity, provision of play materials, maternal involvement, and opportunities for variety of stimulation (Bradley & Caldwell, 1984). Parents who provide verbal stimulation and monitor their children more closely also tend to have close emotional relationships with them.

The behavioural genetic evidence may be interpreted as indicating that parents and their children are a co-evolving system in which passive genotype-environment correlations are of great importance. Children would be expected to benefit differentially from the environments provided by high-investment parents depending on their genotype. Thus far, the evidence does indeed indicate that in early childhood at least passive genotype-environment correlations are more important contributors to the correlations between measures of IQ and the HOME and FES measures of the environment than are active or reactive genotype-environment correlations (Plomin, 1994). The evidence does not show that the environments parents provide are of no importance, but it strongly suggests that the environments that parents provide are effective largely as a result of their being an aspect of a co-evolutionary process in which children are genetically inclined to benefit from the behaviours that parents are genetically inclined to provide (MacDonald, 1997a,b).

There remains controversy surrounding the issue of whether variation in human reproductive strategies is environmentally induced or whether such variation primarily reflects additive genetic variation. The former view, associated with Belsky et al. (1991) and Chisholm (1993, 1996), proposes that low-investment reproductive strategies are a response to resource-poor environments, whereas high-investment strategies are a response to resource-rich environments. Although Belsky et al. (1991) do not rule out a role for heritable genetic variation, they propose that variation in reproductive strategies results from a uniform, species-typical system that provides alternate strategies depending on environmental input. On the other hand, MacDonald (1997a,b) argues that the data are more compatible with supposing that variation in reproductive strategies results mainly from genetic variation and that the opportunity for upward social mobility is the most important contextual influence delaying reproduction and lowering fertility.

CONCLUSION

Overall, the results indicate that evolutionary theory is able to provide a powerful perspective on peer relations. Basic evolutionary theory predicts the importance of reciprocity and similarity in peer friendships. Moreover, the evolutionary theory of sex is a powerful predictor of sex differences in the evolved systems of sensation-seeking/impulsivity, attraction to intimacy, and behavioural inhibition—all of which are assets or liabilities in peer interaction. No other theoretical perspective provides this type of *a priori* predictive power. Other theoretical perspectives are consistent with the descriptive data of peer relationships and with theories on the proximal mechanisms involved. Only evolutionary theory is capable of providing an *a priori* predictive basis for the overall contours of children's social development.

Finally, the entire area of reproductive strategies represents perhaps the largest contribution of an evolutionary perspective because of its unifying effects on the field of children's social development and, indeed, its ability to incorporate other areas of child development, such as IQ data, within an overarching evolutionary paradigm. These general findings do not preclude an important independent role for a variety of evolved systems that evolved to solve discrete adaptive problems in the environment of evolutionary adaptedness, but they do show that developmentalists focusing only on particular systems are, to a considerable extent, missing the forest for the trees.

REFERENCES

Alexander, R. D. (1979). *Darwinism and human affairs.* Seattle, WA: University of Washington Press.

Alexander, R. D. (1987). *The biology of moral systems.* New York: Aldine.

Asher, S. R. (1990). Recent advances in the study of peer rejection. In S. R. Asher & J.D. Coie (Eds.), *Peer rejection in childhood*, (pp. 3–14). New York: Cambridge University Press.

Asher, S. R., Parkhurst, J. T., Hymel, S., & Williams, G. (1990). Peer rejection and loneliness in childhood. In S. R. Asher, & J. D. Coie (Eds.), *Peer rejection in childhood*, (pp. 253–273). New York: Cambridge University Press.

Aukett, R., Ritchie, J., & Mill, J. K. (1988). Gender differences in friendship patterns. *Sex Roles, 19*, 57–67.

Belsky, J., Steinberg, L., & Draper, P. (1991). Childhood experience, interpersonal development, and reproductive strategy: An evolutionary theory of socialization. *Child Development, 62*, 647–670.

Berndt, T. J. (1986). Children's comments about their friendships. In M. Perlmutter (Ed.), *Minnesota Symposia in Child Development. Vol. 18: Cognitive perspectives on children's social and behavioral development* (pp. 189–212). Hillsdale, NJ: Lawrence Erlbaum Associates Inc.

Bourhis, R. Y. (1994). Power, gender, and intergroup discrimination: Some minimal group experiments. In M. P. Zanna & J. M. Olson (Eds.), *The psychology of prejudice: The Ontario Symposium* (Vol. 7) (pp. 171–208). Hillsdale, NJ: Lawrence Erlbaum Associates Inc.

Bowlby, J. (1969). *Attachment and loss. Vol. I: Attachment.* London: Hogarth Press/Institute of Psychoanalysis.

Boyd, R. & Richerson, P. J. (1985). *Culture and the evolutionary process.* Chicago, IL: University of Chicago Press.

Boyd, R. & Richerson, P. J. (1988). An evolutionary model of social learning: The effects of spatial and temporal variation. In T. R. Zentall & B. G. Galef (Eds.), *Social learning: Psychological and biological perspectives* (pp. 29–48). Hillsdale, NJ: Lawrence Erlbaum Associates Inc.

Bradley, R. H. & Caldwell, B. (1984). 174 children: A study of the relationship between home environment and cognitive development during the first 5 years. In W. Gottfried (Ed.), *Home environment and early cognitive development: Longitudinal research* (pp. 5–56). Orlando, FL: Academic Press.

Briggs, S. R. (1992). Assessing the five-factor model of personality description. *Journal of Personality, 60,* 253–293.

Brown, B. B. (1989). The role of peer groups in adolescents' adjustment to secondary school. In T. J. Berndt & G. Ladd (Eds.), *Peer relationships in child development* (pp. 188–216). New York: Wiley.

Buhrmester, D. & Furman, W. (1987). The development of companionship and intimacy. *Child Development, 58,* 1101–1113.

Buss, D. M. (1991). Evolutionary personality psychology. *Annual Review of Psychology, 42,* 459–491.

Buss, D. M. (1994). *The evolution of desire.* New York: Basic Books.

Buss, D. M. (1995). Evolutionary psychology: A new paradigm for psychological science. *Psychological Inquiry, 6,* 1–30.

Buss, D. M. & Schmitt, D. P. (1993). Sexual strategies theory: An evolutionary perspective on human mating. *Psychological Review, 100,* 204–232.

Cairns, R. B., Cairns, B. D., Neckerman, H. J., Gest, S. D., & Gariépy, J. (1988). Social networks and aggressive behavior: Peer support or peer rejection. *Developmental Psychology, 24,* 815–823.

Charlesworth, W. & Dzur, C. (1987). Gender comparisons of preschoolers' behavior and resource utilization in group problem solving. *Child Development, 58,* 191–200.

Charlesworth, W. R. & LaFreniére, P. J. (1983). Dominance, friendship, and resource utilization in preschool children's groups. *Ethology and Sociobiology, 4,* 175–186.

Charlesworth, W. R. (1996). Cooperation and competition: Contributions to an evolutionary and developmental model. *International Journal of Behavioral Development, 19,* 25–38.

Chisholm, J. S. (1993). Death, hope, and sex. *Current Anthropology, 34,* 1–24.

Chisholm, R. (1996). The evolutionary ecology of attachment organization. *Human Nature, 7,* 1–38.

Christopherson, E. R. (1989). Injury control. *American Psychologist, 44,* 237–241.

Cohen, J. (1977). Sources of peer homogeneity. *Sociology of Education, 50,* 227–241.

Coie, J. D., Dodge, K. A., & Coppotelli, H. (1982). Dimensions and types of social status: A cross-age perspective. *Developmental Psychology, 18,* 557–571.

Coie, J. D., Dodge, K. A., & Kupersmidt, J. B. (1990). Peer group behavior and social status. In S. R. Asher & J. D. Coie (Eds.), *Peer rejection in childhood,* (pp. 17–59). New York: Cambridge University Press.

Cosmides, L. & Tooby, J. (1987). From evolution to behavior: Evolutionary psychology as the missing link. In J. Barkow, L. Cosmides, & J. Tooby (Eds.), *The latest on the best: Essays on evolution and optimality*, (pp. 277–306). Cambridge, MA.: MIT Press.

Cowan, G., & Avants, S. K. (1988). Children's influence strategies: Structure, sex differences, and bilateral mother–child influences. *Child Development, 59*, 1303–1313.

Digman, J. M. (1990). Personality structure: Emergence of the five-factor model. In M. R. Rosenzweig & L. W. Porter (Eds.), *Annual Review of Psychology, 41*, 417–470.

DiPietro, J. A. (1981). Rough and tumble play: A function of gender. *Developmental Psychology, 17*, 50–58.

Dodge, K. A., Murphy, R. M., & Buchsbaum, K. (1984). The assessment of intention-cue detection skills in children: Implications for developmental psychopathology. *Child Development, 55*, 163–173.

Eagly, A. H. & Steffen, V. J. (1986). Gender and aggressive behavior: A meta-analytic review of the social psychological literature. *Psychological Bulletin, 100*, 283–308.

Epstein, J. L. (1989). The selection of friends: Changes across the grades in different school environments. In T. J. Berndt & G. Ladd (Eds.), *Peer relationships in child development* (pp. 158–187). New York: Wiley.

Fagen, R. (1981). *Animal play behavior*. New York: Oxford University Press.

Fisher, H. (1992). *The anatomy of love*. New York: Norton.

Flinn, M. V. & Low, B. S. (1986). Resource distribution, social competition, and mating patterns in human societies. In D. I. Ruberstein & R. W. Wrangham (Eds.), *Ecological aspects of social evolution: Birds and mammals* (pp. 217–243). Princeton, NJ: Princeton University Press.

Fulker, D. (1981). The genetic and environmental architecture of psychoticism, extraversion and neuroticism. In H. J. Eysenck (Ed.), *A model for personality* (pp. 88–122). Munich: Springer.

Gangestad, S. W., Thornhill, R., & Yeo, R. A. (1994). Facial attractiveness, developmental stability, and fluctuating asymmetry. *Ethology and Sociobiology, 15*, 73–85.

Gelman, R. & Carey, S. (Eds.) (1991). *The epigenesis of mind*. Hillsdale, NJ: Lawrence Erlbaum Associates Inc.

Gilligan, C. (1982). *In a different voice: Psychological theory and women's development*. Cambridge, MA.: Harvard University Press.

Ginsburg, H. J. & Miller, S. M. (1982). Sex differences in children's risk-taking behavior. *Child Development, 53*, 426–428.

Gray, J. (1982). *The neuropsychology of anxiety*. New York: Oxford University Press.

Gutmann, D. L. (1977). The cross-cultural perspective: Notes toward a comparative psychology of aging. In J. E. Birren & K. W. Shaie (Eds.), *Handbook of the psychology of aging* (pp. 302–326). New York: Van Nostrand Reinhold.

Haan, N. (1978). Two moralities in action contexts: Relationships to thought, ego regulation and development. *Journal of Personality and Social Psychology, 36*, 286–305.

Haan, N. (1985). *On moral grounds*. New York: New York University Press.

Harcourt, A. H. (1992). Cooperation in conflicts: Commonalities between humans and other animals. *Politics and the Life Sciences, 11*, 251–259.

Hartup, W. W. (1989). Behavioral manifestations of children's friendships. In T. J. Berndt & G. Ladd (Eds.), *Peer relationships in child development* (pp. 46–70). New York: Wiley.

Herrnstein, R. J. & Murray, C. (1994). *The bell curve: Intelligence and class structure in American life*. New York: Free Press.

Hinde, R. (1984). Why do the sexes behave differently in close relationships. *Journal of Social and Personal Relationships, 1*, 471–501.

Hogg, M. A. & Abrams, D. (1987). *Social identifications*. New York: Routledge.

Humphreys, A. P. & Smith, P. K. (1987). Rough and tumble, friendship, and dominance in school children: Evidence for continuity and change with age. *Child Development, 58,* 201–212.

John, O. P. (1990). The "big five" factor taxonomy: Dimensions of personality in the natural language and in questionnaires. In L. A. Pervin (Ed.), *Handbook of personality* (pp. 66–100). New York: Guilford Press.

John, O. P., Caspi, A., Robins, R. W., Moffitt, T. E., & Stouthamer-Loeber, M. (1994). The "Little Five": Exploring the nomological network of the Five-Factor Model of personality in adolescent boys. *Child Development, 65,* 160–178.

Kagan, J., Reznick, J. S., & Snidman, N. (1987). The physiology and psychology of behavioral inhibition. *Child Development, 58,* 1459–1473.

Kagan, J., Reznick, J. S., & Snidman, N. (1989). Issues in the study of temperament. In G. A Kohnstamm, J. E. Bates, & M. K. Rothbart (Eds.), *Temperament in childhood* (pp. 133–144). New York: Wiley.

Kanfer, F. H., Stifter, E., & Morris, S. J. (1981). Self-control and altruism: Delay of gratification for another. *Child Development, 52,* 674–682.

Kenrick, D. T. & Trost, M. (1989). A reproductive exchange model of heterosexual relationships: Putting proximate economics in ultimate perspective. In C. Hendrick (Ed.), *Close Relationships* (pp. 92–118). Newbury Park, CA: Sage.

Kiesler, D. J. (1983). The 1982 Interpersonal Circle: A taxonomy for complementarity in human transactions. *Psychological Review, 90,* 185–214.

Kleiman, D. G. (1977). Monogamy in mammals. *Quarterly Review of Biology, 52,* 39–69.

Kleiman, D. G. (1981). Correlations among life history characteristics of mammalian species exhibiting two extreme forms of monogamy. In R. D. Alexander & D. W. Tinkle (Eds.), *Natural selection and social behavior* (pp. 332–344). New York: Chiron.

Kochanska, G., Aksan, N., & Koenig, A. L. (1995). A longitudinal study of the roots of preschoolers' conscience: Committed compliance and emerging internalizationm. *Child Development, 66,* 1752–1769.

LaFreniére, P. J. (1996). Cooperation among peers as a conditional strategy: The influence of family ecology and kin relations. *International Journal of Behavioral Development, 19,* 39–52.

LaFreniére, P. J. & Charlesworth, W. R. (1983). Dominance, affiliation and attention in a preschool group: A nine-month longitudinal study. *Ethology and Sociobiology, 4,* 55–67.

Lancaster, J. B. & Lancaster, C. S. (1987). The watershed: Change in parental-investment and family-formation in the course of human evolution. In J. B. Lancaster, J. Altman, A. S. Rossi, & L. R. Sherrod (Eds.), *Parenting across the life span: Biosocial dimensions* (pp. 187–205). New York: Aldine.

Lang-Takoc, E. & Osterweil, Z. (1992). Separateness and connectedness: Differences between the genders. *Sex Roles, 27,* 277–289.

Leaper, C. (1991). Influence and involvement in children's discourse: Age, gender and partner effects. *Child Development, 62,* 797–811.

Lerner, R. M. & Kauffman, M. B. (1986). The concept of development in contextualism. *Developmental Review, 6,* 309–333.

Lovejoy, O. (1981). The origin of man. *Science, 211,* 341–350.

Lusk, J., MacDonald, K. B., & Newman, J. R. (in press). Resource appraisals among self, friend and leader: Implications for an evolutionary perspective on individual differences. *Personality and Individual Differences, 21.*

MacDonald, K. B. (1988). *Social and personality development: An evolutionary synthesis.* New York: Plenum.

MacDonald, K. B. (1991). A perspective on Darwinian psychology: The importance of domain-general mechanisms, plasticity, and individual differences. *Ethology and Sociobiology, 12,* 449–480.

MacDonald, K. B. (1992). A time and a place for everything: A discrete systems perspective on the role of children's rough and tumble play in educational settings. *Early Education and Development, 3,* 334–355.

MacDonald, K. B. (1993). Parent–child play: An evolutionary analysis. In K. B. MacDonald (Ed.), *Parent–child play: Descriptions and Implications* (pp. 113–143). Albany, NY: State University of New York Press.

MacDonald, K. B. (1994). *A people that shall dwell alone: Judaism as a group evolutionary strategy.* Westport, CT: Praeger.

MacDonald, K. B. (1995). Evolution, the five factor model, and levels of personality. *Journal of Personality, 63,* 525–567.

MacDonald, K. B. (1996). What do children want? An evolutionary perspective on children's motivation in the peer group. *International Journal of Behavioral Development, 19,* 53–73.

MacDonald, K. B. (1997a). The coherence of individual development: An evolutionary perspective on children's internalization of parental values. In J. Grusec & L. Kuczynski (Eds.), *Parenting strategies and children's internalization of values: A handbook of contemporary theory.* New York: Wiley.

MacDonald, K. B. (1997b). Life history theory and human reproductive behavior: Environmental/contextual influences and heritable variation. *Human Nature, 8,* 327–359.

MacDonald, K. B. (in press). The coherence of individual development: An evolutionary perspective on children's internalization of cultural values. In J. Grusec & L. Kuczynski (Eds.), *Parenting strategies and children's internalization of values: A handbook of theoretical and research perspectives.* New York: Wiley.

MacDonald, K. B. & Parke, R. D. (1986). Parent–child physical play: The effects of sex and age of children and parents. *Sex Roles, 15,* 367–378.

McGuire, M. A. (1974). The St. Kitt's Vervet. *Contributions to Primatology, 1,* 1–199.

Marks, I. (1987). *Fears, phobias, and rituals: Panic, anxiety, and their disorders.* Oxford: Oxford University Press.

Miller, E. M. (1994). Paternal provisioning versus mate seeking in human populations. *Personality and Individual Differences, 17,* 227–255.

Minton, C., Kagan, J., & Levine, J. (1971). Maternal control and obedience in the two-year-old. *Child Development, 42,* 1873–1894.

Morgan, W. R. & Sawyer, J. (1967). Bargaining expectations, and the preference for equality over equity. *Journal of Personality and Social Psychology, 6,* 139–149.

O'Brien, M. & Huston, A. C. (1985). Development of sex-typed play in toddlers. *Developmental Psychology, 21,* 866–871.

Öhman, A. (1993). Fear and anxiety as emotional phenomena: Clinical phenomenology, evolutionary perspectives, and information-processing mechanisms. In M. Lewis & J. M. Haviland (Eds.), *Handbook of emotions* (pp. 511–536). New York: Guilford Press.

Overton, W. F. (1984). World views and their influence on psychological theory and research: Kuhn–Lakatos–Lauden. In H. W. Reese (Ed.), *Advances in child development and behavior* (Vol. 18, pp. 191–226) New York: Academic Press.

Park. K. & Waters, E. (1989). Security of attachment and preschool friendships. *Child Development, 60,* 1076–1081.

Parker, J. G. & Gottman, J. M. (1985, April). *Making friends with an "extra-terrestrial": Conversational skills for friendship formation in young children.* Paper presented at the biennial meeting of the Society for Research in Child Development.

Parker, J. G. & Gottman, J. M. (1989). Social and emotional development in a relational context: Friendship interaction from early childhood to adolescence. In T. J. Berndt & G. Ladd (Eds.), *Peer relationships in child development* (pp. 95–132). New York: Wiley.

Pellegrini, A. D. (1988). Elementary-school children's rough and tumble play and social competence. *Developmental Psychology, 24,* 802–806.

Plomin, R. (1994). *Genetics and experience: The interplay between nature and nurture.* Thousand Oaks, CA: Sage.

Rabbie, J. M. (1991). Determinants of intra-group cooperation. In R. A. Hinde & J. Groebel (Eds.), *Cooperation and prosocial behaviour* (pp. 238–262). Cambridge, UK: Cambridge University Press.

Rothbart, M. K. (1989). Temperament and development. In G. A. Kohnstamm, J. Bates, & M. K. Rothbart (Eds.), *Temperament in childhood* (pp. 59–73). Chichester, UK: Wiley.

Rubin, K. H., LeMare, L. J., & Mills, S. (1990). Social withdrawal in childhood. Developmental pathways to peer rejection. In S. R. Asher & J. D. Coie (Eds), *Peer rejection in childhood* (pp. 217–249). New York: Cambridge University Press.

Rushton, J. P. (1988). Race differences in behavior: A review and evolutionary analysis. *Personality and Individual Differences, 9,* 1009–1024.

Rushton, J. P. (1995). *Race, evolution, and behavior: A life-history perspective.* New Brunswick, NJ: Transaction.

Savin-Williams, R. (1987). *Adolescence: An ethological perspective.* New York: Springer.

Shaywitz, S. E. & Shaywitz, B. E. (1988). Attention deficit disorder: Current perspectives. In J. F. Kavanagh & T. J. Truss, Jr. (Eds.), *Learning Disabilities: Proceedings of the National Conference* (pp. 369–528). Parkton, MD: York Press.

Sheldon, A. (1990). Pickle fights: Gendered talk in preschool disputes. *Discourse Processes, 13,* 5–31.

Sherif, M., Harvey, O., White, B. J., Hood, W. R., & Sherif, C. (1961). *Intergroup conflict and cooperation: The robbers' cave experiment.* Norman, OK: University of Oklahoma Press.

Smith, P. K. (1982). Does play matter? Functional and evolutionary aspects of animal and human play. *Behavioral and Brain Sciences, 5,* 135–184.

Smith, P. K. (1991). The silent nightmare: Bullying and victimisation in school peer groups. *The Psychologist: Bulletin of the British Psychological Society, 4,* 243–248.

Smith, P. & Dagliesh, L. (1977). Sex differences in parent and infant behavior in the home. *Child Development, 48,* 1250–1254.

Sroufe, L. A. (1991, April). *Models of relationships and quality of friendships in pre-adolescence: Links to attachment history and pre-school social competence.* Paper presented at the biennial meeting of the Society for Research in Child Development, Seattle, WA.

Sroufe, L. A. & Fleeson, J. (1986). Attachment and the construction of relationships. In W. W. Hartup & Z. Rubin (Eds.), *Relationships and development* (pp. 51–71). Hillsdale, NJ: Lawrence Erlbaum Associates Inc.

Symons, D. (1979). *The evolution of human sexuality.* New York: Oxford University Press.

Trapnell, P. D. & Wiggins, J. S. (1990). Extension of the Interpersonal Adjective Scales to include the Big Five dimensions of personality. *Journal of Personality and Social Psychology, 59,* 781–890.

Trivers, R. (1972). Parental investment and sexual selection. In B. Campbell (Ed.), *Sexual selection and the descent of man* (pp. 136–179). New York: Aldine.

Trivers, R. (1985). *Social evolution.* Menlo Park, CA: Benjamin/Cummings.

Trivers, R. (1991). Deceit and self-deception: The relationship between communication and consciousness. In M. Robinson & L. Tiger (Eds.), *Man and Beast Revisited* (pp. 175–191). Washington, DC: Smithsonian Press.

Tucker, D. M. & Williamson, P. A. (1984). Asymmetric neural control systems in human self-regulation. *Psychological Review, 91,* 185–215.

Tucker, D. M. & Derryberry, D. (1992). Motivated attention: Anxiety and the frontal executive functions. *Neuropsychiatry, Neuropsychology, and Behavioral Neurology, 5,* 233–252.

Turner, B. (1981). Sex-related differences in aging. In B. B. Wolman & G. Stricker (Eds.), *Handbook of Developmental Psychology* (pp. 912–936). Englewood Cliffs, NJ: Prentice-Hall.

Van der Dennen, J. M. G. (1991). Studies of conflict. In M. Maxwell (Ed.), *The sociobiological imagination* (pp. 223–241). Albany: SUNY.

Vine, I. (1987). Inclusive fitness and the self-system. The roles of human nature and sociocultural processes in intergroup discrimination. In V. Reynolds, V. Falger, and I. Vine (Eds.), *The sociobiology of ethnocentrism* (pp. 60–80). Athens, GA: University of Georgia Press.

Weisfeld, G. E. & Billings, R. L. (1988). Observations on adolescence. In K. B. MacDonald (Ed.), *Sociobiological perspectives on human development* (pp. 207–233). New York: Springer.

Weissman, M. M. (1985). The epidemiology of anxiety disorders: Rates, risks, and familial patterns. In A. H. Tuma & J. Maser (Eds.), *Anxiety and the anxiety disorders* (pp. 275–296). Hillsdale, NJ: Lawrence Erlbaum Association Inc.

Wiggins, J. S. & Broughton, R. (1985). The interpersonal circle: A structural model for the integration of personality research. *Perspectives in Personality, 1,* 1–47.

Widiger, T. A. & Trull, T. J. (1992). Personality and psychopathology: An application of the five-factor model. *Journal of Personality, 60,* 363–393.

Wilson, D. S. & Sober, E. (1994). Re-introducing group selection to the human behavioral sciences. *Behavioral and Brain Sciences, 17,* 585–684.

Wilson, E. O. (1975). *Sociobiology.* Cambridge, MA: Harvard University Press.

Wright, P. H. & Scanlon, M. B. (1991). Gender role orientation and friendship: Some attenuation, but gender differences abound. *Sex Roles, 24,* 551–566.

Youniss, J. (1986). Development of reciprocity through friendship. In E. M. Cummings & R. Iannotti (Eds), *Altruism and aggression: Biological and social origins* (pp. 88–106). New York: Cambridge University Press.

Zuckerman, M. (1979). *Sensation seeking: Beyond the optimal level of arousal.* Hillsdale, NJ: Lawrence Erlbaum Associates Inc.

Zuckerman, M. (1984). Sensation seeking: A comparative approach to a human trait. *Behavioral and Brain Sciences, 7,* 413–471.

Zuckerman, M. (1990). The psychophysiology of sensation seeking. *Journal of Personality, 58,* 313–345.

Zuckerman, M. (1991). *Psychobiology of personality.* Cambridge, UK: Cambridge University Press.

3 Genes, environment, and psychological development

David C. Rowe
University of Arizona, Tucson, USA

The theme of this chapter is that genetic influences cannot be ignored if we wish to understand the development of psychological traits. Genes play a major role in the development of most traits (Rowe, 1994). This may surprise some students, who have been taught more about environmental influences on psychological traits than genetic ones.

The chapter considers three ways in which genetic variance can be hidden within social science studies. The first is genetic variance within biological families. In families of biological relatives, inherited genes may create parent–child similarities in psychological traits. The second is genetic variance within social categories such as *social class*. People who adopt different social roles may diverge genetically as well as environmentally. The last is genetic variance between populations that contrast in their evolutionary and historical ancestry. Reproductive isolation of human groups may lead to genetic differences between them.

Only by estimating genetic effects properly can a social scientist learn the true strength of environmental influences on psychological traits. In many cases, estimates of environmental effects will be revised downward, once genetic effects have been allowed. For example, many behaviour geneticists believe that parents may deserve less credit for children who develop positive psychological traits, and less blame for children who develop negative ones. The following vignettes capture essential elements in several common social science research questions. Consider each vignette carefully.

An overweight mother reaches for the cookie jar. As her four-year-old son John watches, she munches down several "full-fat" chocolate chip cookies. Later in the day, her son takes cookies from the same jar. If the boy develops obesity years later, was it his mother's fault?

Mary's parents divorced a year ago. Mary was very upset by the divorce, and cried a lot when it happened. Now, she accepts it, and sees her father on weekends. Despite Mary's emotional recovery, her grades have slipped at school. She also tried sex for the first time, and she is only 14 years old. Are Mary's troubles a product of her parents' divorce?

Kim is fourteen. A second generation Asian American, his parents do not believe in drinking alcoholic beverages. One day, his friends pressure him into drinking a beer. He really does not like the taste. He also turns bright red in the face, and feels a bit ill. If Kim later rebuffs his non-Asian friends, is it because of a clash of their cultural values?

All three vignettes illustrate common situations that social scientists try to explain. In the first vignette, the issue is one of parental influence on a child's weight. The child may learn his parent's eating habits. The second vignette is also about families. Only the children of divorce experience its psychological stresses (see McGurk and Soriano, Chapter 5). The last vignette deals with an Asian American child. The child may not drink because of cultural prohibitions against alcoholic beverages. None of the three vignettes made any mention of effects of genes on development. Yet for each vignette, there is a competing genetic explanation of children's psychological traits, as we shall see in this chapter.

STUDIES OF DEVELOPMENT USING BIOLOGICAL FAMILIES

The first example is one of a family study. In a family study, a trait of a parent is related to a similar trait in a child. What is noticed is the degree of parent–child resemblance. The explanation for familial resemblance is usually sought in some aspect of family environment. In the earlier vignette, the ready environmental explanation of children's obesity is in parental eating habits. One imagines a kitchen filled with cake mixes and cookies—a very inaccurate stereotype of the eating habits of heavier people, but one that captures the popular imagination nonetheless.

The family study, however, is a weak research design for answering questions about family environmental effects (Rowe, 1994). This may seem a surprising statement. You are probably familiar with many dozens of family studies of psychological traits, each one interpreted in terms of some effect of parental treatments on child outcomes. These interpretations could be true, but they also may not be. Two potential sources of parental influence exist in a study of families. The first is parental treatments. The second is parental genes. Children inherit one-half of their genes from their fathers, one-half from their mothers. Most complex traits are not determined by a single gene. Rather, many genes would be involved. Thus, it is unlikely that one common "obesity" gene exists that, if inherited, would doom a child to becoming an overweight adult. There are probably many genes related to the metabolism of fat that determine body weight and the deposition of fat stores. These genes are being discovered at an increasing pace through the new techniques of molecular genetics (e.g. Halaas et al. 1995), but much remains to be learned about them.

You should understand that the genes affecting body weight, or any other trait, come in pairs because for any particular function (e.g. fat storage), one gene was inherited from one's mother, the other, from one's father. For the sake of illustration, suppose that 10 pairs of genes mostly determine variation in weight. In each gene pair, two kinds of gene may exist. Call the one that makes a person overweight a "pro-fat" gene; and the one that makes a person normal weight, an "anti-fat gene". A child could have as many as 0–20 pro-fat genes. Parent–child resemblance in body weight (adjusted for the age difference between them) could be family environmental or genetic in origin. A child of parents burdened by many "pro-fat" genes will tend to inherit them, and vice versa for a child of parents spared them. John's obesity could arise from inheriting his mother's genes, rather than from any social influence of her eating habits.

The same logic extends to psychological traits. Genes, as well as environmental influences, may determine them. The temperamental difference between a frisky Irish setter and a placid basset hound is mainly a genetic one, the result of fixing different genes in the two breeds of dogs by dog breeders. Although we are not (thankfully) subject to artificial selection, people also differ dramatically in temperaments. If there is any continuity to the determination of traits across species, genes must be allowed as one potential influence on human temperament.

In summary, the family study is like a poorly designed experiment that packs too many influences into a single "treatment". A better design would be one that puts each influence into a different condition, so that their effects can be estimated separately. This is the purpose of many behaviour genetic research designs that are described later.

STUDIES OF DEVELOPMENT USING SOCIAL CATEGORIES

Many studies focus on categorical variables, such as divorced vs. married, lower class vs. middle class, teenage mother vs. non-teenage mother, and so on. In studies of development, children belonging to the social categories are compared, with most attention given to how environmental differences among the social categories might affect them. This was the case in the earlier vignette of Mary; her troubles were attributed to a stressful divorce.

What many social scientists seem to miss is that the social categories are composed of people, who may differ in their inherited traits (Udry, 1995). That is, the people counted in the various social categories are not necessarily equivalent in their genes. Suppose the social categories were: (1) attended weight watchers classes; or (2) lived in same community, but did not attend weight watchers classes. One would not be surprised if the men and women in group 1 weighed more than those in group 2. One would also not be surprised if, sometime in the near future, molecular geneticists could genetically type people in both groups and show a greater prevalence of the "pro-fat" genes in the weight watcher group.

The formation of social categories, after all, is unlike that of treatment groups in scientific experiments. In experiments, great care is taken to randomly assign people to different groups. But no omnipotent Supreme Being will dictate randomly who gets divorced or stays married, or who rises to riches or falls into poverty. In an experiment, random assignment equates people in different groups for their genetic traits—for surface traits, like eye colour and for deeper ones, like intelligence and personality. In the human environment of cities, towns, and shopping malls, people select themselves into various social categories; so they may differ in genetically determined traits.

This analysis raises a rather silly idea. I have just implied that genes may distinguish people who are divorced, or not divorced, or people who are poor or rich. Does that mean there is a "gene for divorce"? Or a gene for "poverty" or "wealth"? The answer to this question requires a short digression. The phrases "a gene for trait X" is just a shorthand for a longer phrase, "a gene that contributes to variation in trait X". The gene itself does not cause trait X; a gene, after all, only makes biochemical substances in the body, which are either composed of RNAs or proteins. The best metaphor for gene action is that of a recipe (Dawkins, 1987, p. 295). Many genes go into the recipe that makes a person with different traits. Each gene contributes only a small part to the overall effect, but it may be a critical one. I know of a dinner party where a delicious-looking pecan pie was served. Despite its fine appearance, it tasted terrible. It had been accidentally made with salt instead of sugar. A change in a key ingredient in a recipe can drastically affect how palatable a pie is. The one ingredient alone, of course, does not make the pie—only a complex interaction of many ingredients can do that. In much the same sense, gene substitutions may affect the chances of divorce without literally creating the phenomenon of "divorce". An analysis of these genes would probably proceed to traits associated with divorce. Associated personality traits might include conscientiousness and agreeableness—both genetically influenced trait dimensions (Loehlin, 1992). In so far as people who are less agreeable and less conscientious behave in ways leading to divorce (e.g. arguing, not keeping mutual commitments), their genes may make a contribution to it.

If the people in different social categories differ genetically as well as environmentally, then so can their children. Thus, the comparison of the children of divorced and nondivorced parents would also confound genetic and environmental influences; it is not automatic that any difference between them is solely attributable to environmental influences. Mary's troubles could be attributed to genetic traits, now emerging in adolescence, instead of the stress of the earlier divorce. Again, the separation of genetic and environmental influences is how behaviour genetic designs may provide aid to our understanding of divorce.

STUDIES OF DEVELOPMENT USING RACIAL AND ETHNIC GROUP CATEGORIES

A third kind of social science study compares children of different ethnic or racial groups. Americans of African descent may be compared with those of European descent; Pakistani-born English may be compared with native-born English. Many other ethnic or racial group comparisons have caught the attention of social scientists. They all have the property that the racial and ethnic categories, although socially chosen, may contain genetic information as well.

The genetic information comes from *Homo sapien*'s family tree. Long lines of ancestors separate different populations, some just for a brief period, others for a longer historical and evolutionary time. Whenever such populations are geographically separated and inter-marry only rarely, genetic differences can crop up between them, for two primary reasons (Loehlin, Lindzey, & Spuhler, 1975). One is chance. The proportion of people with a particular gene changes from one generation to another by chance. Without going into the mechanics of Mendelian inheritance, you should understand that by such "genetic drift" alone, a gene that was once common could become rare in a population. The rate of drift for particular genes would typically vary among geographically separated populations. Also, founder effects, where just a small group starts a new population, make populations genetically different by chance. The founders may lack particular genes that were common in their populations of origin.

Another, more powerful evolutionary force is natural selection. Genes can become rare or common depending on how successfully their bearers survive and reproduce. An example of a selected trait is skin coloration.

Any light-skinned Northern European who has vacationed in Africa can appreciate that the effects of sunburn and sun-related cancers make him/ her less well adapted to the tropics than native people. Fortunately, clothes and sunblocks may overcome this maladaptation. Although the details of adaptation for various human physical traits are often unknown, the presumption that some evolutionary adaptation has occurred since the geographical separations of human populations is strong.

Many social scientists find any consideration of racial or ethnic *genetic* differences to be a completely unacceptable idea, for reasons of either politics or morality. They demand, consequently, that nature not produce any genetic differences between populations in the traits of interest to them. Of course, nature need not comply. As we shall see later, research designs for looking at ethnic or racial differences are usually not strong ones so ambiguous conclusions about racial and ethnic differences in genes related to psychological traits are to be expected—without a reliable research design, one cannot produce sound data. Nonetheless, a responsible social scientist must ponder whether trait-relevant genetic differences exist among racial or ethnic group categories, because good science never rejects a hypothesis for reasons of satisfying political or social concerns that are not strictly a part of understanding the origins of trait variation. In our vignette, Kim's dislike of alcohol may arise from ethnic differences in inheritance.

THE FIELD OF BEHAVIOUR GENETICS

The field of behaviour genetics is more than 100 years old (Plomin, DeFries, & McClearn, 1990a). It was founded by the British polymath, Sir Francis Galton. Living in the second half of the 1800s, Galton was a gentleman scientist, able to explore various scientific fields because of a financial inheritance from his family. Among his discoveries were finger prints for the identification of criminals and high and low pressure bars in meteorology. He was intensely interested in the inheritance of psychological traits. At a world's fair-like exposition in London, he gathered data on members of hundreds of families. They paid him to take tests of strength, lung capacity, colour vision, and reaction time, among other measures. Galton noticed that many of these traits were familial; he invented a statistic, the "correlation coefficient", to quantify fully the psychological resemblance of family members. The correlation, given a better mathematical treatment by Galton's student Karl Pearson, is now a standard statistic in all social sciences. Galton also made the first use of twins to infer genetic influences on a trait. In his book, *Hereditary genius* (Galton, 1869, 1962), he also created the idea of an adoption study. As a control for the social benefits of wealth, he recommended looking at the life success of the adopted children of Roman Catholic Popes. He reasoned that the adopted sons of Popes would have received many material and social advantages, without necessarily having genetic ones. Although Galton's proposal does not make for a conclusive study, he gave social science the rudimentary basis of many behaviour genetic research designs.

Since the 1800s, behaviour genetics has grown into a field employing hundreds of researchers world-wide. The field lies at the junction of biology and social science. From biology, it takes the idea that trait variance may be explained partially by genetic variance. Thus, behaviour genetics is distinguished from the field of sociology by an assumption that genetic variance is worth looking for. From social science, it takes an interest in environmental influences. Indeed, behaviour genetic research designs are as informative about environmental variance as they are about genetic variance.

Genetic variance

Many genes serve a particular function but also vary among people. Most physical traits, like eye colour or hair texture, are affected by genes. A lack of pigmentation genes produces albinism, a condition that causes sensitivity to the damaging effects of solar radiation. Psychological traits are also influenced by genes (Plomin et al., 1990a; Bouchard, 1994). Genetic variation is rarely completely determinative of psychological traits—people will differ in their behavioural traits for environmental reasons as well. The strength of the genetic effect depends on how strongly people with different genetic make-ups differ from one another. As in the earlier example of a pecan pie cooked with salt or sugar, the focus is on trait variance—on how people differ in psychological traits—when one set of genes is substituted for another set.

The *heritability coefficient* is a number that summarises the strength of genetic variance in trait variance. The number takes any value from zero to one. A heritability of zero indicates a total absence of genetic variance in the trait in question; one of 1.0 indicates complete genetic determination, a highly unrealistic outcome for most psychological traits.

It is estimated that about 100,000 pairs of genes exist in humans. About 70,000 of them do not vary at all. These genes are exactly identical in all people; they include genes called "housekeeping" genes because they look after cell functions that are essential for life. The other 30,000 genes, according to the best current estimate, are variable ones; thus, combinations of them can contribute to genetic effects on traits. The exact function of far fewer genes is known. Even in a bacteria, *Haemophilus influenzae*, one of the simplest living organisms, the function of about 40 per cent of its newly discovered 1743 genes is unknown today (Nowak, 1995). The genes related to most psychological traits are currently uncharted ones (Mann, 1994). Once a gene is identified, molecular genetic techniques can be used to amplify it from tissue samples (e.g. blood white cells, saliva cheek cells), and also to distinguish whether it contains a particular mutation that alters its function. Theoretically, behaviour genetics could be done with amplified genes alone, if enough were known so that the genes relevant to a particular trait could be amplified and scored properly. As was just noted, however, the number of genes that exist in the human genome is large, and finding those genes relevant to a particular trait is like finding needles hiding in a haystack—a difficult task indeed. For the present, most behaviour genetic work proceeds in the absence of knowledge about individuals' genetic markers.

Environmental variance

A common misunderstanding about behaviour genetic research is to think that it is just about the genes; it is also about environments. Two kinds of environmental influences can be distinguished: those influences shared by pairs of people in a family (e.g. younger brother and older brother, mother and daughter); and those that are nonshared. The latter kind of influence makes individuals in a family different from one another. Table 3.1 presents examples of social science variables that are *potentially* shared and nonshared environmental influences on a particular trait. The word "potentially" is in italics because features of the environment commonly assumed to exert environmental effects may not do so, or may do so only weakly.

Shared environment variance

The environmental variables on the left side of Table 3.1 are usually associated with a pair of individuals in a family. For example, in a family

TABLE 3.1
Potential shared and nonshared influences on behavioural development

Shared influences	*Nonshared influences*
Social class	Birth trauma
Divorce	Car accident
Unmarried vs. married mother	Teacher
Parental alcohol abuse	Peers
Religiosity of the family	Embryological development
Parental vocabulary knowledge	Child-specific parental treatment
Parental love and warmth toward children	
Poverty	

where the father earns $18,000 per year, both siblings are relatively poor by US standards. In one where he earns $50,000, they are relatively well-off. Children share divorce in the sense that siblings in a family are all exposed to the stresses of divorce; those in a family in which the parents remain together avoid these psychological stresses. Another way to think of a shared influence is that it is "correlated across" sibling pairs (or parent–child pairs). The "social address" features of a family, like social class and divorce, are shared most strongly by siblings. But parental treatments also may be shared when parents do not radically change their treatment styles from one child to the next. For example, in a sample of teenage siblings, my colleagues and I correlated the sibling's self-reports about parental treatments; the sibling correlations were 0.43 for maternal warmth, 0.83 for maternal control, 1.0 for parents' drinking of alcoholic beverages, and 0.88 for family religiosity (all values corrected for unreliability of measurement, Rowe, Vazsonyi, & Flannery, 1995). Now, suppose that one of these variables strongly influenced personality development. It would tend to make siblings alike in this trait because each variable is correlated across siblings.

Some students erroneously believe that the "shared environment" is somehow associated with the general cultural landscape. This error occurs, for example, in the false assertion that "identical twins reared apart are alike because they all grow up in England". English rearing may mean that all the twins share a faith in the Queen and a love of country on Guy Fawkes Day. This commonality of experience, however, cannot explain why the twins are *different* from each other. One identical twin in the sample may have an IQ of 107, another an IQ of 88. The variability among twins exists despite their sharing a cultural similarity. Thus, a common culture cannot explain why the twins, on the whole, have different IQ scores, nor why the IQs of two identical twins born as a twin pair happen to match closely (because, by the cultural argument, *all* the twins should score alike). A shared environment is one associated for individuals in a family, but it should differ from one family to another, unlike the cultural background.

Nonshared environment variance

The nonshared environmental influences listed in Table 3.1 may affect each child differently, or have a different effect on a parent and child. For example, oxygen deprivation during delivery may cause permanent brain damage, leading to a lower IQ score in childhood. As one child in a family may have had a bad *in utero* experience, and another a normal one, this influence can be "nonshared" by siblings. Parents may also treat their children differently. Of course, this is a nonshared environmental effect only in so far as the treatment causes the development of particular traits. If the parental choice of treatment is in response to siblings' different traits, then it may express genetic variance. For example, if one boy is genetically conduct-disordered and his brother is not, the fact that the former child receives more punishment by parents is considered to be a genetic effect (see Lytton, 1990 for data on the direction of effects). The same logic applies to peer groups. Peers can be social influences on development, but children also choose to be with friends who they resemble (e.g. on age and race), so that friends' similarity is not always an indicator of mutual influence.

Other nonshared environmental influences are simply idiosyncratic. For example, consider a particularly inspiring teacher. It is probably just chance that one sibling is assigned to this teacher who may affect a life-long career choice because, at that moment, the child was highly receptive to the teacher's message. Darwin almost lost his passage on the ship the *Beagle* because the captain did not like the shape of his nose. A war was waged over Helen of Troy, a very beautiful woman. High chance events do not permit a thorough scientific analysis, if only because they repeat rarely, and under uncontrollable circumstances. The list of nonshared influences in Table 3.1 is certainly incomplete; almost any one-time event, whether social or biological, is a potential nonshared influence.

BEHAVIOUR GENETIC RESEARCH DESIGNS

Behaviour genetic designs involve a type of experimentation. Unlike pure experiments, behaviour geneticists who work with humans cannot create different groups by design. Instead, naturally occurring groups must be sampled and compared. Genetic variance is captured in a comparison of biologically related individuals. If genetic variance contributes to trait variation, then biologically related individuals should show resemblance for the trait, with the strength of the resemblance dependent on the closeness of the biological relationship. Relatives vary in their genetic-closeness. Identical twins are genetically exactly the same because one fertilised egg cell splits early in development and becomes two individuals. Siblings and fraternal twins share half their genes. Half-siblings are the product of one common parent: paternal half-siblings have the same father and maternal ones, the same mother. Half-siblings share one-quarter of their genes. A parent and child share one-half their genes.

For a completely genetically determined trait, the correlation coefficient of pairs of biological relatives would approximately equal the percentage of shared genes. Genetically, the most that a parent and child can correlate is one-half. The most two siblings can correlate is also one-half. The most identical twins can correlate is 1.0 and cousins, a mere 0.125. Relatives

TABLE 3.2
Simple behaviour genetic research designs

Group	Variance estimated
Unrelated siblings reared together	Shared environmental variance
Adoptive parent–child	Shared environmental variance
MZ twins raised apart	Genetic variance
Parent and child raised apart	One-half of genetic variance
Comparison of MZ and DZ twins	Genetic variance and shared environmental variance

MZ, monozygotic; DZ, dizygotic.

typically correlate much less than these maximum values. For one reason, traits are measured imperfectly. Relatives do not share "errors of measurement" and so are less alike than if traits were measured perfectly (e.g. the sibling correlation on weight would be higher if each child were weighed on an accurate scale than if their weights were guessed by a school nurse). The nonshared environmental influences described above also reduce correlations from the value of the percentage of shared genes.

Table 3.2 displays several kinds of behaviour genetic research designs and what influence each one estimates. Unrelated children reared in a family are usually adoptive children from past, successive adoptive placements. Sometimes, one child is the biological child of the adoptive parents and the other is an adoptive child. In this type of family, the two siblings are *biologically* unrelated because the adoptive child's biological parents are not the adopting parents. Both children get their nurture from their adoptive parents, but at least one child receives his/her genes from another set of parents, so that any resulting psychological similarity is a product of shared nurture.

In the next design, the adoptive parent is compared with a biologically unrelated adoptive child. Their trait similarity indexes the effects of shared environmental variance. The same is true of any correlation between features of the adoptive home and adoptive children's traits.

The next two designs deal with genetic influences. The classic design is that of monozygotic (that is, "one-egg", or identical) twins reared apart. Because of the scarcity of identical twins raised apart, this design has been rarely used. However, one recent example is a study carried out in the

United States at the University of Minnesota (Bouchard, Lykken, McGue, Segal, & Tellegen, 1990). This study has generated many anecdotes about monozygotic (MZ) twins reared apart. However, a fictional cartoon best illustrates the spirit of this design. In a Charles Adams drawing, two identical twins raised apart are shown meeting in a patent office, wearing the same clothes, with identical, *Rube Goldberg*-like inventions on their laps. His caption read as "The Mallifert twins meet accidently". For anecdotes on real twins raised apart, you may enjoy a *New Yorker* article presenting several of them (Wright, 1995). Another study of separated twins has received very little press publicity (Pedersen, Plomin, McClearn, & Friberg, 1988). This work was done with a Swedish sample of twins raised part, identified through the records kept in Sweden for tracking citizens' lives. At the time of their rediscovery, the twins were older adults, about 50–70 years old. The logic of this design is based on the contrast of MZ twin's biological and family environmental correlations. They share 100 per cent of their genes (except for rare somatic mutations), so they correlate 1.0 genetically. The family environments of the twins raised apart should correlate zero. Any trait measured on the twins that is shaped strongly by family environment, and not at all shaped by heredity, also should correlate nearly zero.

The last design shown in Table 3.2 is the comparison of MZ and DZ (dizygotic, "two-egg" or fraternal twins) raised together. Estimates of genetic variance and shared environmental variance are gained by comparing the twin correlations. Under certain assumptions, the environmental variance can be calculated as twice the DZ correlation minus the MZ correlation. For example, if $r_{MZ} = 0.40$ and $r_{DZ} = 0.35$, the shared *environmentability* (c^2) would equal 0.30. The heritability (h^2) is twice the subtraction of the MZ and DZ correlations, resulting in this example in $h^2 = 0.10$. When DZ twins are as similar as MZ twins, the heritability estimate is zero. When MZ twins are twice as similar as DZ twins, the *environmentability* is zero. Because of the great number of twins raised together, this design is one of the workhorses of behaviour genetics.

Common criticisms of twin studies

Studies of twins, raised both apart and together, are commonly criticised for two reasons. The first is the similar appearance of twins. Identical twins usually look alike, and are sometimes mistaken for each other by friends and relatives. Young MZ twins are often dressed in identical clothing. When living in different neighbourhoods, with their different adoptive parents, raised-apart twins should retain this similarity of facial and bodily appearance. Figure 3.1 illustrates the facial similarity of a pair of identical twins. Could their remarkable facial alikeness make

FIG. 3.1   Identical twins show facial similarity.

them alike in personality or IQ? For most traits, the short answer is *no* (Hettema, Neale, & Kendler, 1995; Kendler, 1983; Matheny, Wilson, & Dolan, 1976; Plomin, Willerman, & Loehlin, 1976; Rowe, Clapp, & Wallis, 1987). The reason is that appearance differences, in facial features, eye colour, hair colour, and other traits associate weakly, or not at all, with psychological traits. In the 1800s, the phrenologists thought that "primitive" facial features, such as a protruding brow ridge, would lead to criminal behaviour. Actual comparisons of criminals and noncriminals, however, failed to discover any distinguishing facial features. Consider people who look like Prince Charles or President Clinton. It is unlikely that if we collected such people together, they would show much psychological similarity to either famous person. True, some people make money by presenting themselves as being a copy of the king of rock and roll, Elvis Presley. And they probably share the trait of extroversion by their selection into this role—wallflowers need not apply. Yet I doubt that their psychological similarity would be very great, and certainly none have approached the musical talents of the one, true king of rock and roll. The weak relation of appearance to psychological traits means that, in general, the former cannot be used to explain the remarkable psychological similarity of MZ twins, whether reared apart or together.

Placement similarity

The second criticism allots some of the resemblance of reared apart twins to similarities in their adoptive placements. For example, placements may be more similar than chance in the income level of the adoptive parents. This could happen if the separated twins were adopted by relatives (e.g. an uncle adopts one twin and an aunt adopts the other). Or it might happen if adoption agencies were to place each twin with adoptive parents who are similar in social class to the twins' biological parents. Because adoptions are not made for scientific purposes, the assumption of complete "random assignment" to adoptive families is seldom fulfilled.

Nevertheless, whether this criticism warrants our concern depends first on how closely the twins' adoptive families are matched. In the Minnesota study of twins raised apart (Bouchard et al., 1990), the adoptive families did match somewhat for adoptive father's and mother's years of education ($r = 0.13$ and 0.41, respectively) where years of education was used as an index of social class. Second, it depends on whether the social class levels of the adoptive parents *affects* the children's IQs. Remember, each twin raised apart is also usually an *adoptive* child in a new family. In the Minnesota study, father's and mother's years of education failed to influence each adopted twin's IQs ($r = 0.1$ and zero, respectively). It may come as a surprise that parental social class lacked any effect on children's IQs, but you should understand that the environmental effect of social class, which is revealed in an adoption design (see Table 3.2), is very weak. How similar could MZ twins become in IQ from growing up in adoptive families matched somewhat for social class? The maximum value, according to Bouchard's various calculations, was a correlation coefficient of just 0.03. The actual resemblance in IQ of the separated pairs was a hardy $r = 0.70$. Their genetic similarity, not the environments of their adoptive placements, must explain this extraordinary IQ similarity of these twins raised apart.

The assumption of equal environments

The most common kind of twin study, the comparison of MZ and DZ twins reared together, requires an assumption of *equal treatment environments* of the MZ and DZ twin pairs. This assumption seems almost outlandish. Do we really require that MZ and DZ twins be treated *equally* alike, when you can see that MZ twins are more often dressed alike and put on display? The assumption, however, is more subtle than this view. For example, if MZ twins provoked more similar treatments from their parents than DZ twins, this assumption is not violated. The assumption requires that a treatment *causes* the psychological trait in children, instead of being *responsive* to the children's pre-existing traits (Lytton, 1977). The evidence in support of this equal treatment assumption is pretty strong (e.g. Loehlin & Nichols, 1976). Consider dressing twins alike. Few parents would literally think that making a duller sibling wear the same clothes as a brighter brother or sister would equalise their IQs. Parents' dressing twins similarity is not necessarily a problem for the interpretation of twin studies, if that practice does not contribute to variation in IQ.

LIMITS TO THE STRENGTH OF FAMILY ENVIRONMENTAL EFFECTS ON PSYCHOLOGICAL TRAITS

Overweight parents have fat kids. The child of a criminal is more likely a thief than one of a noncriminal. Shy parents have shy kids. The son of a bright parent complains that his cousin does not understand the vocabulary he uses. In each case, the association of these traits in children and parents has been given an environmental interpretation in socialisation science. An alternative explanation, unmentionable in some social science circles, is that genes in the parent partly determine the parental trait and the trait of the child as well, by way of the child's inheritance of copies of those parental genes. Genes for obesity may create parent–child similarity in weight. Genes for aggression and dishonesty may create parent–child similarity in criminality. Genes for shyness may make the shy child similar to her parent. And genes for IQ may fashion the immense vocabulary of a son of smart parents. Of course, as mentioned earlier, a "gene for IQ", just makes a biochemical product in the body. It probably has many functions in metabolism or in the regulation of other genes. It may affect traits other than IQ. It also may not have evolved specifically to make anyone smarter. However, its replacement by another gene with a similar function should change people's IQs; this is the limited meaning of a "gene for trait X".

The astonishing conclusion of behaviour genetic studies is that parent–child (and sibling) resemblance in most traits is entirely, or largely, attributable to genes. This conclusion for the nonpsychological trait of body weight is explained below. More astonishingly, it extends to psychological traits as well. In this brief chapter, space permits only a few illustrations of the weakness (or entire lack) of family environmental effects (see Rowe, 1994 for a fuller treatment). Only a few examples in the domains of intelligence and normal personality traits will be examined.

Family environment and weight

Body weight is a heavily defended trait; the body does what it needs to— from inflicting hunger pains to lowering metabolism—to ensure that no person starves. The world of our ancestors, in which food shortages and famines were frequent if sometimes tragic occurrences, kept people thin. In today's world of abundant food, conveniently packaged and concentrated, genes that efficiently store fat inevitably leave some people overweight.

Studies show the biological control of weight. Thin subjects force-fed food will gain weight, and then lose it once the force-feeding stops. Obese people who lose weight slow their metabolism, making further weight loss more excruciatingly difficult. Monozygotic twins, force-fed, gain and lose weight in similar ways, indicating genetic control over fat deposition and loss. The environment of the rearing family, however, fails to affect body weight. Adoption studies reveal this pattern: The weight of adoptive children tracks that of their biological parents, and is unrelated to that of their adoptive parents.

Figure 3.2 presents some adoption data (Stunkard et al., 1986). The plotted points are body mass indexes (BMIs), a special ratio of weight to height that indicates the degree of "fatness". The ascending line shows the relation of the biological parents' fatness to that of their biological children, who grew up from nearly birth in adoptive families. The heavier the biological parent, the heavier the biological child. The other line, relating the weight of these same adoptive children to that of their adoptive parents, is about horizontal. Heavy adoptive parents have average weight adoptive children. Average adoptive parents have average weight adoptive children. And thin adoptive parents have average weight adoptive children. In the vignette that opened this chapter Mary's mother was eating cookies. The mother can overeat to her heart's content without

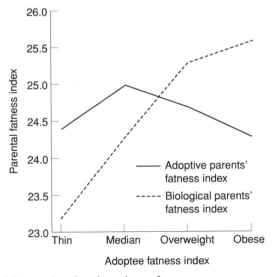

FIG. 3.2   Parental fatness plotted against adoptee fatness.

any worry that her eating habits will make her daughter fat; children will be fat only if they inherit a genetic disposition tending this way.

The trait of intelligence

Intelligence is the ability to learn new things quickly and to reason abstractly. It is partly the product of schooling. Mathematics and advanced uses of language are taught in school. In Western societies, most children receive enough schooling to begin to exercise their intellectual abilities. The behaviour geneticist asks, why is one schooled child brighter or duller than another?

Intelligence certainly requires exposure to books, good conversations, and intellectual problems. One who is an "intellectual" lives best in the milieu of a large urban city with its coffee shops and speciality magazines and with its chances to meet other people of similar interests and expertise. For children, intellectual stimulation consists of the parents' intellectual level, the quality of neighbourhood schools, and parents' direct encouragement of children's intellectual work. Intellectual stimulation levels vary widely among families. For example, even a count of the "number of books" owned by a family is associated with (although not necessarily causative of) children's IQs.

Yet, exposure is not everything. The other side of the coin is what a child does with an "exposure" to a learning opportunity. Suppose a child hears a new word in conversation or reads it in a book. The exposure only adds to the child's knowledge if the child correctly deduces the meaning of the word, and if it does not slip his/her mind later. It is in the rate of learning that variation in the biology of intelligence becomes most important. Many studies now conclude that biological differences in the nervous system, which are not fully understood today, make more intelligent children better able to apprehend and respond to stimuli in their environments (Rowe, 1994).

IQ varies with performance on simple tasks that seem to be more closely tied to neurological functioning than to prior learning or social experience. Consider the inspection time test (Deary, 1995). The auditory version of this task involves presenting two tones in succession. The order varies. On some trials, a high pitched tone precedes a low pitched one (H–L), and on other trials, the order is reversed (L–H). After both tones are presented, another one comes so that the subject cannot mentally rehearse the first two tones. The subject gets a trial correct by giving the correct order of presentation (H–L vs. L–H). The task becomes progressively more difficult because the tones are made briefer and briefer—durations from $\frac{1}{5}$th second to $\frac{1}{20}$th second. The subject's score is the number discrimination errors. This auditory inspection time task is so easy that it can be done by mentally retarded people, or by the mentally ill who have disorganised thought processes. Nonetheless, in normal samples of school aged-students, it is moderately associated with both verbal and nonverbal IQs—a typical correlation between inspection time and IQ is –0.3 to –0.4 (i.e. higher IQ individuals make fewer inspection time errors). Deary interprets inspection time as the time needed to extract information about some perception. High IQ individuals are able to extract information more quickly than low IQ ones, even when tones were presented for just a fraction of a second.

The heritability of IQ

IQ is probably the most heritable psychological trait. In childhood and young adulthood, heritabilities range from about 0.40 to 0.50 (Plomin, Owen, & McGuffin, 1994). The heritability of IQ tends to increase with age, with heritabilities reaching as high as 0.80 later in life. The "genes for IQ" can be understood as resulting in the neurological differences that lead to better performance on simple information-processing tasks, such as inspection time, and ultimately to a greater rate and accuracy of learning that leads to greater intellectual accomplishments.

The limits of family environmental influence on IQ

In the working class to professional class range, variation in family environments only modestly affects young children's IQs. In childhood, the family *environmentability* of IQ ranges from 11 per cent to 35 per cent, depending on the relationship involved (e.g. siblings vs. twins; Chipeur, Rovine, & Plomin, 1990). The IQs of unrelated children, mainly preadolescents, who are reared in the same household correlate 0.32 ($N = 714$ pairs, Bouchard & McGue, 1981). The strength of this family environment effect, however, appears to weaken considerably as children grow up. Dizygotic (DZ) twins get more dissimilar in IQ as they mature, whereas monozygotic (MZ) twins retain their IQ resemblance throughout their lives (McCartney, Harris, & Bernieri, 1990). The reduced DZ twin resemblance increases the heritability of IQ, but reduces its family environmentability. Adoption studies point to the same conclusion. In six recent studies of biologically unrelated adolescent or young adult siblings raised together, the average IQ correlation was about *zero* (both adopted–adopted and adopted–biological pairs were included; McGue, Bouchard, Iacono, & Lykken, 1993).

Table 3.3 illustrates the absence of family environmental effects using the research design of twins reared apart and together. The first three rows of the table show various outcomes expected under different theories of IQ. The first hypothesis is one of family environmental effects. Among twins reared together, identical twins should correlate 0.50 and fraternal twins

TABLE 3.3
Real and expected IQ correlations of twins reared apart and
together

	Group			
	MZ$_t$	DZ$_t$	MZ$_a$	DZ$_a$
Expected correlations				
Family effects only	0.50	0.50	0.00	0.00
Genetic effects only	0.50	0.25	0.50	0.25
Combined family and genetic effects	0.75	0.50	0.50	0.25
Actual correlations				
Pedersen et al. (1992)	*0.80*	*0.32*	*0.78*	*0.23*
N pairs	63	79	45	88

Note: IQ is the first principal component of verbal, spatial,
perceptual speed, and memory tests.

should correlate 0.50. Among twins reared apart, the correlations should drop to zero because the twins are raised in unrelated family circumstances.

The next row shows a genetic hypothesis. The circumstance of rearing does not matter. Among twins reared apart and together, MZ twins correlate 0.50. DZ twins correlate 0.25. DZ twins should correlate less than MZ twins because they share fewer (50%) genes than MZ twins share (100%).

The third row presents a combined family environmental and genetic hypothesis. As expected genetically, DZ twins are less similar than MZ twins (by 0.25). As expected, environmentally, twins reared together are more alike than ones adopted into different families (e.g. $r_{MZt} = 0.75$, $r_{MZa} = 0.50$).

The *Swedish adoption/twin study of aging* (SATSA) provides some relevant data for the last row of Table 3.3 (Pedersen, Plomin, Nesselroade, & McClearn, 1992). A sample of reared together twins was matched for gender, age, and county of birth with a sample of twins who were separated in infancy or childhood. The twins had been separated because of economic and cultural strains in Sweden prior to the Second World War. When they were tested, all the twins were over 50 years of age. All pairs of separated twins had been separated before age 11 years. The findings of SATSA matched the expectations of a genetic hypothesis, but not those of a family environmental hypothesis or a combined one.

Among MZ twins, twins raised together correlated 0.80 and MZ twins raised apart correlated 0.78. Among DZ twins, twins raised together correlated 0.32 and DZ twins reared apart correlated 0.23. A statistical analysis confirmed the general pattern; the heritability of IQ was estimated to be 0.81, the nonshared environmentability, 0.19, and the family (shared) environmentability, *zero*. By the end of the lifespan, experiences in the family had left no visible imprint on IQ variation.

Why does the family have so little influence on the level of IQ that a child finally attains? My interpretation is that many sources of intellectual stimulation exist outside the home and can be tapped by a child with an active, inquiring mind. The child who inherits genes favouring high IQ, but lives with working class parents who are not particularly bright, can shine at school and grow intellectually with the help of supportive teachers and friends, and later, with the help of occupational challenges. The child who inherits genes favourable to a low IQ, even when raised by bright upper class parents, probably will not develop very far intellectually. Although we see the bright parent with the honour-roll child, we should not credit primarily the parents' nurture with the son's or daughter's academic success. Contrary to what most people think, the child's genes, rather than his/her rearing in the family, would deserve the credit. This does not deny that a wealthy family might open some career doors to a child that a poor family could not. Only the wealthy send their children to Britain's best schools, and similarly in the United States. A fancy home computer may be available in one household and not in the other. Nonetheless, the ultimate intellectual development of a child depends less on these experiences in the family than many would wish to believe.

Children "niche-pick". The term "niche" is used in ecology to refer to the environment that best meets the adaptive requirements of a particular organism. Children will discover the environmental niches that best suit their talents and personalities, and then use them. They avoid those environments that tax them unduly. A child who finds arithmetic easy wants more; one who struggles wants less. Parents seem to exert some environmental effects on young children's intellectual growth, but it wanes as children grow and make more choices for themselves. The idea that people ultimately make their own environments is a central one in modern behaviour genetic conceptions of psychological development (Scarr, 1993).

Limited family environmental effects on personality development

Personality researchers have agreed on a consensual system of five personality traits (Goldberg, 1993; see MacDonald, Chapter 2). The first trait in the Five-Factor Model (FFM) system describes the sociability of people, how much they like human contact and get along with others. It is called *extroversion*. A second trait, *neuroticism*, describes the extent to which people are prone to worry and irritability. A third trait, *conscientiousness*, distinguishes people who are future-oriented, organised, and responsible from those who are impulsive and careless. Low conscientiousness is associated with criminal behaviour. A fourth trait, *agreeableness*, marks people who are sympathetic, warm, and kind from those who are quarrelsome, cold, and unfriendly. Agreeableness is prized in a spouse. The last trait in the system, openness to experience, reflects an interest in culture and intellectual sophistication. It may correlate with IQ. The five traits provide a fairly complete description of the broad dimensions of personality.

All five dimensions of personality are heritable (Bouchard, 1994; Loehlin, 1992). According to Loehlin's review of twin and adoption studies, heritabilities range from 0.40 to 0.49. Bouchard's review of three sets of twin studies yields comparably high estimates. Indeed, whereas it was once thought that some psychological traits might be without genetic influence, behaviour geneticists now believe that nearly all psychological traits contain some genetic variance. An effect of genes extends to religiosity, vocational interests, social attitudes (Rowe, 1994), and even to hours of TV viewed (Plomin, Corley, DeFries, & Fulker, 1990b).

Family environment has only a weak, or no, influence on personality traits. In Bouchard's review, an average of 7 per cent of the variation in the FFM traits was attributable to shared *environmentability* ($c^2 = 0.07$). In Loehlin's review, the estimates ranged from 0.02 to 0.09, and were not always statistically significant. These environmentabilities refer to the family environment as shared by siblings. Another estimate of environmentability is for the environment as shared by parent–child. This estimate is obtained from studies of adoptive children. Loehlin, in reviewing the adoptive studies of the FFM, could find no evidence that parents transmit their personality traits environmentally to their children. The estimates of parent–child environmentability nestled around zero.

These data require a rethinking of family effects. This rethinking is difficult because the lay-person's explanation of a troubled adulthood is an abusive childhood. The media constantly promotes the idea that some early trauma or event sets later adult character. Given the lack of personality transmission in families, such theories should be viewed with extreme skepticism. The similarities in the lives of reared apart MZ twins appear despite their different childhoods. In one pair (Rowe, 1994), obsessive cleanliness was a common trait. Each MZ twin believed early parental treatment was to blame for his behaviour. One twin thought he was imitating his adoptive mother's compulsive housekeeping; the other, that he was reacting against a sloppy mother. In neither case does evidence exist that the adoptive mother transmitted a trait to MZ twins; rather, knowing about both twins' behaviour, we can see the common life-line of shared DNA. The fact that childhood explanations of adult behaviour can be easily constructed does not make them true. Behaviour genetic data strongly imply that the true environmental effects lie outside the family, in nonshared environments. For example, these unique environments make MZ twins occasionally discordant for schizophrenia—one twin having a full-blown mental illness, but the other twin has none. The mystery of these nonshared environmental effects has not been solved, but will challenge psychological trait theorists in the future.

GENETIC VARIANCE IN SOCIAL CATEGORIES

The next topic of this chapter is *social categories*, such as divorce status, social class, unwed motherhood, and so on. In many social science fields, these "social address" variables are given an automatic environmental interpretation. A child is said to have a low IQ because of lower class rearing—an environmental interpretation. A child is said to be involved in early sexuality (as in the vignette that opened this chapter) because of the psychological stresses of divorce. Children of unwed mothers are said to fail in school because their mothers lack child-rearing skills. These explanations carelessly assume that no genetic variance exists in measures of social categories. This assumption is seriously flawed.

Genetic variance in divorce

Divorce is the legal separation of a married couple. Divorce rates have not been static in the second half of the 20th century in the Western democracies. In general, divorce has risen substantially. In the United States, the increase in divorce rates parallels changes in state laws, with rates increasing in nearly every state after the passage of "no fault" divorce laws that allowed divorce without proof of infidelity or physical or mental cruelty. The secular trend in divorce clearly is environmental; no one would suggest that a new mutation, a divorce gene, entered these populations and spread to produce divorce. As Udry (1995, p. 1276) notes, social change is a natural focus for environmentally oriented researchers because "rarely does it collide with biology".

Nevertheless, individual variation in divorce may still possess a genetic diathesis. This diathesis is likely to be complex, involving many traits (e.g. low agreeableness, low IQ). Couples possessing this diathesis would tend more to divorce, regardless of the legal restrictions on it. When society places many legal obstacles in the way of divorce, only the most conflictive and unhappy couples would divorce. Let social restrictions ease, and the divorce rate would rise, but couples possessing the strongest genetic diathesis would still tend to be the ones obtaining divorces. Genetic effects on divorce should appear in a behaviour genetic study. First, family members should show resemblance on whether they divorce. Second, more biologically related family members should have more closely tied divorce risks.

McGue and Lykken (1992) completed a study of divorce using 722 MZ and 794 same-sex DZ twins, their parents, and their spouses' parents. Divorce increased if one's biological relative had been divorced. For example, among the offspring of nondivorced parents, 19% were divorced. Among the offspring of divorced parents, 29% were divorced. The increase was far greater, however, for MZ twins. Among the co-twins of nondivorced MZ twins, 13% were divorced. Among the co-twins of divorced MZ twins, 45% were divorced, a threefold increase in rate. McGue and Lykken calculated the risk of divorce in a hypothetical mating of a male MZ twin and a female MZ twin with divorce in both their own co-twins and in their parents. It worked out to 78%. With such negative family histories, it might be best to call off the wedding! In the entire sample, the heritability of divorce was estimated to be 0.53. The family environment-ability was estimated to be zero. This last result is contrary to theories that interpret the intergenerational transmission of divorce as a result of social modelling or of a lessening of the social stigma associated with divorce. The offspring of divorced parents may then have behaviour problems such as precocious sexuality, not because of social modelling, but because they share a genetic diathesis with their parents. This conclusion accords with the observation that children's behaviour problems in families that divorce often precede by several years the actual divorces (Cherlin et al., 1991). This genetic view of divorce puts many findings in a new light.

Genetic variance in social class

Within the Western, industrialised countries, social class is usually measured by parental years of education, occupational status, or income. Other scholars, with wry humour, observe that social class defines preferences for car makes, beer brands, and even salad greens (iceberg among the lower classes, more leafy green lettuce among the upper classes). In England, social classes are marked by difference in regional accents; this is less true in the United States.

Social class also is associated with a variety of life outcomes. Among the upper classes, one finds less divorce (but whether faithfulness is less is unknown), less mental illness, less criminality, and greater intelligence. Physical health also shows a surprisingly robust gradient with social class. In the United States, the annual death rate is five times greater at the bottom of social class levels than it is at the top. Although this gradient may be partly attributable to the drift of ill people into the lower social classes, the actual explanation must be more complex (e.g. Adler et al., 1994).

Genetic variance in social class can be estimated from behaviour genetic studies of a panel of adult twins in which the dependent measure is income or education. About half the variance in social class measures is genetic (Rowe, 1994). For income, most of the remainder is nonshared environmental variance. Years of education, however, shows greater family environmentability (e.g. 0.32 in one study of adult twins in the United States; Taubman, 1976). Scandinavian twin studies show an increase in the heritability of social class in the post-war period (Heath et al., 1985; Tambs, Sundet, Magnus, & Berg, 1989). As in the United States, the effects of family environment were also largest for years of education. In Tambs' study, the environmentability of education was about 0.60 for Swedes born 1931–1935, but fell to only 0.20 in those Swedes born 1958–1960. Family environment effects on occupational status were also weak (<0.10) in the most recent birth group. The loss of family environmental effects in Swedes born more recently may reflect the wealth and equalisation of opportunity within modern Scandinavian societies. If social mobility is less in England, one might expect the estimates of family environmentability to be greater. Unfortunately, twin studies of social class have not been conducted in England.

As with divorce, the genetic diathesis for social class must reflect a heterogeneous combination of traits. Certainly, IQ is one of them. IQ causes social class, not vice versa. We know this because the variation in IQ is primarily genetic, not family environmental, and also because the IQ of children precedes in time their later social class attainments. IQ measures taken in childhood and adolescence predict fairly well children's later social class outcomes (Herrnstein & Murray, 1994). One multivariate genetic study (Tambs et al., 1989) found that many of the same genes underlie the triad of IQ, income, and years of education.

Social mobility is the process that permits genes to become linked to social class. "Social mobility" is movement away from one's social class of origin, either into a higher or lower social class. Imagine a pair of brothers in the moderately prosperous household of Joseph Builder. The father, Mr. Builder, constructs houses in a growing city in Nevada. The two boys, though, differ in IQ. The younger brother has an IQ of 89, below that of his father. The older boy has one of 114, slightly better than his father's. Despite sharing many early experiences in the same family, these boys are unlikely to do equally well in life. The brighter boy is likely to remain in the same social strata as his father, or to rise; let us say that he rises in social status as a well-paid corporate lawyer. The younger boy is likely to fall in social status. Let us say that he becomes a construction worker and never manages to own his own firm. Genes associated with low or high IQ then would "move" with their bearers into the different social classes, making people classified into different social class groups genetically distinct from one another. This pattern of IQ-based social mobility has been documented in empirical studies (Waller, 1971).

The relation of social class to children's psychological traits

The genetic diathesis for social class becomes a confounding factor in studies that relate the social class of parents to the psychological traits of their offspring. For example, social class is often considered to be a major cause of children's IQs. But this ignores the considerable genetic difference among adults classified into different social class strata. In the light of the data reviewed earlier, social class should be considered a good *genetic* variable, a marker for heterogeneous genetic differences among adults, including those in IQ-related genes. Adoptive studies bolster this view of social class. Parental social class is associated more strongly with offsprings' IQ in biological families than in adoptive families. In one of the Minnesota adoption studies, a combination of mother's education and father's occupation and income correlated 0.33 with children's IQs in biological families, but correlated only 0.14 in adoptive families (Scarr & Weinberg, 1978). The effect of family environment would be just the modest association of 0.14. The effect of genes shared by social class and IQ would be 0.14 subtracted from 0.33, or 0.19. (If *one* parent were primarily responsible for the family environment effect, then the genetic effect would be doubled (i.e. 0.28 and 0.38) because a parent and child share only one-half of their genes.) In summary, the genetic effect of social class is stronger than the environmental one. Unfortunately, when studies of social class are interpreted, social scientists rarely acknowledge the role of genes in creating associations between children's social class of rearing and their psychological outcomes.

The problem of interpreting family effects, of course, extends beyond social class to other measures of family environment. These measures always reflect a parent's behaviour, which in turn, may be influenced by genes. I did some of the early work on this topic, showing that adolescents' perceptions of the family environment can be "inherited" (Rowe, 1983). Perceptions of parental warmth, in particular, were heritable, suggesting that either the teenage twins "wore coloured glasses" when observing parental behaviour, or that they had evoked dissimilar parental treatments. On the other hand, little genetic influence was found for the parenting style dimension of control (e.g. whether children must be home by a certain time at night).

Genes also may explain variation in separated MZ and DZ twins' retro-spective perceptions of their childhood family environment—specifically of parental support or nurturance (Hur & Bouchard, 1995). The family "environment" may be considerably less "environmental" than it seems to be. For a full review of studies on the genetics of experience, Robert Plomin's (1994) book should be consulted.

GENETIC VARIANCE IN RACIAL AND ETHNIC GROUP DIFFERENCES

Ethnic and racial groups are clearly heterogeneous in genetics and social history. In recent times, inter-marriage among formerly isolated groups has become fairly common. Through inter-marriage, the genetic distances between racial and ethnic groups is reduced. For instance, in the United States, about 25% of the autosomal genes in Americans of African descent originate from inter-mixing with the Caucasian population of European descent (Chakraborty, Kamboh, Nwankwo, & Ferrell, 1992). Although the exact number of existing racial groupings depends on the particular classifi-cation system used, most ethnic and racial groupings carry some informa-tion about genetic backgrounds, and they carry information about cultural backgrounds as well. The genetic differences that exist among ethnic and racial groups raise the possibility that they may make a modest contribu-tion to group differences in psychological traits.

The degree of group genetic difference, however, must be specified with regard to a particular trait. Between Africans and Asians, gene frequency differences are large for skin colour, but small for some blood groups. Indeed, for genes that do not vary among *Homo sapiens* (about 70,000 of the estimated 100,000 genes in the human body), people are exactly alike genetically, regardless of their geographical or racial origins. Nonetheless, specific traits show large group differences. The genetic disease, sickle-cell anaemia, occurs mostly in Africans, not Europeans; conversely, cystic fibrosis afflicts mainly Europeans, not Africans. Thus, finding a racial genetic difference in one psychological trait would not imply that it exists in another one; each trait must be evaluated separately.

Behaviour genetic research designs for group difference

Earlier in this chapter, several of the major behaviour genetic research designs were described. The adoptive and twin study methods, which were so effective in disentangling genetic and environmental variance in indivi-dual variation, flounder before the group difference problem. For example, MZ twins do not come as a mixed racial pair, one Asian and another

Caucasian, available for scientific comparison. Furthermore, few adoptive children are adopted across racial or ethnic lines (for an exception, see Weinberg, Scarr, & Waldman, 1992). The traditional behaviour genetic research designs are probably inadequate for answering questions about genetic bases of group differences.

New methods of studying group differences in genes have been proposed that would use the offspring of mixed-race marriages (Rowe, Vazsonyi, & Flannery, 1994), but they have not been used to date. Racial differences in early infancy also may return clues as to possible biological differences. This method has had a few applications (e.g. D. G. Freedman & M. Freedman, 1969). Finally, genes related to traits may be identified and their effects compared between populations. Although rarely used because most genes related to psychological traits remain unidentified, this method may have the greatest potential to estimate the true contribution of genes to group differences. In summary, the examination of group differences is not yet a scientifically strong field, and it requires methods that, although not impossible, are difficult to implement as practical research designs.

Genetic effects on group differences in psychological traits: Two examples

Despite the difficulties involved, two well-conducted studies suggest possible between-group genetic effects on psychological traits. The first is a study of behavioural reactivity in infants (Kagan et al., 1994); the second, a study of alcohol consumption in Americans of Asian ancestry (Tu & Israel, 1995).

The study by Kagan and his colleagues compared behavioural reactivity in two Caucasian groups (Irish in Dublin and Americans in Boston) and one Asian group (Chinese in Beijing). Behavioural reactivity is a temperamental trait of ease and intensity of emotional arousal. Considerable data already suggest that this temperament has a partly biological basis. Reactivity is linked to a number of biological pathways involving the amygdala, a structure in the "old brain" that regulates fearfulness and reaction to novelty in other animals. In each country, four-month old infants were put in similar test situations. For example, a balloon was burst directly behind their heads. The babies also were observed responding to the sound of a female voice, and they were shown colourful mobiles. To evaluate their emotional response to a strong odour, a swab of alcohol was placed under their noses. Observers watching the babies recorded fretting, smiling, and crying. The Caucasian babies were fairly similar in reactivity, but differed sharply from the Asian babies. The mean duration of crying was 7.3 seconds in Caucasians, but only 1 second for the Asian babies. Caucasians babbled for about one-third of the session but the Asian babbled for only about one-tenth. The Asian babies were much less fidgety than the Caucasian ones—the *most* active Asian baby was about at the *mean* of the American Caucasian babies. Because it is unlikely that behavioural responsiveness to these arbitrary and novel test situations had been somehow socialised by parents or culture, Kagan and his colleagues advocated the interpretation that the behavioural difference among Caucasians and Asians was genetically based. They noted (p. 345):

> Europeans and Asians have been reproductively isolated for about 30,000 years, or about 1,500 generations; it requires only 15 to 20 generations of selective breeding to produce different behavioral profiles in many animal species...

Thus, plenty of generations existed for Caucasians and Asians to have diverged genetically in temperamental traits, such as behavioural reactivity.

The second study by Tu and Israel (1995) examined the drinking of alcoholic beverages. The amount of alcohol consumed over some period may depend on psychological traits. For instance, it would depend on whether individuals find drinking pleasurable and on whether they see it as socially approved. In the vignette opening this chapter, Kim clearly did not like his body's reaction to a dose of alcohol. There may be a genetic basis for his response. The enzyme, aldehyde dehydrogenase, chemically degrades a toxic substance that is in the metabolic pathway from alcohol to waste products that are flushed out of the body (Crabb, Edenberg, Bosron, & Li, 1989). A mutation occurs in the gene that stops it from working. It is a dominant mutation, so just one copy of the mutant gene, inherited either from a mother or father, will destroy the enzyme's ability to complete the breakdown of alcohol. The enzyme has another side effect; it causes facial flushing when alcohol is consumed. (However, not everyone who flushes red on drinking carries this defective gene—other genes, and the dosage of alcohol, also contribute to the degree of facial reddening.) This gene is rare among Caucasian and African-descended people; however, it is relatively common among many Asians. In Japan, its inheritance strongly discourages the development of alcoholism. Alcoholics are several times more likely to carry normal alleles than abnormal ones; for instance, 2.3% of Japanese alcoholics, as opposed to 41% of the general population in Japan, carried the mutant gene.

The study by Tu and Israel examined how the gene operated in teenagers born in the United States and Canada. Asian-descended males who carried the mutated gene drank one fifth the alcohol of that drunk by Caucasian males and, as shown in Table 3.4, were four times more likely to be abstainers than the Caucasians. Among the three groups, females were less distinctive in drinking, as they tended, on the whole, to be light

TABLE 3.4
Percentage of male Caucasian and Asian abstainers
from drinking alcohol

Group	%	N
Caucasians	11	35
Asians without mutation	13	45
Asians with mutation	39	33

drinkers or abstainers. A most interesting finding was that Asian-descended males without the protective genetic mutation drank about as much as the Caucasian males. Apparently, they were fully acculturated to American and Canadian teenage drinking norms. Astonishingly, this single gene can account for most of the difference in alcohol use between Asians and Caucasians born into a culture that normatively approves the drinking of alcoholic beverages. In the opening vignette, Kim may be one of those Asian males inheriting the protective genetic mutation in aldehyde dehydrogenase, and that, rather than any special psychological resistance to peer pressures or any culturally unique opposition to drinking alcohol, may explain why he decides not to drink.

Although it is unlikely that other single behavioural genes will be as influential as this one, the general argument remains the same. As long as groups were reproductively isolated for many generations, the rarity or commonness of certain genes in the population may account for psychological trait differences between them. The modest effects of these genetic differences, certainly, are played out against many complementary differences in culture and values. Furthermore, it would be short-sighted, as well as prejudicial, not to recall that most genes are the same in all *Homo sapiens* everywhere—people are more alike than they are different (Rowe et al., 1994).

A LOOK AHEAD: SUMMARY AND CONCLUSIONS

It is time to abandon many trusted and influential ideas of socialisation theories. The idea that parents are the "pathogens" for most behaviour disorders deserves the same fate as the harmful and misleading medical advice of prior centuries; it is no more reliable than the burning of incense to ward off plague. The cold, unloving, rejecting mothers, who were once thought responsible for their children's schizophrenia, should be put in with the other arcania of ill-founded medical advice. The notion that "social class" is only an environmental variable deserves the same fate—as does the notion that racial and cultural differences must be only environmental in origin, no matter how fashionable this idea is today. These will be hard transitions for social scientists, but they can be made.

Studies of the environment need to be refocused in entirely new ways. One place to look for strong environmental effects is in secular trends in behaviour that occur far too rapidly to be pushed by underlying genetic changes. Also, I recommend a focus on the current environment, rather than on the childhood one. In adolescence environments that involve sibling mutual influence impact on delinquency and substance use (Rowe & Gulley, 1992). Group memberships also have a strong socialising effect. Although niche-picking means that people choose groups that reinforce their dispositions, groups also nurture, sustain, and amplify behaviours. A new theory of group socialisation contains many provocative ideas (Harris, 1995)and I recommend it to socialisation scientists.

The main distinguishing feature of the behaviour genetic view of people is one of humans as active organisms, carving out environmental niches for themselves. The family of birth origin naturally wanes in influence as children discover peer groups, teachers, the local library, and the local video arcade. Each step away from the family is into a broader world, one replete with both opportunities for growth and with dangers of injury, loss, and misdirection. A parent may recognise a disposition in a child, and with good luck, find ways to direct it. We would all wish that daring and risk-taking children—the children who are high neither on agreeableness nor conscientiousness—take up scuba diving and foreign adventures, instead of taking up a life of crime. Directing children toward complementary social niches may be parents' most natural skill, although even here, success is never guaranteed. Part of maturity is accepting others for who they are, a lesson we learn with regard to our lovers, spouses, and perhaps lastly, with regard to our own children.

REFERENCES

Adler, N. E., Boyce, T., Chesney, M. A., Cohen, S., Folkman, R., Kahn, L., & Syme, S. L. (1994). Socioeconomic status and health: The challenge of the gradient. *American Psychologist, 49*, 15–24.

Bouchard, T. J., Jr. (1994). Genes, environment, and personality. *Science, 264*, 1700–1701.

Bouchard, T. J., Jr., Lykken, D. T., McGue, M., Segal, N. L., & Tellegen, A. (1990). Sources of human psychological differences: The Minnesota study of twins reared apart. *Science, 250*, 223–228.

Bouchard, T. J., Jr. & McGue, M. (1981). Familial studies of intelligence: A review. *Science, 250*, 223–238.

Chakraborty, R., Kamboh, M., Nwankwo, M., & Ferrell, R. (1992). Caucasian genes in American Blacks: New data. *American Journal of Human Genetics, 50*, 145–155.

Cherlin, A. J., Furstenberg, R. F., Chase-Lansdale, P. I., Kiernan, K. E., Robings, P. K., Morrison, D. R., & Teitler, J. O. (1991). Longitudinal studies of effects of divorce on children in Great Britain and the United States. *Science, 252*, 1386–1389.

Chipeur, H. M., Rovine, M., & Plomin, R. (1990). LISREL modeling: Genetic and environmental influences on IQ revisited. *Intelligence, 14,* 11–29.

Crabb, D. W., Edenberg, H. J., Bosron, W. F., & Li, T. (1989). Genotypes for aldehyde dehydrogenase deficiency and alcohol sensitivity: The inactive $ALDH2^2$ is dominant. *Journal of Clinical Investigation, 83,* 314–316.

Dawkins, R. (1987). *The blind watchmaker. Why the evidence of evolution reveals a universe without design.* New York: Norton.

Deary, I. J. (1995). Auditory inspection time and intelligence: What is the direction of causation. *Developmental Psychology, 31,* 237–250.

Freedman, D. G. & Freedman, M. (1969). Behavioral differences between Chinese-Americans and American newborns. *Nature, 224,* 1227.

Galton, G. (1962). *Hereditary genius: An inquiry into its laws and consequences.* Cleveland, OH: World Publishing. (Original work published 1869).

Goldberg, L. R. (1993). The structure of phenotypic personality traits. *American Psychologist, 48,* 26–34.

Halaas, J. L., Gjiwala, K. S., Maffei, M., Cohen, S. L., Chait, B. T., Rabinowitz, D., Lallone, R. L., Burley, S. K., & Friedman, J. M. (1995). Weight-reducing effects of the plasma protein encoded by the obese gene. *Science, 269,* 543–546.

Harris, J. R. (1995). Where is the child's environment? A group socialization theory of development. *Psychological Review, 102,* 458–489.

Heath, A. C., Berg, K., Eaves, L. J., Solaas, M. H., Corey, L. A., Sundet, J., Magnus, P., & Nance, W. E. (1985). Educational policy and the heritability of educational attainment. *Nature, 314,* 734–736.

Herrnstein, R. J. & Murray, C. (1994). The bell curve: Intelligence and class structure in American life. New York: The Free Press.

Hettema, J. M., Neale, M. C., & Kendler, K. S. (1995). Physical similarity and the equal-environments assumption in twin studies of psychiatric disorders. *Behavior Genetics, 25,* 327–335.

Hur, Y. & Bouchard, T. J., Jr. (1995). Genetic influences on perceptions of childhood family environment: A reared apart twin study. *Child Development, 66,* 330–345.

Kagan, J., Arcus, D., Snidman, N., Feng, W. Y., Hendler, J., & Greene, S. (1994). Reactivity in infants: A cross-national comparison. *Developmental Psychology, 30,* 342–345.

Kendler, K. S. (1983). Overview: A current perspective on twin studies of schizophrenia. *American Journal of Psychiatry, 140,* 1413–1425.

Loehlin, J. C. (1992). *Genes and environment in personality development.* Newbury Park, CA: Sage.

Loehlin, J. C., Lindzey, G., & Spuhler, J. N. (1975). *Race differences in intelligence.* San Francisco: Freeman.

Loehlin, J. C. & Nichols, R. C. (1976). *Heredity, environment, and personality: A study of 850 sets of twins.* Austin, TX & London: University of Texas Press.

Lytton, H. (1977). Do parents create, or respond to, differences in twins? *Developmental Psychology, 13,* 456–459.

Lytton, H. (1990). Child effects—Still unwelcome? Response to Dodge and Wahler. *Developmental Psychology, 26,* 705–709.

Mann, C. C. (1994). Behavioral genetics in transition. *Science, 264,* 1686–1689.

Matheny, A. P., Jr., Wilson, R. S., & Dolan, A. B. (1976). Relations between twins' similarity of appearance and behavioral similarity: Testing an assumption. *Behavior Genetics, 6,* 343–351.

McCartney, K., Harris, M. J., & Bernieri, F. (1990). Growing up and growing apart: A developmental meta-analysis of twin studies. *Psychological Bulletin, 107,* 226–237.

McGue, M., Bouchard T. J., Jr., Iacono, W. G., & Lykken, D. T. (1993). Behavior genetics of cognitive ability: A life-time perspective. In R. Plomin & G. McClearn (Eds.), *Nature, nurture, and psychology* (pp. 59–76). Washington, DC: American Psychological Association.

McGue, M. & Lykken, D. T. (1992). Genetic influence on risk of divorce. *Psychological Science, 3*, 368–373.

Nowak, R. (1995). Bacterial genome sequence bagged. *Science, 269*, 468–470.

Pedersen, N. L., Plomin, R., McClearn, G. E., & Friberg, L. (1988). Neuroticism, extraversion, and related traits in adult twins reared apart and together. *Journal of Personality and Social Psychology, 55*, 950–957.

Pedersen, N. L., Plomin, R., Nesselroade, J. R., & McClearn, G. E. (1992). A quantitative genetic analysis of cognitive abilities during the second half of the life span. *Psychological Science, 3*, 346–353.

Plomin, R. (1994). *Genetics and experience: The interplay between nature and nurture.* Thousand Oaks, CA: Sage.

Plomin, R., Corley, R., DeFries, J. C., & Fulker, D. W. (1990b). Individual differences in television viewing in early childhood: Nature as well as nurture. *Psychological Science, 1*, 371–377.

Plomin, R., DeFries, J. C., & McClearn, G. E. (1990a). *Behavior genetics: A primer* (2nd ed.). New York: Freeman.

Plomin, R., Owen, M. J., & McGuffin, P. (1994). The genetic basis of complex human behaviors. *Science, 264*, 1733–1739.

Plomin, R., Willerman, L., & Loehlin, J. C. (1976). Resemblance in appearance and the equal environments assumption in twin studies of personality traits. *Behavior Genetics, 6*, 43–52.

Rowe, D. C. (1983). A biometrical analysis of perceptions of family environment: A study of twin and singleton kinships. *Child Development, 54*, 416–423.

Rowe, D. C. (1994). *The limits of family influence: Genes, experience, and behavior.* New York: Guilford Press.

Rowe, D. C., Clapp, M., & Wallis, J. (1987). Physical attractiveness and the personality resemblance of identical twins. *Behavior Genetics, 17*, 191–201.

Rowe, D. C. & Gully, B. L. (1992). Sibling effects on substance use and delinquency. *Criminology, 30*, 217–233.

Rowe, D. C., Vazsonyi, A. T., & Flannery, D. J. (1994). No more than skin deep: Ethnic and racial similarity in developmental process. *Psychological Review, 101*, 396–413.

Rowe, D. C., Vazsonyi, A. T., & Flannery, D. J. (1995). *Environmental effects on adolescents' alcohol consumption: Parents or siblings.* Unpublished manuscript.

Scarr, S. (1993). Biological and cultural diversity: The legacy of Darwin for development. *Child Development, 64*, 1333–1353.

Scarr, S., & Weinberg, R. A. (1978). The influence of "family background" on intellectual attainment. *American Sociological Review, 43*, 674–692.

Stunkard, A. J., Sorensen, T. I. A., Hanis, C., Teasdale, T. W., Chakraborty, R., Schull, W. J., & Schulsinger, F. (1986). An adoption study of human obesity. *New England Journal of Medicine, 314*, 193–198.

Tambs, K., Sundet, J. M., Magnus, P., & Berg, K. (1989). Genetic and environmental contributions to the covariance between occupational status, educational attainment, and IQ: A study of twins. *Behavior Genetics, 19*, 209–222.

Taubman, P. (1976). The determinants of earnings: Genetics, family and other environments: A study of white male twins. *American Economic Review, 66*, 858–879.

Tu, G., & Israel, Y. (1995). Alcohol consumption by Orientals in North America is predicted largely by a single gene. *Behavior Genetics, 25*, 59–65.

Udry, J. R. (1995). Sociology and biology: What biology do sociologists need to know? *Social Forces, 73*, 1267–1278.

Waller, J. H. (1971). Achievement and social mobility: Relationships among IQ score, education, and occupation in two generations. *Social Biology, 18,* 252–259.

Weinberg, R. A., Scarr, S., & Waldman, I. D. (1992). The Minnesota transracial adoption study: A follow-up of IQ test performance at adolescence. *Intelligence, 15,* 117–135.

Wright, L. (1995). Double mystery. *The New Yorker,* August, 45–62.

4 Cultural influences on development

Gustav Jahoda
University of Strathclyde, Glasgow, UK

WHY BOTHER ABOUT CULTURE?

Wilhelm Wundt did not consider child psychology as relevant to his *Völkerpsychologie*, which dealt with the sociocultural evolution of modes of mental functioning. Current mainstream developmental psychology still does not show a great deal of concern for cultural variations, and it is not uncommon for such variations to be almost completely ignored. It seems likely that the fundamental reason for Wundt's past neglect, and the current one, remains essentially the same. In order to understand it, a brief historical excursion is necessary.

Wundt's thinking on the matter was in line with a tradition going back at least to Montaigne in the 16th century. Its gist may be conveyed in (a "politically correct" version of) the old saw "the child is the mother of the woman"; in other words, the influences on the child will determine the character of the adult. Predominant among these influences were conceived to be "customs and morals", roughly equivalent to our present usage of "culture". Variations in customs and morals, ascribed mainly to climate or later to "race", result in differences between peoples (Jahoda, 1995). The notion that the whole pattern is basically quite simple and obvious was implicit in the stance of Wundt and, I would suspect, in that of some developmental psychologists even nowadays. Hence the tendency to concentrate on what are regarded as evolutionary-based biological universals. There are a number of possible objections to such an emphasis, and I shall focus on some of the main ones.

The first is the danger of ethnocentrism. It is certainly true that by and large all infants are much the same in the human species; yet they soon begin to diverge in different cultures, biological potentials being selectively enhanced in varying eco-cultural settings. For instance, Harris (1992) demonstrated the presence of a small number of innate emotions coupled with distinct facial expressions that infants not merely display, but can recognise in others. However, in the course of further development these become elaborated into sets of increasingly varied emotion patterns that are culturally coded and labelled. Or again, it is now recognised that the old notion of parents simply moulding the child is false (cf. Bell & Harper, 1977), and that there is a mutual influence. The existence of cultural variations complicates this process and can lead to convergences or progressively greater cultural divergences in behaviour. This kind of interactional model was supported by a study tracing changes in infant behaviour over time (Shand & Kosawa 1985a). These considerations make it clear that studies across cultures are necessary in order to differentiate between biological universals and cultural specifics.

A related problem concerns the extent to which, or the level at which, psychological processes remain the same under different conditions of development. The issue was first raised explicitly by Vygotsky (1930/1978, p. 46):

> *Within* a general process of development, two qualitatively different lines of development, differing in origin, can be distinguished: the elementary processes, which are of biological origin, on the one hand, and the higher psychological functions, of socio-cultural origin, on the other. *The history of child behavior is born from the interweaving of these two lines.* (Emphases in original.)

Developmentalists are rightly concerned with evolutionary antecedents, but should be mindful of the fact that in recent discussions of human evolution the role of culture in selection has often been stressed (e.g. by Boyd & Richerson, 1985). However, the undoubtedly intricate nature of the relationship between biology and culture in the context of development remains problematic (Scarr, 1993; Chasiotis & Keller, 1994). Finally, although it is obvious that infants grow into fully fledged members of their society and culture, the manner in which this happens is subtle and complex. Developmentalists could be expected to display some interest in the details of the process.

One consequence of the current marginality of the topic of culture and development is the dearth of relevant texts. Werner (1979) dealt specifically with cultural influences, and M. Cole & S. R. Cole (1993) is an outstanding example of a general text giving full weight to culture. The relevant material is now very abundant (cf. R. L. Munroe, R. H. Munroe, &

Whiting, 1981), albeit scattered widely across the psychological and anthropological literature. An extensive and up-to-date survey of several of the topics dealt with in this chapter will be found in Berry, Dasen, and Saraswathi (1997).

THEORETICAL ORIENTATIONS

The earliest work concerned with culture and development was done by anthropologists, notably Franz Boas and his famous pupil Margaret Mead, rather than psychologists. Mead's (1928) book on *Coming of age in Samoa* was subtitled "A psychological study of primitive youth for western civilization". She was not merely one of the first to document cultural variations in development, but in this and subsequent works espoused the view that human nature is almost infinitely malleable by culture. Such a deterministic model, now considerably modified, also characterised the so-called "culture-and-personality" school during the 1940s and 1950s. Based on neo-Freudianism, it postulated a series of links between types of child-rearing practices and adult personality (cf. Barnouw, 1973; Bock, 1980). Concentrating on the supposed effects of emotional crises, such as weaning, it had very little to say about actual development, which caused Bruner (1974) to dub it "a magnificent failure". Culture-and-personality theory was an early example of a *universalist* approach, aiming at pan-human generalisations concerning the factors influencing personality development.

The use of psychological methods in the ethnographic field originated at the turn of the last century with the Cambridge Expedition to the Torres Straits. Although the work of Rivers and others clearly demonstrated cultural differences in psychological functioning, it did not deal with development and was not followed up until the re-emergence, during the late 1950s, of what became known as "cross-cultural psychology". It was at first largely confined to the description of cultural variations in psychological functioning, including developmental topics. Subsequently its main task became that of systematically exploring the sources of such variations, and if possible identifying underlying universal features. It should be mentioned in passing that "universality" is not a simple concept and certainly cannot be directly equated with biological determination, nor does it necessarily imply a total absence of any differences. Such universals as have been proposed usually remain at a high level of abstraction, as for example LeVine's (1977, p.20) formulation of three universal goals of parenting:

1. The physical survival and health of the child, including the normal development of his reproductive capacity during puberty.

2. The development of the child's capacity for economic self-mainte-
nance in maturity.
3. The development of the child's behavioural capacities for maximiz-
ing cultural values (morality, prestige, wealth, religious piety...).

If one finds broad uniformity across cultures, then there is no problem. In
practice this is rare, and possible universals have to be teased out as
residuals from within the rich texture of cultural variations; Piagetian
developmental studies, further discussed later, are a case in point.
Piagetian theory is also an example of the many issues that cannot be
explored at all without considering a range of variations across cultures
and ecologies wider than those of Europe or America. Sometimes it
becomes necessary to seek out unusual situations that may be regarded as
"natural experiments". For instance, in order to examine the effects of
literacy as such on cognitive functioning, one has to find rare settings
where literacy exists without formal schooling (Scribner & Cole, 1981). In
general, cross-cultural studies entail comparisons of development in two or
more cultures.

Lately a case has also been made out, notably by Shweder (1990), for
intensive studies designed to achieve a fuller understanding of psychological aspects of one particular culture. This is the particularistic version of
so-called "cultural psychology" (cf. Shweder & Sullivan, 1993). Confus-
ingly, there is also another version of "cultural psychology" espoused by
Michael Cole, Wertsch, and others, which is rather different. Inspired by
Vygotsky and the former Soviet sociohistorical school, it focuses on the
cultural context of—mainly cognitive—development in general (LCHC,
1983; Cole, 1996). What both Shweder and Cole have in common is a firm
belief that, as a result of development within a particular context, culture
and mind are inextricably joined. As far as child development is concerned
Valsiner (1987, 1989), while not rejecting cross-cultural comparisons,
regards them as of secondary importance in his "culture-historical theory
of developmental psychology" (1989, p. 5):

> Culture-inclusive developmental psychology is a research paradigm that is
> primarily directed towards explaining how culture organizes the conditions
> for children's development, and how children assimilate these conditions, and
> simultaneously accommodate them.

In actual practice, these conceptual and disciplinary boundaries have
become somewhat blurred. Owing to limitations of resources, many cross-
cultural studies are confined to the comparison of two (usually very
different) cultures, and they often devote a good deal of attention to
cultural features of the kind particularistic "cultural psychologists" are

interested in. Cultural psychologists like Shweder, but not Cole, commonly draw for their background material on ethnographies, and their work is sometimes hard to distinguish from that of anthropologists.

This brings us to the contributions of anthropologists. The old-style ethnographic approach sought to study everything about a specific culture, an aim now recognised as excessively ambitious. In that kind of work one standard topic bearing on development used to be the so-called "life cycle", a description of salient phases from birth to death; hence it was bound to remain rather superficial. But as already mentioned, it was anthropologists who pioneered detailed studies of child development.

After the demise of the culture-and-personality school, similar but less narrow goals were pursued by what came to be known as "psychological anthropology". Initially it was focused mainly on the "hologeistic" approach based on the Human Relations Area Files (HRAF). These consist of a world-wide set of comparative data culled from ethnographies and organised for efficient retrieval (for a discussion of the HRAF, see Jahoda, 1982). Many of the coding categories in the so-called *Ethnographic Atlas* published periodically in the journal, *Ethnology*, relate to child-rearing variables, including for instance sleeping proximity to mother, bodily contact with caretakers, carrying technique, modes of weaning, and age at weaning. Scanning these tables derived from the HRAF provides an insight into the great variety of child-rearing practices across the globe. The material has been widely used, for descriptive, exploratory, and more formal hypothesis-testing purposes. An example will serve to convey the flavour of this kind of approach.

Whiting (1981), one of the foremost researchers in this field, was able by these means to demonstrate a linked chain of eco-cultural phenomena. Ways of carrying infants are related to climate, low mean temperatures being associated with carrying infants in cradles, high ones with carrying them close to the body, usually in some kind of sling. Body closeness in turn is linked with other practices such as sleeping arrangements (with the infant close to the mother), and with late weaning. Under such circum-stances there is a high degree of mother–infant body contact which, it is suggested, leads to a predominance of female role models. Admittedly, the inferences from such lengthy chains of relationships are sometimes rather debatable.

Although HRAF-type studies are informative and often serve to generate ideas, they do not entail any contact with real live children, and some caution in interpreting findings is always indicated. Hence research that combines HRAF work with field studies is to be preferred; an example would be the work of Rohner (1986), who was concerned with the effects of differing types of relationships with parents. Although this line is still being pursued, an increasing number of workers in psychological anthropology have devoted themselves to field studies of child development in particular cultures. As a result of mutual influences, there has been a convergence between their aims and methods and those of cultural and cross-cultural psychologists. Finally, it should be pointed out that cultural practices do not remain constant. This applies both to advanced industrial societies, which have undergone radical transformations over the past century, and to nonindustrial societies influenced by, and to a lesser extent influencing, industrial ones. Hence, there is also an important role for the historian who studies the variations in cultural practices over time (Elder, Modell, & Parke, 1993).

Within the present compass it is, of course, not possible to provide a comprehensive overview of such a vast field. My modest aim will be confined to offering some examples of different types of approach, mainly within three broad areas: infancy; cognitive development, and social development. The selection is bound to be somewhat arbitrary and reflect my personal bias. Nonetheless, it should illustrate both commonalities and diverging lines of development.

INFANCY

In a review of cross-cultural research on infancy, Werner (1988, p. 110) concluded that "we have seen the emergence of an outline of patterns and sequences in infants' mental, motor, and social competencies that appear to be universal and that reflect the canalization of our species' 'early development'". However, this statement was immediately followed by a list of sources of variation in development. Some of the problems of "universality" can be illustrated in relation to the concept of attachment. Bowlby's theory of attachment behaviour was based on the notion that infant–caretaker bonding is a basic human evolutionary adaptation. The first important cross-cultural confirmation came from Ainsworth (1967) in Uganda, followed by a whole series of studies in widely different parts of the world using the "strange situation" procedure, whereby children are exposed to an unfamiliar person in the absence of the mother. Results have been presented by Kagan (1976) and are shown in Fig. 4.1. It will be seen that the curves, although far from identical, do have the same general shape; and that is the kind of universality that can realistically be expected. It is also worth mentioning in passing that Kagan put forward what he regarded as an alternative interpretation of the data, but is probably a complementary one: Namely, that the curves reflect the growth in cognitive capacity enabling the infant to understand that he/she is being abandoned.

With regard to factors responsible for the differences, it has been suggested that the "strange situation" procedure is questionable in cross-

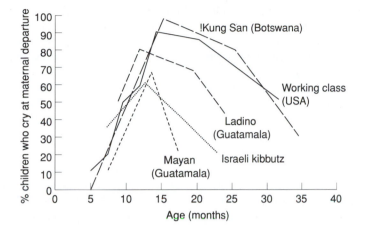

FIG. 4.1 Cross-cultural comparison of the "strange situation" procedure. *Source*: Super (1981). The figure there is in turn adapted from Kagan (1976).

cultural settings (e.g. Gardner, Lamb, Thompson, & Sagi, 1986), mainly owing to the existence in many cultures of multiple caretaking, notably by older siblings. It has also been shown that there are some special cases where bonding with the mother may be low or absent. This was reported to occur among the Hausa, where a posture of avoidance by the wife toward the husband and the first-born male child is prescribed (LeVine et al., 1970, cited in R. H. Munroe et al., 1981, p.236). In several respects, therefore, Bowlby's formulation, based on the assumption of the European norm of mother–infant relations, has had to be modified. Some of the wider implications of attachment in cultural context have been explored by K. E. Grossmann and K. Grossmann (1990).

Numerous other aspects of mother–infant interaction have also been studied cross-culturally, although seldom on a global scale. There are, of course, considerable differences in mothering, of a kind to be illustrated later, between modern industrial countries and traditional villages, which is hardly surprising as not just cultures but environments contrast sharply. The influence of culture as such is more clearly highlighted where technological levels are similar, as in the well-documented comparisons between Euro-American types of countries and Japan (e.g. Shand & Kosawa, 1985b; Norimatsu, 1993, see also Rowe, Chapter 3). Two recent studies will be briefly summarised. Maternal responsiveness was compared by Bornstein et al. (1992) in the United States of America, France, and Japan. The infants themselves behaved in very similar ways in all three settings; mothers' responses also had a great deal in common, but there were significant differences, not merely between Japan and the other two, but also between France and the United States. American mothers more often directed their infants' attention to objects or events in the environment, whereas Japanese mothers focused more exclusively on the dyadic interaction itself; French mothers resembled American ones on some categories, and Japanese ones on others.

Another study dealt with Japanese and American mothers' style of speech to infants (Fernald & Morikawa, 1993). Again certain features were common to both (e.g. linguistic simplification and repetition). But American mothers named objects more often and the children had larger noun vocabularies; in contrast, Japanese mothers often employed objects as instrumental for engaging the infants in social routines. A variety of such differences suggested to the authors (p. 654) that: "From the mother's speech, the infant begins to acquire not only the rules of language, but also the norms of a culture". A variety of other cultures have also been studied, demonstrating the existence of significant differences. Thus, according to Schieffelin (1979) and Ochs (1988) emotion states are salient in language structure and usage in Pacific cultures. In contrast Harkness and Super (1985) carried out an analysis of "cultural scripts" for Kipsigis (Kenyan) mothers' responses to crying episodes involving two-year-old children; they found that the speech and behaviour of the mothers was designed to de-emphasise awareness of inner emotional states. The burden of this and other evidence suggests that over and above the trivial fact that children in different cultures learn different languages, the mode of acquisition is also connected with subsequent styles of communication and interaction according to varying cultural norms. What happens is a process of channelling whereby the originally pan-human potential is progressively narrowed.

Much of the work mentioned so far dealt with relatively circumscribed aspects of development, excluding the wider setting in which interactions between infants and their mothers and other caretakers occur. Super and Harkness (1986) put forward the concept of a "developmental niche" as the focus of a more comprehensive approach which, they suggest (p. 551): "lies at the juncture of the theoretical concerns in psychology and anthropology". The niche is viewed as a system consisting of three major subsystems: (1) the physical and social setting in which the child lives; (2) culturally regulated customs of child care and child rearing; (3) the ethnotheories of child development and educational objectives of the carers. This framework, which includes the adaptive functions of cultural practices, is valuable for the analysis of a wide range of developmental phenomena. For instance, it explains in terms of their different circumstances why children temperamentally inclined to irregular sleeping habits are perceived as "difficult" in the United States and Europe, but not in Kokwet (Kenya). American and European infants usually have their own cot, often in a separate room. Efforts are made to induce sleeping routines that reduce disturbance for parents. In Kokwet, children sleep next to their mothers, who do not mind their wakening every few hours. Hence, what is perceived as a problem in Europe and America, is part of a normal pattern in Kokwet.

The Kokwet material can also be used to illustrate a common tendency for authors of textbooks to write about culture-specific behaviours as though they were true of all children. Thus, both Dworetzky (1990, p. 403) and Kaplan (1991, p.401) state that from kindergarten onwards children play mostly with same-sex fellows; the fact that the groups will consist of children of about the same age is so much taken for granted that it is not even mentioned. Yet here is what Harkness and Super (1985b, cited in Super & Harkness, 1986, p. 553) report:

> In Kokwet ... children from late infancy through middle childhood spent most of their time in mixed-age, mixed-sex groups of children from the same or neighbouring households. The tendency for boys and girls to associate more with same-sex peers did not emerge until after the age of six, when they were considered old enough to leave their own homesteads to seek companions. Thus, it appears that the question of developmental trends in children's choice of companions cannot be addressed independently of the settings of their daily lives.

The trouble is that genuinely universal features, such as the existence of some form of attachment, are apt to be indiscriminately juxtaposed in many texts with culture-bound ones. The fact that numerous facets of development are a function of specific cultural practices is often insufficiently considered.

Customs of child rearing are usually connected with ethnotheories about what develops "naturally" and what has to be taught. There are, for example, often beliefs about motor development, leading to postural manipulations designed to create or advance certain skills. Bril (1986) has analysed this for Bambara babies in Africa, and Stork (1986) in India.

There are, of course, other spheres where parental expectations are well-nigh universal. Rogoff et al. (1975) have shown that the age range within which children are considered to have attained rationality or "common sense" is in most cultures between the ages of about five and seven. They are then considered capable of looking after younger children, tending animals, carrying out household tasks, and so on. They are considered to have become responsible for their social behaviour and more readily teachable. It is noteworthy that this age range corresponds fairly closely to Piaget's transition period to concrete operations.

Generally, the importance of parental beliefs, values, and expectations has come to be increasingly recognised (but see Rowe, Chapter 3), and their cultural variations have been documented (e.g. Goodnow 1984; Gergen, Golger-Tippelt, & Berkovitz, 1990). This, of course, applies also to the inculcation of sex roles, where some cases have been found running counter to the conventional wisdom. Thus Goodale (1980) reports as follows about the Kaulong of Papua New Guinea (p. 135):

> ...from infancy girls are encouraged to behave aggressively towards males, and men are taught to submit to such attacks without retaliation, or run. Should a man initiate an act of courtship toward a woman, it is considered rape...

In this instance there is an obvious link between early childhood training and adult behaviour. The same is true of certain aspects of mother–child interaction, described earlier, in Japan and the United State, respectively. There is now considerable evidence indicating that not merely deliberate training, but also the taken-for-granted modes of interaction with infants and children are culturally variable. It has also been suggested that this results in distinctive "cognitive styles", which have adaptive functions in relation to the eco-cultural environment (Witkin & Goodenough, 1981).

COGNITIVE DEVELOPMENT

There is no question that cognition subserves adaptation to eco-cultural conditions, but what this implies regarding cognitive development remains a somewhat moot issue. I shall outline the positions of three major contenders in this field: traditional intelligence and ability testing; Piagetian theory; and the sociohistorical school inspired by Vygotsky and Luria.

It is well known that IQ tests were originally regarded as objective measures, allegedly proving that "primitive" children and adults are relatively stupid. What is less well known is the fact that it was anthropologists who first threw doubt on such a view (Nadel, 1939, p. 185): "In tests standardized on European children, natives belonging to groups whose social efficiency and adjustment to environment cannot be doubted obtain a score so low as to be absurd". Although the early simplistic notions have long been abandoned, the lower scores obtained by children in some non-European cultures were until the recent past often attributed to an intellectual *deficit* (cf. Cole & Bruner, 1974). This is the result of the still widespread tendency to think of "intelligence" as an objective entity with a genetic basis, present in all normal humans but varying in quantity. Even sophisticated discussions of nature of "intelligence" and the various theories concerning it usually suffer from a powerful Western bias. For instance Sternberg and Powell (1983), in their detailed and lengthy review, devote only a single short paragraph to cultural differences. I do not, of course, wish to deny the influence of genetic factors, but strongly dissent from extreme views, such as those of Lynn (1991), who assert the genetic inferiority of some other "races". As regards genetic factors, most (cross-) cultural psychologists would agree with Vernon that "they are probably small and we have no means of proving them" (Vernon, 1969, p.215) (see Rowe, Chapter 3).

An alternative perspective on cultural differences starts from the observation that the very *concepts* vary across cultures. The kinds of terms in many non-European languages usually glossed as "intelligence" have been shown to refer in reality rather more to what we would call wisdom and social skills (for details, cf. Segall, Dasen, Berry, & Poortinga, 1990) . This suggests the likelihood that in different cultures somewhat divergent lines of cognitive development might be adaptive and hence fostered by socialisation practices. (These comments are not intended to suggest that the use of tests in non-European cultures is always inappropriate. For instance, efforts have been made to identify common factors—in the statistical sense—across cultures, and tests can also be useful in certain contexts such as education, see, for example, Irvine, 1981; Van de Vijver & Poortinga, 1991).

The assumption that cognitive development is a universal that follows the same path everywhere was originally shared by Piaget. As already mentioned, the opposite view was taken by the sociohistorical school of Vygotsky and his American followers as far as the higher cognitive functions were concerned. As is often the case, what at one time appeared to be polar opposites turned out not to be so as research data accumulated. But this is anticipating the outcome of a story that in itself is instructive.

When, in the 1950s, Piaget took part in a series of discussions on child development, his position was still what he himself called "psycho-biological". The formidable Margaret Mead criticised his neglect of cultural influences, and this was probably at least in part responsible for his later change of tone. At any rate, in 1966 he published an article whose concluding paragraph began as follows (Piaget, 1966/1974, p. 309):

> Psychology elaborated in our environment, which is characterized by a certain culture and a certain language, remains essentially conjectural as long as the necessary cross-cultural material has not been gathered as a control.

Piaget envisaged that cross-cultural work would deal with three main issues. Two of these concern the question of the universality of some of his postulates: (a) whether the same stages are found everywhere and follow each other in the same order of succession; and (b) whether the relative difficulty of particular tasks remains constant. In addition, he wanted to know (c) the relative weights of the several factors (biological, equilibration, interpersonal co-ordination, and specific learning) which he regarded as governing cognitive development (Jahoda, 1980). The article stimulated a burgeoning of research in this sphere, which became something of a growth industry reaching into every corner of the world. Some of it was flawed due to shortcomings of method or misinterpretations of Piagetian theory. There remained a solid core of research reports, widely scattered in the literature. Some important examples are to be found in Dasen (1977) for children in a range of cultures and Seagram and Lendon (1980) for Australian Aboriginal cultures. The overall picture that emerged will now be summarised.

As regards (a), the main stages were identifiable in every culture, although few researches dealt with formal operation, most of the work being focused on the transition to concrete operations. However, in traditional cultures compared with modern industrial ones there was commonly a time lag of about two years before concrete operations came to be attained. In many cultures, individuals were encountered who did not seem to reach that stage at all, a finding whose interpretation was controversial (for a review, see Price-Williams, 1981). Subsequent research suggested that it was not simply a matter of "deficiency", as training studies showed that most children became quite capable of functioning at the level of concrete operations (Dasen, 1982).

As regards (b), the outcome was quite clear-cut: There were wide performance variations in different task domains, so that relative difficulty does not remain constant. Piaget's questions about the relative importance of his factors remain largely unanswered, as the research required would have to be on a very large scale as well as longitudinal, needing vast resources. However, some progress has been made in trying to understand the causes of variations. Berry (1975) put forward an eco-cultural theory which postulates that ecology and associated modes of subsistence will selectively enhance relevant cognitive skills, whereas others may fail to develop fully. He predicted that among nomadic hunters, spatial ability will be relatively high as compared with those of agriculturists, whereas the latter are likely to display other skills. This was put to the test by Dasen (1975) employing Piagetian tasks, such as conservation of liquids and horizontality, which taps spatial ability. Among the populations he studied were Arunda (Australian Aboriginal hunters) and Baoulé (West African agriculturists). Results, shown in Fig. 4.2, clearly confirmed these predictions.

There are numerous other factors that can affect cross-cultural work with Piagetian-type tasks. In spheres involving social cognition, direct comparisons are often not possible because of differences in social structure. For instance, LeVine and Price-Williams (1974) could not

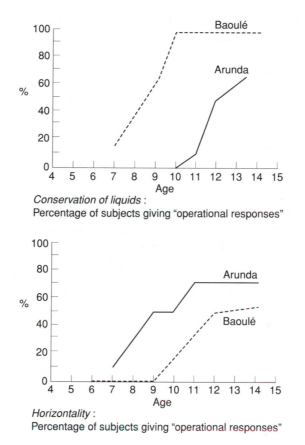

Conservation of liquids :
Percentage of subjects giving "operational responses"

Horizontality :
Percentage of subjects giving "operational responses"

FIG. 4.2 Comparisons of performances of Baoulé (agriculturists) and Arunda (hunters) on conservation of liquids and horizontality tasks. Adapted from Dasen (1975).

directly replicate Piaget's studies on the understanding of kinship, because in the Hausa there are no strict equivalents to terms like "family" or "sister". Or again, the development of number concepts takes a special form in parts of New Guinea where an association between numbers and body parts has interesting consequences. Saxe (1981) worked with the Oksapmin, where traditional counting begins with the thumb of the right hand, continues along the arm, head, and down the arm again and so on; this means that the fingers of the left hand go from 23 to 27. He showed that although in some respects the acquisition of number concepts paralleled that in the United States, the system produced some culture-specific variations. For example, among Oksapmin children there was a stage when they believed that symmetrical body parts meant numerical equivalence.

Similar issues have been examined among other populations by Lancy (1983) and Wassmann and Dasen (1994).

Several conclusions may be drawn from this large, if somewhat heterogeneous body of work. The original Piagetian tasks dealing with physical and mathematico-logical problems are not suitable for cross-cultural studies, because they presume a background of Western-type schooling; even adapted, they are probably not much more "culture-fair" than similarly adapted IQ tests. The lesson of all this for developmental psychology in general is that cognitive development is powerfully influenced by culture-specific experiences, a lesson that has been accepted by neo-Piagetians. This has taken them much closer to the sociohistorical theorists like Cole and his associates (LHCH, 1983). Without, of course, denying the existence of central processes they, unlike Piagetians, do not view them as internal structures closely linked to the successive emergence of cognitive skills. The manner they view this is as follows (LHCH, 1982, p. 698):

> The engine of change is experience of a very special kind—experience tailored to the child's current level of understanding, experience that provokes contradictions of just the right kind. These contradictions are invitations to form a next-higher-order generalization.

Such a formulation bears a striking resemblance to Piaget's concept of "equilibration", again indicating the convergence of the two schools. The stress on relevant experience also helps to account for the fact that non-European children, given either intelligence tests or Piagetian tasks, usually perform less well.

When the tables are turned, the opposite can be found. For instance, small trading by children is common in Africa but practically nonexistent in Britain. This difference provided an opportunity for assessing the effects of direct experience on corresponding aspects of development. A game-like "shopping" or "trading" situation was set up for the purpose of comparing children's understanding of the concept of "profit" in Britain and Zimbabwe. It was found that most Zimbabwean children were at least two years ahead of Scottish ones in their grasp of this notion (Jahoda, 1983).

Kohlberg's theory of moral development was originally derived from Piaget, and cross-cultural research on moral dilemmas revealed similar problems to those of Piagetian tasks. In his extensive review of 45 studies, Snarey (1985) accepted that some elements seem to be universal, but also identified major problems. It is possible that even the apparent universality may at least partly be due to the form of the instrument employed for testing. This is suggested by the work of Shweder, Mahapatra, and Miller (1990) in India which, unlike most others, was preceded by a close ethnographic study of local community life. In discussing their results they state that although abstract ideas of moral law might be universal, the ideas of both Indian and American children about more concrete issues were much like those of adults in their respective cultures. Moreover, they found that (p. 173): "Over the entire set of cases, the judgements of our Oriya and American informants about right and wrong are virtually unrelated".

Generally, there does appear to be tension between "top-down" approaches which necessarily have to seek common denominators across cultures, and "bottom-up" ones concentrating on the features of particular cultures. The type of approach selected is largely, but by no means exclusively, governed by whether the researchers are psychologists or anthropologists. Among the latter there are universalists, as for instance the Whitings (1975), who collected systematic child behaviour samples in six different cultures. Their aim was to examine the relationship between sociocultural types, and dimensions of social behaviour in children. However, most anthropologists prefer to confine themselves to particular cultures and study these in depth. Not many have concentrated on children, but those who did have provided valuable insights of a kind that will now be illustrated.

ANTHROPOLOGICAL STUDIES OF SOCIAL DEVELOPMENT

A century ago it was generally believed that the children of "primitives" are much the same everywhere, and facile generalisations abounded (Schurtz, 1900):

> On the whole there is little to be said about the upbringing [of children] by primitives, since even the older generation has little to transmit, neither much knowledge nor much self-discipline.

With the onset of relevant field research during the 1930s, such complacent feelings of civilised superiority have given way to greater modesty and better understanding of the manifold ways in which children are helped to develop into effective members of their culture. The classic ethnographic study is that of Meyer Fortes (1938) in Taleland (now Northern Ghana). He had originally been trained as an educational psychologist, which accounts for his clear awareness of methodological problems and his apologetic statement that (p. 7): "It is impossible ... to follow up a special psychological problem in a manner commensurate with the criteria of experimental research in England". However, he spent a whole year in careful observation, and his description of phases of development from infancy onwards is still a model of its kind. Fortes is most illuminating on social development, the ways in which Tale children become integrated into their culture. For instance, each person and clan has prohibitions against eating certain animals, and (p. 39): "a 5-year-old knows his or her personal or clan taboo, and can state it emphatically". Adults never constrain their conversations because of the presence of a child, which results in (p. 27): "comprehensive and accurate sexual knowledge of a 6-year-old, though direct instruction in these matters is never given". Tale parents have an expectation of "natural development" which means that explicit teaching is rare (p. 26): "Everybody takes it for granted that any person participating either already knows, or wants to know, how to behave in a manner appropriate to the situation and in accordance with his level of maturity". So, for instance, there is no deliberate toilet training and mothers are content to wait until the child independently attains control. It is an approach that has come into fashion recently in Euro-American culture!

Fortes also showed in detail how children spontaneously enact in play the survival skills and ritual practices of their society. The following extract illustrates this and involves a group of children with ages of about 6 or 7 years and one, Ton, aged about 10 (exact ages cannot usually be ascertained) whose task was to scare birds away (Fortes, 1938, p. 50):

> Gomna had wandered off a few yards and now came running up with three locusts. 'These are our cows' said Gomna, 'let's build a yard for them'. Zoo and the little girl foraged around and produced a few pieces of decayed bark. The children, Gomna dominant ... set about building a 'cattle yard' of the pieces of bark. Ton ... also squatted down to help. He and Gomna constructed an irregular rectangle with one side open ... The little girl stood looking on. Gomna carefully pushed the locusts in ... and declared 'We must make a gateway'. Rummaging about, the boys found two pebbles which they set up as gate posts ... suddenly the whole structure collapsed and Ton started putting it up again. The little girl meanwhile had found a pair of stones and a potsherd and was on her knees 'grinding grain'. Suddenly the two boys dashed off into the growing grain, shouting to scare the birds.

The relevance of such play rehearsal of what will become their adult tasks is clear; moreover, they do it without prompting and find evident enjoyment in it. Similarly, young boys build shrines for themselves in the cattle yard, and if they construct play houses, "shrines" are added as in a real house. If they catch a mouse, they "sacrifice" it to their miniature shrine. Thus, the ritual duties of adults are enacted in play. Let me mention in passing that close involvement of children with the beliefs and practices of their elders can have its darker side. In Ashanti I have come across a child aged about 10 who believed herself to be a witch, and many such cases are well documented (Field, 1960).

Returning to the "rehearsal" elements in children's play, this applies in some other cultures to the functioning of social institutions as with the Ngoni of Central Africa (Read, 1959, p. 84):

A perennial amusement among Ngoni boys of five to seven was playing at law courts. They sat round in traditional style with a 'chief' and his elders facing the court, the plaintiffs and defendants presenting their case, and the counsellors conducting proceedings and cross-examining witnesses. In their high squeaky voices the little boys imitated their fathers whom they had seen in the courts, and they gave judgments, imposing heavy penalties, and keeping order in the court with ferocious severity.

My examples may have conveyed the impression that in traditional cultures children are always encouraged to follow adults models from an early age; but although common, this is by no means a general rule. Even within a relatively small geographical area, practices may differ sharply. For instance, within the Bismarck Archipelago of New Guinea, Mead (1930) said of the Manus that there was a gulf between the worlds of adults and children, who enjoyed a carefree existence until early adulthood. They took no part in economic activities of their elders except that girls carried out some domestic tasks. The important ceremonial cycle was of no interest to them, and they were unconcerned with the world of spirits. A contrasting pattern was described by Epstein (1992) for the Tolai: Young children help their mothers in the gardens, and on ceremonial occasions when tambu (shell money) is distributed, children are not merely present but receive a share.

With a few exceptions, most of the earlier studies dealing with child development had been more or less a by-product of more general ethnographic work. More recently, a number of investigations in Africa and elsewhere have been specifically directed at early social development. It should be stressed, once again, that African practices are by no means uniform. For instance, weaning can sometimes be very harsh, the mother applying hot pepper to her nipples, or quite gentle as among the Wolof of West Africa. (Some earlier writers such as Ritchie, 1944, attributed the alleged deficiencies of "African personality" to traumatic weaning!) Zempleni-Rabain (1973) conducted an admirable study of Wolof mother–infant relations. She looked at these in terms of two components, namely "mother-as-food" and "mother-as-support", showing that both aspects are extended to other caretakers prior to weaning, so that the transition is usually a smooth one. From weaning onwards, caretakers start transmitting to the infant the basic rules of ritual exchanges that play a key part in the culture. This is mainly done by associating the child with the sharing-out process, directly in the course of interaction with her own group, and indirectly by adults jokingly bringing her into exchanges between different categories of adults, such as kinsmen, or host and guest. For instance, a mother asked her three-year-old child if she had a fiancé, and she named her maternal uncle who lived in the compound. On being asked what she would give him, the child said "some rice and some *laax u bissap*"; aston-ishingly for one so young, this was the correct type of food prestation. At the same time, rules and prohibitions concerning food are rarely spelled out directly, behaviour being inculcated by the framework of exchanges that binds siblings together. Thus, when a small boy took some sugar from his mother's hut, she did not reproach him or say he should return it. She merely said that his little brother was going to eat it, or that the older brother was going to look after it. Here is another illustration of the manner in which conflict situations are handled (Zempleni-Rabain, 1978, p. 228[1]):

> A quite violent altercation took place between Yirim (4 years and 6 months) and his grandmother over a small box belonging to the child which the grandmother wanted to give to his small brother. Yirim cried wildly and his mother protested to the grandmother. After the child had remained disconso-late for more than half an hour, the grandmother calls out to him suddenly, in a lively way, saying "come and give me some mangoes !" Everyone burst out laughing.

The grandmother succeeds in consoling this very small child by asking him to make her a gift, rather than giving him something. Zempleni-Rabain shows in detail how the symbolism as well as the actual giving of food are, in Wolof culture, tied to the nature of relationships between different types of people, and can also change the nature of these relation-ships. The surprising fact is that one so young has already become integrated into that system. At later ages, the control of behaviour is taken over more and more by siblings and age-mates. But the fundamental rules of the culture begin to be inculcated from weaning onwards, and Zempleni-Rabain argues that the period of infancy should be studied (p. 22): "in the light of ulterior relationships"; and as may be seen from the earlier discussion, this injunction is now being taken seriously.

The indirect mode of socialisation, as also described by Fortes, is common among non-Western cultures, sometimes taking rather subtle forms. My next case is drawn from the work of Nicolaisen (1988) in Sarawak, which contains an account of the following scene: A boy aged between five and six years comes into a room where the family has already

---

[1]Reproduced with kind permission of the International African Institute.

had some coffee and biscuits, and is told by his grandmother that she also has some for him—a rare treat usually reserved for special occasions. Instead of going to the mat where the food is waiting, the boy retreats to the sleeping platform on the side of the room and one can see from his looks that he is sullen with anger. None of those present say anything. Then the grandfather gets up, goes to sit down on the mat and begins to sing a song of praise of the kind reserved for honoured guests. Whereupon, the boy immediately starts screaming with fury, while everybody else laughs.

In order to understand what has happened here one has to know something about the wider sociocultural system, and in particular that Punan Bah society is highly stratified by age and rank. It is customary for men to be called from their gallery when food is available and the boy, well aware of this rule, had not been called; thus he felt that the proper respect due to him had not been paid. However, in reality he had prematurely assumed that he had the rights of an adult man. Note that no one lectured him about this in so many words ("You are still a small boy", as we would probably have done). Instead, the grandfather treated him as though he were an important personage, which was obviously absurd, and the boy reacted with shame and fury to being humiliated by laughter, a powerful sanction in the culture. Thus, by a manipulation of the context, the boy was being socialised into appreciating his current status.

My last example also concerns a highly stratified culture, and the study breaks new ground by focusing on symbolism. Anthropologists are interested in ritual and symbolism because these serve to cement the unity of a society, define hierarchies of status, and control behaviour in social contexts. The numerous detailed studies of these salient aspects of social life have been invariably restricted to adults. Children, although usually present, tend to play no active part. A quarter of a century ago Audrey Richards (1970, p. 12) raised the question: "At what stages of childhood and adolescence are the deeper levels of meaning associated with each symbol passed on?". It is a hard question to answer, and the challenge was not taken up until recently, when Christina Toren (1991, 1993) studied the development of understanding of the *kava* ritual in Fiji.

The *kava* ceremony is highly complex and subtle, so that my bald summary can only indicate certain salient features. The raw plant is infused and drunk as part of virtually every important ritual, and the sequence in which people partake of *kava* reflects an intricate hierarchy of status based on rank, seniority, and gender. Moreover, just as we refer symbolically to a "social ladder", so in Fiji these hierarchical relations are expressed spatially in terms of seating arrangements whereby certain parts of a house or meeting hall are designated as "above" or "below". In general, older are above younger, chiefs above commoners, and men above women. This, of course, does not constitute a simple ordering but embodies an inherent ambiguity (e.g young men vs. old women) which makes the system more difficult to grasp.

The main method employed by Toren in order to explore the development of children's concepts in this sphere was by getting them to make drawings of ritual occasions and discussing with them their representations of different categories of people. From this it became clear that some rough notion of the link between hierarchy and the above/below axis emerges before the age of about six years (Toren, 1993, p. 156):

> The data suggest that it is not before 8/5 at the earliest that children become aware that it is *relative status* that is expressed on the above/below axis. The youngest children merge status and above/below only in the crude sense that they "know" that the high chief sits above and women, or women and young men, sit below with married men in between. An enlightened merging of the spatial axis with an awareness that status may be derived from contexts independent of it, occurs for many children around the age 11/0, when their drawings reveal a conflict between rank/seniority and gender in status differentiation.

An appreciation of the subtleties of the status system thus starts to become manifest at the stage of transition (in Piagetian terms) to formal operations. Toren also analysed the cues used by the children in constructing their increasingly elaborate concepts, as for instance certain aspects of the physical arrangements at rituals which divide people of differing status. In sum, there was a progression by successive constructions from a mere perception of people's relations in space, to an eventual full understanding of space as symbolic of multifaceted status relations that could vary with contexts (1993, p. 156).

> The children's data show that the high salience of above/below as constitutive of differential status is the foundation for complex adult notions of hierarchy with repect to kinship and political relations across clans, villages and chiefdoms...

A sophisticated grasp of the system is therefore essential for effective functioning within the culture, and Toren has shown how it comes to be attained (full details are given in Toren, 1991).

These abbreviated accounts do less than justice to the richness of the material that helps us to understand the processes whereby children come to be socialised into cultures very different from Western ones. They serve as a corrective to the common assumption in developmental psychology that social development is much the same everywhere.

CONCLUSION

The burden of the argument presented here is that, just as much of social psychology is "college sophomore" psychology (Sears, 1986), so much of developmental psychology is EuroAmerican child psychology. At one time, this might have been understandable owing to the lack of relevant research, but this is no longer the case and it is therefore difficult to justify the frequent neglect of cultural variations in the framing of theories or the writing of texts.

Saying this does not imply any intention of pitting cultural against genetic factors or claiming that one is more important than the other— there is an intricate interplay that remains to be more fully explored. Trevarthen (1983) has put forward the bridging notion of "innate intersubjectivity", a genetically determined readiness to acquire culture in interaction with others. The intimate relationship between genetics and culture is very clear in the case of language: Very young infants are capable of discriminating between similar sounds whether or not these belong to the mother tongue; but in the course of the first year the infant "loses" the capacity to discriminate sounds that are not part of it (Werker & Tees, 1984). Just as an infant learns a particular language, so the infant grows up within a particular culture, resulting in culture-specific behaviour. Of course, this neither precludes the existence of significant communalities, nor does it assume extreme cultural relativism. Variation is bound to remain "within the limits provided by biology" (Konner, 1977, p.70), and it is the task of genetic and evolutionary theorists to specify what these limits are.

REFERENCES

Ainsworth, M. D. (1967). *Infancy in Uganda*. Baltimore, MA: Johns Hopkins University Press.

Barnouw, V. (1973). *Culture and personality*. Homewood, IL: Dorsey.

Bell, R. Q. & Harper, L. V. (1977). *Child effects on adults*. Hillsdale, NJ: Lawrence Erlbaum Associates Inc.

Berry, J. W. (1975). *Human ecology and cognitive style*. New York: Sage.

Berry, J. W., Dasen, P. R., & Saraswathi, T. S. (Eds.) (1997). *Handbook of cross-cultural psychology: Vol. 2. Basic processes and human development* (2nd ed.). Boston, MA: Allyn & Bacon.

Bock, P. K. (1980). *Continuities in psychological anthropology*. San Francisco: Freeman.

Bornstein, M. H., Tamis-LeMonda, C. S. et al. (1992). Maternal responsiveness to infants in three societies: the United States, France and Japan. *Child Development, 63*, 808–821.

Boyd, R. & Richerson, P. J. (1985). *Culture and the evolutionary process*. Chicago, IL: University of Chicago Press.

Bril, B. (1986). Motor development and cultural attitudes. In M. G. Wade & H.T.A. Whiting (Eds.), *Themes in motor development*. Dordrecht: Martinus Nijhoff.

Bruner, J. (1974). Concluding comments. In J. L. M. Dawson & W. J. Lonner (Eds.), *Readings in cross-cultural psychology* (pp. 392–397). Hong Kong: Hong Kong University Press.

Chasiotis, A. & Keller, H. (1994). Evolutionary psychology and developmental cross-cultural psychology. In A.-M. Bouvy, F. J. R. Van de Vijver, P. Boski & P. Schmitz (Eds.), *Journeys into cross-cultural psychology* (pp. 68–82). Lisse, The Netherlands: Swets & Zeitlinger.

Cole, M. (1996). *Cultural psychology*. Cambridge, MA: Harvard University Press.

Cole, M. & Bruner, J. (1974). Cultural differences and inferences about psychological processes. In J. W. Berry & P. R. Dasen (Eds.), *Culture and cognition* (pp. 231–246). London: Methuen.

Cole, M. & Cole, S. R. (1993). *The development of children*. New York: Freeman.

Dasen, P. R. (1975). Concrete operational development in three cultures. *Journal of Cross-Cultural Psychology, 6*, 156–172.

Dasen, P. R (Ed.) (1977). *Piagetian psychology: Cross-cultural contributions*. New York: Gardner.

Dasen, P. R. (1982). Cross-cultural aspects of Piaget's theory: The competence-performance model. In L. L. Adler (Ed.), *Cross-cultural research at issue* (pp. 163–170). New York: Academic Press.

Dworetzky, J. P. (1990). *Introduction to child development*. St. Paul, MN: West Publishing.

Elder, G. H., Jr., Modell, J., & Parke, R. D. (1993). *Children in time and place*. Cambridge, UK: Cambridge University Press.

Epstein, A. L. (1992). *In the midst of life*. Berkeley, CA: University of California Press.

Fernald, A. & Morikawa, H. (1993). Common themes and cultural variations in Japanese and American mother's speech to infants. *Child Development, 64*, 637–656.

Field, M. J. (1960). *Search for security*. London: Faber.

Fortes, M. (1938). *Social and psychological aspects of education in Taleland* (Memorandum XVII). London: International Institute of African Languages and Cultures.

Gardner, W., Lamb, M. E., Thompson, R. A., & Sagi, A. (1986). On individual differences in strange situation behavior. *Infant Behavioral Development, 9*, 355–375.

Gergen, K. J., Golger-Tippelt, G., & Berkovitz, P. (1990). Everyday conceptions of the developing child. In G. Semin & K. J. Gergen (Eds.), *Everyday understanding social and scientific implications*. London: Sage.

Goodale, J. C. (1980). Gender, sexuality and marriage: A Kaulung model of nature and culture. In C. MacCormack & M. Strathern (Eds.), *Nature, culture and gender* (pp. 119–142). Cambridge, UK: Cambridge University Press.

Goodnow, J. J. (1984). Parents' ideas about parenting and development. In M. E. Lamb, A. E. Brown, & B. Rogoll (Eds.), *Advances in developmental psychology*. Hillsdale, NJ: Lawrence Erlbaum Associates Inc.

Grossmann, K. E. & Grossmann, E. (1990). The wider concept of attachment in cross-cultural research. *Human Development, 33*, 31–47.

Harkness, S. & Super, C. M. (1985). Child-environment interactions in the socialization of affect. In M. Lewis & C. Saarni (Eds.), *The socialization of emotions*. New York: Plenum.

Harkness, S. & Super, C. M. (1985b). The cultural context of gender segregation in children's peer groups. *Child Development, 56*, 219–224.

Harris, P. (1992). *Children and emotion*. Oxford: Blackwell.

Irvine, S. H. (1981). Culture, cognitive tests and cognitive models: Pursuing cognitive universals by testing across cultures. In M. Friedman, J. P. Das, & N. O'Connor (Eds.), *Intelligence and learning*. New York: Plenum.

Jahoda, G. (1980). Theoretical and systematic approaches in cross-cultural psychology. In H. C. Triandis & W. W. Lambert (Eds.), *Handbook of cross-cultural psychology* (Vol. 1) (pp. 69–141). Boston, MA: Allyn & Bacon.

Jahoda, G. (1982). *Psychology and anthropology*. London: Academic Press.

Jahoda, G. (1983). European 'lag' in the development of an economic concept: A study in Zimbabwe. *British Journal of Developmental Psychology, 1*, 113–120.

Jahoda, G. (1995). The ancestry of a model. *Culture and Psychology, 1*, 11–24.

Kagan, J. (1976). Emergent themes in human development. *American Scientist, 64*, 186–196.

Kaplan, P. S. (1991). *A child's odyssey*. St. Paul, MN: West Publishing.

Konner, M. J. (1977). Evolution of human behavior development. In P. H. Leiderman, S. R. Tulkin, & A. Rosenfeld (Eds.). *Culture and infancy. Variations in human experience*. New York: Academic Press.

(LCHC) Laboratory of Comparative Human Cognition (1982). Culture and intelligence. In R. J. Sternberg (Ed.), *Handbook of human intelligence*. Cambridge, UK: Cambridge University Press.

(LCHC) Laboratory of Comparative Human Cognition (1983). Culture and cognitive development. In W. Kessen (Ed.), *Handbook of child psychology* (Vol. 1) (pp. 295–356). New York: Wiley.

Lancy, D. F. (1983). *Cross-cultural studies in cognition and mathematics*. New York: Academic Press.

LeVine, R. A. (1977). Child rearing as cultural adaptation. In P. H. Leiderman, S. R. Tulkin, & A. Rosenfeld (Eds.), *Culture and infancy. Variations in the human experience*. New York: Academic Press.

LeVine, R. A., LeVine, S., Iwagana, M., & Marvin, R. (1970). Child care and social attachment in a Nigerian community. Paper presented at the meeting of the American Psychological Association, Miami.

LeVine, R. A. & Price-Williams, D. R. (1974). Children's kinship concepts: Cognitive development and early experience among the Hausa. *Ethnology, 13*, 25–44.

Luria, A. R. (1976). *Cognitive development: Its cultural and social foundations*. Cambridge, MA: Harvard University Press.

Lynn, R. (1991). Race differences in intelligence: A global perspective. *The Mankind Quarterly, XXXI*, 255–296.

Mead, M. (1928). *Coming of age in Samoa*. New York: William Morrow.

Mead, M. (1930). *Growing up in New Guinea*. London: Routledge.

Munroe, R. H., Munroe, R. L., & Whiting, B. B. (Eds.) (1981). *Handbook of cross-cultural human development*. New York: Garland.

Nadel, S. F. (1939). The application of intelligence tests in the anthropological field. In F. C. Bartlett, M. Ginsberg, E. J. Lindgren, & R.H. Thouless (Eds.), *The study of society*. London: Kegan Paul, Trench, Trubner.

Nicolaisen, I. (1988). Concepts and learning among the Punan Bah of Sarawak. In G. Jahoda & I.M. Lewis (Eds.), *Acquiring culture* (pp. 193–221). London: Croom Helm.

Norimatsu, H. (1993). Development of child autonomy in eating and toilet training: One- to three-year-old Japanese and French children. *Early Development and Parenting, 2*, 39–50.

Ochs, E. (1988). *Culture and language development*. Cambridge, UK: Cambridge University Press.

Piaget, J. (1974). Needs and significance of cross-cultural studies in genetic psychology. In J. W. Berry & P. R. Dasen (Eds.), *Culture and cognition: Readings in cross-cultural psychology* (pp. 299–309). London: Methuen. (Original work published 1966).

Price-Williams, D. R. (1981). Concrete and formal operations. In R. H. Munroe, R. L. Munroe, & B. B. Whiting (Eds.), *Handbook of cross-cultural human development* (pp. 403–422). New York; Garland.

Read, M. (1959). *Children of their fathers*. London: Methuen & Co.

Richards, A. (1970). Socialization and contemporary British anthropology. In P. Mayer (Ed.), *Socialization. The approach from social anthropology* (pp. 1–32). London: Tavistock.

Ritchie, J. (1944). The African as a grown-up nursling. *Rhodes-Livingstone Journal, 1*, 55–60.

Rogoff, B., Sellers, M. J., Pirrotta, S., Fox, N., & White, S.H. (1975). Age of assignment of roles and responsibilities to children. *Human Development, 18*, 353–369.

Rohner, R.P. (1986). *The warmth dimension.* Beverly Hills, CA: Sage.

Saxe, G. B. (1981). Body parts as numerals: A developmental analysis of numeration among the Oksapmin in Papua New Guinea. *Child Development, 52*, 306–316.

Scarr, S. (1993). Biological and cultural diversity: The legacy of Darwin for development. *Child Development, 64*, 1333–1353.

Schiefellin, B. (1979). Getting it together: An ethnographic approach to the study of developmental communicative competence. In E. Ochs & B. Schieffelin (Eds.), *Developmental pragmatics.* New York: Academic Press.

Schurtz, H. (1900). *Urgeschichte der Kultur.* Leipzig: Biographisches Institut.

Scribner, S. & Cole, M. (1981). *The psychology of literacy.* Cambridge, MA.: Harvard University Press.

Seagram, G. N. & Lendon, R. J. (1980). *Furnishing the mind.* Sydney: Academic Press.

Sears, D. O. (1986). College sophomores in the laboratory: Influences of a narrow data base on social psychology's view of human nature. *Journal of Personality and Social Psychology, 51*, 515–530.

Segall, M. H., Dasen, P. R., Berry, J. W., & Poortinga, Y. H. (1990). *Human behavior in global perspective.* New York: Pergamon.

Shand, N., & Kosawa, Y. (1985a). Culture transmission: Caudell's model and alternative hypotheses. *American Anthropologist, 87*, 862–871.

Shand, N. & Kosawa, Y. (1985b). Japanese and American behavior types at three months: Infant and infant-mother dyad. *Infant Behavior and Development, 8*, 225–240.

Shweder, R. A. (1990). Cultural psychology—what is it? In J. W. Stigler, R. A. Shweder, & G. Herdt (Eds.), *Cultural psychology* (pp. 1–43). Cambridge, UK: Cambridge University Press.

Shweder, R. A., Mahapatra, M., & Miller, J. G. (1990). Culture and moral development. In J. W. Stigler, R. A. Shweder, & G. Herdt (Eds.), *Cultural psychology.* Cambridge, UK: Cambridge University Press.

Shweder, R. A. & Sullivan, M. A. (1993). Cultural psychology: Who needs it ? *Annual Review of Psychology, 44*, 497–523.

Snarey, J. R. (1985). Cross-cultural universality of social-moral development: A critical review of Kohlbergian research. *Psychological Bulletin, 97*, 202–232.

Sternberg, R. J. & Powell, J. S. (1983). The development of intelligence. In P. Mussen (Ed.), *Handbook of child psychology* (4th ed.) (Vol. III). New York: Wiley.

Stork, H. (1986). *Enfances Indiennes.* Paris: Le Centurion.

Super, C. M. (1981). Behavioral development in infancy. In R. H. Munroe, R. L. Munroe, & B. B. Whiting (Eds.), *Handbook of cross-cultural human development* (p. 234). New York: Garland.

Super, C. M. & Harkness, S. (1986). The developmental niche: A conceptualization at the interface of child and culture. *International Journal of Behavioral Development, 9*, 545–569.

Toren, C. (1991). *Making Fijian hierarchy: Social and cognitive processes in the construction of culture.* London: Athlone Press.

Toren, C. (1993.) Sign into symbol, symbol as sign: Cognitive aspects of a social process. In P. Boyer (Ed.), *Cognitive aspects of religious symbolism* (pp. 147–164) Cambridge, UK: Cambridge University Press.

Trevarthen, C. (1983). Interpersonal abilities of infants as generators for transmission of language and culture. In A. Oliverio & M. Zapella (Eds.), *The behavior of human infants.* New York: Plenum.

Valsiner, J. (1987). *Culture and the development of children's actions.* Chichester, UK: Wiley.

Valsiner, J. (1989). *Human development and culture*. Lexington, MA: Heath.

Van de Vijver, F. J. R. & Poortinga, Y. H. (1991). Testing across cultures. In R. K. Hambleton & J. N. Zaal (Eds.), *Advances in educational and psychological testing: Theory and applications*. Dordrecht: Kluwer.

Vernon, P. (1969). *Intelligence and cultural environment*. London: Methuen.

Vygotsky, L. S. (1978). *Mind in society*. Cambridge, MA: Harvard University Press. (Original work published 1930)

Wassman, J. & Dasen, P. R. (1994). Yupno number system and counting. *Journal of Cross-Cultural Psychology, 25*, 78–94.

Werker, J. F. & Tees, R. C. (1984). Cross-language speech perception: Evidence for perceptual reorganization during the first year of life. *Infant Behavior and Development, 7*, 49–63.

Werner, E. E. (1979). *Cross-cultural child development*. Monterey, CA: Brooks-Cole.

Werner, E. E. (1988). A cross-cultural perspective on infancy. *Journal of Cross-Cultural Psychology, 19*, 96–113.

Whiting, J. W. M. (1981). Environmental constraints on infant care practices. In R. H. Munroe, R. L. Munroe, & B. B. Whiting (Eds.), *Handbook of cross-cultural development* (pp. 155–179). New York: Garland.

Whiting, B. B. & Whiting, J. W. M. (1975). *Children of six cultures*. Cambridge, MA: Harvard University Press.

Witkin, H. & Goodenough, D. (1981). *Cognitive styles: essence and origins*. New York: International Universities Press.

Zempleni-Rabain, J. (1973). Food and the strategy involved in learning fraternal exchange among Wolof children. In P. Alexandre (Ed.), *French perspectives in African studies*. London: Oxford University Press.

II Agents

5 Families and social development: The 21st century

Harry McGurk and Grace Soriano
Australian Institute of Family Studies, Melbourne, Australia

Bronfenbrenner's (1979) repeated pleas for developmental psychologists to inform their thinking about developmental processes by consideration of the entire ecological context in which development occurs, have by and large, fallen on deaf ears. Even in the area of social development, there are few investigations or overviews that have adopted an ecological orientation.

Readers will recall Bronfenbrenner's four-level model of the psychosocial ecosystem in which the human individual is embedded (Bronfenbrenner, 1982). The *microsystem* refers to the pattern of activities, roles and interpersonal relationships experienced by the developing person in a given setting with its own particular physical and material characteristics; the family home provides an obvious example. The *mesosystem* comprises the interrelationships between two or more settings in which the developing person is an active participant, such as home, day-care centre, and peer group.

An *exosystem* refers to one or more settings in which the developing person is not an active participant but within which events and processes occur that influence or are influenced by what happens in the immediate setting, the microsystem, containing the developing person. Obvious examples here are the parent(s) workplace(s), or the family day-care setting attended by a sibling.

Finally, the *macrosystem* refers to consistencies, in the form and content of the lower order systems, that exist or could exist at the level of the culture (or subculture) as a whole, along with the ideology underlying such consistencies (Bronfenbrenner, 1979). For example, the majority of children in Australia, as in the United Kingdom, are educated in the public school system. However, the education systems of the two countries are quite different and, within both of them, the quality of educational experience of children from middle class backgrounds is different from that experienced by youngsters of poverty.

Most psychological investigations of social development have been restricted to the levels of the individual child and the microsystem comprising the individual child and his/her immediate caregivers. However, even this representation of the field overstates the case with respect to the extent to which the ecosystem in which development occurs is *ever* taken into account in social development research. Indeed, much of the current corpus of psychological research on social development would be accurately described as context-free! Analogous to the concept of the transportability of the principles of concept-free management, it seems to be assumed that the accounts and interpretations of social development reported in the psychological research literature are true for all times and all places. Accordingly, context barely gets a mention (see Jahoda, Chapter 4). Alternatively, it appears to be assumed that the social settings in which social development occurs are so standard and so widespread as to be universal for all intents and purposes, and therefore not worthy of attention. The default setting appears always to be that of the "traditional" Western middle class nuclear family comprising a once-married couple and their biological children.

The fact of the matter is, of course, that in the contemporary post-industrial world there is great diversity within and between different societies with respect to the structure and composition of families and, by corollary, with respect to the principal microsystems in which children are reared. Similarly there is diversity in the meso-, exo-, and macro-systems within which family microsystems are embedded.

This chapter presents an account of at least some of the diversity in familial and related settings of social development to which children growing up in contemporary, post-industrial societies are exposed and highlights the need for research on social development to be informed by awareness of its context. For too long developmental researchers have largely ignored the social context of social development. The chapter has been written as a plea for future research on social development to be designed in ways that will increase the probability of outcomes being generalisable to the real, messy world in which children and their families live.

CHANGING FAMILY DEMOGRAPHY

As indicated earlier, families constitute the primary setting within which childhood social development occurs. However, families are not static entities. Different cultures have given rise to different family forms and, within cultures, family structures evolve and adapt over time in response to changing social and economic conditions. The statistical and related information presented in this section is drawn in the main from census material and research data collected in Australia. Australia is a modern, post-industrial society and the kinds of demographic changes which Australia has experienced in recent decades are discernible to greater or lesser degree in all Western countries. Accordingly, recent changes in family demography in Australia are to that extent illustrative of changes in evidence throughout the *developed* world.

Politicians, clerics, social science researchers, and others who ought to know better are prone to speak about "the family" as if it were a static, stable, unchanging entity. In fact, throughout social history, human families and family structures have been in a state of dynamic transition as they have sought to respond more or less adaptively to changes in the external conditions that affect their roles and functions in providing for the care, nurture, and well-being of their members.

Different periods in social history are characterised by differences in the rates of change in the factors affecting family functioning and in the responses of families thereto. Currently, families and family structures seem to be subject to unprecedented rates of change. In consequence, families are now characterised by diversity rather than homogeneity of structure. This is as true of Australia as it is of other countries in the developed world.

For example, prior to 1975, rates of divorce in Australia were relatively low. However, in 1975, Australia, for the first time, introduced the possibility of "no fault" divorce into family law. Immediately thereafter there was a surge in the frequency of divorce which peaked around 1981 and has remained fairly stable since then (see Fig. 5.1).

The current overall annual rate of divorce in Australia is about 12 per thousand married couples. However, the risk of a marriage ending in divorce is greater during the early years of marriage. Ten per cent of all registered marriages in Australia are likely to end in divorce within 6 years, 20 per cent within 10 years, 30 per cent by 20 years, and 40 per cent after 30 years. The risk of divorce is significantly higher for second and subsequent marriages (ABS, 1994a).

As indicated earlier, the processes leading to change in family structures are in operation to a greater or lesser extent throughout the world, although local factors influence their manifestation from one country to

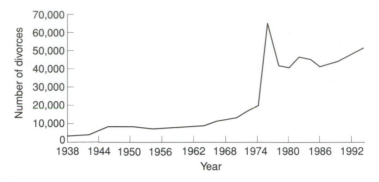

FIG. 5.1   Number of divorces in Australia, 1938–93. *Source*: McDonald et al. (1987) in *Australians: Historical Statistics* and Australian Bureau of Statistics (various years), *Divorces Australia*.

another. For example, the comparative data presented in Table 5.1 provide a kind of international league table of the prevalence of divorce. The lowest levels occur in countries where the population is predominantly Catholic and in the more traditional societies of Asia. Divorce rates in

TABLE 5.1
Crude divorce rate in selected countries

Country	Reference year	Crude divorce rate
Italy	1993	0.39
Brazil	1990	0.53
Mexico	1992	0.58
Poland	1993	0.68
Hong Kong	1990	0.97
Portugal	1992	1.26
Singapore	1993	1.33
Japan	1992	1.44
France	1992	1.89
Austria	1992	2.07
Norway	1992	2.38
Sweden	1992	2.53
Australia	*1992*	*2.61*
New Zealand	1992	2.65
Canada	1990	2.94
United Kingdom	1991	2.96
Cuba	1992	4.15
Russian Federation	1992	4.30
United States	1993	4.60

Source: United Nations (1995). *1993 Demographic Yearbook*. New York: Author.

Australia, along with those of the other predominantly English-speaking member states of the Commonwealth are intermediate, whereas the highest rates are to be found in the Russian Federation and the United States.

Increase in the divorce rate has been accompanied by decrease in rates of marriage. Twenty years ago the annual crude marriage rate for Australian men was 62.9 per thousand and 61.1 for women; currently the respective rates are 38.2 and 36.4. However, decline in marriage has been accompanied by increase in cohabitation and so-called *de facto* relationships. Over the decade 1982–92 the proportion of such relationships increased from 4 per cent to 8 per cent of all couple relationships. However, *de facto* status is increasingly serving as a transition into rather than as a substitute for marriage; more than half of all Australian marriages are now preceded by a period of cohabitation compared with 16 per cent 20 years ago.

Demographic changes like these have profound significance for family structure and for children's experiences of family life and family relationships. For example, it is clearly unjustified for developmental psychology to continue to theorise about parent–child relationships as if these were exclusively, or even normatively, experienced within the context of the "traditional" nuclear family comprising two parents and their biological children.

As illustrated in Fig. 5.2, there is now a wide variety of family structures. In Australia as elsewhere, couples with children continue to be the predominant family form; they account for 85 per cent of the 4.8 million Australian families (ABS, 1992). However, increasing proportions of these households comprise blended and step-families. Moreover, the fastest growing family type is that comprising a sole parent and his/her children; these increased by 42 per cent in the 10 years to 1992 to constitute 13 per cent of all families (ABS, 1992), see Fig. 5.2.

There are marked differences between Australia on the one hand and the United States and United Kingdom on the other, with respect to the factors responsible for the increase in sole-parent households. Much of the increase in the two latter countries is caused by rapid growth in the number of births to unmarried women under 25, whereas in Australia the dominant route to sole parenthood is through divorce/separation.

Looking at these data from the perspective of the children involved, 17 per cent of Australian children live in one-parent families and 11 per cent live either in blended families, step-families, or families with other children.

WORK AND FAMILIES

There is an ingrained tradition in human social discourse for us to hanker after a Golden Age when things were done not only differently but better than they are today. Even Socrates' complaint about the

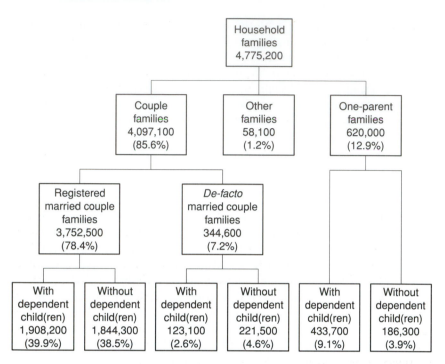

FIG. 5.2   Composition of Australian family households, 1992. *Source*: Australian Bureau of Statistics (1992), *Australia's Families: Selected Findings*.

youth of his day has a contemporary ring to it! (quoted by Brande, 1957, p. 96):

> The children now love luxury; they have bad manners, contempt for authority, they show disrespect for their elders and love to chatter in places of exercise. They no longer rise when elders enter the room. They contradict their parents, chatter before company, gobble up dainties at the table, cross their legs and are tyrants over their teachers.

So it is with family life. Here the Golden Age, as it is presently extolled, was the era of "traditional" families and "traditional" family values, when fathers provided for the material needs of the entire family and mothers provided for the care and nurture of their children at home. In fact, the period in social history when working men were paid enough for their labour to enable an average size family to exist in frugal comfort on the basis of one income alone was very short lived (McGurk, 1995).

It was in Australia perhaps in the early 20th century, that formal recognition was first accorded to the need for nuclear families to be properly resourced to fulfil their caring functions. This occurred in 1907 when Justice Higgins, then President of the Commonwealth Conciliation and Arbitration Court, in handing down his judgement in the Mackay–Harvester case, defined the concept of a fair and reasonable wage. Such a wage, he argued, was one which would enable a household comprising a man, wife, and three children (the average size of Australian families at the time) to meet their needs for housing, basic commodities, and clothing—in other words to meet normal minimum needs—and, in addition, to maintain at least a frugal standard of comfort. Judge Higgins arrived at his decision about the definition and magnitude of a fair and reasonable wage after collecting information on household expenditure from a number of Melbourne families (Jamrozik, 1994).

The concept of the fair and reasonable, or basic living wage, whereby enough could be earned by one man to maintain a family, influenced the determination of wages in Australia for 60 years. However, in 1967 the Conciliation and Arbitration Court redefined its function more narrowly as the prevention or settling of specific disputes. From the 1970s, acceler-ated by the processes of wage deregulation introduced in the 1980s, the concept of the living wage has been abandoned. During the same period interest rates soared. Thus, by 1994, in order to achieve a comparable start in the housing market, an average family would have needed to earn about 1.7 times the equivalent salary required in 1970 (Yates, 1994).

In response to such economic pressure, with increasing frequency since the 1960s onwards, increasing numbers of Australian couple families have been obliged to adopt a dual-earner lifestyle. This has resulted, of course, in a marked increase in participation in the paid labour force by women of all ages, as illustrated in Table 5.2.

There are two additional factors that are contributing to the increased participation by women in the paid labour force. One is the increase in the

TABLE 5.2
Participation of Australian women in the paid labour force

Age	1970	1980	1990	1995
15–19	58.5	60.6	59.6	60.3
20–24	62.9	71.1	78.4	78.9
25–34	41.3	52.5	66.1	68.2
35–44	43.4	58.2	72.4	70.8
45–54	40.4	47.6	61.1	67.7
55–59	28.7	28.8	32.3	39.3
60–64	14.9	12.8	15.9	17.2
65 +	3.6	2.8	2.2	2.6

Source: Australian Bureau of Statistics (1996), *Labour Force Australia.*

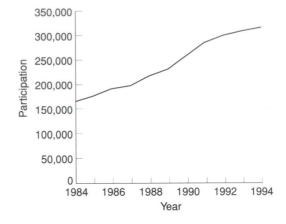

FIG. 5.3   Australian women's participation in higher education, 1984–94. *Source*: Australian Bureau of Statistics (1995a). *Australian Women's Yearbook*.

rates of participation by women in higher education, illustrated in Fig. 5.3. The other, widely experienced throughout the entire world, is the overall increase in women's demand and expectation for greater gender equity in participation in social and economic life. The two are not independent of each other but, on the contrary, are complexly and intimately interrelated. Both have combined with economic necessity to lead to increasing numbers of women, at all ages including the primary child-bearing years, being involved in paid employment outside the home.

In two-parent families where both parents are engaged in employment outside the home, alternative arrangements must be made for the care and well-being of children while parents are at work. A similar situation obtains for the children of sole parents who work away from home. The demands and conflicts created by parents' work engagement and responsibilities together with the arrangements they make for their children while they are at work can each have significant impacts on the quality of family life as well as on the social development of children. Let us consider each of these in turn.

The parent employee: Achieving a balance

Employed parents, men and women alike, experience difficulty in balancing the dual responsibilities of work and family life (Edgar & Glezer, 1992; Russell, 1993). Among the more obvious conflicts between the roles of parent and employee are that time spent at work reduces the time available to be with children; the time available for joint leisure activities; and the energy to do household chores. These stresses occur across the spectrum of trades and professions, for parents in high as well as low status jobs (Glezer, 1991). Not surprisingly, the challenges of achieving a balance between work and family fall primarily on women. The "new men", willing to share in household and family chores on a basis of equity, are slow in arriving on stream and the overwhelming responsibility for carrying out these tasks continues to fall on mothers, regardless of their employment status (ABS, 1994b).

On the other hand, even for those men who are motivated to share more equitably in discharging household and family obligations, the culture of the workplace has been slow to recognise the relevance of fatherhood in men's lives. Thus, men in a recent Melbourne study reported that there was not enough time for them to be the kind of father they would ideally like to be because they experienced work demands as non-negotiable, with time commitments more likely to be expected to shift in response to work demands rather than in response to family demands; families simply got whatever time was left over (Holland, 1994, p.11). Similar pressures and attitudes are revealed in other countries. For example, men in a number of European states are reported to be reluctant to use paternity leave or parental leave to its full extent because they fear that it would contribute to a loss of their job or damage their career prospects if they prioritised family responsibilities over work (Conference of European Ministers responsible for Family Affairs, 1995).

Most of us would agree that, in the context of trying to achieve an optimum balance between the demands of family life and work, parents would be assisted by the support of a sympathetic external environment, one that recognised and acknowledged the desire and responsibility of parents to provide adequately for the well-being of their children. Enlightened employers and employment policies would surely wish not to compromise the welfare of children in favour of company or economic policy? Employers, trade unions, and governments as well as individual parents all have parts to play in this context. For families to be able to harmonise family and work responsibilities will require the co-operation of players at different levels in the eco-system of the developing child. The extent to which such co-operation is achieved, and effective outcomes result, will impact directly and indirectly on the lives of children in the families affected. We see in this kind of example an illustration of the further significance of Bronfenbrenner's ecological approach to the study of human development; the need to consider the interactions between processes at *micro-*, *meso-*, *exo-*, and *macro-*levels of the child's eco-system.

In Australia, successive governments have enacted a range of legislative arrangements in place which, cumulatively, have a bearing on work–family harmonisation. The passing of Equal Opportunity Laws in the 1960s and

Equal Pay Provision in the 1970s recognised and provided further impetus for the transition away from the traditional male breadwinner/female home maker mode of nuclear family composition. Maternity leave benefits have been widely available to Australian female employees since 1979 (Glezer, 1988, p. 3); in 1991 that right, to leave of up to 12 months following the birth of a child, was extended to include fathers, thus introducing parental leave to Australia for the first time. Parental leave can be distributed, according to preference, between mother and father although both may not be away from work at the same time; to date, however, such leave carries no entitlement to salary and is therefore a practical option for a very few families.

Income-tested subsidies for child-care expenses have been in place in Australia since 1991 (Wangmann, 1995, p. 29), bringing public and private child-care provision within the reach of many parents who would otherwise be unable to afford formal child care for their children while they are at work.

In 1990, the Australian Government ratified International Labour Organisation Convention 156: *Workers with Family Responsibilities* (ILO, 156), whereby signatories undertook to ensure that no employee in their jurisdiction would be discriminated against at work on grounds of family obligations and responsibilities. In 1994, the Industrial Relations Court awarded employees the right to use sick leave and related entitlements for purposes of caring for a family member; previously the Court had legislated for employees to be able, as of right, to take up to four weeks of unpaid leave per year, without compromising any of their entitlements as full-time employees, and to have their reduced salaries paid in equal instalments over the full 52-week year. Known as the "48/52 arrangement", it is used by many families to allow parents to take leave so as to be at home with children during school holiday periods.

By these and other means, Australian governments have contributed to the development of so-called "family friendly" work practices as a means of easing the parental task of combining the demands of work and family life in a manageable manner. There is also a great deal of current rhetoric among employers about the importance of the family friendly workplace. However, although some progress towards this end has been made in the corporate sector, overall rhetoric far outstrips achievement (Wolcott & Glezer, 1995). Indeed, in Australia, the duration of the working week for full-time employees is increasing rather than decreasing; in 1989 it averaged 39.9 hours, whereas it is currently 40.9 hours (ABS, 1996). Moreover, the contemporary trend towards deregulation and casualisation of labour throughout the post-industrial world is likely to make it more rather than less difficult for parents to achieve the balance they would prefer between employment and parenting.

Children and parental employment

As indicated earlier, parents' workplaces are part of the *exosystem* for most children (Bronfenbrenner, 1979). With the exception of the small proportion who accompany their parents to work or whose parents work from home the majority of children rarely enter their parents' workplace. Nonetheless, parental presence there and the experiences parents have at work profoundly impact on the lives of the children.

By and large, developmental research in this area has tended to dwell on the potentially negative impact of parental employment on children's lives. Thus, there is an entire research literature on the effects on child social development of "father absence", whether through desertion, or military service, or employment circumstances. For example, "father absence" has been causally associated with male delinquency and aggression, with reduced or confused male gender identity and with lowered self-esteem (Carlsmith, 1964; Lynn, 1974).

Similarly, there is an extensive research literature on the "problem of working mothers" to whom is attributed responsibility for, *inter alia,* failures of infant–mother bonding, childhood aggression, and such other childhood behavioural manifestations as stubbornness and lack of compliance with adult authority (McGurk, Caplan, Hennessy, & Moss, 1993).

Before we go on to consider some of these issues in detail, we would do well to remind ourselves of the ethnocentricity of such concepts as "absent fathers" and the "problem of working mothers". Both have their origins in and stand in contrast to the "traditional" Western nuclear family of two heterosexual parents and their biological offspring living together in a single occupancy household in which the male parent is the breadwinner and the female parent the home-maker. It takes only a little reflection to realise that in terms of the ethnic and cultural diversity of family forms, the Western nuclear family is only one among an extensive and diverse range of functional forms (see Jahoda, Chapter 4). The concepts in question also entail the implicit assumption that exclusive rearing by mother is the "natural" way to bring up children. Again, little reflection is required to realise that such a form of rearing is experienced only by a minority of the world's children and that nature has privileged no single mode of child rearing (McGurk et al., 1993).

We need to remind ourselves also of the positive advantages that can accrue to children from parental employment. For many families, the only realistic alternative to dual earner status is poverty. Poverty and its associated disadvantages are among the most powerful predictors of poor developmental outcomes for children (see the section on poverty, p. 126). In addition, having parents who successfully combine family and employment responsibilities can be a positive resource for children who, through parents' involvement in work, are exposed to positive models for effective time and value management and self-direction, all of which can contribute to children's own self-esteem and well-being (Parcel & Menagham, 1994, pp. 13–14).

Maternal employment and child care

This is the area of greatest controversy with respect to the influences of parental employment on developmental outcomes for children. Is it damaging to the development of children for persons other than their mothers to be extensively involved in child care, especially during the first months of life? Are "working mothers" therefore exposing their children to harm? Is day care harmful to children?

Although these issues have frequently been addressed over the past half century, and although the research evidence consistently confirms that there is little reason to believe that negative developmental consequences are associated with work-related, nonparental child care, it is a controversy which seems destined not to go away! The most recent formulations of the controversy have their primary origins in a series of papers published by Jay Belsky and his colleagues in the late 1980s and early 1990s (see Fox & Fein, 1990).

Belsky focused his concerns about nonparental day care on its consequences for the development of early social and emotional attachments and the sequelae of these consequences on later development. His position can be summarised as follows: (1) exposure to more than 20 hours per week of nonmaternal child care during the first year of life is argued to be associated with an increased probability of infants being classified as insecurely attached to their mothers when attachment is assessed using the Ainsworth Strange Situation (Ainsworth & Wittig, 1969); (2) infants assessed as insecurely attached to their mothers are argued, on theoretical grounds, to be at increased risk for subsequent maladjustment; (3) thus, children who, as infants, experienced more than 20 hours per week of nonmaternal care are argued to be at risk of manifesting more symptoms of maladjustment than children with histories of reduced nonmaternal care or none at all.

The evidence adduced by Belsky to support his case was largely indirect and circumstantial but he nonetheless concluded that infants, who during the first year of life experience more than 20 hours per week of nonmaternal care, are at risk for later psychosocial maladjustment (Belsky, 1988, 1989, 1992).

Following the publication of Belsky's controversial conclusions, each of the three steps in his argument, as just outlined, were subject to careful scrutiny and evaluation in a succession of research and review papers, many of which were published in the *Early Childhood Research Quarterly*, Volumes 3 and 4, 1988 (see also Fox & Fein, 1990). By and large, Belsky's conclusions were shown to overstate the case for any strong association between early experiences of nonparental day care and quality of mother–infant attachment or between early day care and subsequent developmental pathology.

Despite the lack of direct empirical support for the position advanced by Belsky, the issues raised by the controversy over the effects of early nonmaternal day care were considered by researchers and policy-makers in the United States to be of sufficient theoretical and practical importance to merit investment in a major normative, longitudinal investigation of the issues. Accordingly, under the auspices of the US National Institutes of Child Health and Development (NICHD), a consortium of 10 teams of American developmental researchers has been engaged in a long-term national follow-up study, from birth through to the first year of school, of the social, emotional, and cognitive development of representative samples of infants with and without experience of day care.

Preliminary findings from this important study, reported when the children were around four years of age, reveal no adverse effects on mother–child attachment attributable to exposure to day care. Findings have confirmed, however, that where the quality of interaction between mothers and their children is already poor, exposure to day care may further weaken attachments (NICHD Early Child Care Research Network, 1996).

These findings, albeit preliminary, from a carefully designed prospective investigation of the effects of early day care on later development, represent an important contribution to the day-care debate. What has been missing from this debate until now has been evidence from large scale, longitudinal studies. Outcomes from the NICHD project afford encouragement to researchers, policy-makers, early childhood professionals, and parents alike to shift their focus of attention away from putatively damaging effects of nonparental child care, towards a focus on how we can ensure delivery of child-care services that will support the development and well-being of young children and their families. The NICHD findings should also facilitate a shift away from questions about "the problem of working mothers", towards determining what has to be done to ensure that employed parents, mothers and fathers alike, are better enabled to combine family and work responsibilities in ways that are fulfilling for all the participants.

POVERTY AND CHILDHOOD SOCIAL DEVELOPMENT

Increase in the frequencies of dual-earner lifestyles and in women's participation in the paid labour force have both been occurring at a time when, in many countries, there has also been growing unemployment. Indeed, in Australia as elsewhere in the post-industrial world, children are increasingly living in households where either *both* parents or *no* parent is employed (ABS, 1995b); consequently, increasing numbers of children, both relatively and absolutely are being reared in poverty. In Australia, this condition affects about 13 per cent of the children in couple families and more than 50 per cent of children in single-parent households (McDonald, 1993).

Children reared in poverty are frequently disadvantaged both materially and socio-emotionally. For example, such children are likely to live in less desirable neighbourhoods, in overcrowded conditions, and in homes lacking in books and toys (McDonald, 1995; Boss, Edwards, & Pitman, 1995). Australian research indicates that housing (street, neighbourhood, and type of house) is a predictor of childhood emotional and social adjustment (Burns & Homel, 1984). Moreover, the demands of coping with economic hardship can create stress and induce a sense of helplessness in some parents, reduce the emotional resources they have available for child rearing, and render them less responsive to their children (Parcel & Menagham, 1994).

Infants reared under conditions of poverty may be at particular risk in this respect because parents, especially mothers, who are required to shoulder the main responsibility for economic management as well as caring for children, feel emotionally as well as materially undermined by poverty. Thus, quality of child care may deteriorate and parents may become less supportive of their infants (Fox & Fein, 1990).

It is not only infants who are developmentally disadvantaged by poverty. A large body of international research demonstrated strong associations between poverty and negative outcomes for children at all ages (e.g. Amato, 1987; Elder, 1974; Elder, Conger, Foster & Ardelt, 1992; Isralowitz & Singer, 1986; Patterson, Griesler, Vaden & Kupersmidt, 1992; Slaughter, 1988; Werner & Smith, 1989). In his review, Amato observed that family socioeconomic status (SES) is positively associated with child competence (Hess, 1970; Kagan, 1979; White, 1982; Marjoribanks, 1979). Children in high SES families were at an advantage because they have access to a broader range of resources and higher levels of parental support; they grow up in environments that encourage independence, achievement, and self-control. These, in turn promote increased self-esteem, self-efficacy, and intrinsic motivation to achieve goals (Amato, 1987).

In addition to relative lack of competence and lowered self-esteem, other adverse developmental outcomes associated with poverty include behaviour problems and difficulties with peer relationships. Adjustment problems in adolescence, such as delinquency, are frequent. Moreover, young people reared in poverty are less likely to pursue secondary or further education and more likely to become unemployed on leaving school or to be in part-time employment compared with their more fortunate peers (Bolger, Patterson, Thompson, & Kupersmidt, 1995; Ochiltree, 1990b). The stage is thus set for the developmental disadvantages associated with poverty to be continued into subsequent generations.

It is very important to recognise in this context that good developmental outcomes are not predicated necessarily on material advantage, nor are poor outcomes an inevitable and necessary consequence of poverty. As noted earlier, it is the coping stresses associated with poverty that can make it difficult, even for otherwise well-intentioned parents, to function as effectively as they would wish. As Amato (1987) has also noted, in the review already referred to, children born into families with economic and material advantage as well as disadvantage may both fail to develop optimal levels of competence if parents show little support or warmth and employ unpredictable or authoritarian methods of control.

DIVORCE AND CHILDHOOD SOCIAL DEVELOPMENT

In the section on changing family demography (p. 115), reference was made to the trend for significant numbers of children to experience disruption to their lives as a consequence of the divorce of their parents. There is now a substantial body of research to document and interpret the impact of these events on the lives of the children involved. Reviews by Hetherington (1989), and by Kurtz and Derenvensky (1994), indicate that transitions and complications associated with divorce—the restructuring of living arrangements, changes in family lifestyle, rules, and relationships—all affect the emotional, social, and academic development of children.

Longitudinal research (Kurtz & Derevensky, 1994) has identified three consistent findings concerning the effects of divorce on young children. First, children invariably experience short-term adverse effects in post-divorce adjustment regardless of age including reduced academic performance, low self-esteem, problems in peer relationships, and difficulties with emotional well-being. However, many children prove to be remarkably resilient and, following the initial crisis period, a majority go on to develop coping strategies which can serve them well in the long term. Second, the nature and course of children's post-divorce adjustment varies according to a number of important factors, including their developmental level, gender, birth order, and degree of dependence on parents. The third general finding is that, five years after marital break up, childhood depression is the most frequent clinical diagnosis, together with increase in the frequency of conduct and behavioural disorders (Kurtz & Derevensky, 1994).

There is an extensive range of other factors which can affect children's post-divorce adjustment. For example, the level of marital hostility prior to divorce is significantly related to post-divorce functioning and well being. Children from families characterised by intense parental conflict tend to make poorer adjustments than those from backgrounds less marred by such conflict (McFarlane et al., 1995; Stolberg, Camplair, Currier, & Wells, 1987). These authors also report that mothers' confidence in their child-rearing skills, their actual skills, and even the perception of children about the presence or absence of external controls can influence the levels of aggression displayed by children from divorced families.

Children of divorce experience disruption not only to their immediate family life. Divorce is often accompanied by other changes such as a move to a new house, a new neighbourhood, and a new school. These changes place demands for adjustment on young children at a time when their coping strategies are already under pressure. Children's level of social maturity and their skills in social interaction are important predictors of the ease with which they accommodate these changes.

The divorce of their parents presents children with cognitive as well as social challenges. For example, for young children, common residence is a necessary condition for family membership (Gilby & Pederson, 1982; Piaget, 1961; Wynn & Brumberger, 1982). It is not until around 11 or 12 years of age that children spontaneously identify consanguinity and legal relationships as defining characteristics of families. Consequently, younger children are likely to have difficulty in coming to terms with the idea that a nonresident parent can remain a family member beyond divorce and may also fail to appreciate that the parental relationship continues beyond divorce. Thus, for young children, divorce may be experienced as the loss of a parent.

This issue was investigated in a study by McGurk and Glachan (1987) in which three levels in children's understanding of the continuity of parenthood following divorce were identified. The study involved almost 300 children aged between 4 and 14 years from intact and divorced family backgrounds. By means of doll-play, children were presented with a series of vignettes in which various members of a nuclear family comprising parents and two children were absent from the family home for a variety of reasons ranging from attending school, shopping or going on holiday, to divorce. After each account of a departure from the family home the children were asked about the continuity of the familial relationship between the person who had left and the other members of the family.

Children's responses to the vignettes were classified according to their cognitive complexity into three levels, the second and third of which were divided into additional subcategories. Levels and associated subcategories are presented in Table 5.3; the proportions of children at different age levels whose judgements fell into the different levels and categories are illustrated in Tables 5.4 and 5.5 for children from intact and divorced families, respectively.

The first level of response involved simple, *matter of fact assertion of the continuity of the parental relationship* unsupported by any justification

TABLE 5.3

Response categories

Level I: *Continuity of parenthood unquestioned*
1. Naïve affirmation: Justified by reference to irrelevant characteristics of parents

Level II: *Continuity of parenthood denied*
2. Conditional on location
3. Conditional on affection
4. Conditional on subsequent marital/step-parent status
5. Conditional on sex of parent

Level III: *Continuity of parenthood affirmed: Justified by reference to procreation and permanence of consanguinity*
6. Marital and parental relationships clearly differentiated
7. Parental relationships and roles differentiated

Source: H. McGurk and M. Glachan (1987).

TABLE 5.4

Children of intact families: Percentage frequency of response

		Age (years)					
Level	Category	4 (%)	6 (%)	8 (%)	10 (%)	12 (%)	14 (%)
I	1	48	30	6			
	2	43	46	9			
	3	9	15	9			
II	4		9	28	37		
	5			16	5		
	6			32	52	88	58
III	7				6	12	42
	N	42	43	32	38	42	50

Source: H. McGurk and M. Glachan (1987).

TABLE 5.5
Children of divorced/separated parents: Percentage frequency of response

		Age (years)					
Level	Category	4 (%)	6 (%)	8 (%)	10 (%)	12 (%)	14 (%)
I	1						
	2	38	57	19			
	3	62	43	25			
II	4			12	10		
	5						
	6			44	90	88	
III	7					12	
	N	8	6	16	10	8	

Source: H. McGurk and M. Glachan (1987).

other than fiat or by reference to irrelevant characteristics such as the physical size of the parties involved. Children who responded in this way did not seem to perceive divorce as representing any kind of threat to the continuity of parenthood.

Responses at the second level came from children who denied the continuity of parenthood beyond divorce or whose appreciation of such continuity was conditional. Four kinds of justifications or conditions were offered. (i) *Parenthood is conditional on residence*. A parent remains such when co-residing with his or her children but not when living elsewhere. For these children a parent of either sex who lives in a different house from them is seen as a mother or father when visiting them but not otherwise. (ii) *Parenthood is conditional on evidence of affection*; if the mother or father maintains his/her love for the children he/she continues to be a parent, even when living far away, but not otherwise. (iii) *Parenthood is dependent on subsequent marital or parental or step-parental status*. If a departed parent remarries and/or has other children or becomes a step-parent to other children, he/she ceases to be the parent of the original children, regardless of his/her affection for the latter. (iv) *Continuity depends on the gender of the parent*. Whenever children's judgements differentiated between parents on the basis of gender, it was with respect to mothers that the continuity of parenthood was first seen as surviving divorce, regardless of whether she had other children or became a step-parent. Such differentiation was based on the argument that because, as babies, the children had come from the mother's womb, they would always be hers.

The third level of response came from children whose affirmation of the continuity of parenthood beyond divorce was unconditional, justified by reference to both parents' involvement in procreation and to the permanence of consanguinity. At this level, however, responses could be divided into two further subcategories: (a) marital and parental relationships are clearly differentiated; the former can be severed but the latter cannot; (b) parental roles and genetic relationships are differentiated; the former may not be maintained but the latter remains intact after divorce.

Development in children's responses to questions about the continuity of parenthood after divorce are apparent in Tables 5.4 and 5.5. Responses increase in cognitive complexity with increasing age. Conceptualising the permanence of parenthood beyond divorce presents children of 8 years or less with considerable intellectual challenges. Thereafter, however, belief in the permanence of parenthood regardless of residential or marital status becomes modal and is universal by 12 years of age. Interestingly, children whose parents are divorced appear to reach higher level judgements about the continuity of parenthood at an earlier age than their peers from intact families. Thus, the experience of parental divorce influences children to think more maturely about this aspect of the nature of parenthood.

How children adjust to their parents' divorce in the medium to long term is influenced by a number of factors. Among them are children's relationships with both parents, before and after divorce, and the divorced parents' relationship with each other. Weirson, Forehand, Fauber, and McCoombs (1989) reported that warm relationships with both parents was associated with higher levels of cognitive functioning and served as a buffer against some of the harmful effects of divorce. Inter-parental relationships and the quality of parent–child relationships are better predictors of the social behaviour of children than marital status or family type (Amato, 1986). Cooper, Holman, and Braithwaite (1983) in a study of Australian primary schoolchildren found that parent conflict and parent–child conflict were associated with low self-esteem among children of both intact and divorced families. Where there are continuing high levels of conflict between parents following divorce children tend to be adversely affected. Such conflict is associated with behaviour problems and difficulty in social adjustment in children; parental conflict post-divorce has also been associated with the occurrence of childhood somatic and psychosomatic symptoms (Johnston, Kline, & Tschan, 1989; Kelly, 1993; Kilne & Pew, 1992).

To the extent that they provide children with a safe, supportive, structured, and predictable environment, external settings such as day-care centres, kindergartens, and schools, can provide children adapting to divorce with some relief from family stresses and, in the process, can facilitate children's social and cognitive adjustment (Stolberg et al., 1987). The

study by McGurk and Glachan (1987) illustrated how children's appreciation of the continuity of parenthood beyond divorce can be modified by
experience. This finding offers some support to the proposal that adults at
school can help these youngsters to arrive at a better understanding of
their situation. However, for this to be achieved would require staff in
these settings to be reasonably well informed about children's home situations. This, in turn, will depend on the relationships between home and
kindergarten or other setting and the degree to which relationships have
been established which facilitates shared confidence (McGurk, 1995).

Their peer groups have also proved to be important sources of support
to youngsters coming to terms with their parents' divorce, although this
function is more readily provided by older childrens' and adolescents' peer
groups than in the case of younger children (Hetherington, 1989).

Findings from a long-term follow-up study of the consequences of
divorce, carried out at the Australian Institute of Family Studies (AIFS),
demonstrate that just as there is an extensive range of factors in the
immediate environment of the home, in settings external to the home and
in the wider society which influence children's adjustment to divorce, so
also is there an extensive range of individual pathways which children and
young people take in their transitions through their parents' divorce and
beyond (Funder, 1996; Funder, Harrison, & Weston, 1993; McDonald,
1986). Outcomes from the AIFS study combine with those from other
investigations to reveal that, with reasonable support, children can make
satisfactory post-divorce adjustments and are able to get on with their lives
(Amato, 1987; Skewes & Kelly, 1989). Clinical and research evidence alike
confirm that children are hurt and grieve over their parents' divorce and
would prefer for it not to happen and for their parents to find other
solutions to their difficulties (Cockett & Tripp, 1994). On the other hand,
children do survive divorce and there is some evidence in the work, just
referred to by Amato (1987) and by Skewes and Kelly (1989), to suggest
that many emerge with enhanced emotional maturity, self-confidence, and
independence.

The consequences of relationship breakdown between parents whether
through divorce, separation, or the disruption of a previously stable
cohabitation are giving rise to concern in many societies. The costs to
human suffering of such relationship breakdown, in terms of the sadness
and distress they cause to adults and children alike, are immeasurable but
are comparable to, possibly greater than, those associated with bereave-
ment. There are also financial costs, direct and indirect, to the individuals
involved as well as to the larger society. These include, at the individual
level, legal costs, costs of conveyancing, loss of income, reduced financial
support. The greatest burden of these individual costs falls on women and
children who, in the immediate aftermath of divorce, often make a rapid

transition into poverty (McDonald, 1986; Funder et al., 1993). At a societal level there are also legal costs as well as costs associated with providing housing and income support to women and children and collecting child support contributions from nonresident parents, primarily men. For example, 1989, it was estimated that the cost to government of supporting separated parents with at least one dependent child under 16 years of age was 1.9 billion (Wolcott & Glezer, 1989).

Many societies, including Australia and the United Kingdom, are currently making two kinds of response towards reducing both the personal and financial costs associated with divorce. One is preventative and involves investing resources in the development of relationship and marriage education, the long-term objective of which is to reduce the frequency of divorce by providing individuals and couples with increased understanding and skill in the development and maintenance of harmonious and fulfilling interpersonal relationships (Utting, 1995).

The second response is directed, through the provision of Court-based mediation and conciliation services, towards the promotion of the "good" divorce, based on mutual respect for and consideration of the well-being and integrity of the former partner and, particularly, on parental recognition to make adequate provision for the material, psychological, and social well-being of their children beyond divorce (Funder et al., 1993).

There are two points to be made here that require the serious consideration of developmental researchers. The first concerns, once more, the importance of contextualising the study of developmental processes within the larger socio-ecological framework within which they are embedded. The second concerns the importance of developmental researchers engaging themselves in evaluations of the impact of these kinds of provision on developmental processes and of designing studies of the effects of these provisions on developmental outcomes for children, thereby positioning themselves to contribute to the knowledge-based development of policies and services intended to promote child and family well-being.

Lone-parent households

Lone-parent households, mainly comprising divorced or separated mothers and their dependent children, represent an increasingly frequent type of family in Australia and elsewhere; currently such families represent just under 13 per cent of all Australian families. Almost 15 per cent of children and young people under 25 years of age are living in a lone-parent family, mainly with mothers although a small minority, 2.1 per cent, live with lone-parent fathers (ABS, 1992).

It is important to note that lone parenthood and living in a lone-parent household is a transitory process for most of the adults and children involved. Within 6 years from the end of a previous marriage 69 per cent of women and 81 per cent of men remarry; in any one year about 25 per cent of divorced persons aged between 25 and 40 years will remarry (McDonald, 1993).

Lone parenthood is not an enviable status. For many women in particular the transition to lone parenthood is accompanied by a transition into increased or unaccustomed poverty (McDonald, 1986; Funder et al., 1993). Thus, in addition to the stresses created by having to assume sole responsibility for the security and well-being of vulnerable children, the lone female parent has also to cope with economic deprivation. For many such families the only route out of poverty is through entering the paid work force but this can increase stress further by the requirement to achieve a balance between the responsibilities of being an employee with those of being a lone parent, by having to juggle with child care and work schedules and by having to find the energy to face the night shift of work at home when the day shift of paid work is over. It is perhaps more impressive that so many women and their children cope at all with this situation than that some have difficulty in doing so. Contemporary employment arrangements are even less friendly to single-parent families than they are to two-parent families (see the section on work and families, p. 117).

Research on the impact of rearing in a sole-parent family on children's development and well-being indicates, not surprisingly, that, once more, many factors require to be taken into account. Parenting style is an important characteristic. Hetherington (1989) has identified authoritative parenting, involving a combination of warmth and firm but responsive control, as particularly effective in enabling the children of single parents to achieve social competence and to enable them to overcome the adverse effects of marital transitions. Hetherington argues that the supportive, structured, predictable parent–child relationships promoted by such a parenting style plays a critical role.

Weiss (1979) has argued that, in single-parent households, children are required to "grow up" a little faster than their peers. They are expected to take on more domestic responsibilities, share in decision making, and sometimes have to act as confidant of the lone parent. The consequent reduction in generational boundaries can serve to bolster children's sense of responsibility and self-esteem. But there is a need for lone parents to strike a balance in this respect. However, as Devall, Stoneman, and Brody (1986) have pointed out, such increased responsibilities may foster self-reliance and high self-esteem, and enhance self-perceptions of competence, such demands, if not controlled carefully, may also serve to overburden the children and isolate them from their peers due to the limited time they have to engage in activities outside the home and to develop friendships.

The lone parent's adjustment to his/her situation is an important predictor of the adjustment of children. For example, Poehlmann and Fiese (1994) report that, in general, divorced mothers felt that they had less social support and were less satisfied with their life situation than married mothers. It is therefore not surprising, perhaps, that lone parents generally provide less stimulating environments for their children or that their children have increased levels of social and behavioural difficulties (Guidobaldi, Cleminshaw, Perry, Nastasi, & Lightel, 1986; Poehlmann & Fiese, 1994).

On the other hand, recent studies have shown that children whose lone-parent mother's were employed had higher self-esteem and showed increased social and mental well-being compared with children whose lone-parent mothers were not in the paid labour force (Kurtz & Derevensky, 1994; Silburn et al., 1996). Such findings are to be explained in part by increased self-esteem and well-being on the part of the employed mothers as well as the socioeconomic advantages that come with employment and the increased expectation on children to be more independent.

Step-families

As indicated earlier, for most divorced parents and their children, life in a sole-parent household is only a temporary condition, frequently by a transition out of lone parenthood into step and blended family relationships.

In 1992, the latest year for which data are available, about 7 per cent of Australian children were living in step or blended family situations (ABS, 1992). Step-families come in a range of shapes and sizes including: children, their natural mother and a spouse/step-father; children, their natural father and a spouse/step-mother; children and their natural mother along with other children and their natural father—in this constellation both parents have a step-child or children and each child has one or more step-siblings as well as a step-parent. Blended families incorporate the features of each of the three constellations just described but also include the natural children of the relationship between the spouses.

The creation of harmonious step and blended families thus present adjustment challenges for all family members. The step-parents in such households are confronted by the necessity to develop a *modus vivendi* with children who themselves may resist step-parents' overtures out of the conflict they may engender over relationships with the absent natural parent. For most adults this is unfamiliar territory and few approach the task prepared by relevant prior experience.

Children who have made a successful transition to having a lone parent may resent the intrusion into their lives of a new adult who has become a competitor for the previously exclusive attention and affection of the natural parent. Moreover, some children have also to adjust to the presence in their home of other youngsters of whom they have little previous experience and with whom they have had no hand in choosing as intimates. Little wonder, then, that the initial stages of step-family life are fraught with tension (Cherlin, 1978; Connolly, 1983; Webber, 1986; E. Visher & J. Visher, 1983).

On the other hand, despite the early tensions and associated problems, the entry of a step-parent can result in improvement in family functioning and well-being. For previously lone-mother households, for example, there is very frequently an immediate increase in the standard of living (McDonald, 1986, p. 238). For both men and women there is an increase in well-being and self-esteem as a consequence of the emotional support and companionship provided by a new partner who can also provide increased emotional resources to children, especially if their noncustodial parent has severed contact with the family.

For example, both Hetherington, M. Cox, and R. Cox (1982) and Wallerstein and Kelly (1980) found that the entry of a step-father into their family had positive effects on young boys, leading to improvements in general family functioning. Amato (1987) reported that relationships with step parents generally improve, with step-fathers coming to take on many of the parental functions and responsibilities of biological fathers. Findings from the AIFS's study on the Economic Consequences of Marriage Breakdown (ECMB) indicate that when children develop good relationships with their step-father, these are not necessarily at the expense of relationships with their natural but nonresident father; the latter are also maintained and children do not seem to swap one father for another.

Children who live in step-families have experienced more disruption and change in their lives than those living in lone-parent families who, in turn, have experienced more than children from intact families. For example, an Australian study revealed that primary schoolchildren from step-families have experienced more changes of residence than their sole-parent counterparts, whereas the latter have moved house more often than children from intact two-parent families. These disruptions place demands on the social skills of young children, requiring them to settle into new schools, to cope with discontinuities in friendships, and to make new friends. Children who undergo many such disruptions are vulnerable to becoming socially isolated (cf. Ochiltree, 1990; Wertsch, 1993).

Like their counterparts from lone-parent households, children in step-families also report a relatively high level of involvement with domestic chores and in household decision making. The latter are, in all probability, directly attributable to their prior experience of the former (Amato, 1987).

The disruptions to children's lives discussed in this section of the present chapter all come about as the consequences of decisions taken by adults to which children are only rarely first parties. At this point in the development of post-industrial society adults seem to be seeking increasingly less restricted and increasingly more fulfilling personal lives. The decisions made by many parents in pursuit of these adult objectives have profound implications for the happiness and well-being of their children. As a society we need to invest more effort in ensuring that adult objectives are not being achieved at the expense of children (cf. Guidobaldi, Cleminshaw, Perry, Nastasi, & Lightel, 1986).

CONCLUSIONS

Human infants come into the world already equipped with a prosocial orientation in the sense that their perceptual systems seem to be especially attuned to the differentiation of such specifically human stimuli as the configuration of the human face, the sound of the human voice, and the odours of the human body. Infants soon begin to deploy these perceptual capacities in the service of differentiating between one person and another and to support selective attention towards some individuals over others.

Families represent the primary loci of social development for children more or less from birth onwards. It is within the context of their families that the newborn's prosocial capacities are capitalised on by caregivers so as to facilitate the infant's integration into the social world (Kaye, 1983). It is within the family that the vast majority of young infants form the initial socio-emotional attachments that provide them the bases of security they need from which to explore the larger material and social world and which serve to underpin subsequent social relationships.

It is within families too that infants and young children are exposed to models for the day to day management of intimate relationships and, in many instances, through the arrival of a sibling, families provide children with their initial experiences of encounters with other youngsters. The families in which they are embedded therefore constitute the very crucible of social development.

In this concluding section of our chapter we have used the plural form, families, mindfully and intentionally. Nature has privileged no one family structure and no one model for the parenting of children over other alternative structures or models over others. It is the quality of care they receive that is critical to the well-being of infants and young children rather than the particular social structure within which that care is provided. That said, the evidence suggests that each child prospers best when there is at least one caring adult in his/her immediate environment who has an unconditional commitment to his/her well-being and when there is a system in place which supports the committed adult in fulfilling his/her caring role and shares in that role. We would do well to remember that neither individual parents nor families, whatever their structure, have gone it alone in the rearing of their children, and to have a mind also to the African proverb: that "It takes the whole village to rear a child" (see McGurk et al., 1993).

Accordingly, in order to understand the nature of social development it is necessary also to understand something of the nature of the family systems within which social development is framed. Moreover, because families themselves are embedded within a larger social context, the reciprocal ways in which family functioning influences and is influenced by the operation of that larger context needs to be understood.

That is the orientation we have tried to elaborate in this chapter. Employing Bronfenbrenner's ecological model as an organising principle we have endeavoured to illustrate how the study of childhood social development can be most meaningfully investigated within the context of all the complexities of the ordinary, everyday world in which ordinary children from ordinary families live and move and have their being. We believe that it is only by conducting itself in this manner that developmental psychology will be able to create a knowledge base from which to contribute effectively to the formation of practices, policies, services, and programmes to promote the optimum development of all our children.

REFERENCES

Ainsworth, M. & Wittig, B. (1969). Attachment and exploratory behaviour of one-year-olds in a strange situation. In B. M. Foss (Ed.), *Determinants of infant behaviour*, (Vol. IV, pp. 111–136). London: Methuen.

Amato, P. (1986). Marital conflict, the parent–child relationship and child self-esteem in *Family Relations*, *35*, 403–416.

Amato, P. (1987). *Children in Australian families: The growth of competence*. Englewood Cliffs, NJ: Prentice Hall.

ABS (Australian Bureau of Statistics) (1992). *Australia's families: Selected findings from the survey of families in Australia* (4418.0). Canberra: Australian Government Publishing Service.

ABS (Australian Bureau of Statistics) (1993). *Divorces Australia* (3307.0). Canberra: Australian Government Publishing Service.

ABS (Australian Bureau of Statistics) (1994a). *Marriages and divorces Australia* (3310.0). Canberra: Australian Government Publishing Service.

ABS (Australian Bureau of Statistics) (1994b). *Focus on families, family life, Australia* (4425.0). Canberra: Australian Government Publishing Service.

ABS (Australian Bureau of Statistics) (1995a). *Australian women's yearbook* (4124.0). Canberra: Australian Government Publishing Service.

ABS (Australian Bureau of Statistics) (1995b). *Labour force status and other characteristics of families Australia* (6224.0). Canberra: Australian Government Publishing Service.

ABS (Australian Bureau of Statistics) (1996). *Labour force, Australia* (6203.0). Canberra: Australian Government Publishing Service.

Belsky, J. (1988). The "effects"of infant day care reconsidered. *Early Childhood Research Quarterly, 3,* 235–272.

Belsky, J. (1989). Infant–parent attachment and day-care: In defense of the Strange Situation. In J. S. Laude, S. Scarr, & N. Gunzenhauser (Eds.), *Caring for Children: Challenge to America* (pp. 83–94). Hillsdale, NJ: Lawrence Erlbaum Associates Inc.

Belsky, J. (1992). Consequences of child care for children's development: A deconstructionist view. In A. Booth (Ed.), *Child care in the 1990s: Trends and consequences.* Hillsdale, NJ: Lawrence Erlbaum Associates Inc.

Bolger, K., Patterson, C., Thompson, W., & Kupersmidt, J. (1995). Psychosocial adjustment among children experiencing persistent and intermittent family economic hardship. *Child Development, 66,* 1107–1129.

Boss, P., Edwards, S., & Pitman, S. (Eds.) (1995). *Profile of young Australians: Facts, figures and issues.* Melbourne: Churchill Livingstone.

Braude, J. (1957). *Encyclopaedia of stories, quotations and anecdotes.* Englewood Cliffs, NJ: Prentice Hall.

Bronfenbrenner, U. (1979). *The ecology of human development: Experiments by nature and design.* Cambridge, MA: Harvard University Press

Bronfenbrenner, U. (1982). Children and families: The silent revolution. *Australian Journal of Sex, Marriage and Family, 3,* 111–123.

Burns, A. & Homel, R. (1984). Neighbourhood quality and child adjustment. In *Australian family research conference proceedings: Vol. 6. Family life,* (pp. 70–104). Melbourne: Australian Institute of Family Studies.

Carlsmith, L. (1964). Effect of early father-absence on scholastic aptitude. *Harvard Educational Review, 34,* 3–21.

Cherlin, A. (1978). Remarriage as an incomplete institution. *American Journal of Sociology, 84,* 23–30.

Cockett, M. & Tripp, J. (1994). *The Exeter family study: Family breakdown and its impact on children.* Exeter, UK: University of Exeter Press.

Conference of European Ministers responsible for Family Affairs MMF–XXIV (1995). *National replies to the questionnaire: "The status and role of fathers–family aspects" for the Conference of European Ministers responsible for Family Affairs, Collection* XXIVth Session, (2nd ed.) Helsinki, Finland.

Connolly, J. (1983). *Stepfamilies.* Condell Park, New South Wales: Corgi.

Cooper, J., Holman, J., & Braithwaite, V. (1983). Self esteem and family cohesion: The child's perspective and adjustment. *Journal of Marriage and the Family, 45,* 153–159.

Devall, E., Stoneman, Z., & Brody, G. (1986). The impact of divorce and maternal employment on pre-adolescent children. *Family Relations, 35,* 153–168.

Edgar, D. & Glezer, H. (1992). *Reconstructing family realities: Men do matter.* Paper presented at the International Council of Women International Conference on Changing Families in Changing Societies, Brussels, Belgium.

Elder, G., Jr. (1974). *Children of the great depression.* Chigaco, IL.: University of Chicago Press.

Elder, G. M., Conger, R. D., Foster, E. M., & Ardelt, M. (1992). Families under economic pressure. *Journal of Family Issues, 13,* 5–37.

Fox, N. & Fein, G. (Eds.) (1990). *Infant day care: The current debate.* Norwood, NJ: Ablex.

Funder, K. (1996). *Remaking families.* Melbourne: Australian Institute of Family Studies.

Funder, K., Harrison, M., & Weston, R. (1993). *Settling down: Pathways of parents after divorce.* Monograph No. 13. Melbourne: Australian Institute of Family Studies.

Gilby, R. & Pederson, D. (1982). The development of the child's concept of the family *Canadian Journal of Behavioural Science, 14*, 110–121.

Glezer, H. (1988). *Maternity leave in Australian employee and employer experiences: Report of a survey.* Melbourne: Australian Institute of Family Studies.

Glezer, H. (1991). Cycles of care: Support and care between generations. *Family Matters, 30.* Melbourne: Australian Institute of Family Studies.

Guidobaldi, J., Cleminshaw, H., Perry, J., Nastasi, B., & Lightel, J. (1986). The role of selected family environment factors in children's post divorce adjustment. *Family Relations, 35*, 141–151.

Hess, R. (1970). Social class and ethnic influences upon socialization. In P. H. Mussen (Ed.), *Carmichael's manual of child psychology* (pp. 457–557). New York: Wiley.

Hetherington, M. (1989). Coping with family transitions: Winners, losers and survivors. *Child Development, 60*, 1–14.

Hetherington, E., Cox, M., & Cox, R. (1982). Effects of divorce on parents and children. In M. Lamb (Ed.), *Non-traditional families* (pp. 233–288). Hillsdale, NJ: Lawrence Erlbaum Associates Inc.

Holland, A. (1994). Fathers' involvement in child rearing: Chasing an ideal or challenging barriers. *Children Australia, 19*, 9–13.

Isralowitz, R. & Singer, M. (1986). Unemployment and its impact on adolescent work values. *Adolescence, 21*, 145–158.

Jamrozik, A. (1994). From harvester to de-regulation: Wage earners in the Australian welfare state. *Australian Journal of Social Issues, 29*, 162–170.

Johnston, J., Kline, M., & Tschan, J.M. (1989). Ongoing post divorce conflict: Effects on children of joint custody and frequent access. *American Journal of Orthopsychiatry, 59*, 576–592.

Kagan, J. (1979). *The growth of the child.* Hassocks, Sussex, UK: Harvester Press.

Kaye, K. (1983). *The mental and social life of babies.* London: Methuen.

Kelly, J. (1993). Current research on children's post divorce adjustment. *Family and Conciliation Courts Review, 31*, 29–49.

Kline, K. & Pew, S. (1992). *For the sake of the children: How to share your children with your ex-spouse in spite of your anger.* Rocklyn, WA: Prima Publishers.

Kurtz, L. & Derevensky, J. (1994). Family configuration and maternal employment: Effects on family environment and children's outcomes. *Journal of Divorce and Remarriage, 22*, 137–154.

Lynn, D. (1974). *The father: His role in child development.* Belmont, CA: Brooks-Cole.

Marjoribanks, K. (1979). *Families and their learning environments.* London: Routledge & Kegan Paul.

McDonald, P. (1986). *Settling up: Property and income distribution on divorce in Australia.* Sydney: Prentice Hall.

McDonald, P. (1993). *Family trends and structure in Australia.* Australian Family Briefings, No.3. Melbourne: Australian Institute of Family Studies.

McDonald, P. (1995). *Families in Australia: A socio-demographic perspective.* Melbourne: Australian Institute of Family Studies.

McDonald, P., Ruzicka, L., & Pyne, P. (1987). Marriage, fertility and morality. In W. Vamplew (Ed.), *Australians: Historical statistics* (pp. 42–61). NSW: Fairfax, Syme and Weldon.

McFarlane, A., Bellisimo, A., & Norman, G. (1995). Family structure, family functioning and adolescent well-being: The transient influence of parental style. *Journal of Child Psychology and Psychiatry, 34*, 3–23.

McGurk, H. (1995). *Children, schools and families in the 21st Century.* Opening Plenary Address, Teacher Assistant National Conference, Perth, Western Australia.

McGurk, H., Caplan, M., Hennessy, E., & Moss, P. (1993). Controversy, theory and social context in contemporary day care research. *Journal of Child Psychology and Psychiatry, 34,* 3–23.

McGurk, H. & Glachan, M. (1987). Children's conception of continuity of parenthood following divorce. *Journal of Child Psychology and Psychiatry, 28,* 427–435.

Ochiltree, G. (1990). *Children in stepfamilies.* Englewood Cliffs, NJ: Prentice Hall.

Ochiltree, G. (1990b). *Children in Australian families.* Melbourne: Longman Cheshire.

NICHD Early Child Care Research Network (1996). *Infant child care and attachment security: Results of the NICHD study of early child care.* Symposium presented at the 10th Biennial International Conference on Infant Studies, Providence, Rhode Island.

Parcel, T. & Menagham, E. (1994). *Parents' jobs and children's lives.* New York: Aldine.

Patterson, C.J., Griesler, P. C., Vaden, N. A., & Kupersmidt, J. B. (1992). Family economic circumstances, life transitions and children's peer relations. In R. D. Parke & G. W. Ladd (Eds.), *Family-peer relationships, modes of linkage* (pp. 385–424). Hillsdale, NJ: Lawrence Erlbaum Associates Inc.

Piaget, J. (1961). *Judgement and reasoning in the child.* Patterson, NJ: Littlefield, Adams.

Poehlmann, J. & Fiese, B. (1994). The effects of divorce, maternal employment and maternal social support on toddler's home environments. *Journal of Divorce and Remarriage, 22,* 121–135.

Russell, G. (1993). *Work and family: Audits of Australian workplaces: An employee perspective.* Paper presented at the Work and Family: The Corporate Challenge Conference, Melbourne. Australia.

Silburn, S., Zubrick, S., Garton, A., Gurrin, L., Dalby, R., Shepherd, C., & Lawrence, D. (1996). *Western Australian child health survey: Family and community health.* Perth: Australian Bureau of Statistics and the Institute for Child Health Research.

Skewes, A. & Kelly, S. (1989). *The journey from first family to stepfamily: Tracing changes in the quality of parent–child relationships.* Paper presented at the Third Australian Family Research Conference, Australian Institute of Family Studies, Ballarat.

Slaughter, D. (Ed.) (1988). *Black children and poverty: A developmental perspective.* San Francisco: Jossey-Bass.

Stolberg, A., Camplair, C., Currier, K., & Wells, M. (1987). Individual, familial and environmental determinants of children's post divorce adjustment and maladjustment. *Journal of Divorce, 11,* 51–70.

Utting, D. (1995). *Family and parenthood: Supporting families, preventing breakdown.* York, UK: Joseph Rowntree Foundation.

Visher, E. & Visher, J. (1983). Step-parenting: Blending families. In H. I. McCubbin & C. R. Figley (Eds.), *Stress and the family: Vol. I. Coping with normative transitions* (pp. 133–146). New York: Brunner/Mazel.

Wallerstein, J. & Kelly, J. (1980). *Surviving the break-up. How children and parents cope with divorce.* New York: Basic Books.

Wangmann, J. (1995). *Towards integration and quality assurance in children's services.* AIFS Early Childhood Study Paper No. 6. Melbourne: Australian Institute of Family Studies.

Webber, R. (1986). *Living in a stepfamily: An educative program for step-parents.* Proceedings of the Making Marriage and Family Work National Conference, University of Melbourne, Australia.

Weirson, M., Forehand, R., Fauber, R., & McCoombs, A. (1989). Buffering young male adolescents against negative divorce influences: The role of good parent–adolescent relationships. *Child Study Journal, 19,* 101–116

Weiss, R. (1979). *Going it alone: The family life and social situation of the single parent.* New York: Basic Books.

Werner, E. E. & Smith, S. (1989). *Vulnerable, but invincible: A longitudinal study of resilient children and youth*. New York: Adams, Bannister, Cox.

Wertsch, M. (1993). *Military brats: Leagues of childhood inside the fortress*. New York: Harmony Books.

White, K. R. (1982). The relation between socioeconomic status and academic achievement. *Psychological Bulletin, 91*, 461–481.

Wolcott, I. & Glezer, H. (1989). *Marriage counselling in Australia: An evaluation*. Melbourne: Australian Institute of Family Studies.

Wolcott, I. & Glezer, H. (1995). *Work and family life: Achieving integration*. Melbourne: Australian Institute of Family Studies.

Wynn, R. & Brumberger, L. (1982, June). *A cognitive developmental analysis of children's understanding of family membership and divorce*. Paper presented at the Twelfth Symposium of the Jean Piaget Society, Philadelphia, PA.

Yates, J. (1994). Is the current level of home ownership in Australia sustainable? *National Housing Action, 10*, 27–35.

6

The company they keep: Friendships and their developmental significance

Willard W. Hartup
University of Minnesota, Minneapolis, USA

On 16 February 1995, in the small Minnesota town of Delano, a 14-year-old boy and his best friend ambushed and killed his mother as she returned home. The circumstances surrounding this event were described in the next edition of the *Minneapolis Star Tribune* (18 February 1995): The boy had "several learning disabilities including attention deficit disorder". He had been "difficult" for a long time and, within the last year, had got in trouble with a step-brother by wrecking a car and carrying a gun to a cinema. The mother was described as having a wonderful relationship with her daughter but having "difficulties" with her son. The family dwelling contained guns.

Against these child, family, and ecological conditions is a significant social history: The boy was:

> ...a lonely and unliked kid who was the frequent victim of schoolmates' taunts, jeers, and assaults. He had trouble with school work and trouble with other kids... He was often teased on the bus and at school because of his appearance and abilities.... He got teased bad. Every day, he got teased. He'd get pushed around. But he couldn't really help himself. He was kind of skinny... He didn't really have that many friends.

This chapter has been reproduced from *Child Development, 67*, 1–13.

The boy actually had two good friends: One appears to have had things relatively well put together. But with this friend, the subject "...passed [a] gun safety course for hunting; they took the class together". The second friend (with whom the murder was committed) was a troublesome child. These two boys described themselves as the "best of friends", and spent much time together. The boys have admitted to planning the ambush (one saying they had planned it for weeks, the other for a few hours). They were armed and waiting when the mother arrived home from work. One conclusion seems relatively certain: This murder was an unlikely event until these two antisocial friends reached consensus about doing it.

An important message emerges from this incident: Child characteristics, intersecting with family relationships and social setting, cycle through peer relations in two ways to affect developmental outcome: (1) through acceptance and rejection by other children in the aggregate; and (2) through dyadic relationships, especially with friends. Considerable evidence now tells us that "being liked" by other children (an aggregate condition) supports good developmental outcome; conversely, "being disliked" (another aggregate condition) is a risk factor (Parker & Asher, 1987). But the evidence concerning friendships and their developmental significance is weak—mainly because these relationships have not been studied extensively enough or with sufficient differentiation.

On the too-rare occasions in which friendships are taken into account developmentally—either in diagnosis or research—children are differentiated merely according to whether or not they have friends. This emphasis on having friends is based on two assumptions. First, making and keeping friends requires good reality-testing and social skills; "having friends" is thus a proxy for "being socially skilled". Second, friendships are believed to be developmental wellsprings in the sense that children must suspend egoism, embrace egalitarian attitudes, and deal with conflict effectively in order to maintain them (Sullivan, 1953). On two counts, then, having friends is thought to bode well for the future.

Striking differences exist, however, among these relationships—both from child to child and companion to companion. First, enormous variation occurs in who the child's friends are: Some companions are outgoing and rarely get into trouble; others are antisocial; still others are good children but socially clumsy. These choices would seem rather obviously to contribute to socialisation—not only by affecting reputations (as the adage admonishes) but through what transpires between the children. Knowing that a teenager has friends tells us one thing, but the identity of his/her friends tells us something else.

Second, friendships differ from one another qualitatively, that is, in their *content* or normative foundations (e.g. whether or not the two children engage in antisocial behaviour), their *constructiveness* (e.g. whether conflict resolution commonly involves negotiation or whether it involves power assertion), their *closeness* (e.g. whether or not the children spend much time together and engage in many different activities), their *symmetry* (e.g. whether social power is vested more or less equally or more or less unequally in the two children), and their *affective substrates* (e.g. whether the relationship is supportive and secure or whether it is nonsupportive and conflict-ridden). Qualitative differences in these relationships may have developmental implications in the same way that qualitative variations in adult–child relationships do (Ainsworth, Blehar, Waters, & Wall, 1978).

This chapter begins, then, with the argument that one cannot describe friendships and their developmental significance without distinguishing between *having friends, the identity of the child's friends* (e.g. personality characteristics of the child's friends), and *friendship quality*. In the sections that follow, these relationship dimensions are examined separately and in turn. Three conclusions emerge. First, having friends is a normatively significant condition during childhood and adolescence. Second, friendships carry both developmental advantages and disadvantages, so that a romanticised view of these relationships distorts them and what they may contribute to developmental outcome. Third, the identity of the child's friends and friendship quality may be more closely tied to individual differences than merely whether or not the child has friends.

HAVING FRIENDS

Measurement issues

Children's friends can be identified in four main ways: (1) by asking the children, their mothers, or their teachers to name the child's friends and determining whether these choices are reciprocated; (2) by asking children to assess their liking for one another; (3) by observing the extent to which children seek and maintain proximity with one another; and (4) by measuring reciprocities and co-ordinations in their social interaction. Concordances among various indicators turn out to be substantial, but method variance is also considerable; the "insiders" (the children themselves) do not always agree with the "outsiders" (teachers) or the observational record (Hartup, 1992; Howes, 1989).

Some variation among measures derives from the fact that social attraction is difficult for outsiders to know about. Method variance also derives from special difficulties connected with self-reports. First, children without friends almost always can name "friends" when asked to do so (Furman, 1996). Second, friendship frequently seems to investigators to be a dichotomous condition (friend vs. nonfriend), whereas variation is more continuous (best friend/good friend/occasional friend/not friend). Third, whether these categories form a Guttman scale has not been determined, although researchers sometimes assume that they do (see Doyle, Markiewicz, & Hardy, 1994). Fourth, the status of so-called unilateral or unreciprocated friendship choice is unclear. Sometimes, when children's choices are not reciprocated, social interaction differs from when friendship choices are mutual; in other respects, the social exchange does not. Unilateral friends, for example, use tactics during disagreements with one another that are different from the ones used by mutual friends but similar to those used by nonfriends (e.g. standing firm). Simultaneously, conflict *outcomes* among unilateral friends (e.g. whether interaction continues) are more similar to those characterising mutual friends than those characterising nonfriends (Hartup, Laursen, Stewart, & Eastenson, 1988).

Developmental significance

The developmental significance of having friends (apart from the identity of the child's friends or the quality of these relationships) has been examined in three main ways: (i) comparing the social interaction that occurs between friends and between nonfriends; (ii) comparing children who have friends with those who don't; and (iii) examining the extent to which having friends moderates behavioural outcomes across certain normative transitions.

Behaviour with friends and nonfriends

Behaviours differentiating friends from nonfriends have been specified in more than 80 studies (Newcomb & Bagwell, 1995); four are cited here. In the first of these (Newcomb & Brady, 1982), school-aged children were asked to explore a "creativity box" with either a friend or a classmate who was not a friend. More extensive exploration was observed among the children with their friends; conversation was more vigorous and mutually oriented; the emotionality exchange was more positive. Most important, when tested individually, the children who explored the box with a friend remembered more about it later.

Second, Azmitia and Montgomery (1993) examined problem solving among 11-year-olds (mainly their dialogues) working on "isolation of variables" problems either with friends or acquaintances (the children were required to deduce which pizza ingredients caused certain characters in a series of stories to get sick and die). Friends spontaneously justified their suggestions more frequently than acquaintances, elaborated on their partners' proposals, engaged in a greater percentage of conflicts during their conversations, and more often checked results. Most important, the children working with friends did better than children working with nonfriends on the most difficult versions of the task. Clearly, "a friend in need is a friend indeed". The children's conversations were related to their problem solving through engagement in transactive conflicts. That is, task performance was facilitated to a greater extent between friends than between nonfriends by free airing of the children's differences in a co-operative, task-oriented context.

Third, we recently examined conversations between friends and nonfriends (10-year-olds) in an inner-city magnet school while the pairs wrote stories collaboratively on a computer (Hartup, Daiute, Zajac, & Sholl, 1995). Stories dealt with the rain forest—subject matter that the children had studied during a six-week science project. Baseline story writing was measured with the children writing alone; control subjects *always* wrote alone. Results indicate that friends did not talk more during collaboration than nonfriends but, nevertheless: (a) engaged in more mutually oriented and less individualistic utterances; (b) agreed with one another more often (but did not disagree more readily); (c) repeated their own and the other's assertions more often; (d) posed alternatives and provided elaborations more frequently; (e) spent twice as much time as nonfriends talking about writing content, the vocabulary being used, and writing mechanics; and (f) spent less time engaged in "off-task" talk. Principal component analyses confirm that the structure of friends' talk was strongly focused on the task (i.e. the text) and was assertively colla-borative—reminiscent of the dialogues used by experts and novices as discovered in other social problem-solving studies (Rogoff, 1990). Our stories themselves show that, overall, the ones collaboratively written by friends were better than the ones written by nonfriends, a difference that seems to rest on better use of Standard English rather than the narrative elements included in the text. Results suggest, overall, that the affordances of "being friends" differ from the affordances of "being acquaintances" in social problem solving (Hartup, 1996).

Fourth, we examined conflict and competition among school-aged children playing a board game when they had been taught different rules (Hartup, French, Laursen, Johnston, & Ogawa, 1993). Disagreements occurred more frequently between friends than between nonfriends and lasted longer. Conflict resolution, however, differed by friendship and sex: (a) boys used assertions *without rationales* more frequently than girls—but only when friends were observed; (b) girls, on the other hand, used asser-tions *with rationales* more frequently than boys but, again, only with friends. Sex differences in conflict talk, widely cited in the literature (see Maccoby, 1990), thus seem to be relationship manifestations rather than manifestations of individual children.

Based on these and the other available data sets, a recent meta-analysis identified significant friend versus nonfriend effects across four broad-band categories (Newcomb & Bagwell, 1995): *positive engagement* (i.e. talk, smiling, and laughter); *conflict management* (i.e. disengagement and negotiation vs. power assertion); *task activity* (i.e. being oriented to the task as opposed to being off-task); and *relationship properties* (i.e. equality in the exchange as well as mutuality and affirmation). Behaviourally speaking, friendships clearly are "communal relationships" (Clark & Mills, 1979). Reciprocity constitutes their deep structure.

Existing data suggest that four cognitive and motivational conditions afford these distinctive interactions: (1) friends know one another better than nonfriends and are thus able to communicate with one another more efficiently and effectively (Ladd & Emerson, 1984); (2) friends and nonfriends have different expectations of one another, especially concerning assistance and support (Bigelow, 1977); (3) an affective climate more favourable to exploration and problem solving exists between friends than between nonfriends—namely, a "climate of agreement" (Gottman, 1983); and (4) friends more readily than nonfriends seek ways of resolving disagreements that support continued interaction between them (Hartup & Laursen, 1992).

Unfortunately, the developmental significance of these differences is not known. Only fragmentary information tells us about short-term consequences in problem solving and behavioural regulation. Recalled events (Newcomb & Brady, 1982), deductive reasoning (Azmitia & Montgomery, 1993), conflict rates (Hartup & Van Lieshout, 1988), creative writing (Hartup et al., 1995), and social/moral judgements (Nelson & Aboud, 1985) are better supported by transactions with friends than by transactions with nonfriends. But only a small number of investigations exists in each case—sometimes only one. The bottom line: Process-outcome studies are badly needed to tell us whether friends engage in better scaffolding than nonfriends, or whether it only seems as if they do. Once process/outcome connections are established, we can then—and only then—conclude that friendships have *normative* significance (i.e. that children employ their friends adaptively on a daily basis as cognitive and social resources).

Having friends vs. not having friends

Does having friends contribute to developmental differentiation (i.e. contribute to individual differences)? For the answer to this question to be affirmative, children who have friends must differ from those who do not.

Cross-sectional comparisons show that, first, children who have friends are more socially competent and less troubled than children who do not; they are more sociable, co-operative, altruistic, self-confident, and less lonely (Hartup, 1993; Newcomb & Bagwell, 1996). Second, troubled children (e.g. clinic-referred children) are more likely to be friendless than nonreferred control cases (Rutter & Garmezy, 1983).

Friendlessness is not always assessed in the same manner in these studies, but the results are consistent: Not one data set suggests that children with friends are worse off than children who do not have them. Although friended/friendless comparisons are consistent across data sets, the results are difficult to interpret. First, having friends in these studies usually means having good supportive friends; thus having friends is confounded with friendship quality. Second, causal direction is impossible to establish: Friendship experience may contribute to self-esteem, for example, but self-confident children may make friends more readily than less confident children.

Longitudinal studies can be more convincing concerning developmental significance. Unfortunately, few exist. Short-term studies suggest that certain benefits accrue across school transitions: First, attitudes toward school are better among kindergarteners (5-year-olds) who have friends at the beginning and who maintain them than those who do not. Making new friends also predicts gains in school performance over the kindergarten year (Ladd, 1990). Second, with data collected from 10-year-olds across a one-year interval, friendship experience enhanced self-esteem (Bukowski, Hoza, & Newcomb, 1991). Third, psychosocial disturbances have been reported less frequently when school changes occur in the company of good friends than when they do not (Berndt & Hawkins, 1991; Simmons, Burgeson, & Reef, 1988). Having friends thus seems to contribute specifically to affective outcomes across normative school transitions.

One long-term investigation (Bagwell, Newcomb, & Bukowski, in press) raises questions, however, about "having friends" as a developmental predictor: 11-year-old children were identified as either befriended or friendless on two separate occasions; subjects were re-evaluated at 23 years of age. Having friends and sociometric status (i.e. social acceptance) *together* predicted school success, aspirations, trouble with the law, and several other outcomes. Unique contributions to adult adjustment, however, were verified only for sociometric status. And even then, when stability in the childhood adjustment measures was taken into account, neither sociometric status nor friendship predicted adult outcomes.

Comment

Overall, the developmental significance of having friends is far from clear. Social interaction between friends differs from social interaction between nonfriends, but this does not tell us much more than that these relationships are unique social entities. Correlational studies are difficult to interpret because the effects of having friends are difficult to disentangle from the effects of friendship quality. Short-term longitudinal studies suggest that having friends supports adaptation during normative transitions, but more substantial evidence is needed concerning these effects. Child differences may interact with friendship experience in relation to developmental outcome rather than being main effects. Having friends, for example, may differentiate mainly among children who are vulnerable in some way prior to the transition. Stress associated with developmental transitions is known to accentuate differences among vulnerable children to a greater extent than among nonvulnerable ones (Caspi & Moffitt, 1991). Similarly, developmental interventions often have greater effects on vulnerable than on nonvulnerable individuals (see Crockenberg, 1981).

THE IDENTITY OF THE CHILD'S FRIENDS

We turn now to the identity of the child's friends. Several questions can be asked: With whom does the child become friends? Can the identity of a child's friends be forecast from what we know about the child? What is the developmental significance of the company a child keeps?

Who are children's friends?

Consider, first, that children make friends on the basis of common interests and common activities. Common ground is a *sine qua non* in friendship relations throughout childhood and adolescence, suggesting that friends ought to be similar to one another in abilities and outlook. Folklore sometimes suggests that "opposites attract", but this notion has not found general support in the empirical literature. The weight of the evidence suggests that, instead, "Beast knows beast; birds of a feather flock together" (Aristotle, *Rhetoric*, Book 11).

Similarities between friends, however, vary from attribute to attribute, in most cases according to *reputational salience* (i.e. according to the importance of an attribute in determining the child's social reputation). Considerable evidence supports this "reputational salience hypothesis": Behaviour ratings obtained more than 60 years ago by Robert Challman (1932) showed that social co-operation (an attribute with considerable reputational salience) was more concordant among friends than nonfriends; intelligence (an attribute without reputational salience among young children) was not. Among boys, physical activity (reputationally salient among males) was more similar among friends than nonfriends. Among girls, attractiveness of personality and social network size (both more reputationally salient among females than among males) were more similar among friends than nonfriends.

More recent data also suggest that behavioural concordances among school-aged children and their friends are greater than among children and nonfriends (Haselager, Hartup, Van Lieshout, & Riksen-Walraven, in press). Peer ratings were obtained in a large number of fifth-grade classrooms centring on three constructs: prosocial behaviour, antisocial behaviour, and social withdrawal (shyness). First, friends were more similar to one another than nonfriends within each construct cluster (i.e. mean difference scores were significantly smaller). Second, correlations between friends were greater for antisocial behaviour (i.e. fighting, disruption, and bullying) than for prosocial behaviour (i.e. co-operation, offering help to others) or social withdrawal (i.e. shyness, dependency, and being victimised). These differences may reflect differences among these three attributes in reputational salience: Fighting, for example, is more consistently related to reputation than either co-operation or shyness (Coie, Dodge, & Kupersmidt, 1990). Our results also show important sex differences: (a) friends were more similar to one another among girls than among boys in both prosocial and antisocial behaviour (see also Cairns & Cairns, 1994); and (b) friends were more similar among boys than among girls in shyness. These gender variations are consistent with the reputational salience hypothesis, too: Being kind to others and being mean to them have greater implications for girls' social reputations than boys', whereas shyness/withdrawal has more to do with boys' reputations than girls' (Stevenson-Hinde & Hinde, 1986).

Concordance data from other studies are consistent with the reputational salience notion: Among adolescents, friends are most similar to one another in two general areas: (a) school-related attitudes, aspirations, and achievement (Epstein, 1983; Kandel, 1978b); and (b) normative activities such as smoking, drinking, drug use, antisocial behaviour, and dating (Dishion, Andrews, & Crosby, 1995; Epstein, 1983; Kandel, 1978b; Tolson & Urberg, 1993). Sexual activity among adolescents is also consistent with the reputational salience hypothesis. Among girls (both African-American and white) in the United States, friends have been found to be similar in sexual behaviour and attitudes, even when age and antisocial attitudes are taken into account. Among boys, however, sexual activity (especially engaging in sexual intercourse) was not concordant (Billy, Rodgers, & Udry, 1984). The authors argue that sexual activity is more closely related to social reputation among adolescent girls than it is among boys, thus accounting for the gender differences in the results. Still other investigators, employing the social network as a unit of analysis, have discovered that members of friendship networks are concordant on such salient dimensions as sports, academic activities, and drug use (Brown, 1989). Antisocial behaviour also distinguishes social networks from one another beginning in middle childhood (Cairns, Cairns, Neckerman, Gest, & Garieppy, 1988).

Friendship concordances: Sources and developmental implications

Similarities between friends are one thing, but where do they come from and where do they lead? Developmental implications cannot be specified without understanding that these similarities derive from three sources: (1) *sociodemographic conditions* that bring children into proximity with one another; (2) *social selection* through which children construct relationships with children who are similar to themselves rather than different; and (3) *mutual socialisation* through which children become similar to their friends by interacting with them.

Sociodemographic conditions

Demographic conditions determine the neighbourhoods in which children live, the schools in which they enrol, and the classes they attend. Concordances among children and their friends in socioeconomic status, ethnicity, and chronological age thus derive in considerable measure from social forces that constrain the "peer pool" and the child's access to it. One should not underestimate, however, the extent to which some of these concordances derive from the children's own choices. Among children attending schools that are mixed-age, mixed-race, and mixed-socioeconomically, friends are still more similar to one another in these attributes than nonfriends are (Goldman, 1981; McCandless & Hoyt, 1961).

Selection

Some similarities among friends derive from the well-known tendency among human beings (not alone among the various species) for choosing close associates who resemble themselves. Recent studies confirm that the similarity-attraction hypothesis applies to children: Among elementary schoolchildren who began an experimental session as strangers, differential attraction was evident in some groups (40%). Within them, more social contact occurred between preferred than between nonpreferred partners, and correlations were higher between preferred than nonpreferred partners in sociability and the cognitive maturity of their play (Rubin, Lynch, Coplan, Rose-Krasnor, & Booth, 1994).

But friendship selection is embedded in assortative processes occurring in larger social networks. Dishion and his colleagues (Dishion, Patterson, & Griesler, 1994) believe that these network concordances emerge through a process called "shopping" in which children and adolescents construct relationships that maximise interpersonal payoffs. Children are not believed to choose friends who are similar to themselves on a rational basis so much as on an experiential one. Accordingly, relationships become established when they "feel right". Similar individuals cleave to one another more readily than dissimilar individuals because they are more likely to find common ground in both their activities and their conversations. Antisocial children are thus most likely to make friends with other antisocial children and, in so doing, their common characteristics merge to create a "dyadic antisocial trait". Similarly, soccer players or musicians make friends, merge themselves dyadically, and set the stage for becoming even more similar to one another.

Selection thus acts simultaneously to determine the identity of the child's friends through two interlocking processes: (1) similarity and attraction occurring within dyads; and (2) assortative network formation occurring within groups. These processes undoubtedly combine differently from child to child in affecting developmental outcome. Co-operative, friendly, nonaggressive children can choose friends resembling themselves from a wide array of choices; antisocial children can also choose their friends on the basis of similarity and attraction—but frequently from a more restricted range of social alternatives.

Mutual socialisation

What behavioural outcomes stem from mutual socialisation? The weight of the evidence suggests, first, that children and their friends who ascribe to conventional norms move further over time in the direction of normative behaviour (Ball, 1981; Epstein, 1983; Kandel & Andrews, 1986). But does antisocial behaviour increase over time among children in antisocial networks? Does troublesome behaviour escalate among children— especially into criminal activity—through membership in these networks? Answers to these questions have been surprisingly difficult to provide, especially as children perceive their friends as exerting more pressure toward desirable than toward undesirable conduct (Brown, Clasen, & Eicher, 1986). Nevertheless, increases in undesirable behaviour through antisocial friends among children who are themselves at risk for antisocial behaviour is now relatively well documented (Ball, 1981; Berndt & Keefe, 1992; Dishion, 1990; Dishion et al., 1994). Conversely, "desisting" is forecast as strongly by a turning away from antisocial friends as by any other variable (Mulvey & Aber, 1988).

What occurs on a day-to-day basis between aggressive children and their friends? Jocks and their friends? "Brains" and their friends? One guesses that children model normative behaviours *for* their friends and simultaneously receive reinforcement *from* them. Antisocial children, for example, are known to engage in large amounts of talk with their friends—talk that is deviant even when the children are being videotaped in the laboratory

(Dishion et al., 1994, 1995). Ordinary children talk a lot with their friends, too, but the content is not generally as deviant (Newcomb & Bagwell, 1995). Antisocial children use coercion with one another (Dishion et al., 1995); ordinary children, on the other hand, are freewheeling with their criticisms and persuasion but are less likely to be coercive (Berndt & Keefe, 1992; Hartup et al., 1993). Finally, one guesses that friends support one another in seeking environments that support their commonly held world views, although not much is known about this.

Other results show that selection *combines* with socialisation to effect similarity between friends. Kandel (1978a) studied changes over the course of a year in drug use, educational aspirations, and delinquency in early adolescence, discovering that similarity stemmed from both sources in approximately equal amounts. Relative effects, however, vary according to the norms and the children involved (see Hartup, 1993).

Comment

Children and their friends are similar to one another, especially in attributes with reputational salience. One must acknowledge that effect sizes are modest and that friends are not carbon copies of one another. One must also acknowledge that the reputational salience hypothesis has never been subjected to direct test and it needs to be. Nevertheless, the identity of the child's friends is a significant consideration in predicting developmental outcome. Friends may be generally intimate, caring, and supportive, thus fostering good developmental prognosis. At the same time, the activities in which they support one another (the relationship *content*) may be extremely deviant, suggesting an altogether different prognosis.

FRIENDSHIP QUALITY

Conceptual and measurement issues

Qualitative assessment of child and adolescent friendships currently involves two main strategies: (1) *dimensional analysis* through which one determines whether certain elements are present or absent in the social interaction between friends (e.g. companionship, intimacy, conflict, or power asymmetries), and (2) *typological* or *categorical* analysis through which one identifies patterns in social interaction believed to be critical to social development and adaptation (Furman, 1996).

Dimensional assessment

Most current dimensional assessments are based on "provisions" or "features" that children mention when talking about these relationships

(Berndt & Perry, 1986; Bukowski, Hoza, & Boivin, 1994; Furman & Adler, 1982; Furman & Buhrmester, 1985; Parker & Asher, 1993); most instruments tap five or six domains. Domain scores, however, are correlated with one another (Berndt & Perry, 1986; Parker & Asher, 1993), and most factor analyses yield two-factor solutions. Both Berndt (1996) and Furman (1996) argue that "positive" and "negative" dimensions adequately describe most dimensional assessments, although some data sets suggest that more elaborate solutions are warranted (e.g. Ladd, Kochenderfer, & Coleman, 1996).

Typological assessment

Typological assessment is evolving slowly because the functional significance of friendships remains uncertain. Can one, for example, regard friendships as attachments? Probably not. No one has demonstrated that "the secure base phenomenon", so common among children and their caregivers, constitutes the functional core of children's friendships. Friends have been shown to be secure bases in one or two instances (Ipsa, 1981; Schwartz, 1972), but one is not overwhelmed with the evidence that children and their friends are bound to one another as attachment objects. Children describe their relationships with friends differently from their relationships with their caregivers—as *more* companionable, intimate, and egalitarian, and, simultaneously, as *less* affectionate and reliable (Furman & Buhrmester, 1985). For these reasons, some writers describe friendships as affiliative relationships (Weiss, 1986). The challenge, then, is to describe what good-quality affiliative relationships are.

One new classification system has been devised on the basis of family systems theory (Shulman, 1993). Well-functioning friendships are considered to be balanced between closeness and intimacy, on the one hand, and individuality, on the other. The family systems model suggests three friendship types: (i) *interdependent* ones, with co-operation and autonomy balanced; (ii) *disengaged* ones, in which friends are disconnected in spite of their efforts to maintain proximity with one another; and (iii) *consensus-sensitive* or *enmeshed* relationships, in which agreement and cohesion are maximised. Empirical data are based largely on children's interactions in a co-operative task adapted from family systems research (Reiss, 1981) and document the existence of interdependent and disengaged relationships—a promising beginning. Once again, however, caution should be exercised: Friendship networks may not revolve around the same equilibrative axes as families do.

Developmental significance

Cross-sectional studies

Among the various qualitative dimensions, *support* (positivity) and *contention* (negativity) have been examined most extensively in relation to child outcomes. Support is positively correlated with school involvement and achievement (Berndt & Hawkins, 1991; Cauce, 1986) and negatively correlated with school-based problems (Kurdek & Sinclair, 1988); positively correlated with popularity and good social reputations (Cauce, 1986); positively correlated with self-esteem (Mannarino, 1978; McGuire & Weisz, 1982; Perry, 1987) and psychosocial adjustment (Buhrmester, 1990); as well as negatively correlated with identity problems (Papini, Farmer, Clark, Micke, & Barnett, 1990) and depression—especially among girls (Compas, Slavin, Wagner, & Cannatta, 1986). Results are thus consistent but, once again, impossible to interpret. We cannot tell whether supportive relationships contribute to the competence of the individual child or vice versa.

Longitudinal studies

Longitudinal studies dealing with friendship quality (positive vs. negative) emphasise school attitudes, involvement, and achievement. Studying children across the transition from elementary to junior high school, Berndt (1989) measured the size of the friendship network, friendship stability, and self-reported friendship quality (positivity) as well as popularity, attitudes toward school, and achievement. First, network size was negatively related to friendship support as reported by the children, suggesting that children recognise what researchers have been slow to learn, namely, that friendships are not all alike. Second, several nonsignificant results are illuminating: Neither number of friends nor friendship stability contributed to *changes* in school adjustment—either across the school transition or across the first year in the new school. School adjustment was relatively stable across the transition and was related to friendship stability cross-sectionally but not with earlier adjustment factored out. Third, the self-rated supportiveness of the child's friends, assessed shortly after entrance to the new school, predicted increasing popularity and increasingly positive attitudes toward classmates over the next year, suggesting that positive qualities in one's friendship relations support a widening social world in new school environments.

Other investigations focus on friendship qualities as predictors of school adaptation within the school year. Among 5-year-olds enrolled in kindergarten (Ladd et al., 1996), for example, those having friendships characterised by "aid" and "validation" improved in school attitudes over the year with initial attitudes toward school factored out. Perceived conflict in friendships, on the other hand, predicted increasing forms of school maladjustment, especially among boys, including school loneliness and avoidance as well as school liking and engagement.

One other investigation (Berndt & Keefe, 1992) focused on both positive and negative friendship qualities and their correlations across time with school adjustment and self-esteem among adolescents (Berndt & Keefe, 1992). Students with supportive, intimate friendships became increasingly involved with school, whereas those who considered their friendships to be conflict-ridden and rivalrous became increasingly disruptive and troublesome. Friendship quality was not correlated with changes in self-esteem, possibly because self-esteem was relatively stable from the beginning to the end of the year. Additional analyses (Berndt, 1996) suggest that developmental prediction is better for the negative dimensions in these relationships than the positive ones.

Other investigators have examined the interactions between stress and social support as related to behavioural outcome. With elementary schoolchildren, increases in peer support over several years predict both increasingly better adaptation and better grade point averages (Dubow, Tisak, Causey, Hryshko, & Reid, 1991). Other results, however, suggest that support from school personnel was associated with decreases in distress across a two-year period but not support from friends (controlling for initial adjustment). Regression models showed that, actually, school grades predicted changes in friends' support rather than the reverse (DuBois, Felner, Brand, Adan, & Evans, 1992). Among adolescents, however, results are more complex: Windle (1992) reported that, among girls, friend support is positively correlated with alcohol use but negatively correlated with depression (with initial adjustment levels factored out). Among boys, friendship support is associated with outcome depending on stress levels: When stress is high, friend support encourages both alcohol use and depression; when stress is low or moderate, both alcohol use and depression are associated with having *nonsupportive* friends.

The dissonances encountered in these results would be reduced considerably were the identity of the children's friends to be known. Children and adolescents with behaviour difficulties frequently have friends who themselves are troublesome (Dishion et al., 1995). These friends may provide one another with emotional support, but the interactions that occur between them may not be the same as those occurring between nontroubled children and their friends. Knowing who the child's friends are might account for the empirical anomalies.

Other difficulties in accounting for these results derive from the fact that the referents used in measuring social support in these studies (except in

Berndt's work) consisted of friendship networks (the child's "friends") rather than a "best friend". And still other complications arise from the use of one child's assessments of relationship qualities (the subject's) when the evidence suggests that discrepancies between partners may correlate more strongly with adjustment difficulties than the perceptions of either partner alone (East, 1991). Nevertheless, these studies provide tantalising tidbits suggesting that friendship quality bears a causal relation to developmental outcome.

Comment

What kinds of research are needed to understand better the developmental implications of friendship quality? One can argue that we are not urgently in need of cross-time studies narrowly focused on friendships and their vicissitudes. Rather, we need comprehensive studies in which interaction effects rather than main effects are emphasised and that encompass a wide range of variables as they cycle through time: (a) measures of the child, including temperament and other relevant early characteristics; (b) measures of early relationships, especially their affective and cognitive qualities; (c) measures of early success in encounters with relevant institutions, especially the schools; (d) status and reputation among other children (sociometric status); *and* (e) friendship measures that simultaneously include whether a child has friends, who the child's friends are, and what these relationships are like.

Coming close to this model are recent studies conducted by the Oregon Social Learning Center (e.g. Dishion et al., 1994; Patterson, Reid, & Dishion, 1992). Child characteristics and family relations in early childhood have not been examined extensively by these investigators, but their work establishes linkages between coerciveness and monitoring within parent–child and sibling relationships, on the one hand, and troublesomeness and antisocial behaviour among school-aged boys on the other. These studies also establish that poor parental discipline and monitoring predict peer rejection and academic failures, and that these conditions, in turn, predict increasing involvement with antisocial friends. Among children with these early histories, the immediate connection to serious conduct difficulties in adolescence now seems to be friendship with another deviant child. Exactly these conditions existed in the social history of that Minnesota teenager who, together with his best friend, killed his mother early in 1995.

CONCLUSION

Friendships in childhood and adolescence would seem to be developmentally significant—both normatively and differentially. When children have friends, they use them as cognitive and social resources on an everyday basis. Normative transitions and the stress carried with them seem to be better negotiated when children have friends than when they don't, especially when children are at risk. Differential significance, however, seems to derive mainly from the identity of the child's friends and the quality of the relationships between them. Supportive relationships between socially skilled individuals appear to be developmental advantages, whereas coercive and conflict-ridden relationships are developmental disadvantages, especially among antisocial children.

Nevertheless, friendship and its developmental significance may vary from child to child. New studies show that child characteristics interact with early relationships and environmental conditions, cycling in turn through relations with other children to determine behavioural outcome (Hartup & Van Lieshout, 1995). The work cited in this chapter strongly suggests that friendship assessments deserve greater attention in studying these developmental pathways than they are currently given. These assessments, however, need to be comprehensive. Along with knowing whether or not children have friends, we must know who their friends are and the quality of their relationships with them.

ACKNOWLEDGEMENTS

The author is grateful to W. Andrew Collins, Rosemary K. Hartup, Gary W. Ladd, Brett Laursen, and Andrew F. Newcomb for their comments on this chapter.

REFERENCES

Ainsworth, M. D. S., Blehar, M. C., Waters, E., & Wall, S. (1978). *Patterns of attachment: A psychological study of the Strange Situation.* Hillsdale, NJ: Lawrence Erlbaum Associates Inc.

Azmitia, M. & Montgomery, R. (1993). Friendship, transactive dialogues, and the development of scientific reasoning. *Social Development, 2,* 202–221.

Bagwell, C., Newcomb, A. F., & Bukowski, M. W. (in press). *Pre-adolescent friendship and peer rejection as predictors of adult adjustment. Child Development.*

Ball, S. J. (1981). *Beachside comprehensive.* Cambridge, UK: Cambridge University Press.

Berndt, T. J. (1989). Obtaining support from friends during childhood and adolescence. In D. Belle (Ed.), *Children's social networks and social supports* (pp. 308–331). New York: Wiley.

Berndt, T. J. (1996). Exploring the effects of friendship quality on social development. In W. M. Bukowski, A. F. Newcomb, & W. W.Hartup (Eds.), *The company they keep: Friendships in childhood and adolescence* (pp. 346–365). Cambridge, UK: Cambridge University Press.

Berndt, T. J. & Hawkins, J. A. (1991). *Effects of friendship on adolescents' adjustment to junior high school.* Unpublished manuscript, Purdue University, IN.

Berndt, T. J. & Keefe, K. (1992). Friends' influence on adolescents' perceptions of themselves in school. In D. H. Schunk & J. L. Meece (Eds.), *Students' perceptions in the classroom* (pp. 51–73). Hillsdale, NJ: Lawrence Erlbaum Associates Inc.

Berndt, T. J. & Perry, T. B. (1986). Children's perceptions of friendship as supportive relationships. *Developmental Psychology, 22,* 640–648.

Bigelow, B. J. (1977). Children's friendship expectations: A cognitive developmental study. *Child Development, 48,* 246–253.

Billy, J. O. G., Rodgers, J. L., Udry, J. R. (1984). Adolescent sexual behavior and friendship choice. *Social Forces, 62,* 653–678.

Brown, B. B. (1989). The role of peer groups in adolescents' adjustment to secondary school. In T. J. Berndt & G. W. Ladd (Eds.), *Peer relationships in child development* (pp. 188–215). New York: Wiley.

Brown, B. B., Clasen, D. R., & Eicher, S. A. (1986). Perceptions of peer pressure, peer conformity dispositions, and self-reported behavior among adolescents. *Developmental Psychology, 22,* 521–530.

Buhrmester, D. (1990). Intimacy of friendship, interpersonal competence, and adjustment during preadolescence and adolescence. *Child Development, 61,* 1101–1111.

Bukowski, W. M., Hoza, B., & Boivin, M. (1994). Measuring friendship quality during pre- and early adolescence: The development and psychometric properties of the Friendship Qualities Scale. *Journal of Personal and Social Relationships, 11,* 471–181.

Bukowski, W. M., Hoza, B., & Newcomb, A. F. (1991). *Friendship, popularity, and the "self" during early adolescence.* Unpublished manuscript, Concordia University, Montreal.

Cairns, R. B. & Cairns, B. D. (1994). *Lifelines and risks.* Cambridge, UK: Cambridge University Press.

Cairns, R. B., Cairns, B. D., Neckerman, H. J., Gest, S., & Garieppy, J. L. (1988). Peer networks and aggressive behavior: Peer support or peer rejection? *Developmental Psychology, 24,* 815–823.

Caspi, A. & Moffitt, T. E. (1991). Individual differences are accentuated during periods of social change: The sample case of girls at puberty. *Journal of Personality and Social Psychology, 61,* 157–168.

Cauce, A. M. (1986). Social networks and social competence: Exploring the effects of early adolescent friendships. *American Journal of Community Psychology, 14,* 607–628.

Challman, R. C. (1932). Factors influencing friendships among preschool children. *Child Development, 3,* 146–158.

Clark, M. S. & Mills, J. (1979). Interpersonal attraction in exchange and communal relationships. *Journal of Personality and Social Psychology, 37,* 12–24.

Coie, J. D., Dodge, K. A., & Kupersmidt, J. B. (1990). Peer group behavior and social status. In S. R. Asher & J. D. Coie (Eds.), *Peer rejection in childhood* (pp. 17–59). Cambridge, UK: Cambridge University Press.

Compas, B. E., Slavin, L. A., Wagner, B. A., & Cannatta, K. (1986). Relationship of life events and social support with psychological dysfunction among adolescents. *Journal of Youth and Adolescence, 15,* 205–221.

Crockenberg, S. B. (1981). Infant irritability, mother responsiveness, and social support influences on the security of mother–infant attachment. *Child Development, 52,* 857–865.

Dishion, T. J. (1990). The peer context of troublesome child and adolescent behavior. In P. Leone (Ed.), *Understanding troubled and troublesome youth* (pp.128–153). Newbury Park, CA: Sage.

Dishion, T. J., Andrews, D. W., & Crosby, L. (1995). Anti-social boys and their friends in early adolescence: Relationship characteristics, quality, and interactional process. *Child Development, 66,* 139–151.

Dishion, T. J., Patterson, G. R., & Griesler, P. C. (1994). Peer adaptations in the development of antisocial behavior: A confluence model. In L. R. Huesmann (Ed.) *Current perspectives on aggressive behavior* (pp. 61–95). New York: Plenum.

Doyle, A. B., Markiewicz, D., & Hardy, C. (1994). Mothers' and children's friendships:

Intergenerational associations. *Journal of Social and Personal Relationships*, *11*, 363–377.

DuBois, D. L., Felner, R. D., Brand, S., Adan, A. M., & Evans, E. G. (1992). *Child Development*, *63*, 542–557.

Dubow, E. F., Tisak, J., Causey, D., Hryshko, A., & Reid, G. (1991). A two-year longitudinal study of stressful life events, social support, and social problem-solving skills: Contributions to children's behavioral and academic adjustment. *Child Development*, *62*, 583–599.

East, P. L. (1991). The parent–child relationships of withdrawn, aggressive, and sociable children: Child and parent perspectives. *Merrill-Palmer Quarterly*, *37*, 425–444.

Epstein, J. L. (1983). Examining theories of adolescent friendship. In J. L. Epstein & N. L. Karweit (Eds.), *Friends in school* (pp. 39–61). San Diego, CA: Academic Press.

Furman, W. (1996). The measurement of friendship perceptions: Conceptual and methodological issues. In W. M. Bukowski, A. F. Newcomb, & W. W. Hartup (Eds.), *The company they keep: Friendships in childhood and adolescence*. (pp. 41–65). Cambridge, UK: Cambridge University Press.

Furman, W. & Adler, T. (1982). *The Friendship Questionnaire*. Unpublished manuscript, University of Denver, CO.

Furman, W. & Buhrmester, D. (1985). Children's perceptions of the personal relationships in their social networks. *Developmental Psychology*, *21*, 1016–1022.

Goldman, J. A. (1981). The social interaction of preschool children in same-age versus mixed-age groupings. *Child Development*, *52*, 644–650.

Gottman, J. M. (1983). How children become friends. *Monographs of the Society for Research in Child Development*, *48*, (Serial No. 201).

Hartup, W. W. (1992). Friendships and their developmental significance. In H. McGurk (Ed.), *Childhood social development* (pp. 175–205). Hove, UK: Lawrence Erlbaum Associates Ltd.

Hartup, W. W. (1993). Adolescents and their friends. In B. Laursen (Ed.), *Close friendships in adolescence* (pp. 3–22). San Francisco: Jossey-Bass.

Hartup, W. W. (1996). Cooperation, close relationships, and cognitive development. In W. M. Bukowski, A. F. Newcomb, & W. W. Hartup (Eds.), *The company they keep: Friendships in childhood and adolescence* (pp. 213–231). Cambridge, UK: Cambridge University Press.

Hartup, W. W., Daiute, C., Zajac, R., & Sholl, W. (1995). *Collaboration in creative writing by friends and nonfriends*. Unpublished manuscript, University of Minnesota.

Hartup, W. W., French, D. C., Laursen, B., Johnston, K. M., & Ogawa, J. (1993). Conflict and friendship relations in middle childhood: Behavior in a closed-field situation. *Child Development*, *64*, 445–454.

Hartup, W. W. & Laursen, B. (1992). Conflict and context in peer relations. In C. H. Hart (Ed.), *Children on playgrounds: Research perspectives and applications* (pp. 44–84). Albany, NY: State University of New York Press.

Hartup, W. W., Laursen, B., Stewart, M. I., & Eastenson, A. (1988). Conflict and the friendship relations of young children. *Child Development*, *59*, 1590–1600.

Hartup, W. W. & Van Lieshout, C. F. M. (1995). Personality development in social context. In J. T. Spence (Ed.), *Annual review of psychology*, *46*, 655–687.

Haselager, G. J. T., Hartup, W. W., Van Lieshout, C. F. M., & Riksen-Walraven, M. (in press). Similarites between friends and nonfriends in middle childhood. *Child Development*.

Howes, C. (1989). Peer interaction of young children. *Monographs of the Society for Research in Child Development*, *53* (Serial No. 217).

Ipsa, J. (1981). Peer support among Soviet day care toddlers. *International Journal of Behavioral Development*, *4*, 255–269.

Kandel, D. B. (1978a). Homophily, selection, and socialization in adolescent friendships. *American Journal of Sociology*, *84*, 427–436.

Kandel, D. B. (1978b). Similarity in real-life adolescent pairs. *Journal of Personality and Social Psychology, 36*, 306–312.

Kandel, D. B. & Andrews, K. (1986). Processes of adolescent socialization by parents and peers. *International Journal of the Addictions, 22*, 319–342.

Kurdek, L. A., & Sinclair, R. J. (1988). Adjustment of young adolescents in two-parent nuclear, stepfather, and mother-custody families. *Journal of Consulting and Clinical Psychology, 56*, 91–96.

Ladd G. W. (1990). Having friends, keeping friends, making friends, and being liked by peers in the classroom: Predictors of children's early school adjustment? *Child Development, 61*, 1081–1100.

Ladd, G. W. & Emerson, E. S. (1984). Shared knowledge in children's friendships. *Developmental Psychology, 20*, 932–940.

Ladd, G. W., Kochenderfer, B. J., & Coleman, C. C. (1996). Friendship quality as a predictor of young children's early school adjustment. *Child Development, 67*, 1103–1118.

Maccoby, E. E. (1990). Gender and relationships: A developmental account. *American Psychologist, 45*, 513–520.

Mannarino, A. P. (1978). Friendship patterns and self-concept development in preadolescent males. *Journal of Genetic Psychology, 133*, 105–110.

McCandless, B. R. & Hoyt, J. M. (1961). Sex, ethnicity and play preferences of preschool children. *Journal of Abnormal and Social Psychology, 62*, 683–685.

McGuire, K. D. & Weisz, J. R. (1982). Social cognition and behavior correlates of preadolescent chumship. *Child Development, 53*, 1478–1484.

Mulvey, E. P. & Aber, M. S. (1988). Growing out of delinquency: Development and desistance. In R. Jenkins & W. Brown (Eds.), *The abandonment of delinquent behavior: Promoting the turn-around* (pp. 99–116). New York: Praeger.

Nelson, J. & Aboud, F. E. (1985). The resolution of social conflict between friends. *Child Development, 56*, 1009–1017.

Newcomb, A. F. & Bagwell, C. (1995). Children's friendship relations: A meta-analytic review. *Psychological Bulletin, 117*, 306–347.

Newcomb, A. F. & Bagwell, C. (1996). The developmental significance of children's friendship relations. In W. M. Bukowski, A. F. Newcomb, & W. W. Hartup (Eds.), *The company they keep: Friendship in childhood and adolescence* (pp. 289–321). Cambridge, UK: Cambridge University Press.

Newcomb, A. F. & Brady, J. E. (1982). Mutuality in boys' friendship relations. *Child Development, 53*, 392–395.

Papini, D. R., Farmer, F. F., Clark, S. M., Micke, J. C., & Barnett, J. K. (1990). Early adolescent age and gender differences in patterns of emotional self-disclosure to parents and friends. *Adolescence, 25*, 959–976.

Parker, J. G. & Asher, S. R. (1987). Peer relations and later personal adjustment: Are low-accepted children at risk? *Psychological Bulletin, 102*, 357–389.

Parker, J. G. & Asher, S. R. (1993). Friendship and friendship quality in middle childhood: Links with peer group acceptance and feelings of loneliness and social dissatisfaction. *Developmental Psychology, 29*, 611–621.

Patterson, G. R., Reid, J. B., & Dishion, T. J. (1992). *Antisocial boys*. Eugene, OR: Castalia.

Perry, T. B. (1987). *The relation of adolescent self-perceptions to their social relationships*. Unpublished doctoral dissertation, University of Oklahoma.

Reiss, D. (1981). *The family's construction of reality*. Cambridge, MA: Harvard University Press.

Rogoff, B. (1990). *Apprenticeship in thinking*. New York: Oxford University Press.

Rubin, K. H., Lynch, D., Coplan, R., Rose-Krasnor, L., & Booth, C. L. (1994). "Birds of a feather...": Behavioral concordances and preferential personal attraction in children. *Child Development, 65,* 1778–1785.

Rutter, M. & Garmezy, N. (1983). Developmental psychopathology. In E. M. Hetherington (Ed.), P. H. Mussen (Series Ed.), *Handbook of Child psychology: Vol. 4. Socialization, personality, and social development* (pp. 775–911). New York: Wiley.

Schwartz, J. C. (1972). Effects of peer familiarity on the behavior of preschoolers in a novel situation. *Journal of Personality and Social Psychology, 24,* 276–284.

Shulman, S. (1993). Close friendships in early and middle adolescence: Typology and friendship reasoning. In B. Laursen (Ed.), *Close friendships in adolescence* (pp. 55–72). San Francisco: Jossey-Bass.

Simmons, R. G., Burgeson, R., & Reef, M. J. (1988). Cumulative change at entry to adolescence. In M. Gunnar & W. A. Collins (Eds.), *Minnesota symposia on child psychology, 21,* 123–150. Hillsdale, NJ: Lawrence Erlbaum Associates Inc.

Stevenson-Hinde, J., & Hinde, R. A. (1986). Changes in associations between characteristics and interaction. In R. Plomin & J. Dunn (Eds.), *The study of temperament: Changes, continuities and challenges* (pp. 115–129). Hillsdale, NJ: Lawrence Erlbaum Associates Inc.

Sullivan, H. S. (1953). *The interpersonal theory of psychiatry.* New York: Norton.

Tolson, J. M. & Urberg, K. A. (1993). Similarity between adolescent best friends. *Journal of Adolescent Research, 8,* 274–288.

Weiss, R. S. (1986). Continuities and transformations in social relationships from childhood to adulthood. In W. W. Hartup & Z. Rubin (Eds.), *Relationships and development* (pp. 95–110). Hillsdale, NJ: Lawrence Erlbaum Associates Inc.

Windle, M. (1992). A longitudinal study of stress buffering for adolescent problem behaviors. *Developmental Psychology, 28,* 522–530.

7 Social life in the primary school: Towards a relational concept of social skills for use in the classroom

Peter Kutnick and Iain Manson
Roehampton Institute, London, UK

Children of primary school age are under contradictory pressures regarding the development of prosocial skills. Primary schools claim to be aware of the social aspects of learning and take grouping as a norm; but teach in a predominantly didactic way. Although children are expected to show prosocial skills, media-borne and other derivative role models promote a nonsocial individualism (Kline, 1994). Children who do not develop prosocial skills are in danger of being labelled antisocial (or worse). These children will have limited ability to interact in the grouped seating pattern which predominantly characterises primary school classrooms. They will also have limited opportunity to develop the cognitive understanding necessary in problem solving.

The traditional way of handling school-aged children without prosocial skills has been to offer them a form of social skills training (SST). This chapter challenges the theoretical assumptions behind social skills training, questions a range of results from SST, and offers a theoretical rationale for an alternative model of social development that can be engendered within classrooms. We also present some preliminary results to show how the social developmental model is constructed and how it works. The chapter brings together three strands of investigation which have been treated separately in the literature: (1) classroom pedagogy—specifically the use of groups in the classroom as a means of promoting learning and prosocial behaviour; (2) SST—currently employed as a means of case-specific clinical intervention for children with perceived abnormal behavioural patterns; and (3) developmental psychological theory relating to the emergence of social relationships.

CLASSROOM GROUPING AND PEDAGOGY

To a great extent, effectiveness in promoting learning and social behaviour in the classroom will depend on the "ethos" or structure of action of the classroom and school. A major contributor to the ethos will be the teacher's use of groups. The role of grouping in pedagogy is recognised in the National Curriculum in England and Wales (DES, 1989). Grouping of pupils also coincides with current socially based theories of learning and development (especially as espoused by Newman, Griffin, & Cole 1989; Vygotsky, 1978).

Current social psychological studies concerning the use of groups in the classroom generate the following findings: shared perspective taking within groups increases the likelihood of enhanced cognitive understanding; effective small groups promote more achievement in the classroom through co-operation than comparative whole class or individualised grouping approaches; co-operative groups also enhance proschool norms and within-class friendships across ability, gender, and racial divides; effective groups engender a sense of security, trust, and identity among members (for a fuller review, see Kutnick & Rogers, 1994).

The understanding of social interactive influences on cognitive development has progressed far beyond the simple teaching of Piaget's cognitive stages (Davis, 1991) to emphasise the importance of socio-cognitive conflict and the joint resolution of conservation problems (Doise, 1990; Light & Littleton, 1994; Perret-Clermont, 1980). Cognitive problem solving necessarily requires the ability to share perspectives for the joint/ social resolution of new and difficult problems (Damon & Phelps, 1989). Yet, telling children to resolve a problem collaboratively ignores recent work on social facilitation and social comparison within cognitive development. Monteil (1992) acknowledges that the nature of children's social pairings (used to promote cognition) will be affected by the pupil's emotional and social responses to the "working conditions" in which they undertake the assigned cognitive tasks.

Simply sitting children around tables, however, does not mean that they will or can work as a small group (Galton & Williamson, 1992). A child's ability to work within groups will be limited by previous experiences of working with groups, liking of others within the group, and the general "cultural" support for groupwork in the classroom (Cowie & Ruddock, 1988). Experience of working in small groups may be alienating for the child who is teacher-dependent. The threat of working with other pupils who are not supportive may force the child into a passive role. Unease, lack of direction or suspicion of group effectiveness from the teacher causes some children to be "fence-sitters" in their lack of commitment (Galton & Williamson, 1992). If the children fear being "put-down" by the group, then they may not take the risk of explaining their ideas or making contributions to effective group learning (Galton, 1990).

Groups do have their positive points for pupils. According to Dunne and Bennett (1990), pupils familiar with the ideas being discussed and the materials available will have little need of teacher attention and are very capable of looking after each other. Pupils who experience effective groupwork understand that they can learn from one another, and find security in doing so (Cullingford, 1988). Children's liking for groupwork is strongly associated with the legitimacy and structure given to group work in the classroom (Cowie & Rudduck, 1988). Their liking is also affected by the relationships that children engender among themselves. For groups to be effective, pupils must feel secure, have the ability to communicate effectively among themselves, and understand that the teacher approves of such behaviour—as shown in the co-operative group-work strategy to overcome bullying (Smith, Cowie, & Berdondini, 1994).

Many studies find that small groups rarely work effectively the first time. These groups may include children who do not have the skills to work with others or have children who reject the presence of a particular child. The studies suggest that training of pupils for group work is necessary. Training can be undertaken in a number of ways. Minimally, the pupils must have and use skills of listening, questioning, challenging, helping and providing explanations to others (Bennett & Dunne, 1990). These skills can be approached by direct training exercises or as part of a social skills programme that emphasises security, communication and joint problem solving (Hall, 1994; Kutnick & Marshall, 1993). If allowed to develop effective group-work skills, children find these groups also provide social and emotional benefits (Biott, 1987).

SOCIAL SKILLS TRAINING (SST)

The traditional approach to SST is founded on a nonproblematic notion of the "normal" and is, therefore, implicitly normative. Children who noticeably deviate from the expected norms of behaviour within the social system in which they participate (in the main, the school classroom) are the subjects of study. The classroom is implicitly viewed as an integrative mechanism in the socialisation of the child. Within the literature scant attention is paid to what constitutes this normalcy, either in terms of its description or its development; it is taken for granted. The assumption appears to be made that children will develop "good" social behaviour as a norm and that in cases of deviation from it, intervention will be needed in order to ensure an effective return to it. Working on a pro-active principle, the aim of SST is to prevent the compounding of current dysfunctional behaviours and the subsequent development of even more deviant behaviours by ensuring that the deviant child is equipped with the means to integrate with their peers.

Overwhelmingly, research in SST is carried out within what Harré and Gillet (1994) have termed the "Old Paradigm" (i.e. within the behavioural model). The situation is observed, its elements analysed, the dysfunctional elements isolated, further analysed, and suggestions for remedies investigated. Two clearly discernible areas of research can be seen in the literature. The first, which we shall term the "sociobehavioural approach", is concerned with the identification and evaluation of techniques designed to remedy perceived social deficits. The second, the sociocognitive approach, concerns itself with the analysis of cognitive processes, deemed to underlie the behavioural deficit.

Within the sociobehavioural approach, the analysis with regard to the individual is ahistorical and nonprocessual. The sociocognitive approach is theoretically more complex but retains the same behavioural orientation. It draws on other theoretical dimensions (i.e. developmental psychology and interactional analysis), in order to broaden its understanding and further its applicability. Certain elements of the sociocognitive approach aspire to an overt reductionism (Dodge, Pettit, McClaskey, & Brown, 1986). As we have argued, both approaches share a foundation in the paradigm of the normal—there is an agreed set of behaviours that the child must fulfil to be considered normal; if any of these behaviours are missing, underpresent or overly-present then specific SST may be called upon to correct the situation.

The aim of SST from the sociobehavioural approach, is isolating and making good any deficiency in the target child's repertoire of behaviours by means of behaviour modification and training. It is seen as a means of intervention at a remedial level and is used to help children fit into their peer group (and, hence, into the classroom, thus facilitating classroom learning). The value placed on these skills is derived from the use of groups in the classroom (see earlier), and the "conspiracy", described by Maras and Messer (1995) of some teachers and psychologists to remove children from the classroom if their nonsocial behaviours are deemed too extreme.

Behind this aim is a considerable body of research, both in the United Kingdom and the United States. The research is supportive of the view that poor social skills are contributory factors in academic under-achievement (Cartledge & Milburn, 1980; Hughes & Sullivan, 1988; Michelson,

Sugai, Wood, & Kazdin, 1983). In a recent review of the effectiveness of SST with both children and adolescents, Ogilvy (1994, p. 73) states:

... the evidence suggests that childhood social deficits are strong predictors of subsequent academic, social and psychological functioning. Associated problems include delinquence, dropping out of school, low academic achievement, anti-social behaviour, alcoholism and adult psychoses.

Problems with SST begin early in its consideration. Ogilvy notes the lack of a commonly agreed definition of either social skill or social competence. Social skills have been defined either in terms of ability or behaviour. The problem with a purely behavioural definition is a lack of any objective means by which to identify which behaviours are of key importance (Ogilvy, 1994, p. 74, our italics).: "The problem is that *there is no theoretical model of social skills development* to provide guidance in the selection of which skills to target". The lack of such a model has led to confusion over which behaviours to train. Ogilvy offers two extremes of error: either choosing specific behaviours that have only limited contextual relevance; or setting a general aim which is so vague as to lack any specific behavioural component. She notes, of the two, the former seems the most common. Specific behaviours, such as question asking or eye contact, may be trained. However, the purpose of the training lacks any notion of higher order integration. On the other hand, more general behaviours such as playing co-operatively may be targeted by SST but these lack specific behavioural reference as they are not broken down into a full complement of component behaviours. Even if the general behaviours could be broken down, there is no certainty that the component behaviours would be socially valid for the child. Further, the operant model refers solely to specific outcome behaviours with no reference to underlying abilities which, in themselves, may be the roots for the desired operant behaviour.

Following a review of some common definitions, Ogilvy favourably quotes the work of Gresham and Elliot (1984) which places emphasis on the social validity of the behaviour. She concludes that (p. 75):

Social skills appear to have three main elements: cognitive, behavioural and environmental (i.e. they may be performed in one context but not another). These are, furthermore, most adequately defined in terms of their functional relationship with socially valued outcomes.

It is this latter element which is of most interest to us. The key element to be derived from her conclusion is that children themselves define what is or is not deemed as an acceptable behavioural profile for others wishing to enter into a particular peer group—without reference to an externally imposed notion of "normal" behaviour. Whatever the cognitive and

behavioural elements are that may be involved in attaining social competence, these are subservient to their social validation by the emergent
group norm. This recognition leads Ogilvy to conclude (p. 81):

> Whilst SST may be a necessary component in bringing about change in chil-
> dren's and adults' social lives, it may not always be sufficient. The child's
> interpersonal competence occurs within a specific network of social relations
> and any attempts to improve the individual's social functioning must take
> into account contextual factors. As well as targeting the observed deficits in
> the child's individual behaviour, attempts should also be made to restructure
> the social environment.

The change in primary emphasis from altering the child to the recognition that altering the environment may be necessary is reached also by
Bierman and Furman (1984) whose work is favourably cited by Ogilvy.
They compared, over time, four different treatment conditions: (1) individual coaching; (2) peer experience under super-ordinate goals; (3) individual coaching and peer involvement; and (4) a no treatment control.
Bierman and Furman found that the individual coaching and peer involvement condition was most effective in altering the subjects' feelings of social
efficacy. They argue that this may be due to the subjects' perceptions of
their peers' responses, leading Bierman and Furman to suggest changes in
self-efficacy may be more likely to occur "in peer involvement programs
where peer responses have been modified". They go on to make the point
that (p. 160):

> By pre-adolescence, peer acceptance may be affected increasingly by peer
> norms. If so, changes in children's behaviour may have less impact on their
> acceptance by the group. Consequently, it may be important to supplement
> skill training for adolescents with environmental manipulations that
> maximize the probability that peers will recognize and accept the new compe-
> tencies of the coached children.

There is no elaboration on the possible nature of these proposed "environmental manipulations". In these remarks there is an implicit recognition
of the theoretical limitations of SST as practised by them. As with Ogilvy,
the emphasis changes from the individual to the context in which the
individual acts.

Although researchers still continue to work on social behaviour as the
root of SST, others have concentrated on the sociocognitive elements in
social interaction. The rationale is clearly stated by Pellegrini (1985, p.
254): "Our therapeutic efforts would most likely be more efficient if we
could target specific socio-cognitive training programs for specific sociobehavioural deficits". Pre-eminent here is the work of Dodge and his

various associates. Over the past 10 years Dodge has published over 50 articles in this area and it is beyond the scope of this chapter to do any more than present a very brief outline of its findings. Dodge et al. (1986) present a general model of social functioning. An individual child's response to a given social stimulus involves the child in a five stage process of analysis. The stages are: (1) encoding the stimulus; (2) interpreting the stimulus; (3) searching for a suitable response; (4) evaluation of the response once found; and (5) enactment of the response. These five stages occur rapidly and in real time, often at a nonconscious level. They are continually repeated in any social interaction. The child's response, once enacted, forms the stimulus for the peers' processing judgement about the behaviour, which involves the five elements outlined above, and leads to the peers' social behavioural response. This in turn leads to the target child's response, again involving the five elements and so on in a processual and reciprocal manner. As Gottman's (1986) commentary on the monograph points out, by introducing this general model, Dodge and his associates are able to progress from general considerations of social competence to the study of specific social tasks thus creating a welcome link between research on social cognition and research on social behaviour.

Utilising an ingenious and novel methodology in this and subsequent studies (Dodge & Crick, 1990; Dodge & Tomlin, 1987), Dodge undertook an incremental study of each of the five stages. Whereas previous studies by other authors tended to concentrate on single elements in the response process, the approach outlined · by Dodge and colleagues enables researchers to analyse each of the stages—thus describing the relationship between behaviour and social information processing in each single instance. By holding preceding steps constant, regular patterns emerging in processing can be assessed. The authors hypothesise that successful processing results in social competence, conversely, unsuccessful processing results in the consequent behaviour being categorised as deviant by the peer. In subsequent studies, Dodge and his associates have attempted to analyse in what ways social interaction processes (described earlier) may be skewed and what reasons may lead to this. What emerges from this work is a model based on a notion of deficient socialisation, its reasons (e.g. socio-economic status, family discord, physical abuse), and its effects on social information processing. We would raise two points:

1. The studies all involve children who to some extent have been labelled as deviant. Identification of the subjects ranges from teacher observation in the case of rejected or neglected children, to subjects whose violent behaviour has led them to be imprisoned in secure institutions. There has been extensive sociological study of the social organisation of juvenile justice (Cicourel, 1976; Gilroy, 1983) which raises questions about the

simple relationship between behaviour and labelling which Dodge appears to envisage; this has been similarly considered in the social psychology of schooling (Rogers, 1982). We do not deny that children can and do engage in aggressive or violent behaviour. We do assert, however, that the reasons for the application of a public label are seldom simple and are not countenanced by Dodge.

2. Our second point is related to the first. There does not appear to be in Dodge's work a notion of "normal" social development beyond the implicit assumption of functional success. If the child successfully processes social information then the child is integrated into the peer group. Some children do this very well and are popular (as measured by sociometric indices). Some (the majority?) do it adequately and are "normal" children. The processes of socialisation involved in "normal" children are discussed only by default (i.e. they are not those involved in the socialisation of children judged to be deficient). Dodge's work makes the assumption of "normal" socialisation and development but does not discuss it. Given the task that Dodge and other sociocognitive psychologists set themselves (i.e. what are the processes involved in the apprehension of social reality and how are these related to social behaviour), we do not think this an unfair criticism. The general model of social functioning offered by Dodge et al. (1986) looks only at individual slices of interaction taken out of processual context.

As with the studies mentioned in the previous section on specific behavioural approaches to SST, the theoretical approach of this orientation cannot place social interaction on any other than a static and ahistorical foundation. To use a film analogy, although 48 pictures when placed end to end give information, it is not the same information given as when they are projected continuously on a screen to give two seconds of moving picture. It may be that the individual pictures can give valuable insights but they do not describe movement. Similarly, the behavioural approach may well describe a moment in time, but time moves on. Neither the sociobehavioural nor sociocognitive approaches have as yet succeeded in describing the processes involved in development.

There are further limitations to such an approach. Some of them are raised by the authors of the various studies themselves. Dodge and Coie (1987) specifically alert their readers to the limitations of generalisability from the study of a sample of a specific population of black, male first- and third-graders. Rabiner and Gordon (1993) conclude that the elements they separated out for study, prosocial concerns and strategies, are best seen as interrelated and that future work should attend to that relationship.

There are, however, more serious limitations which cannot be self-corrected. Gottman (1986) praises the research for moving away from a general consideration of social competence to the study of specific social tasks (in this case, the provocation of aggression and social acceptance and rejection) as creating a link between social cognition and behaviour. He then proceeds to criticise the work for its lack of developmental orientation. He wonders why children were studied at all, let alone 7- to 9-year-olds. From his own work on the development of children's friendships, Gottman (1983) hypothesises that this age group was studied because of the particular context of social development that the middle-school years represent. In brief, he argues that there is a major transition in the complexity of the social world that children must apprehend between preschool and the early elementary school years. The child must learn to function in a peer social world which includes such issues as power and influence and notions of "what to be like". Gottman's criticism is clear and reiterates the point that we have previously made. In this type of cross-sectional study, the context is taken for granted. The social construction of the context is not seen as problematic and the social processes, prior to and after the events studied, although of putative interest, are defined out of the study. Also lacking in this type of study, argues Gottman, is any consideration of the emotional context in which the socio-cognitive activities take place. As the authors of this chapter, we would add to this criticism by questioning whether teachers are able to undertake fully an individually oriented programme of SST while they simultaneously maintain responsibility for all other pupils in the classroom.

DEVELOPMENTAL THEORY

In contrast to the predominantly operant nature of SST, this section now draws on a theory of the development of social relationships and seeks to show its effects on children's social and learning competencies. The social developmental model is summarised by Kutnick (1988), who charts close social relationships which underlie both social and learning behaviours. The model identifies stages in the development of social relationships. These stages are found in both ideal–typical child–adult and child–peer relationships. The stages are analytically independent (deep structure) from their mode of expression as they emerge in the social context (surface structure). The deep structures are representative of the socio-cognitive–relational mode operating at a given time. The surface structures are the means by which the specific modes are exhibited and the degree of operational autonomy that they impart to the actor within a culturally based, social relational context. Co-construction is the fundamental process, both in the formation of these relationships and their development. The theoretical underpinning of the theory draws on notions of the social construction of understanding as espoused by Vygotsky (1978) and the progression toward autonomy described by Piaget (1995). The advantage of the developmental sociorelational approach to be propounded is that it can be used with groups within the classroom, scaffolded by teachers but interacted by pupils. The importance of drawing on such a sociorelational theory for establishing this alternative approach to social skills development is the potential to embody these developments within classroom relationships—the point where "abnormal" is identified. Clarification of a developmental model of social relationships (see Table 7.1) leads to the construction of a programme to enhance their development in classrooms.

The programme itself was created in response to requests from primary school head teachers facing the following pupil-based problems. (1) A local head teacher was concerned about "antisocial" behaviour among the infants (aged 5–6 years) in her school. By antisocial she meant fighting and causing distress to others, whether in the company of teacher or peers, as well as poor concentration and communication. (2) Another head teacher requested a programme to create conditions to enhance children's (aged 10–11 years) ability to work in small groups on microcomputers. The school wished to maximise children's opportunities to work with computers but, like most primary schools in the United Kingdom, there were only enough computers in the school to place one or two per classroom (Jackson, Fletcher, & Messer, 1986). To allow all children access to the computer, pupils had to work in groups—they had to co-operate with each other and avoid antisocial and nonsocial behaviours. (3) A teacher of 9- to 10-year-olds expressed concerns that her class of 32 pupils had a number of strong cliques which did not allow children to work with others outside their own clique. Pupils refused to share equipment, understanding, and insight among themselves, while the teacher was at pains to introduce co-operative working practices. These three requests represent children's refusal or limited ability to work, share, and co-operate with classmates. The behaviours are seen to disrupt the learning and social experience of particular children (those who have traditionally been labelled as "abnormal") yet, because these behaviours are exhibited within the classroom they are disruptive to all the members of the classroom—who in their turn may exclude, reject, or refuse to work with any disruptive child.

The theoretical basis of the programme may be briefly outlined as follows. Children's relationships with both adults and peers follow a similar deep structural pattern that manifests itself in different modes (surface structures) of relational interaction as the cognitive apprehension and organisation of the relationship and its context increases in complexity. The deep structural stages can be promoted within any culture through quality interactions with adults and peers. Stages are displayed in Table 7.1 and can be described as:

1. A primary stage of sensori-motor affect, which, once established, is sustained by the development of a complementarity of dependency (Hinde, 1979).
2. The child's reflection on the mode of interaction, which gives rise to:
3. A cognitive ordering of the experience in terms of pre-operative rules or regularities.
4. Further interaction concretises these socially constructed rules and this, in turn, forms the basis of:
5. Formal operational rule construction and manipulation—the basis for autonomous behaviour.

The deep structural stages and the occurrence of surface manifestations of the stages within the cultural experience of the child are alluded to in Piaget's (1995) sociological study of development. Table 7.1 identifies and portrays each stage more clearly for the reader. Having identified the stages and cultural presentation, an explanation for their development can be made.

The study of adult–child relationships provides strong empirical evidence for the existence of deep structures. The importance of the attachment bond with its reciprocal disposition to obedience, trust, and dependency is identified by Ainsworth, Bell, and Stayton (1974) and Stayton, Hogan, and Ainsworth (1971). Development of the child–adult relationship is exemplified in an increasingly sophisticated understanding of the world as a social milieu with systemic qualities, where regularities of behaviour exist as does a differential right to exercise power (Damon,

TABLE 7.1
Structural representation of social relational stage development

Deep structure	Surface	Structure
	Adult-based	Peer-based
Sensori-motor affect	Sensori-affective contacts	Sensori-affective contacts
Development of dependent relation	Obedience	Peer-oriented
Early rule application	Unilateral respect	Sharing
Concrete/rational rule application	Legitimisation of expert	Mutuality
Reflective rule application	Collaboration	Negotiation through need/co-operation

Source: adapted from Kutnick (1988).

1977; Selman, 1980; Turiel, 1980; Youniss, 1992). The traditionally close child–adult relationship has been identified as a necessary condition for effective learning (Barrett & Trevitt, 1991) and further development of relationships with others.

The existence of deep structures in child–peer relationships is more anecdotal. This is in part accounted for by the manner in which childhood is both constituted and constructed in Western society (Kessen, 1991), which results in children rarely being allowed the quality of early interactive experience necessary to develop fully their potential for creating close peer relationships until late in adolescence (Youniss, 1978). On the other hand, simply stating that the conditions of Western child upbringing makes it unlikely that children will develop early sensori-affect-based peer relations misconstrues their potential. Peer-orientated deep-structure processes can be inferred from the literature. Freud and Dann (1951) identified the existence of peer-based attachment among a small group of child concentration camp survivors brought to London just after the Second World War. These children were brought up communally from birth, and they later showed a closeness, trust, and dependence within the group that Freud termed "peer attachment". Sensori-affective relationships have also been observed among some very young children who are provided with the opportunity to interact with one another (Howes, 1983; Vandell & Mueller 1980). Peer-oriented dependency is found in participation in valued group interaction (Rubin & Pepler, 1980) within which the early rule-application stage of sharing is the predominant mode (Hartup, 1978; Maxwell, 1990; Youniss, 1980). Concrete and formal modes of relational expression may be negotiated in advanced friendships and early work relations (Selman, 1980; Sullivan 1953). According to this model, if children are given the opportunity to develop close child–peer relationships, then similar cognitive and social benefits will accrue to those found in close child–adult relationships.

From this information a developmental model to promote prosocial skills based on the sociorelational stages can be constructed. In the model, early relationships develop from schemes that promote an affective tie between child and specific others, to a realisation of dependence and attachment, to communicative understanding of rules (especially respect for others), and ability to change and develop new perspectives and rules. What is unusual about the model is the identification that close relationships may develop between the child and adult as well as the child and peers. Educators of young children would note that pupils may readily transfer their ability to form close relationships with adults from home to the classroom teacher but many children may not have the ability to transfer close relationships to peers due to lack

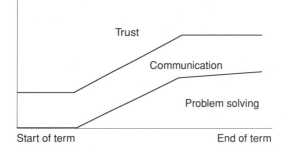

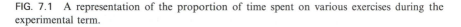

Start of term   End of term

FIG. 7.1 A representation of the proportion of time spent on various exercises during the experimental term.

of opportunity and experience. The model suggests that effective and close social relationships are based on a trust/dependence which sensitivity exercises may facilitate, followed by increased communication skills to extend affective ties and understanding of interaction, and the promotion of problem-solving skills. A sociorelational programme based on this developmental model assumes that most children will have experience of adult-based relationships although they will need to enhance the quality of their peer relations to promote socialisation and learning in school. More specifically, the programme developed for use in primary schools adapted its training procedure from sensitivity–trust exercises (e.g. see Pfeiffer & Jones, 1976), with appropriate modifications made for such concerns as children's size, age, strength, communicative ability (Pattisson, 1987) and problem-solving capacity (Spivak, Platt, & Shure, 1976). The choice and ordering of these exercises were specifically designed to reflect a natural course of development of close social relationships among children. Such a programme can only develop over time and is obviously experiential in nature. Figure 7.1 shows how the model may be laid out in the form of activities and how they develop over a term. The programme is spiral in nature (specific social skills being repeated, extended, and applied over time—a pre-operative assumption such that the learning of these skills does not take place in a one-off situation). Without this structured basis to close social relationships, children's interactions among peers may be perceived as threatening, especially in the primary school classroom (Bennett, 1994; Galton & Williamson, 1992). Unstructured relationships that characterise classrooms in the main may act as a hinderance to the development of a suitable socio-emotional climate (Light & Littleton, 1994) thereby limiting the socio-interactional basis of cognitive development (Dawes, Fisher, & Mercer, 1992; Doise, 1990).

What is the sociorelational programme expected to do?

The organisation of the programme is informed by criteria for the effective testing of social skills training programmes (Ogilvy, 1994). These criteria are the following: (1) That the programme is able to promote a range of social skills. (2) The promoted skills can be generalised to real-life settings and that the effects can be maintained over time. (3) The skills make a difference to the child's life in terms of some socially valued outcome. These criteria are pragmatic, sensible, and transposable to other theoretical approaches. They also set parameters by which the programme for the development of social relations can be evaluated, although the theory supporting the design of the programme reverses the normal "operant" route in SST. Instead of operationalising a specific behaviour, reinforcing that behaviour and testing for its occurrence, the developmental programme provides a relational structure which should promote prosocial behaviour and cognition.

The programme is likely to promote the following. (1) The enhancement of cognitive ability with regard to specific tasks. (2) The development of co-operative interaction, again relating to specific tasks. (3) The development of co-operative and sociomoral reasoning, measured in each child's predisposition to co-operative behaviour and empathic concern for others.

HAS THE SOCIORELATIONAL PROGRAMME BEEN EFFECTIVE?

To meet criteria for the evaluation of the effectiveness of the developmental sociorelational programme, small-scale studies were undertaken in each of the three schools identified earlier. Because the studies were undertaken with real children (exhibiting social and educational needs) we could not assess effectiveness by purely experimental methods which often, mistakenly, are used to identify psychological research (Harré and Gillet, 1994). The small-scale studies briefly reported later draw on the involvement of teachers and children in both "action research" and quasi-experimental orientations (see Cohen & Manion, 1994). These orientations will always depend on the presence and judgement of teachers.

Social skills training in the infant school

The programme was initially used with children identified as being antisocial. Eight year 1 children, drawn from two classes, participated in the programme. Programme sessions took the place of "remedial" lessons (to which the pupils would have been assigned due to poor classroom performance) and lasted one hour per week over a 12-week term. As described previously, the programme sessions evolved from predominantly trust and communication exercises (the start of the term) to communication and problem-solving exercises by the end of the term. Aside from the initial, global teacher identification of the experimental pupils, individual social/ antisocial behaviours were identified on a 12-item rating scale (adapted from Osborn & Milbank, 1987) concerning learning and social skills. Teachers rated all members of their classes including the eight children at the start of the term. At the end of the term all pupils were re-rated by their teachers. Table 7.2 presents average scores for the antisocial pupils at

TABLE 7.2
Average ratings and changes in behaviour for infants in the programme

Rated behaviour	Av. score before programme	Av. score after programme	Change
General knowledge	2.625	2.375	No change
Interaction with peer when confronting a classroom problem	2.000*	2.125	Improvement
Communication with teacher	2.500	2.376	No change
Concentration on educational tasks	2.125	1.750	Decline
Pay attention in class	2.125	2.250	Improvement
Interaction in working group	1.375**	1.500**	Improvement
Solitary/social when working in class	1.625*	2.500	From solitary to sociable worker
Dependence on teacher	2.250	2.375	Improvement
Popularity with peers	2.000**	2.125**	Improvement
Bold/shy with peers	2.000	2.000	No change
Co-operative with peers	2.250**	2.750	Improvement
Adjustment to social demands of playtime	1.750**	2.000	Improvement

Ratings made on a 5-point scale (1, antisocial performance to 5, highly social performance).

* and ** denote .01 and .001 levels of difference between the children who participated in

the start and end of the term for each rated behaviour as well as direction of change over the term and differences between the experimental children's behaviours and their classmates. When comparing these children to the rest of their classmates, behaviour was significantly different in six areas at the start of the term and in only two at the end. Within those two areas of difference (popularity with peers and ability to work with peers in the classroom) there was an improvement in the children's behaviour. Although the sociorelational programme was not successful in all areas of behaviour (decline in concentration and general knowledge), the general improvement clearly met evaluational guidelines of promoting social skills within the real-life context of the classroom—where these skills centred on co-operative interaction. Anecdotally, a follow-up visit to the school nine months later found that the eight pupils were no longer a cause of concern for their teachers.

Social skills and cognitive development (on the microcomputer) in a junior school

This study explored how the programme would affect both co-operative classroom behaviours as well as cognitive skills displayed on a problem-solving computer task. It was undertaken with two, parallel year 5 classes over the course of a term in a quasi-experimental design. At the start of the term, each teacher completed the rating scale (described earlier) for every child in his/her class. Pupils were divided into small groups and undertook the simulation "Water Game" (CWDE, 1989) on a microcomputer—a cognitive problem-solving task that required small groups of pupils to transport various amounts of water via various routes to support a Third World farm. Pupil interaction and game results were recorded by an observer. During the term, one (experimental) class undertook the programme during twice-weekly physical education sessions while the other (control) class maintained its ordinary physical education routine. At the end of the term the teachers re-rated their pupils' behaviour and the small groups were asked to play the Water Game again. Behavioural and game outcome results are presented in Table 7.3.

   Pupils who undertook the programme showed significant prosocial and prolearning changes, especially when compared to the control class. With regard to the prosocial skills, pupils in the experimental class improved on positive interaction with peers when confronting a classroom problem, working productively within classroom groups, maintaining a sociable presence (as opposed to solitary) when working in class, popularity with peers, and ability to co-operate with peers. Teacher-rated improvements of learning skills for the experimental class showed improved concentration on tasks and attention paid to the teacher. The second sitting of the

TABLE 7.3

Average behavioural ratings and amount of water carried (game score) of experimental (Exp.) and control (Con.) classes in the junior school (before, after and change scores)

Rated behaviour	Class	Av. score before programme	Av. score after programme	Change
General knowledge	Exp.	2.567	2.533	n.s.
	Con.	2.100	1.867^{+}	
Interaction with peer when confronting a classroom problem	Exp.	3.667	4.100	Exp.>
	Con.	4.067	3.900	Con.**
Communication with teacher	Exp.	2.800	2.933	n.s.
	Con.	2.333^{+}	2.533	
Concentration on educational tasks	Exp.	3.000	3.400	Exp.>
	Con.	2.700	2.633^{++}	Con.**
Pay attention in class	Exp.	2.133	2.367	Exp.>
	Con.	2.467	2.267	Con.**
Interaction in working group	Exp.	2.633	3.133	Exp.>
	Con.	2.667	2.467^{++}	Con.**
Solitary/social when working in class	Exp.	3.267	3.500	Exp.>
	Con.	3.067	3.200	Con.*
Dependence on teacher	Exp.	2.867	2.866	n.s.
	Con.	2.400^{++}	2.400^{++}	
Popularity with peers	Exp.	2.467	2.900	Exp.>
	Con.	2.500	2.400^{++}	Con.**
Bold/shy with peers	Exp.	4.067	3.333	Exp.<
	Con.	3.467	3.400	Con.**
Co-operation with peers	Exp.	2.500	3.667	Exp.>
	Con.	2.267	2.333^{++}	Con.**
Litres of water carried	Exp.	71.689	129.414	Exp.>
	Con.	101.517	118.286	Con.**

$^{+}$ and $^{++}$ denote levels of difference (.05 and .01, respectively) between the two classes based on the raw data collected at the start and end of the term.

* and ** denote significant levels of difference (.05 and .01, respectively) in the amount of change within each class over the term.

microcomputer Water Game showed a significant improvement in understanding and ability to handle the programme (cognitive understanding) by the experimental class. While working on the microcomputer, subtle differences in the conversation and actions of the children in the experimental class were found. Compared to the start of term, children in the experimental class became more focused in their communication. They spent less time asking general questions, making general responses, and directing others in keyboard use. They increased the time spent on keyboard use, supporting skills necessary to move the litres of water. The experimental class significantly decreased "superfluous conversation" which may have threatened or derogated other members of the group. The control class improved their keyboard use but increased superfluous conversation as well. One interpretation for the difference in performance between the two classes on the microcomputer task is that the experimental class was able to draw on "elaborating skills" (see Webb, 1989) while providing a supportive (nonthreatening) atmosphere. This quasi-experimental study showed a promotion of social, communicative, and co-operative skills that coincided with enhanced cognitive performance on the microcomputer.

Social skills in junior class with strong cliques

This year 5 class followed the same action research orientation as the year 1 class except that the study was undertaken by a whole class instead of specifically identified pupils. At the start of term the teacher rated each pupil in the class on the scale (described earlier). Additionally, the children were asked to undertake a sociometric task (to identify classroom cliques) which asked the children to imagine themselves stranded on a desert island with enough equipment to assemble a raft to sail back home. Each child was asked to select and name classmates with whom they would like to build a raft (adapted from Hall, 1994). The class undertook the programme once a week over a term. At the end of the term, the teacher re-assessed the children on the rating scale and the children were asked to undertake the sociometric task again. The rating of behaviours and significance of change are reported in Table 7.4.

The teacher rating clearly showed improvements in a range of behaviours over the term, promoting both interpersonal and learning skills. Evidence of change and development from the sociometric data are not so clear-cut or well defined. The first desert island task showed that among the 30 pupils (13 male and 17 female) there were 8 cliques, composed on average of 3 pupils. The cliques were predominantly single sex; of the male choices, 92 per cent were to work with other males and of the female choices 91 per cent were to work with other females. There were 6 "loners" in the class that no one chose. At the end of term, the number of cliques decreased and the average number of children within each clique rose to 4.3. Sadly, the male–female mix of the cliques did not change; males chose other males 93% of the time and females chose other females 90% of the time. Loners decreased in number to 4. Thus, although the

TABLE 7.4
Average ratings and changes in behaviour for juniors in the programme

Rated behaviour	Av. score before programme	Av. score after programme	Change
General knowledge	2.897	3.172	Improvement*
Interaction with peer when confronting a classroom problem	3.345	3.172	No change
Communication with teacher	2.207	3.793	Improvement**
Concentration on educational tasks	2.138	2.862	Improvement**
Pay attention in class	2.517	3.1379	Improvement*
Interaction in working group	2.689	3.276	Improvement*
Solitary/social when working in class	2.035	3.069	Improvement**
Dependence on teacher	4.276	3.689	Improvement**
Popularity with peers	3.172	3.483	No change
Bold/shy with peers	2.586	3.069	No change
Co-operative with peers	3.034	3.621	Improvement*

Ratings made on a 5-point scale (1, antisocial performance to 5, highly social performance).

* and ** denote .05 and .01 levels of significance as tested on matched pair t-tests.

learning and co-operative atmosphere of the classroom improved there is clearly more work to be undertaken in this programme.

CONCLUSION

This chapter has outlined an approach to social skills training (SST), based on developmental theory. It has argued that common stages in the development of relationships exist in both child–adult and child–peer relations. It contends that although the surface structures of these stages have different manifestations in child–adult and child–peer relations, the deep structures of affect, dependency, and the concomitant cognitive organisation of the relationship in terms of rule application at preconcrete,

concrete, and formal levels is common to both. From the theoretical stand-point adopted, a developmental approach has been adduced that concentrates on enhancing the affective element of relationships through the use of trust and sensitivity exercises (building on this via the use of communication exercises and using the gains made to facilitate problem solving and hence cognitive growth). We contend that this approach has a clear practical advantage over the more usual behavioural approach to SST in that it allows for whole classes to be involved and takes place within the classroom. We also claim a theoretical advantage over the behavioural perspective in that the developmental approach bases itself on a coherent model of the emergence and nature of child–peer relationships rather than attending to isolated individual elements of behaviour.

The chapter has also set out criteria by which the effectiveness of such an approach may be judged. Evidence for effectiveness as presented from the small-scale studies that have been undertaken so far is by no means unequivocal, but lends support to the potential effectiveness of the programme. Each of the studies reported shows a positive result in terms of promoting a range of social skills. With regard to whether these skills generalise to real-life settings and whether the effects can be maintained over time, the evidence is weaker. All of the studies were classroom (real-life) based and teachers reported increases in prosocial behaviour at the end of the experimental period. But none of the studies were longitudinal. Some anecdotal evidence (study 1) exists that the programme was able to effect change over time, but the sample size was small. Perhaps the most difficult criterion of success to satisfy is that the skills make a difference to the child's life in terms of some socially valued outcome. Again, the lack of longitudinal evidence is apparent. Indeed, in order to satisfy this, possibly the most rigorous of the criteria, a formal evaluative study would be needed. However, we do not think it unreasonable to claim that the programme clearly has the potential to fulfil this criterion, by providing a structured base and a set of experiences from which future relationships might be structured and enhanced. If the programme, as outlined, is able to generate a nonthreatening and structured basis for social relationships, then it can be used as a template for the organisation of future relationships and will have fulfilled this criterion.

The sociorelational programme, although following a developmental path and being based on close relationships that support social and learning development, is something that teachers will need to consider in relation to the time given to the UK National Curriculum. If teachers wish to improve social and learning skills in their pupils, they cannot simply match interesting and curricularly meaningful work to their pupils' levels of ability. Time, effort, and legitimacy must be given to social skills and social relations in the classroom. For social scientists, we hope to show that developmental principles can be adapted to promote practical and valid classroom improvements. Finally, we must not draw conclusions that are too grand from the programme described here. Although having been planned in a developmental manner, as distinct from other programmes, more time should be given to assessing immediate impact on pupils and teachers, but also initiating long-term follow-ups to ascertain whether these skills are retained by pupils.

REFERENCES

Ainsworth, M., Bell, S., & Stayton, D. (1974). Infant–mother attachment and social development: "socialisation" as a product of reciprocal responsiveness to signals. In M. Woodhead, R. Carr, & P. Light (Eds.), *Becoming a person*, pp. 30–55. London: Routledge.

Barrett, M. & Trevitt, J. (1991). *Attachment behaviour and the school child.* London: Routledge.

Bennett, N. (1994). Co-operative Learning. In P. Kutnick & C. Rogers (Eds.), *Groups in schools*, pp. 63–78. London: Cassell.

Bennett, N. & Dunne, E. (1990). Implementing co-operative groupwork in classrooms. In V. Lee (Ed.), *Children's learning in school.* London: Hodder & Stoughton.

Bierman, K.L. & Furman, W. (1984). The effects of social skills training and peer involvement in the social adjustment of preadolescents. *Child Development, 55,* 151–162.

Biott, C. (1987). Co-operative group work: Pupils' and teachers' membership and participation. *Curriculum, 8,* 5–14.

Cartledge, G. & Milburn, J. F. (1980). *Teaching social skills to children.* New York: Pergamon.

Cicourel, A. V. (1976). *The social organization of juvenile justice.* London: Heinemann.

Cohen, L. & Manion, L. (1994). *Research methods in education.* London, Routledge.

Cowie, H. & Ruddock, J. (1988). *Co-operative groupwork: An overview.* London: BP Education Service.

Cullingford, C. (1988). Children's views about working together. *Education, 16,* 29–34.

CWDE (1989). *The water game.* London: CWDE Software.

DES (Department of Education and Science) (1989). *National curriculum from policy to practice.* London, HMSO.

Damon, W. (1977). *The social world of the child.* San Francisco: Jossey-Bass.

Damon, W. & Phelps, E. (1989). Critical distinctions among three approaches to peer education. *International Journal of Educational Research, 13,* 9–19.

Davis, A. (1991). Piaget, teachers and education: Into the 1990s. In P. S. Light, S. Sheldon, & M. Woodhead (Eds), *Learning to think*, pp. 16–31. London: Routledge/Open University.

Dawes, L., Fisher, E., & Mercer, N. (1992). The quality of talk at the computer. (cited in Light & Littleton, 1994).

Dodge, K. A. & Coie, J. D. (1987). Social information processing factors in reactive and proactive aggression in children's peer groups. *Journal of Personality and Social Psychology, 53,* 1146–1158.

Dodge, K. A. & Crick, N. R. (1990). Social information-processing bases of aggressive behaviour in children. *Personality and Social Psychology Bulletin, 16,* 8–32.

Dodge, K. A., Pettit, G. S., McClasky, C. L., & Brown, M. (1986). Social competence in children. *Monographs of the Society for Research in Child Development, 213,* 3–51.

Dodge, K. A. & Tomlin, A. M. (1987). Utilization of self-schemas as a mechanism of interpretational bias in aggressive children. *Social Cognition, 5,* 280–300.

Doise, W. (1990). The development of individual competences through social interaction. In H. Foot, M. Morgan, & R. Shute (Eds.), *Children helping children*, pp. 43–64. Chichester, UK: Wiley.

Dunne, E. & Bennett, N. (1990). *Talking and learning in groups*. London: Macmillan.

Freud, A. & Dann, S. (1951). An experiment in group upbringing. *Psychoanalytic Study of the Child*, *6*, 127–168.

Galton, M. (1990). Grouping and groupwork. In C. Rogers & P. Kutnick (Eds.), *The social psychology of the primary school*, pp. 11–30. London, Routledge.

Galton, M. & Williamson, J. (1992). *Groupwork in the primary school*. London: Routledge.

Gilroy, P. (1983). Police and thieves. In *The Empire strikes back*, Centre for Contemporary Cultural Studies. London: Hutchinson.

Gottman, J. (1983). How children become friends. *Monographs of the Society for Research in Child Development*, *48*, 3.

Gottman, J. (1986). Commentary on Dodge et al. (1986). *Monographs of the Society for Research in Child Development*, *212*, 51.

Gresham, F. N. & Elliot, S. N. (1984). Assessment and classification of children's social skills. *School Psychology Review*, *13*, 292–301.

Hall, E. (1994). The social relational approach. In P. Kutnick & C. Rogers (Eds.), *Groups in Schools*, pp.129–142. London: Cassell.

Harré, R. & Gillet, G. (1994). *The discursive mind*. Thousand Oaks, CA: Sage.

Hartup, W. (1978). Children and their friends. In H. McGurk (Ed.), *Issues in childhood social development*, pp. 130–170. London: Methuen.

Hinde, R. A. (1979). *Towards understanding relationships*. London: Academic Press.

Howes, C. (1983). Patterns of friendship. *Child Development*, *53*, 217–226.

Hughes, J. N. & Sullivan, K. A. (1988). *Assessment and training of isolated children's social skills*. Paper presented at the biennial meeting of the Society for Research in Child Development, New Orleans.

Jackson, A., Fletcher, B., & Messer, D. (1986). A survey of microcomputer use and provision in primary school. *Journal of Computer Assisted Learning*, *2*, 45–55.

Kessen, W. (1991). The American child and other cultural inventions. In M. Woodhead, P. Light, & R. Carr (Eds.), *Growing up in a changing society*, pp. 26–37. London: Routledge/ Open University.

Kline, S. (1994). *Out of the garden: Children, toys and television in the age of marketing*. London: Verso.

Kutnick, P. J. (1988). *Relationships in the primary school classroom*. London: Paul Chapman.

Kutnick, P. & Marshall, D. (1993). Development of social skills and the use of the microcomputer in the primary school classroom. *British Educational Research Journal*, *19*, 517–533.

Kutnick, P. J. & Rogers, C. (Eds.) (1994). *Groups in schools*. London: Cassell.

Light, P. & Littleton, K. (1994). Cognitive approaches to group work. In P. Kutnick & C. Rogers (Eds.), *Groups in schools*, pp. 87–103. London: Cassell.

Maras, P. & Messer, B. (1995). What are EBD's? *A summary review of medical, cognitive, social and societal perspectives*. London: Greenwich University Press.

Maxwell, W. (1990). The nature of friendship in the primary school. In C. Rogers & P. Kutnick (Eds.), *The social psychology of the primary school*, pp. 169–189. London, Routledge.

Michelson, L., Sugai, D. P., Wood, R. P., & Kazdin, R. E. (1983). *Social skills assessment and training with children*. New York: Plenum.

Monteil, J-M. (1992). Towards a social psychology of cognitive functioning. In M. von Granach, W. Doise, & G. Mugny (Eds.), *Social representation and the social representation of knowledge*. Berne: Hubert. As cited in Light, P. J. & Littleton, K. (1994).

Newman, D., Griffin, D. & Cole, M. (1989). *The construction zone: Working for cognitive change in school.* London: Cambridge University Press.

Ogilvy, C. M. (1994). Social skills training with children and adolescents: A review of the evidence on effectiveness. *Educational Psychology, 14,* 73–83.

Osborn, A. F. & Milbank, J. E. (1987). *The effects of early education.* Oxford: Oxford University Press.

Pattison, P. (1987). *Developing communication skills.* Cambridge, UK: Cambridge University Press.

Pfeiffer, J. W. & Jones, J. E. (1976). *Handbook of structured exercises for human relations training.* La Jolla, CA: University Associates.

Pellegrini, D. S. (1985). Social cognition and competence in middle childhood. *Child Development, 56,* 253–264.

Perret-Clermont, A. (1980). *Social interaction and cognitive development in children.* London: Academic Press.

Piaget, J. (1995). *Sociological studies.* London: Routledge.

Rabiner, D. L. & Gordon, L. V. (1993). The relationship between children's concerns and their social interaction strategies: Differences between rejected and accepted boys. *Social Development, 2,* 83–96.

Rogers, C. (1982). *A social psychology of schooling.* London: Routledge & Kegan Paul.

Rubin, K. H. & Pepler, D. J. (1980). The relationship of play to social-cognitive growth and development. In H. Foot, A. J. Chapman, & J. R. Smith (Eds.). *Friendship and social relations in childhood,* pp. 209–234. Chichester, UK: Wiley.

Selman, R. (1980). *The growth of interpersonal understanding.* New York: Academic Press.

Smith, P. K., Cowie, H., & Berdondini, L. (1994). Co-operation and bullying. In P. Kutnick & C. Rogers (Eds.), *Groups in schools.* London: Cassell.

Spivak, G., Platt, J. J., Shure, M. M. (1976). *The problem-solving approach to adjustment.* San Francisco: Jossey-Bass.

Stayton, D., Hogan, R., & Ainsworth, M. S. (1971). Infant obedience and maternal behaviour: The origins of socialization reconsidered. *Child Development, 42,* 1057–1069.

Sullivan, H. S. (1953). *The interpersonal theory of psychiatry.* New York: Norton.

Turiel, E. (1980). The development of social-conventional and moral concepts. In M. Windmiller, N. Lambert, & E. Turiel (Eds.), *Moral development and socialization,* pp. 69–106. Boston, MA: Allyn & Bacon.

Vandell, D. L. & Mueller, E. C. (1980). Peer play and friendship during the first two years. In H. Foot, A. J. Chapman, & J. R. Smith (Eds.), *Friendship and social relations in children,* pp. 181–208, Chichester, UK: Wiley.

Vygotsky, L. S. (1978). *Mind and society: The development of higher mental processes.* Cambridge, MA: Harvard University Press.

Youniss, J. (1978). The nature of social development: A conceptual discussion of cognition. In H. McGurk (Ed.), *Issues in childhood social development,* pp. 203–227. London: Methuen.

Youniss, J. (1980). *Parents and peers in social development.* Chicago, IL: Chicago University Press.

Youniss, J. (1992). Parent and peer relations in the emergence of cultural competence. In H. McGurk (Ed.), *Childhood social development: Contemporary perspectives,* pp. 131–147. Hove, UK: Lawrence Erlbaum Associates Ltd.

Webb, N. (1989). Peer interaction and learning in small groups. *International Journal of Educational Research, 13,* 21–39.

8 Technology, media, and social development

Charles Crook
Loughborough University, Loughborough, UK

In this chapter, I shall discuss the relationship between two particular topics. On the one hand, a certain class of modern communications media; on the other, preparations during childhood for participating in a social world. Within traditions of theorising psychological development, technology and media exist rather on the sidelines. Taking them seriously may require us to adopt a somewhat different orientation to the business of theorising—but I believe this challenge is a useful one.

First, consider "technology". The term suggests material things—video recorders, walkmen, games consoles, and so forth. In contemplating these as topics within the study of social development, we must orient towards things themselves—enquiring how cultural artefacts get "fitted" into a socially organised world. In particular, we must enquire how social behaviour adjusts to allow various kinds of harmony between ourselves and such technology. Starting from things themselves is an unusual (but challenging) strategy for students of social development. Second, consider "media". This also requires a distinctive research orientation. A typical definition of the term might be (Meyrowitz, 1985, p. 331): "...all channels and means through which information is transmitted among people except direct, face-to-face modes of communicating". Obviously, any history of a human culture will very much be about the growth and elaboration of such *mediated* (as opposed to "im-mediate") modes of communication. In short, if understanding social development requires studying our early experience of the social world, then researchers must notice that, for each generation, such experience is transformed by new forms of mediated encounter with that world. Of course, this is a general claim about the study of any social behaviour—a concern with "mediational means" must be central to all our accounts of human communication. Yet, this concern has never been rigorously explored within the study of social *development*.

So, the principal terms within my chapter title encourage, first, what we might call an "ecological" orientation—taking seriously the material environment in which social behaviour gets organised and social development thereby takes place. Second, there is encouragement for an orientation towards mediational means—taking seriously the ways in which our communications within a social world are mediated by the various technologies and rituals of cultural practice. How does this compare with a more orthodox approach towards studying social development? I suggest that the orthodox approach has been preoccupied with psychological processes that too often refer only to the individual actor. They are insufficiently "social"—or, where this seems not to be the case, any social dimension that is described seems to exist independently of a cultural context. The main stuff of theorising has thereby become either individual social skills and cognitions, or the dynamics of relatively decontextualised relationships. To be sure, the concepts that arise within such theory have done some useful work. However, they have encouraged a narrow focus on the *individual* as the unit of analysis or, at best, a focus on social relations that are made to function freely of historical or cultural circumstances. Perhaps this reflects a certain "laboratory" ethos that pervades much scientific psychology. Privileged accounts are those that identify "pure" psychological processes—those that might be made visible in relatively controlled environments, protected by research design from too much contextual "noise". Yet, it is not clear that this kind of abstraction has worked. It is not clear that the contexts of social action can be put aside for consideration later in the research enterprise, as if context was merely a package of environmental variables to be grafted back on after the laboratory work has been done on the "basic processes".

In case this perspective should itself suffer from lack of context, I shall briefly recast the argument by reference to a concrete example; one already well worked through in another area of developmental psychology. I have in mind the analysis of *literacy*, a topic of some interest to students of cognitive development. What literacy is about, of course, is reading and writing. For many psychologists, the study of literacy has entailed the study of how children decode the sophisticated symbol systems we recognise as "text"; how they master reading—as a skill. To a lesser extent, it has also been about documenting children's discovery and deployment of various textual resources for self-expression—how they become skilled writers. This much is well and good as far as it goes, but it does not go far enough towards identifying literacy as a significant force within cognitive development. The story remains incomplete perhaps because the mainstream of psychological theorising resists locating reading and writing within a broader framework of socially organised activity.

Now consider literacy from within the kind of ecological or mediational framework that I have introduced earlier. In the spirit of a thought experiment, consider this simple situation: Someone reads a list of words that must be remembered (it might be a psychology experiment, but it might be a shopping list). In these circumstances, a child with a pencil may have a better memory than an adult without one. If we are a little uneasy at this way of talking, it could be because of our immersion in orthodox psychological thinking. The orthodoxy requires that "memory" is a private cognitive function. It encourages dismissing the adult–child performance difference in my example as having been contrived from a trivial sleight of hand. Yet, a child's superior remembering under these circumstances does confront us with something that it is important to understand and important to incorporate into our theorising. I mean the idea that higher cognitive functions are mediated activities. What we achieve—what we remember, for example—will often depend on our histories of appropriating the use of certain technologies. Although it may now sound eccentric to refer to pencil-and-paper as "technology", that is surely what it still is. In relation to the development of cultures—and thus on the scale of *historical* time—the impact of literacy and literate practices has been thoroughly studied (e.g. Goody & Watt, 1968; Ong, 1977). Certainly, the making of lists and the recording of events in writing brought about radical changes in social relations. The availability of written records also challenged the authoritative basis of knowledge within cultures. Finally, some will argue that the individuals within literate cultures come to think in different ways, that is, think differently even at times when the technology is not to hand (Luria, 1976). A number of psychologists (e.g. Olson, 1986) have extrapolated this historical analysis to describe the effects of literacy within individual lifetimes (i.e. its effects on children growing up in a literate culture).

The presence of this "cultural" tradition of analysis within research on (cognitive) development is encouraging—even if its influence still remains modest. It represents a willingness to characterise intelligent action as mediated; as action always needing to be organised in relation to a material and social world. Thus, it is a view that takes seriously the context of action, making it central to any framework of explanation. It should be clear that a comparable perspective could be mobilised to support the study of *social* development. This might be expected if we are now more comfortable with this situated analysis of children's *cognitive* functioning; an analysis requiring us to see intelligence as activity-in-context, activity always organised in relation to certain technologies and rituals (including, for example, writing and written messages). However, in practice, we seem slow to construct a similar orientation towards the topics of social development. This position—that we must conceptualise early social experience in relation to its historical, material and cultural circumstances—is implicit in the analysis that follows. Others have explored the conceptual framework more fully elsewhere (e.g. various essays collected by Elder, Modell, & Parke, 1993).

My arguments predict that the topic of electronic media will be pursued only on the margins of research in developmental psychology. This seems to be the case. Consider its representation, at the time of writing, in two leading periodicals. Volume 66 (1995) of *Child Development* contains 122 articles, only one of which takes media as a concern. Volumes 59–60 (1995) of the *Journal of Experimental Child Psychology* contains 46 articles, none of which have this concern. Of course, I do not mean to imply that there is *no* literature on this topic, but that literature is scattered across the disciplines of, in particular, communication, sociology, education, and cultural studies. At an earlier time, developmental psychologists did occupy this territory. Now they have retreated—leaving a rather modest impact. Part of my purpose in this chapter, is to make the case for returning. I have argued above that the study of social development must be the study of action-in-contexts. Technology and media provide rich and pervasive examples of that context—in particular, determining the manner in which human communication takes place. The following discussion slowly moves towards examples of research that is attempting a more "situated" form of study in this area.

That said, what follows cannot be construed as a *comprehensive* review of the literature that is available. My more modest aim is to suggest a geography for the hazardous landscape of discourse about media and its impacts on development. I shall endeavour to make some summary judgements and to point any interested reader towards more detailed sources that are more thorough in their review. Certainly, I shall identify the texts that I have found most useful for navigating this territory. As declared earlier, the focus of interest is electronic media. In practice, much research has been on television and my own discussion will reflect this. New information technology will be the second most represented theme. I have organised the discussion in relation to three perspectives that I judge to be relatively distinct in the literature. The first orients to electronic media as sources of social representations. Here, the recurring question has been: What are the psychological effects on children of exposure to particular forms of such representation? The second perspective orients to media as a form of cultural artefact around which social life must get organised. This is an ecological orientation: It asks how children's social development is influenced by the various designs for social living that these technologies afford. The third perspective orients to media as a resource for discourse and social negotiation. Here, we are interested in how the content of media spreads into social life to influence the sense people make of their broader experience. As the discussion proceeds across these three sections, the empirical data becomes gradually scarcer whereas, arguably, the theoretical dimension becomes more sophisticated. Then, in a final section, I identify a theme on which I believe much of the discussion sensibly converges— namely, how exposure to electronic media may bear on children's own status as psychologists of social life.

ELECTRONIC MEDIA AND THE DELIVERY OF SOCIAL REPRESENTATIONS

Popular perceptions of how media relate to social life tend to dwell on the issue of social representation—we tend to worry about (or, occasionally, celebrate) the manner in which our ways of living are portrayed. There has always been a subversive dimension to the mass distribution of cultural knowledge. As is often noted, even Plato predicted dangerous consequences of exposing the populace to communications media. He expressed concern over the potentially uncertain impact of *writing* on society; in particular its potential for corrupting youthful minds. That the young are vulnerable when exposed to mass media has been a persistent concern of adults, although one particularly visible within the last 100 years. Plato's worry about the dangers of writing was never a pervasive concern. Indeed, some have argued (e.g. Postman, 1982) that print literacy actually sharpened (rather than undermined) the separation between childhood and the adult world. However, starting at the turn of the century with an interest in the impact of dime novels (Barker, 1989; Kline, 1993), the modern mass media have been frequently identified as a subversive influence on a vulnerable youth. Parents, teachers, and other adults have been surprised and disheartened to discover that children's spontaneous preferences are often for the more bland or the less wholesome media products on offer. Spigel (1992) documents the lively public debate that has surrounded these apparent preferences, and the widespread belief that media producers have failed to create a balanced range of material for children. She suggests that one side effect of this concern was the invasion of family life by "experts", causing a curious but lasting professionalisation of parenthood.

Certainly, popular concern has demanded political responses. There have been a number of public inquiries into the issue of "media effects", including some that have sponsored substantial new research initiatives. The 1930s Payne Fund studies of children and cinema urged caution over the undesirable effects of too much exposure to the movies. Given that "regular" exposure at that time might amount to no more than once a week for teenagers (Dale, 1935), it is understandable that the growth of television—with much more frequent viewing—came to be cause for a greater concern. Much of that concern has focused on the possible impact of exposure to violent programming during early childhood. As research has accumulated on this issue there has been a growing sense of frustration that either researchers could not agree or that they fell back on too heavily qualified conclusions. A much-cited example is the judgement reached in a review by Schramm, Lyle, and Parker (1961):

> For *some* children, under *some* conditions, some television is harmful. For *other* children under the same conditions, or for the same children under other conditions, it may be beneficial. For *most* children, under *most* conditions, *most* television is probably neither particularly harmful nor particularly beneficial.

This pleases nobody. Naturally, the popular press will be dissatisfied—typically, they exercise a rhetoric of damning "so-called experts" (usually without naming offenders). Buckingham (1994) discusses this reaction at length and expresses his own irritation with it. Unfortunately, the media scholars themselves are similarly uneasy over the state of their colleagues' research. For example, Buckingham makes a vigorous attack on television effects studies, leaving a strong impression of "so-calledness" about expertise in this area. In short, the experts also are at odds. Indeed, it is common for reviews of the topic simply to write off the bulk of relevant research (Buckingham, 1994, p. 81): "...much of it based on simplistic forms of behaviourism, and functionalist theories of socialisation... Children are perceived here as mere blank slates on which television scrawls its harmful and indelible messages". Like journalists, dissatisfied scholars are also coy about naming offenders. Of course, the reality is that very few media effects researchers actually declare that they are behaviourists and none state that children are blank slates or that the messages of television are indelible. The critical observer of this literature has to judge whether researchers are acting *as if* they believed such things—and, it must be said, sometimes that does seem to be the case.

Perhaps this bickering and inconclusiveness is part of the reason why research on media and social development attracts little respectability within the mainstream of psychology. A typical—and telling—attitude is captured within one eminent experimental psychologist's view, as expressed in the science pages of an up-market UK newspaper (Morgan, 1994, p. 9). Morgan summarises the status quo on television violence research as follows:

The problem with most socially important questions is that they are virtually impossible to solve by good experiments... Such questions should be left alone until new methods are invented to deal with them. And where opinion is more important than scientific evidence, it would be useful if experts learned to say 'Ignoramus—we don't know'... A period of silence on this topic from the experts would be welcome.

This piece is interesting for the insight it offers into a (psychology) establishment's perception of social science research—that it can only be based on controlled experiments. The piece is less bullish in offering advice for those concerned laypeople who remain uneasy about the role of mass media in children's lives. The reality is that this popular debate will continue. Therefore, the public have a right to expect social scientists to inform the manner in which it is carried out. In short, the experience and findings of researchers should enjoy significant notice within the arenas where such things are discussed—however imperfect their methods.

I have two further comments on the methodological worries articulated by Morgan. The first is that it is not the case that this area is bereft of experiments. The second is that it is misleading to suggest the experiment is the only—or indeed the preferred—method for casting light on how media influences social development. On the first point, we should note that there are three species of experiment that have been reported in the literature. First, there is the tradition of laboratory study in which the short-term effects of watching certain film or video programming is evaluated. Control and experimental groups of children are observed in structured play following a period of such viewing (e.g. Bandura, Ross, & Ross, 1963). The force of these studies is to demonstrate significant short-term carry-over of both violent and prosocial programming. Second, there is a tradition of "field experiments" which counter some of the criticisms attracted by the laboratory work: In particular, that the laboratory scenario tends to suggest to participants that the experimenters are condoning—even encouraging—violence. In field experiments, the research context and purpose is kept carefully concealed: Participants do not know they are under study. Behaviour subsequent to various exposures to television material is monitored in an unconstrained social situation. Wood, Wong, and Chachere (1991) have reported a meta-analysis of 28 studies conducted in this manner. They conclude that there are reliable short-term effects on behaviour when young people are exposed to violent programming. In the framework of psychosocial research, these effects are typically "small to moderate" (although, of course, this says nothing of the magnitude of *cumulative* exposure to such programming). Third, there is a tradition of "natural experiments". These arise from very unusual opportunities to observe a community before, during, and after a transition to adopting television. Two such cases have been documented where television arrived late to a community for arbitrary geographical reasons (Murray & Kippax, 1978; Williams & Handford, 1986). In both cases, there is evidence for changes in children's behaviour, including evidence of more violent forms of play. So, in sum, there is experimental research on this topic and it does tend to show an impact of television violence on children's attitudes and behaviour.

My second reaction to Morgan's methodological worries (outlined earlier) was to suggest that experimental method is not the only route towards being more confident about causal relations. The work of Eron and colleagues illustrates how sophisticated statistical analysis (cross-lagged correlations) can help establish the direction of effects between television viewing and aggressive behaviour. Starting with a cohort of 8-year-olds, they found on 10-year follow-up a significant impact (for boys) of earlier TV viewing on aggressiveness in play (Lefkowitz, Eron, Walder, & Huesmann, 1977). A 22-year follow-up (Huesmann, Eron, Lefkowitz, & Walder, 1984) found a similar association between early television viewing and seriousness of convicted crimes. Singer and Singer (1981) report a study of nursery schoolchildren in which the same statistical techniques are used to establish a causal relation between violent content of television programming and subsequent aggressiveness in playground encounters.

Even though the methodological rigour of these examples is impressive, extrapolation from their findings must still be carried out with care. Yet the majority of those who have reviewed the massive corpus of research in this area are in general agreement that there are impacts of media violence on the behaviour, attitudes and cognitions of children (Rubinstein, 1983; Surgeon General's Report, 1972). Although, as indicated earlier, there do remain dissenting voices in this debate (e.g. Cumberbatch & Howitt, 1989). More recently, the terms of interest in this issue have been extended by the considerable popularity of interactive video games—many of which involve violent themes (Provenzo, 1991). Early reviews of research in this area suggest that there are similar effects on the behaviour of regular users (Griffiths, 1991). Moreover, the active nature of the engagement with this material may serve to heighten its impact. One study shows that users (compared with mere observers) experience greater cognitive and physiological after effects from a violent virtual reality game (Calvert & Tan, 1994).

Despite a certain consensus of opinion, the findings of "media effects" research has not had a dramatic impact on the public, on media professionals, or on politicians. Indeed, a survey of media researchers themselves revealed that they resisted the findings of their peers—downplaying the relevance of television as an influence on their own children's development (Bybee, Robinson, & Turow, 1985). Perhaps the reality is that these conclusions about an impact of media-portrayed violence just do not feel right to us. Instead, what may be felt is that, if there is truth in the findings, then this truth must apply to other people's families and children. Such personal responses suggest shortcomings in the way we react to children's media habits—on a casual basis. First, our own more informal observations of children and media may suffer from a failure to *integrate* the significance of children's sustained and repetitive exposure to certain material (each individual viewing occasion seems trivial enough in itself). Second, we may fail to take into account the ways in which these experiences may be elaborated and developed at other times, when the programming is over (a point to which I shall return later). Both of these observations are echoed in (and may be reinforced by) a certain rigid style of thinking promoted by the dominant research paradigms, especially the factorial experiment. This style of investigation may encourage us to conceptualise the issues in terms of discrete, localised "effects"—instead of influences that may be more cumulative, incremental, or counterbalancing. Moreover, the terminology of the experiment encourages naïve analysis of media content into a taxonomy of "inputs" and, thus, we may overlook the interpretative contribution of the observers themselves in defining what is actually experienced.

I will illustrate these claims more fully. This requires a widening of the present discussion to embrace research themes additional to the popular ones of violence and aggression. If a focus on the experiment as favoured methodology introduced one set of constraints on our conceptual thinking, then a focus on the violence issue created another class of constraint. However, during the 1970s, research interest spread to include the impact of media on two other dimensions of social development: first, the formation of social stereotypes and, second, the development of prosocial behaviour.

By "stereotype", I mean some broad theory about the nature of people in a given societal setting. One issue we might worry about in a media-rich society is whether the mass media systematically promote stereotypes in the form of particular world views—particular templates for interpreting the people, places, and times we live in. There is an influential tradition of television effects research that is based on this model of the medium's impact. It is termed "cultivation theory" (e.g., Gerbner & Gross, 1976). This theory supposes that media effects take place via their impact on structures of belief, rather than through processes of identification or through simple translations into specific behaviours. Moreover, such influences of media are gradual and cumulative. For example, one belief that might arise from intensive exposure to television is: "The world is a violent place". The theory would expect some such particular belief to be cultivated if research reveals that the media are promoting such a world view. So, the first move in a research strategy is to conduct content analysis of media programming. The second move involves applying correlational techniques to determine if heavy users of the media in question also report attitudes that are consistent with the particular world view shown to be cultivated. In behavioural terms, the direction of psychological effect is not then always straightforward. For example, a cultivated belief that the world is a dangerous place might encourage individual aggression but it might also lead to passivity.

So, cultivation theory goes beyond the framework of much "effects" research by: (1) acknowledging the potentially cumulative effect of media exposure, and (2) acknowledging the inherent complexity of outcomes that arise because of the personal meanings and interpretations that individuals bring to the theories that might be cultivated. There are grounds for recognising that media can influence social development in this general way. For example, Signorielli (1991) has shown interesting effects for young people. Heavy television viewing adolescents have distorted ambitions in relation to the world of work: These are correlated with portrayals of employment in this media (they expect high status work and expect the demands of work to be relatively easy). Other kinds of distortion in social understanding (e.g. of expectations of marriage) were also traced to TV portrayals and intensive exposure to them (Signorielli, 1993).

A second recent research theme that is helpful in sharpening our perception of influence mechanisms in this area is work on prosocial effects. Some years ago, beleaguered media representatives began to respond to arguments about the dangers of violent programming by raising the possibility that media might have a set of parallel influences that were socially constructive (prosocial) rather than socially destructive. *Sesame Street* (seeded by the Head Start preschool intervention initiative) was one much-cited example of a successful and engaging programme with prosocial ambitions. Moreover, programming need not be explicitly "educational" to be successful in this respect. Some of the more wholesome TV drama series also enjoyed favourable analyses—programmes such as *The Waltons* for instance (Baran, Chase, & Courtright, 1979). Yet, still there has been much more research on the impacts of aggression than there has on other potential psychological impacts. I suggest one reason for this is that prosocial influences are far harder to conceptualise in the preferred analytic language of media "input". That is, recognising, categorising and evaluating particular media instances of prosocial exposure is not such an easy exercise for researchers. Probably, we feel it is easier to do such systematising for the case of violence: Violent acts *seem* more readily definable in terms of their surface (behavioural) characteristics. However, that impression may be seductive but, in the end, misleading. *All* psychologically interesting portrayals may demand more careful analysis prior to any categorisation of their putative content. In practice, what this entails is greater sensitivity by the researcher to the nature of viewers' interpretative attitudes.

These observations help us progress beyond the research traditions that have dominated the earlier literature on media effects, and they help us notice why the outcomes of that research are often hard for us personally to appropriate, or to live by. If findings seem too coarse-grained, too fragmentary, or simply too unconvincing, it has to do with a lack of conceptual sophistication on the part of researchers. The core problem has been one of failing to conceptualise the "viewer" as actively engaged with media—as making a personal investment of interpretation (rather than merely being a recipient of stock inputs with their supposedly universal meanings). As Buckingham (1993a, p. 19) puts it for television: "The narrow focus on the isolated encounter between the individual child and the all-powerful screen that characterises a great deal of academic research does not begin to do justice to the complexity of this process". Arguably, our collective perception of contact with modern media has been too influenced by vivid but misleading metaphors, such as Winn's (1977) "plug-in drug" and Marcuse's (1966) "one-dimensional mind". This is not to take a relaxed position on the final impact of mass media on social development, rather it is to discourage lazy analysis based only on the rhetoric of narcotics or human vulnerability.

If we take seriously the idea that children are active interpreters of media experiences, then we cannot be surprised that the preferred research designs generate heavily qualified conclusions of the kind cited earlier (i.e. "...some effects on some children some of the time..."). At most, existing studies furnish findings that give us cause for concern. Yet, as a resource for guiding policy, the bulk of research barely scratches the surface of a complex developmental problem. So, what is the route for penetrating this surface—such that we might acquire greater insights into electronic media and social development? The active-viewer diagnosis implies that solutions will be difficult. If what makes the difference is how individual children *experience* media programming, then this suggests any "effects" will be predictable only in the light of knowing rather particular things about those individual children. Yet it may not be helpful if the research tradition *only* becomes a catalogue of case studies. Claims at some level of generality must be sought.

What I have been arguing might be recruited to the view that media effects are "a cognitive issue". That is, what happens depends upon the sense-making of individual children as they engage with media. However, it would be unfortunate if this encouraged a form of analysis that was preoccupied with the individual, "cognitive" child considered as an isolated unit. For I believe the way to make progress must be to recognise that media use is located within (and contributes to) a wider context of social experience. If television is the most popular media encounter, then the most common representation of the most popular medium is the "plugged-in" child, absorbed by a screen. Perhaps it is therefore not surprising that research on media effects should take this isolated viewer as its main preoccupation. Certainly, psychological theorising in this area has been relatively asocial in its terms of reference. Ideas about how the impact of televison is mediated certainly have focused on the individual: The key processes are either associationist (imitation and reinforcement), psychodynamic (identification), or cognitivist. In the last case, those processes might adopt the computational flavour of semantic networks (Berkowitz, 1984) or the more activity-based flavour of script theory (Huesmann, 1986). I do not mean to imply that such over-arching theorising is necessarily unhelpful. However, it is unlikely to take us very far as long as it decouples the individual child from a wider social context of meaning-making in which media experiences are situated.

In the following sections, I take up this point and illustrate research traditions that have been more socially oriented in this sense. First, I shall consider the ways in which electronic media exist as technologies, influencing the organisation and orchestration of social interaction. These are artefacts that enter into and re-configure those relations. Second, I shall consider another form of intrusion: How the content of media programming furnishes narratives and representations that serve as a recognised reference point in children's more discursive interactions with other people. The line dividing these two discussions is not sharp. Both concern the way in which experience with electronic media intrudes into the broader organisation of children's social life either with a greater orientation to the material artefact itself and adjustments of social life around it (next section), or with a greater orientation to the content of media programming and how it is mobilised in social interactions at other times (the section after next).

ELECTRONIC MEDIA AND CONFIGURATIONS OF SOCIAL LIFE

Research discussed in the preceding section suggests (albeit in heavily qualified terms) that media may exert an influence on social development through furnishing particular representations of a viewer's societal context. In contrast, in this section, the influence to be examined arises more from the way in which engagement with media configures distinctive possibilities for interaction with other people. Lull (1980) in the United States and Morley (1986) in the United Kingdom have been particularly clear in encouraging an analysis of media effects that stress the way in which these technologies enter into an existing pattern of social life—the way in which they afford or deny certain forms of interaction with others. Research guided by this concern has, again, largely concerned television although we shall make some reference below to the significance of new information technology.

The simplest way in which media exerts such influences is through being a "thief of time" (Condry, 1993). Andreason (1994) collates some telling survey statistics relating to the penetration of television into US homes and, thus its place within children's leisure time. The 1950s was the period when television ownership increased most dramatically—from around 9 per cent in 1950 to around 87 per cent in 1960. Perhaps surprisingly, the hours spent viewing in the typical family has not changed greatly since those early days; a shallow upward trend hovering around an average of five hours per day. However, for children, this is a significant portion of their spare time. Condry (1989) estimates that it is the third most common-place activity for American children, after sleeping and school. Kline (1993) argues that it was this massive disturbance to the dynamic of family life that catalysed the early concerns about television effects on children, that is, the theme of this section rather than the (now more familiar) "content" themes of my preceding section. What seems to have been most striking to early commentators was the simple time-consuming nature of the medium—the content of programmes was less of an issue. After all, people argued, children watching television appeared well enough aware it was not "real". Evidently, the pattern of public concern has altered. On the one hand, it seems we now fail to notice the sheer presence of this medium in our lives; on the other hand, we certainly no longer take for granted the benign nature of programming merely because it is recognised as fictional.

Television does seem to have become a pervasive feature of family life. Of course, the fact that it is switched on does not mean that it gets contin-uous attention. Viewing of the viewers themselves suggests that young children at home are only attending to the programmes between 50 per cent and 70 per cent of the time they are in sight of them (Anderson, Field, Collins, Lorch, & Nathan, 1985). However it is noteworthy that, when they are viewing, the patterns of television use from an early age are quite stable. One two-year longitudinal study revealed that within a sample of children between 3 and 5 years and 5 and 7 years, there were consistent individual viewing patterns and preferences (Huston, Wright, Rice, Kerkman, & St. Peters, 1990). This same study also showed striking varia-bility among children in terms of how much time they spent viewing: From children watching not at all, to children watching up to 76 hours per week. There was a slight drop in viewing during the 5 to 7 years period (perhaps reflecting more time in school). Other studies have shown another significant age-correlated drop to be in the adolescent years (Barwise & Ehrenberg, 1988).

Observations about time allocation begin to matter when we ask questions about children's total budgeting of time in relation to all other sources of social experience. In particular, it will be of interest to know how far other significant activities are squeezed out for some children by this substantial investment in television viewing. Unfortunately, this is a difficult question to answer empirically. The best guidance we have comes from the studies of those communities where television was introduced relatively late (because, for geographical reasons, signal transmission was blocked). Observing such introductions (with controlled comparisons) Williams and Handford (1986, p. 182) comment: "Television apparently has little if any impact on the number of community activities available, but it has a noticeable negative effect on participation in those activities". Effects were particularly apparent for children's active involvement with sports. These researchers also comment that, on the arrival of television, older citizens seemed especially vulnerable to becoming dislocated from the local community; the researchers speculate that this has an indirect effect on children, who would grow up with less chance of informal contact with this group. In short, a "stay-indoors" effect was documented. Possibly such a trend rings true for us. We might expect it to emerge from a simple tracing of time use in society at large over the full period of television adoption. However, effects documented only in that way could be due to a variety of influences (e.g. suburbanisation or parents being more cautious about a more dangerous world). The "natural experiment" described earlier is important in directly implicating television.

More "staying indoors" does not entail for children a more socially impoverished experience; it might give rise to stronger family bonds. Spigel (1992) provides a scholarly and engaging account of how television did influence family routine in its early years. She draws on representations of television and family life as portrayed at that time in other media; particularly popular women's magazines. One observation she makes is that television came to play a role in the management of family discipline. Here is a quote taken from a 1955 article in *Better Homes and Gardens* (Spigel, 1992, p. 57): "After performing the routine of dressing, tidying up his room ... Steve knows he can ... watch his favourite TV show. His attitude is now so good he has volunteered to set the table for breakfast and help his little sister dress". It is unlikely that the medium is now such an effective device for domestic engineering! Yet, we may assume issues of access and choice will surface within families and, thereby, sharpen children's sensitivity to authority, fairness, and family affiliations. In interviews with London 7- to 12-year-olds and (separately) with their parents, Buckingham (1993b) reports that the parents vigorously profess commitments to monitoring and policing what gets viewed—although often what was claimed did not match well with their own children's account of the same events. Interestingly, the children themselves most often talked about "television-and-family" in terms of disputes with siblings. The "unjustly wounded" and "peace-making parent" scenarios were commonly described. The sibling reference is interesting as it illustrates well my argument for adopting an ecological orientation towards the technology. When we do this, we note that television has characteristics that ensure it will often become the focus for a certain variety of social dispute and negotiation. For example, it offers (age-variable) choice, yet allows at a given time for the viewing of only one channel. So, experiences relevant to children's social development get organised in relation to the properties of this domestic artefact: Social life is fashioned to fit some of its demands. Dunn's (1988) claims regarding the psychological potency of sibling social dynamics make this particular example all the more significant.

Time allocation and negotiated viewing are not the only senses in which media enter into the dynamic of family interaction. Another point of influence will be co-viewing; the extent and manner in which children share their media involvement with others. To what extent does this living room technology support joint activity and talk among members of a domestic community? Timme, Eccles, and O'Brien (1985) report that it is the most frequently shared activity within American families. However, such observations (made in 1981) need cautious treatment. The advent of video recorders and inexpensive second television sets may mean that domestic viewing is becoming more solitary. One recent family diary study involving 271 3- to 5-year-olds reveals that the majority of child-oriented television programmes (around 75 per cent of them) were viewed without parents being present (St. Peters, Fitch, Huston, Wright, & Eakins, 1991). Is this modest level of co-viewing to be regretted? Messaris has argued (e.g. Messaris & Sarett, 1981) that shared television is potentially a significant reference point for developing conversation with young children. Yet, at the present stage of research, we can do no more than recognise that this is a tantalising dimension of difference among families. Much has been made of the significance of talk with young children mediated by reading books with adults. Lemish and Rice (1986) demonstrate that joint watching of television can sustain just as rich conversational opportunities. Moreover, compared with joint book reading, it is sustained further into childhood and is more naturally knitted into a stream of local activity (rather than being a special, put-aside time). Although these observations about circumstances for mediated talk are usually made in the context of language development, participation in organised, interpretative conversation must be relevant to the broader course of social development.

Some of the "thief of time" worries discussed above are more keenly voiced in relation to young people's use of computers. In the 1970s, MIT computer scientist Weizenbaum (1976) highlighted the phenomenon of "hollow-eyed youths" absorbed with computer technology. Turkle (1984) documented and interpreted their obsessions in an influential book written from within this community. Yet, the fears projected from such accounts have not proved to be true. Computer enthusiasts certainly still exist but accounts of their interests and lifestyles suggest something relatively innocent—even misunderstood (Shotton, 1989). Moreover, the uses to which that technology is put have changed: Powerful user interfaces have deflected some of the interest (and need for) absorption in writing code. These machines are more "convivial tools" than seductive mechanisms to be programmed. This shift finds some support in surveys of young people who are "heavy users". Rocheleau (1995) describes a five-year study covering a stratified sample drawn from 51 primary and secondary schools. One trend reported was a decline in heavy use across this period. Another was the disappearance of gender differences in this measure. This suggests that the technology is becoming a (gender-neutral) benign feature of the domestic environment, rather than a source of obsessive absorption.

An exception to this might be suspected for one species of computer-related activity; namely, interactive video games. Although use of these games has greatly increased (Provenzo, 1991) and there are reported cases of extreme involvement, there is little evidence that their use is having a serious effect on social engagement. Lin and Lepper (1987) studied 210 children in grades 4–6 asking them questions about computer and game use as well as other questions about their leisure time. Their teachers described these same children in terms of their intellectual and social dispositions. First, no grounds were found for concluding that video game use was supplanting other forms of recreation. Second, few teacher ratings correlated with computer or game use—except that video arcade users were rated as more impulsive in school. Third, there were only small negative correlations between game use and measures of academic achievement and no relations with sociability. Sakamoto (1994) studied 500 primary schoolchildren and also found no correlation between video game use and measures of social skill and social understanding.

Information technology is evolving so rapidly that it feels dangerous to draw conclusions at this point in time. In terms of the traditional fears of children becoming socially isolated through computer and game use, there is very little basis for believing this is yet a widespread problem. The direction in which the technology is currently developing is particularly interesting in relation to our considerations of social development. For it is the application to communication (e.g. the Internet) that is currently so fashionable. At present, very few young people enjoy regular use of network-based interaction. Yet where they do (in school), studies suggest that this can be a potent basis for extending children's sensitivity to the circumstances of other children's lives (Crook, 1994; Riel, 1995). It is difficult to anticipate how far children will be drawn into computer-mediated communication, and hard to anticipate the forms it might take. However, a sense of the possible future is conveyed in Stone's (1995) review of network systems for creating communities of interacting computer users.

In this section I have considered electronic media as technology around which social life gets organised. I have suggested that significant aspects of children's interaction with others (particularly in the family) does get configured in relation to their contact with these technologies. The following section pursues this theme of locating media experiences in a broader social context, but does so more in relation to content—media programming—and the various uses to which such material gets put in the elaboration of relations with other people.

ELECTRONIC MEDIA AS RESOURCE WITHIN SOCIAL RELATIONS

Although I have identified "social relations" as a focus for the present section, a starting point for this discussion might be the general concept of "play". The limited scope of much media effects research has prompted many commentators to argue for more concern with how the media influences childhood *imagination*, as it gets expressed in their playful lives—solitary and social (cf. Cullingford, 1984; Kline, 1993). Observational study of early play suggests two lines of influence from media. One arises from the dramatic narratives that are the currency of much programming; the other arises from the defining of certain material objects as playthings (i.e. their becoming toys).

The former influence is the most straightforward. The dominant mass media (films and television) tell stories and, as with all storytelling, children are thereby given access to possible circumstances, possible worlds. The developmental significance of such experiences has been widely recognised within psychology (Bettelheim, 1976; Humphrey, 1984). Modern mass media, being a rich source of such material, may therefore serve to resource children's imaginative exploration. Observational studies suggest that children freely mobilise television characters and television scenarios in the development of their own sociodramatic play (Davie, Hutt, Vincent, & Mason, 1984; Singer & Singer, 1981). Just how *well* served children are in this respect is a matter for debate. The early innovators seemed sensitive to such opportunities. Walt Disney referred to his own enterprise in animation as "imagineering". However, television opened up markets for a rather less challenging product. Designers and technicians recognised how the animated cartoon format could be diluted to allow more economical production: simpler, movements against a fixed background allowed reduction in costs, while character recognition was kept strong through stylised voices with easy-to-identify catchphrases (Huckleberry Hound, Yogi Bear, and so forth). The children seemed to love it, but there has been little opportunity to assess the loss (or gain) to fantasy play of the shift away from a more idealistic, narratively subtle form of "imagineering".

One outgrowth of these developments that has received some modest research attention is the particular phenomenon of toy tie-ins. The appropriation of "things" into playful exploration is a familiar aspect of childhood life. Through such representations, it is possible for children to experiment with reality—a dramatisation that is an important part of the developmental process (Erikson, 1964). However, it is easy to forget that the *manufactured* toy is a relatively recent cultural invention. Even 100 years ago, children would most typically make do with "found" objects to resource their experimentation. Mass media have increasingly acted to define children's preferences in respect of the modern toy. It is likely that, for example, trends in (media) character-marketing are influencing the scope and content of children's pretence. Kline (1993) argues that character toys (Power Rangers, Care Bears, and so forth) are shown to lead to very rigid styles of play (such as war or fashion games) that minimise a creative dynamic, maximising instead the imitative, reproductive dimension of play. Kinder (1991) has explored children's awareness of the "intertextuality" that emerges from a cross-referencing of topics across different media (as in the marketing of Ninja Turtles).

These remarks about pretend play are most relevant to the social development of younger children. Yet, beyond the early years, similar themes relating to the influence of media arise. However, that influence will later be manifest more discursively; more in the *conversational* elaboration of shared media experiences. This might apply particularly to children's interactions with their peers. Within those arenas, participants explore areas of mutual knowledge; from such explorations arise enriched social understandings. The point at issue here is how far media programming serves to resource this form of discursive exploration.

A number of researchers have investigated this question through analysis of how small groups of children talk about their media understanding, particularly in relation to television (Buckingham, 1993b; Hodge & Tripp, 1986). Such material is often gathered in school-based conversations with visiting researchers (Buckingham, 1993b, p. 63) "...interested in finding out what children think about television". Naturally, such orchestration limits the inferences that should be made. In particular, it is hard to infer how far media events and characters populate the *spontaneous* talk of these young people as it occurs outside of interviews. However, the clarity and vigour of their opinions suggest that media programming is likely to be a significant discursive resource in this sense. What is also clearly documented through this research is how the articulation of views about media characters and events permit children to explore aspects of their own personal identity. Buckingham illustrates how media programming creates reference points for various positionings and counter-positionings in relation to issues of class, gender, race, or other personal attributes.

In this chapter I have argued that the inertia of much media effects research can only be overcome by orienting to the broader social context of media exposure. As Buckingham (1993b, p. 99) puts it: "...what children choose to talk about, and the ways in which they do so, needs to be understood in terms of the context in which the talk occurs". Unfortunately, this worthy sentiment applies just as forcefully to the circumstances of talking to researchers. The analysis of semi-structured conversations with children is useful but problematic. It is a useful way forward in that it helps us recognise young people's interpretative sophistication and, thereby, to understand why the "active viewer" is a necessary conception for enriching any analysis of media "input". However, this small group research technique is also problematic. Although motivated by a concern for respecting context, it tends to overlook the constraints arising from the settings that it creates itself. Neither the group nor the individual participants are ascribed any kind of "history"; the conversations typically take place in schools and are configured to the format of intimate class discussions. Even though the resulting talk can be very telling, one is bound to worry how far it manifests merely the kind of discourse understood by the children to be normally required in this form of encounter.

How else might the reach of media into children's broader social lives be studied? One solution is to adopt an ethnographic approach. This would involve researchers in a more intimate relation to children's everyday lives—with a view to identifying the spontaneous mobilisation of media themes into routine social interactions. There are a small number of studies conceived in this spirit. An interesting example is an observer's account by Walkerdine (1993) of how a video-recorded movie (*Annie*) acts as a point of reference for the members of one chaotically stressed family, resourcing them to negotiate understandings of their circumstances. Walkerdine recounts how an alcoholic central character in the film triggers for the daughter in this family an observation about her mother ("Mummy's drunk") and then services the mother's own extended conversation with the researcher about how she herself is misrepresented and misunderstood ("...they say I'm drunk but I'm not"). The idea is that the media presence in this situation provides a vehicle for some mutual sense-making of their predicaments. This form of participant analysis gives a compelling impression of how media may indeed impinge on the development of children's social understandings. However, interpretations are inherently difficult in these contexts. In this case, for example, the relevant sense-making has been anchored to a moment of attention to events in the film. Yet, from the account given, all of the talk reported might equally have been anchored to another (media-irrelevant) moment—the researcher refusing the child's offer of a lager ("...she says no thank you very much"). Perhaps this interpretation is not convincing to anyone with the researcher's full knowledge of the circumstances. But the basis for deriving an interpretation remains problematic.

I believe this last example of research on media in children's lives illustrates the most promising (but neglected) format for serious study of the topic. Yet the example also illustrates that the research required must be careful and rigorous in authenticating its claims. When this is achieved, it offers the best opportunity for revealing the dynamics of media presence in social life. These then might form the inspiration for a more effective deployment of other traditional techniques—many of which, I have argued here, have so far been applied to this topic in a rather heavy-handed manner. These are personal remarks about methodology. I shall finish my discussion with some similarly personal comments about theory. In particular, I wish to highlight a relatively unexplored link between electronic media and fashionable ideas in the mainstream of psychological theorising about social development.

ELECTRONIC MEDIA AND CHILDREN'S PSYCHOLOGICAL THEORISING

What I term (at the time of writing) "fashionable" psychological thinking is the lively interest in children's own theorising about other people and their mental lives. Naturalistic observations of children's domestic worlds has led some researchers to emphasise the child's curiosity about human emotions, intentions, and motivations (Dunn, 1988). They suggest, in fact, that children's natural interest in the world is best described by viewing them as little psychologists (Bennett, 1993) rather than as little physicists (arguably the metaphor inherited from a Piagetian tradition of developmental thinking). The idea that media representations are relevant for such a childhood agenda might be derived from considering the ideas of two rather different theory-makers, each working on broad canvasses. Nicholas Humphrey is concerned with the origins of consciousness and, in particular, the cultivation of self-knowledge through exposure to culturally organised story-telling rituals (Humphrey, 1984). Joseph Meyrowitz is concerned with the role of electronic media in challenging traditional barriers between the childhood world and the psychological complexity of adult life (Meyrowitz, 1985).

Humphrey (1984) explores an evolutionary approach to the origins of human consciousness. He argues that the capacity for predicting the behaviour of other members of the species would have had great survival value within certain forms of socially organised living. The peculiarly human capacity to theorise about other people's minds (their desires, expectations, beliefs, etc.) is linked to the emergence of a reflective form of self-understanding. Humphrey argues that family relations, dreaming, and play each evolved to resource the developing child's opportunity to gather data about, and experiment with, the psychological dimension of human life. Moreover, culture follows nature in this venture. Humphrey links the development of the performance arts and of formalised story telling to the need to enrich and further extend our resource base for cultivating self-knowledge (Humphrey, 1984, p. 94): "...when spectators outnumber actors, the institution is presumably serving the interests of the former as well as the latter". So, the role of spectator provides opportunities for vicarious forms of emotional experience. It also provides material that, Humphrey argues, can be richly elaborated later in playful extensions and explorations. Of course, I have already indicated in the previous section that this playful elaboration of media themes is something that is commonly observed in naturalistic studies of childhood. My point here will be merely to suggest that for considerations of social development, the role of media representations of psychological themes is particularly interesting. The "resourcing" that they provide might be especially potent.

Meyrowitz (1985) places a particular judgement on the role of modern media in transforming social development through routes very much of the kind I am introducing (i.e. through presenting children with significant resources for thinking psychologically). He mobilises a rich documentation of how electronic media have developed in the last 50 years, arguing that they have served to remove some of the barriers that conceal the intimate world of adulthood from children's experience. The vivid and probing forms in which society is portrayed on television (in particular) allows children more readily to encounter the "backstage" world of adult life. His thesis is sophisticated and carefully argued but it is also controversial. Some may find the thesis encourages misplaced nostalgia and questionable censorship. Such implications might well be derived from Postman's (1982) more popular version of these ideas, but they are less evident in Meyrowitz's work. However, this is less important than the more general point that emerges: Namely, that modern mass media furnish for children a particularly rich basis for identifying and analysing the psychological world.

Such a claim, if made at all, would normally be made in relation to the *content* of media programming—the particular events portrayed. However, I would like to conclude by making this same point in relation to modern media *style*—the very process of dramatic representation. It has been observed that children are increasingly media-wise in the sense of being alert to the technical and stylistic devices of production. From his discussions with young people, Buckingham (1993b) notes their awareness of the organised fiction that comprises television drama. He comments about their "reading" of television (Buckingham, 1993b, p.100): "It may be through this oscillation between engagement and distance that children become aware of at least some of the range of possible reading strategies that are open to them as viewers, and thus extend their range of viewing competencies". I think it would be unfortunate only to appropriate this observation about media sophistication to a point about "viewing competencies"—as if identifying only some form of cognitive skill. The formats of contemporary media drama may be relevant to more than this. They may develop in children a kind of analytic attitude that bears more directly on social development. Consider another example. In the Walkerdine (1993) case study described earlier, a child was watching *Annie*. The participant researcher recounts and comments on the child's one verbal reference to events in the film (p. 84): " 'She's supposed to be drunk, but she ain't'. I ask her why not, to which she replies 'cos it's water' ". Walkerdine is struck by how this reference to the film exposes its role as a sense-making narrative for the child's own family circumstances. Perhaps so. However, the reference certainly also exposes a particular analytic attitude on the part of this young viewer: It allows her to articulate and share her own capacity for reading the medium (not really alcohol, only water). Much fiction offers these chances, even comics. Barker (1989) reminds us how comic strip artists sometimes represent their own presence through intrusions outside and around the actual frames ("...notice, dear reader..."). However, television and cinema drama may offer children particularly dense and particularly vivid examples of this tension between reality and representation. My point is merely that the reflection that this provokes in a viewer forces a more acute exercise of psychological analysis and sensitivity.

Moreover, modern television is increasingly reflective about the management of relations between reality and representation: Increasingly commenting on this feature of what it does. Actors and presenters make asides about their status in the "acting" or "presenting" role. So, for example, an actress appears in a soap opera but she is also performing pop songs, and talking on chat shows, about being in soap operas ... and so on. If young viewers recognise and share this self-consciousness of the medium then, indeed, they may develop greater "viewing competencies", as suggested by Buckingham. But they may also be indirectly exposed to (and become intrigued by) the underpinnings of what is involved in the taking of roles or the telling of tales. They may be forced to be more conscious of the psychological dimension of social life.

In sum, what is suggested here is that electronic media may be particularly effective in confronting children with "the diverse relationships between reality and its representations" (Buckingham, 1993b). Through dense exposure to these media, children are being enculturated into particular (psychological) practices for making sense of the social world. Perhaps there is a useful parallel with the medium I cited at the very start of this chapter—the written word. In accounts of *cognitive* development, it has been argued that literacy influences the way in which children think—cultivating a certain form of analytic attitude that arises from attention to "the words themselves". Accounts of social development might need us to consider more how the style of modern media influences the way in which children relate to and understand other people—cultivating a degree of interest in and sensitivity towards "psychological status". This arises from the intertextuality of media (Kinder, 1991) and from its self-conscious referencing of ambiguities arising from roles, performances, and reality.

CONCLUDING COMMENTS

This has been a brief overview of a large and fragmented research literature. What can be said by way of summary? The enterprise of looking for "media effects" (see p. 193) has been much criticised. Yet, our impatience with a way of talking that seemed to fracture and decontextualise the phenomena should not cause us totally to overlook findings from this tradition. In which case, it is hard to avoid the conclusion that children do derive attitudes and ways of acting from media representations. It is also important to note that these may be prosocial or antisocial in nature. The apparent ease with which media programming can be categorised in terms of the antisocial dimension may have biased our interests as well as caused us to neglect the active, interpretative role adopted by the young viewer. Plenty of evidence suggests this is a role children readily exercise. The "effects" orientation also led researchers to neglect the broader context in which media exposure rests. When we attend to this, we notice the way in which early social interaction has become significantly configured in relation to media technologies (see p. 200) . We also notice that the programming thereby encountered enters in various and significant ways into young people's play and their exploratory talk with others (see p. 205).

This last point is important. For it addresses the manner in which, for example, television becomes a real part of young people's lives. I have resisted generalisations about the impact of this form of presence, beyond noting that children are sophisticated in how they use media experience for finding shared reference points. Perhaps the route towards deriving more compelling generalisations is to dwell on the possible *variation* in this activity as a social enterprise. For example, it would be wrong to equate media "entering people's lives" with the idealised phenomena of children sitting around discussing television with their families. Walkerdine (1993) makes this point before presenting a less self-conscious form of media appropriation. However, in seeking to systematise this topic, perhaps the caricature of the media-discursive family does offer a point of entry. For example, I concluded earlier with some remarks concerning how electronic media furnish a rich resource for children's psychological thinking. Yet what is it that determines whether this actually "happens" (whether their media-based sensitivity spills out to support thinking about their real world of personal relationships)? This *might* depend on how far other people (parents, siblings, peers) say and do things that facilitate such continuities. In any case, an important research line for the future will be to study more closely variation in this active weaving of media experiences into everyday life—including everyday exploratory discourses.

This chapter has converged on somewhat speculative possibilities. However, it is fair to say that the topic of technology, media, and development has attracted a good deal of such speculation. This is some reflection of the interest it arouses across a broad constituency of academic researchers—as well as among the public at large. It is unfortunate that developmental psychologists have maintained a polite distance from the topic for I believe it offers great challenges to theory and method. Stronger than that, I believe it is improper to attempt a comprehensive account of social development without attending to the mediated nature of all social relations.

REFERENCES

Anderson. D. R., Field, D. E., Collins, P. A., Lorch, E. P., & Nathan, J. G. (1985). Estimates of young children's time with television: A methodological comparison of parent reports with time-lapse video home observation. *Child Development, 56,* 1345–1357.

Andreason, M. S. (1994). Patterns of family life and television consumption from 1945 to the 1990s. In D. Zillman, J. Bryant, & A. Huston (Eds.), *Media, children and the family* (pp. 19–36). Hillsdale, NJ: Lawrence Erlbaum Associates Inc.

Bandura, A., Ross, D., & Ross, S. (1963). Imitation of film-mediated aggressive models. *Journal of Abnormal and Social Psychology, 66,* 3–11.

Baran, S.J., Chase, L. J., & Courtright, J. A. (1979). Television drama as a facilitator of prosocial behavior: "The Waltons". *Journal of Broadcasting, 23,* 277–284.

Barker, M. (1989). *Comics: Ideology, power and the critics.* Manchester, UK: Manchester University Press.

Barwise, P. & Ehrenberg, A. (1988). *Television and its audience.* London: Sage.

Bennett, M. (1993). *The child as psychologist.* New York: Harvester-Wheatsheaf.

Berkowitz, L. (1984). Some effects of thoughts on anti- and prosocial influences of media events: A cognitive-neoassociation analysis. *Psychological Bulletin, 95*, 410–427.

Bettelheim, B. (1976). *The uses of enchantment*. London: Thames & Hudson.

Buckingham, D. (1993a). *Changing literacies: Media education and modern culture*. London: Tufnell.

Buckingham, D. (1993b). *Children talking television: The making of television literacy*. London: Falmer.

Buckingham, D. (1994). Television and the definition of childhood. In B. Mayall (Ed.), *Children's childhoods: Observed and experienced,* (pp. 79–96). London: Falmer.

Bybee, C., Robinson, J. D., & Turow, J. (1985). The effects of television on children: What the experts believe. *Communication Research Reports, 2,* 149–154.

Calvert, S. L. & Tan, S-L. (1994). Impact of virtual reality on young adults' physiological arousal and aggressive thoughts: Interaction versus observation. *Journal of Applied Developmental Psychology, 15,* 125–139

Condry, J. (1989). *The psychology of television*. Hillsdale, NJ: Lawrence Erlbaum Associates Inc.

Condry, J. (1993). Thief of time, unfaithful servant: Television and the American child. *Daedalus, 122,* 259–278.

Crook, C. K. (1994). *Computers and the collaborative experience of learning*. London: Routledge.

Cullingford, C. (1984). *Children and television*. Aldershot, UK: Gower.

Cumberbatch, G. & Howitt, D. (1989). *A measure of uncertainty: The effects of the mass media*. London: Libbey.

Dale, E. (1935). *Children's attendance at motion pictures*. New York: Macmillan.

Davie, C. E., Hutt, S. J., Vincent, E., & Mason, M. (1984). *The young child at home*. Windsor, UK: NFER.

Dunn, J. (1988). *The beginnings of social understanding*. Oxford: Blackwell.

Elder, G. H., Modell, J., & Parke, R. D. (1993). *Children in time and place. Developmental and historical insights*. Cambridge, UK: Cambridge University Press.

Erikson, E. H. (1964). *Childhood and society*. New York: Norton.

Gerbner, G. & Gross, L. (1976). Living with television: The violence profile. *Journal of Communication, 26,* 173–199.

Goody, J. & Watt, J. P. (1968). The consequences of literacy. In J. Goody (Ed.), *Literacy in traditional societies* (pp. 27–68). Cambridge, UK: Cambridge University Press.

Griffiths, M. D. (1991). Amusement machine playing in childhood and adolescence: A comparative analysis of video games and fruit machines. *Journal of Adolescence, 14,* 53–73.

Hodge, R. & Tripp, D. (1986). *Children and television. A semiotic approach*. Cambridge, UK: Polity Press.

Huesmann, L. R. (1986). Psychological processes promoting the relation between exposure to media violence and aggressive behavior by the viewer. *Journal of Social Issues, 42,* 125–139.

Huesmann, L. R., Eron, L. D., Lefkowitz, M. M., & Walder, L. O. (1984). Stability of aggression over time and generations. *Developmental Psychology, 20,* 1120–1134.

Humphrey, N. (1984). *Consciousness regained*. Oxford: Oxford University Press.

Huston, A. C., Wright, J. C., Rice, M. L., Kerkman, D., & St. Peters, M. (1990). Development of television viewing patterns in early childhood: A longitudinal investigation. *Developmental Psychology, 26,* 409–420.

Kinder, M. (1991). *Playing with power in movies, television and video games: From muppet babies to teenage mutant turtles*. Berkeley, CA: University of California Press.

Kline, S. (1993). *Out of the garden. Toys and children's culture in the age of TV marketing*. London: Verso.

Lefkowitz, M. M., Eron, L. D., Walder, L. O., Huesmann, L. R. (1977). *Growing up to be violent*. New York: Pergamon.

Lemish, D. & Rice, M. L. (1986). Television as a talking picture book: A prop for language acquisition. *Journal of Child Language, 13*, 251–274.

Lin, S. & Lepper, M. R. (1987). Correlates of children's usage of videogames and computers. *Journal of Applied Social Psychology, 17*, 72–93.

Lull, J. (1980). The social uses of television. *Human Communication Research, 9*, 3–16.

Luria, A.R. (1976). *Cognitive development. Its cultural and social foundations*. Cambridge, MA: Harvard University Press.

Marcuse, H. (1966). *One-dimensional man*. London: Routledge & Kegan Paul.

Messaris, P. & Sarett, C. (1981). On the consequences of television-related parent–child interaction. *Human Communication Research, 7*, 226–244.

Meyrowitz, J. (1985). *No sense of place*. New York: Oxford University Press.

Morgan, M. J. (1994). Sexpert schmexpert. *The Guardian OnLine*, 30 June, p. 9.

Morley, D. (1986). *Family television: Cultural power and domestic leisure*. London: Comedia.

Murray, J. P. & Kippax, S. (1978). Children's social behavior in three towns with differing television experience. *Journal of Communication, 28*, 19–29.

Olson, D. (1986). Intelligence and literacy: The relationships between intelligence and the techniques of representation and communication. In R. Sternberg (Ed.), *Practical intelligence* (pp. 338–360). Cambridge, UK: Cambridge University Press.

Ong, W. J. (1977). *Interfaces of the word. Studies in the evolution of consciousness and culture*. Ithaca, NY: Cornell University Press.

Postman, N. (1982). *The disappearance of childhood*. New York: Random House.

Provenzo, E. F. (1991). *Video kids: Making sense of Nintendo*. Cambridge, MA: Harvard University Press.

Riel, M. (1995). Cross-classroom collaboration in global learning circles. In S. Star (Ed.), *The cultures of computing* (pp. 219–242). Oxford: Blackwell.

Rocheleau, B. (1995). Computer use by school-age children: Trends, patterns, and predictors. *Journal of Educational Computing Research, 12*, 1–17.

Rubinstein, E. A. (1983). Television and behavior. Research conclusions of the 1982 NIMH report and their policy implications. *American Psychologist, 38*, 820–825.

Sakamoto, A. (1994). Video game use and the development of sociocognitive abilities in children: Three surveys of elementary school students. *Journal of Applied Social Psychology, 24*, 21–42.

Schramm, W., Lyle, J., Parker, E. B. (1961). *Television in the lives of our children*. Stanford, CA: Stanford University Press.

Shotton, M. (1989). *Computer addiction: A study of computer dependency*. London: Taylor & Francis.

Signorielli, N. (1991). Adolescents and ambivalence towards marriage. *Youth and Society, 23*, 121–149.

Signorielli, N. (1993). Television and adolescent's perception about work. *Youth and Society, 24*, 314–341.

Singer, J. L. & Singer, D. G. (1981). *Television, imagination and aggression: A study of preschoolers*. Hillsdale, NJ: Lawrence Erlbaum Associates Inc.

Spigel, L. (1992). *Make room for TV. Television and the family ideal in post-war America*. Chicago, IL: Chicago University Press.

St. Peters, M., Fitch, M., Huston, A. C., Wright, J. C., & Eakins, D. J. (1991). Television and families: What do young children watch with their parents. *Child Development, 62*, 1409–1423.

Stone, A. R. (1995). Sex and death among the disembodied: VR, cyberspace, and the nature of academic discourse. In S. Star (Ed.), *The cultures of computing* (pp. 243–255). Oxford: Blackwell.

Surgeon General's Report (1972). *Television and growing up: The impact of televised violence.* Washington, DC: United States Government Printing Office.

Timme, S. G., Eccles, J., & O'Brien, K. (1985). How children use time. In F. T Juster. & F. P. Stafford (Eds), *Time, goods, and well-being* (pp. 106–123). Ann Arbor, MI: Institute for Social Research, University of Michigan.

Turkle, S. (1984). *The second self.* New York: Simon & Schuster.

Walkerdine, V. (1993). 'Daddys gonna buy you a dream to cling to (and mummy's gonna love you just as much as she can)': Young girls and popular television. In D. Buckingham (Ed.), *Reading audience* (pp. 74–88). Manchester, UK: Manchester University Press.

Weizenbaum, J. (1976). *Computer power and human reason.* San Fancisco: Freeman.

Williams, T. M., & Handford, A. G. (1986). Television and other leisure activities. In T. Williams (Ed.), *The impact of television: A natural experiment in three communities* (pp. 143–213). London: Academic Press.

Winn, M. (1977). *The plug-in drug.* New York: Viking.

Wood, W., Wong, F. Y., & Chachere, J. G. (1991). Effects of media violence on viewers' aggression in unconstrained social interaction. *Psychological Bulletin, 109,* 371–383.

Substance

9 The developmental origins of social understanding

Dale F. Hay
Cambridge University, Cambridge, UK
Helen Demetriou
Institute of Psychiatry, London, UK

Social life requires thought as well as action, knowledge as well as feeling—but action and emotion are the elements of social life that children must come to know and understand. Our aim is to describe some of the ways in which infants and very young children begin to understand their social worlds. At earlier ages, understanding is limited by the infant's immature cognitive and linguistic abilities; but, at all ages, social understanding is either enhanced or obscured by particular experiences in important personal relationships. In the pages that follow, we shall chart some important first steps in social understanding.

There are many dimensions of the social world that humans must learn about in the course of growing up. Adults must have at least a reasonable understanding of the economic and political processes at work in their societies. They must be sensitive to the dynamics of their important personal relationships, and grasp the moral codes and social etiquettes that govern conventional interaction in their day-to-day lives. In the language of the social sciences, social understanding can be studied at both a "micro" and a "macro" level. Most developmental psychologists who study social cognition have focused on the "micro" level of the dyad, asking what children understand about individual persons in particular situations. In particular, psychologists have placed great emphasis on children's guesses about other people's internal experiences (i.e. their feelings, thoughts, plans, and beliefs). These influential studies of children's "theories of mind" concentrate primarily on the years between the second and sixth birthdays, when many important changes in social understanding are taking place (e.g. see Astington, Harris, & Olson, 1988; Baron-Cohen, 1994). Nonetheless, long before children are able to answer psychologists' questions about story characters' feelings, desires, and beliefs, experiences with parents, siblings, peers, and other people provide children with key information about the social world. Infants' and toddlers' actions and speech may reveal precursors to a more mature social understanding (see Frye, 1993; Moore, 1996).

When studying the developmental origins of social understanding, it is indeed important to look for early signs of an appreciation of the internal lives of fellow humans. One of our major aims is to describe very young children's understanding of internal experience. However, if we are to understand the full dimensions of what very young children manage to work out about social life, it is important to go beyond the "micro" level and ask, what understanding do very young children have about social interaction, relationships, and group processes? To what extent can the young child be characterised as a social, as well as a social cognitive psychologist? Our second aim is to provide some preliminary answers to that latter question.

THE "MICRO" LEVEL: HUMANS AND THEIR INNER WORLDS

Successful decoding of the internal lives of others is necessary for harmonious interaction. In this chapter, we focus on several dimensions of the internal worlds of human actors, and ask, how do children come to share the basic human assumption that members of our species have hearts and minds that govern action? How do children's guesses and claims about the internal worlds of others eventually consolidate into a coherent understanding of the reasons why other people act as they do?

One of the most basic assumptions that humans make about fellow humans is that we all have internal selves—unseen entities that are related to but not reducible to our brains, which guide our actions and give meaning to our feelings. This species-characteristic assumption about the internal reality of human existence is itself a developmental attainment. Some would claim that ontogeny recapitulates the way psychology has been studied in the 20th century: It has been claimed that children start out as behaviourists and only gradually become cognitive theorists (see Meerum Terwogt and Stegge, Chapter 10). We may therefore ask, when in development do children become at all aware of internal experience?

Baldwin (1895) believed that development consisted of a dialectical process, whereby children become aware of the minds of others through the perception of their own mental states and, conversely, become more aware of the dimensions of the self by observing and imitating others. This notion of a reciprocal relation between self-awareness and understanding of the minds of others continues to influence contemporary thinking about the growth of social understanding (e.g. Moore, 1996). Hardly any topic in developmental psychology has received more scrutiny in recent years than children's understanding of other people's internal states. The development of such understanding has itself been understood as analogous to the activity of a scientist; children are described as constructing and then testing their own theories about other people's minds (see Baron-Cohen, 1994; Frye, 1993; but see Hobson, 1991, for a counter-view).

Such accounts of social cognitive development derive from the primary axiom that people in fact have minds, and the actions they choose to perform are done with reference to internal states. Thus, to understand what people do, children must make guesses about what those people feel, want, or believe. Not all human children acquire theories of mind. Difficulty in understanding of other people's mental states—in particular, their beliefs, but also their desires—is one of the telling features of autism (see Baron-Cohen, 1994; Phillips, Baron-Cohen, & Rutter, in press).

The first signs of a theory—or, at the least, a set of primitive axioms about the mind—emerge in late infancy. In the second year of life, as children begin to acquire language, they begin to refer to many different internal states—to perceptions, feelings, preferences, desires, intentions, and beliefs (Bretherton & Beeghly, 1982; Dunn, 1988). For example, in a case study of six second-born toddlers, observed at two-month intervals over the third year of life, the children talked about emotions and mental states, and use of terms such as *want*, *know* and *forget* increased over that year (Brown & Dunn, 1991). The pattern of developmental change in that case study was reminiscent of the dialectical process imagined by Baldwin (1895). Initially, the children mainly talked about their own mental states, perhaps as part of a process of appreciating and exploring a newly developing sense of self. Later, by the end of the year, over a quarter of their contributions to conversation with their mothers and siblings referred to other people's internal states (Brown & Dunn, 1991).

The acquisition of internal state language does not seem to be a case of simple, rote imitation, although learning by listening to other people is probably involved. In a short-term observational study, mothers who used mental state terms more than other mothers were likely to have one-year-olds who used such terms more than other toddlers (Hay, Castle, & Stimson, 1990). The mothers mainly talked about *knowing*, whereas the children talked about *feeling, liking*, and *wanting*. In other words, the mothers made reference to the mental state of belief whereas the children were talking about their preferences and desires.

On the basis of such studies of children's spontaneous talk about the internal worlds of themselves and others, as well as other, experimental evidence, we propose that the human awareness of internal states develops in the following progression, at least for children in the Western world who have been the subjects of most studies. Initially, in the first year of life, infants begin to be aware of other people's *perceptions* and *emotions*. During the second and third years, they reveal their awareness of other people's *preferences*, *desires* and, gradually, *intentions*. As Wellman (1990) has claimed, the very young child is a "desire psychologist" who only gradually comes to an understanding of other people's beliefs. The understanding of belief emerges and consolidates during the fourth and fifth years of life, so that by the fifth birthday many children pass experimental tests assessing their "theories of mind" (see Baron-Cohen, 1994).

Another way to describe this progression is one from an understanding of *perception* to *affect* to *conation* to *cognition,* in terms of the classic dimensions of psychological phenomena that children must eventually come to understand. It is important to note, however, that development in one dimension of social understanding may begin sooner and progress faster than in another, but it does not necessarily stop in the year it begins. For example, the understanding of other people's emotions may begin in the first months of life, but remains a life-long task.

Because there are many excellent reviews of the later developments in this progression, notably the understanding of false belief (e.g. Astington et al., 1988; Baron-Cohen, 1994), we shall concentrate here on the earlier steps along this developmental pathway. We shall now chart some early achievements in understanding the attention, the emotions, the desires, and the intentions of other people.

Understanding what people pay attention to

Attention to internal states begins with an awareness of another person's *perception* and *attention*. An important feature in infants' social interactions with other people, particularly their mothers or other caregivers, is joint attention to objects in the environment (e.g. Bakeman & Adamson, 1984). At six months of age, infants tend to look in the same direction their mothers are looking, but may not be able to pinpoint the particular object of their mother's gaze. They are, however, sensitive to the mother's attention in so far as her change of gaze from one object to another triggers the baby's own search for an interesting object to look at (Butterworth & Jarrett, 1991). Butterworth argues that the achievement of joint visual attention does not necessarily require that the baby has a *theory* of mind, but may be an important social experience that lays the groundwork for more sophisticated beliefs about other minds.

Around eight or nine months of age, human infants begin drawing their companions' attention to objects the infants find of interest in the environment, by pointing to those objects or holding them up for other people to see (Rheingold, Hay, & West, 1976). These actions have been interpreted as precursors to language and a more mature understanding of other people's mental states (e.g. Baron-Cohen, 1994; Sigman & Mundy 1993). Detailed longitudinal home observations have indicated that early points occur by nine months of age (Rheingold et al., 1976), but the ability to point with an extended index finger is gradually refined over the next months (Butterworth & Cochran, 1980; Leung & Rheingold, 1981). Such studies demonstrate a clear distinction between reaching for objects for one's own use and pointing them out for others to look at. The frequency of pointing is reliably increased if additional decorations are placed in a room (Rheingold et al., 1976), but virtually all children point out features of their worlds to parents, peers, and other people. In a very large prospective study of autism, it was found that children who later received a diagnosis of autism had not pointed to objects at 18 months of age, as reported by their parents and confirmed in laboratory assessments (Charman et al., 1995). This link with later failure to understand mental states further validates pointing in infancy as a measure of understanding of another's perception and attention.

The ability to appreciate where another person is looking underlies some of the conventional social "games" played by infants with their parents and other adults. Early parent–infant interaction is often characterised by "games" of alternating gaze (for a review see Reddy, Hay, Murray, & Trevarthen, 1997) and later in the first year of life infants begin deliberately to direct and control their companions' gaze through conventional games of "peekaboo". Thus, an emergent understanding of joint attention facilitates social interaction in infancy, and experience with such conventional games may feed back to sharpen children's understanding of perception and attention.

The young child's understanding that the expression of the eyes may convey quite critical information about other internal states is an important developmental achievement. There is good reason to believe that some underlying problems with gaze as a vehicle of social interaction contribute to the problems autistic individuals have with the understanding of other people's mental states and social interaction. It is possible that autistic individuals do not understand that the direction of another person's gaze provides cues about his/her internal states (Baron-Cohen, Campbell, Karmiloff-Smith, Grant, & Walker, 1995). To test this possibility, Baron-Cohen and his colleagues presented cartoon faces to three groups: (1) individuals with a diagnosis of autism who were attending special schools; (2) other pupils at special schools with learning difficulties, some of whom had a diagnosis of William's syndrome; (3) and a group of normal four-year-olds, attending nursery classes. They were asked to judge which of a pair of cartoon faces was looking at them or away, which was silly (the eyes being portrayed in impossible positions), and which expressed happiness and sadness. There were no differences among the groups in assessing the direction of gaze, the impossibility of a certain position of the eyes, or the imputation of emotion. In follow-up experiments, however, the autistic individuals were unable to make correct inferences about a cartoon character's desires, goals, or state of being sunk in thought on the basis of eye direction. In contrast, the majority of individuals with learning disabilities and most of the four-year-olds could make such inferences.

These findings suggest that much information about the emotions and mental states of others is indeed conveyed in the course of mutual gaze (i.e. in the context of face-to-face interaction with one's companions). We now turn to one of the most important dimensions of social interaction in infancy as well as adulthood, the emotions felt and expressed by oneself and others. We believe that understanding of emotion is fundamental for all other dimensions of social understanding, and so examine the evidence in some detail.

Understanding what other people feel

Understanding distress

Children are exposed to the emotions of others from the moment of birth onwards. Even newborns perceive and react to other people's emotions: They can imitate emotional expressions (Field, Woodson, Greenberg, & Cohen, 1982) and they cry when they hear the cries of other infants (Sagi & Hoffman, 1976; Simner, 1971). Much research on children's understanding of emotion has been undertaken with respect to the construct of *empathy*. Empathy is often thought to have two components: (1) a perceptual-cognitive recognition of another's emotions, from facial expressions, tone of voice, or situational cues; and (2) a vicarious emotional reaction, so that the witness of a person's emotion comes to experience the same feeling. Different researchers have tended to focus on one or other of these dimensions of empathy. In the beginning, however, an infant's understanding of another's emotion may be assessed by the infant's vicarious reaction.

Humans react to their distressed companions in many different ways: with wonder, disinterest, repugnance, or pity, to name but a few possibilities. At the simplest level, one may ask if infants and very young children even notice the distress of others. At times young children may ask an adult why another child cries (e.g. Murphy, 1937). In addition, their imitation of characteristic features of another child's distressed behaviour attests to their ability to attend to, recall and recreate such events— Piaget's (1951/1972) classic example of his 16-month-old daughter's deferred imitation of a temper tantrum is such an instance.

Theorists have long speculated that the origins of sympathy lie in infants' own early distress experiences and some confusion between the self and the distressed other (e.g. Darwin, 1877; Preyer, 1889). Murphy (1937) and Hoffman (1975) suggested that very young infants do not really distinguish between themselves and others. Consequently, the cry of another infant would be as effective in promoting distress as the infant's own cry. This notion of a blurred boundary between the self and others in early infancy is also echoed in psychoanalytic writings, in terms of Freud's notion of the primary process of infancy and the later work of the object relations theorists such as Winnicott, who famously declared: "There is no such thing as an infant".

Although the infant's confusion between self and others is probably impossible to ascertain directly—it being more of an axiom than a theorem—infants are indeed likely to cry if they are exposed to the prolonged crying of other infants (Hay, Nash, & Pedersen, 1981; Sagi & Hoffman, 1976; Simner, 1971). In an observational study of six-month-olds, the longer an infant cried, the more likely another infant was to cry as well (Hay et al., 1981). At 12 months of age, infants reacted in an agitated manner to another's distress (Radke-Yarrow & Zahn-Waxler, 1984). The young child's own distress in response to another's is not only seen in the case of contagious crying. For example, Preyer (1889) reported that his son wept "if human forms cut out of paper were in any danger of mutilation". Other children have been reported to weep when confronted with the Thanksgiving or Christmas turkey, Stern's (1924) son protesting: "But poor turkey has no clothes...". Such more complex vicarious reactions in toddlers would be hard to explain entirely in terms of a classical conditioning process.

Hoffman (1975) argued that, over the course of the first two years of life, an initial biologically based, species-characteristic form of empathy, as reflected in this vicarious response to another person's distress, transmutes into a more mature sympathetic reaction, which encompasses both cognitive understanding of the other's emotion and instrumental attempts to alleviate the distress. This achievement is seen as a function of cognitive development. Hoffman claimed that the acquisition of a cognitive understanding of the other as distinct from the self, which he put at about 12 months of age, led to the early empathic distress being (p. 615): "gradually transformed into a more reciprocal, sympathetic concern for the victim".

Hoffman does not provide independent evidence for a new distinction between self and other, but it is clear that instrumental attempts to help or comfort distressed persons emerge in the second year of life. At that point in early childhood, children not only respond vicariously to the distress of others but begin to comfort them, for example, by bringing a teddy bear to a crying friend (Hoffman, 1975; Radke-Yarrow & Zahn-Waxler, 1984; Zahn-Waxler, Radke-Yarrow, & King, 1979). Very young children comfort their parents (Zahn-Waxler & Radke-Yarrow, 1984), siblings (Dunn & Munn, 1986), and peers (Murphy, 1937).

The descriptive studies of children's reactions to distress reveal a host of emotional and behavioural responses (Dunn, 1988). Many of their actions may actually aggravate rather than relieve the other's distress, especially if they have themselves caused the other person to become distressed in the first place (Demetriou, in prep.). For example, in one observational study, siblings tended to laugh at or try to aggravate distress that they themselves had caused (Dunn & Brown, 1991). Children gradually seem to acquire an understanding of the social norms governing reactions to distress. For example, when three- and four-year-olds were observed in their nursery classes, most tried to help a distressed classmate at least once, but the frequency of such attempts to alleviate distress was not high (Caplan & Hay, 1989). The children were then interviewed individually and shown a video record of a distress incident that had occurred during the course of observations. All the children had a great deal to say about how the child in the video could be helped, but they did not see it as their own responsibility to provide the help required. When asked who should tend to the distressed classmate, most said: "The teacher", and a few invoked their own mothers. In other words, by the age of three, these children were showing a "diffusion of responsibility norm" similar to that voiced by adult witnesses of distress (Darley & Latane, 1968). Understanding may impel action, but need not do so.

Bridges (1932) argued that emotional development consists of a gradual differentiation of discrete emotions, so that feelings of sadness, fear, anger, and disgust eventually emerge out of a primordial capacity for distress. Although contemporary theorists of emotion have called our attention to the infant's tendency to express discrete emotions in the same way that adults do (see Izard et al., 1995), we might still ask whether the infant as perceiver of emotion only gradually differentiates amongst various kinds of distress. When do children come to understand fear, sadness, and anger?

Fear. Infants' responsiveness to adults' distress acquaints them with the sorts of situations in which their caregivers become distressed and thus alerts them to potential dangers in the environment. As young mammals follow their mothers around the environment, they come to appreciate the value objects in the environment hold for their mothers and generally for members of their species (Bindra, 1974). In particular, the young animals learn to avoid those objects and situations that provoke fear in adults. Similarly, in the last quarter of the first year of life, human infants use adults' expressions of fear and apprehension to guide their own actions. This process has been referred to as "social referencing" (Campos & Stenberg, 1981).

Social referencing can be detected when infants are placed in an ambiguous situation, such as a "visual cliff"—a clear, firm plexiglass surface that is placed over a checkerboard surface that has two levels. The infant can in fact crawl securely along the upper, clear surface, but the checkerboard pattern appears to drop off sharply, and so the situation creates uncertainty: Most infants pause at the edge of the visual cliff before venturing forth. If mothers pose facial expressions of joy or interest, their infants carry on across the cliff; if, on the contrary, the mothers express fear or anger, the vast majority of infants do not venture on. The infants thus consult the mothers' emotional expressions to determine whether their course of action is dangerous or not.

Conversely, situations that might induce some apprehension in infants can be transformed by a caregiver's emotional reactions. For example, some toys (such as a noisy robot walking across the floor or a garish jack-in-the-box jumping out of its box at random intervals) might provoke either fear or interest in a toddler. Mother's positive reactions to such toys promote the infant's own positive interest in such potentially frightening objects (Gunnar & Stone, 1984; Hornik, Risenhoover, & Gunnar, 1987). Infants who show an immediately fearful reaction to objects such as a toy spider are less influenced by the mothers' posed expressions than are those infants who are uncertain about how to respond (Zarbatany & Lamb, 1985).

Infants' use of other people's emotions as guides to their own goes beyond the mother–infant relationships. Infants are influenced by the emotions of other familiar caregivers. If fathers pose emotional expressions in experimental settings, infants use this information; however, if the parents are together, behaving naturally, the infants are more likely to consult their mothers' reactions than their fathers' (Hirshberg & Svejda, 1990). Infants who spend time in day care are influenced by their familiar caregivers' reactions in social referencing tasks (Camras & Sachs, 1991). Social referencing can also be directed to unfamiliar adults who may be particularly knowledgeable in a given situation. For example, six-month-olds confronted with the distress of a peer were more likely to look at the peer's mother's face than at their own mothers (Hay et al., 1981).

Infants' attention to the emotions of other people guides their reactions to the social as well as the physical environment. So-called "fear of strangers" has sometimes been thought of as a developmental milestone (Sroufe, 1977), but actually depends on the infant's degree of control over the interaction with the stranger (Rheingold & Eckerman, 1973) and the stranger's behaviour (Ross & Goldman, 1977). It also depends on emotions expressed by familiar persons in interaction with the stranger. If parents speak positively about a stranger, 10-month-olds show more friendly overtures to that person (Feinman & Lewis, 1983). If two previously acquainted mothers are interacting positively together, infants do not protest being left in the care of the other mother (Nash, 1988).

Infants' capacities for social referencing emerge in the first year of life and consolidate over the second year (Walden & Ogan, 1988). Its emergence has been linked to successful understanding of causality on Piagetian tasks (Desrochers, Ricard, Decarie, & Allard, 1994). However, the ability to use another person's emotions to guide one's actions probably rests on earlier responsiveness to the emotional expressions of caregivers. Infants as young as 10 weeks of age are able to react in different and appropriate ways when mothers pose different emotional expressions in face-to-face interactions (Haviland & Lelwica, 1987). Responsiveness to expressions of fear in particular seems to be greatest in the second year of life (which is of course the period when newly locomoting infants begin to venture farther into a potentially dangerous environment on their own).

Sadness. Just as attention to caregivers' fearful expressions may arise out of a prior responsiveness to another's distress, so children's eventual understanding of sadness may rest on their initial tendencies to become distressed or disorganised by an adult's own distress. As early as 10 weeks of age, infants are reported to react differently to the mother's posing of sadness, happiness and anger: Posed happiness was associated with the infants looking happy and interested; sadness was reacted to with more mouth movements and looking at the floor (Haviland & Lelwica, 1987). In the visual cliff paradigm, the mother's posing of sadness made it less likely that the infant would cross the divide, although about a third of the infants tested still did so; their crossing of the cliff was accompanied by behavioural signs of ambivalence and confusion (Campos, 1981).

Such a vicarious response to another person's emotion may promote empathy (Hoffman, 1975), but may also consolidate into a negative reaction to and perhaps distrust of the social world. Some infants may become excessively caught up in the sadness of their companions. This tendency has been remarked in the infants of depressed mothers, who come to show "depressed" behaviour themselves (Cohn & Tronick, 1983). Infants of depressed mothers are more likely to fuss or cry and less likely to engage in a lively, positive manner with their caregivers (Field, Healy, & Goldstein, 1988; Murray, 1992). The reactions of infants' to their depressed mothers' expressions of emotion are at least partly a function of gender. Boys are more likely than girls to show dysregulated emotion in response to their depressed mothers' emotions; however, once girls have begun expressing sadness, they are likely to carry on doing so (Tronick & Weinberg, 1997).

Infants' reactions to their depressed mothers' emotions may lead to more fundamental problems with social understanding, which affects their relationships with persons other than the mother, including nondepressed caregivers. The infants' negative affect and disengagement continues to be shown, even when they are cared for by other people; indeed, those alternative caregivers themselves then start to show "depressed" affect (Field et al., 1988). Some children of depressed mothers appear to be acutely sensitive to the distress of others and may thus appear to be more "empathic" than other children (Radke-Yarrow et al., 1994).

Anger.   It is not uncommon for infants to witness or experience their parents' and siblings' anger, and so they soon become sensitive to the characteristic features of expressions of anger. Ten-week-old infants reacted to their mothers' posed angry expressions by crying or by producing their own angry looks (Haviland & Lelwica, 1987). Mothers' posed anger prevented infants crossing the visual cliff (Campos, 1981).

Observational studies of young children's reactions to anger have shown that children react in diverse ways. True expressions of anger are difficult to capture in laboratory settings, and so Radke-Yarrow and her colleagues trained mothers to keep diary records of their one- and two-year-old children's reactions to anger and other intense emotions in the course of ordinary domestic life (Cummings, Zahn-Waxler, & Radke-Yarrow 1981). These records showed that children were highly aroused and distressed by other people's expressions of anger in the course of physical fights and verbal arguments. The children were especially likely to become distressed when they witnessed physical attacks.

These home observations were followed up by the development of an experimental paradigm in which children are exposed to simulated conflict and expressions of anger (e.g. Cummings, Iannotti, & Zahn-Waxler, 1985; Cummings, Ballard, El-Sheikh, & Lake, 1991). In a study of very young children, pairs of two-year-olds were exposed to simulated anger whilst they and their mothers were engaging in a free play session in a research flat (Cummings et al., 1985). Over the course of a half an hour, two research workers who were working in another part of the flat engaged in friendly interaction, then had a quarrel about work left undone, and then reconciled their differences. The children became distressed by the expressions of anger in the background, and were more likely to show aggressive behaviour with each other. Boys and children who had previously been classed as particularly likely to show aggression were especially likely to react aggressively to the adults' expressions of anger.

Just as persistent exposure to sadness and depression influences children's general understanding of the social world, so does their persistent exposure to anger and violence. Repeated witnessing of violent acts may distress children and promote their own aggression, and may furthermore lead to their adopting a "world view" of the social environment as a hostile, violent place (e.g. Richters & Martinez, 1993). For example, inner-city preschoolers who were directly exposed to the Los Angeles riots were more likely than children from other inner-city communities to tell stories that were filled with references to aggression and destruction (Farmer & Frosch, 1996).

Very young children's sensitivity to other people's sadness and anger is finely honed in the ordinary conflicts of family life. In the course of these conflicts, they also become increasingly aware of their companion's motivation, as well as their overtly expressed emotion. Thus, over the second and third years of life, children grow to understand some additional mental states, notably that of desire.

Understanding of desire

People communicate their desires to others partly through the expression of emotion, and so the young child's appreciation of the desires of others emerges in parallel with the understanding of emotion. At the same time, much social interaction in early childhood involves negotiating one's desires with caregivers, siblings, and peers. Thus, very young children's understanding of desire is partly advanced through the interactions they witness and partly through those in which they participate and are asked to suppress or regulate their own desires.

Early awareness of the desires of others

As we have seen, very young children, in contrast to their mothers, talk more about what they want than what they know (Hay et al., 1990), which underscores Wellman's (1990) claim that the two- to three-year-old is a "desire psychologist" who only gradually acquires an understanding of people's beliefs (Wellman & Wooley, 1990). In the second and third years of life, children are able to move beyond shared attention and awareness of another's distress or happiness to an appreciation of the value certain objects and events hold for other persons. Thus, the young "desire psychologist" acquires a more general understanding that different people may want different things, and the same person may want different things at different times.

Children's awareness of the desires of others is probably stimulated first by the simple behavioural exchanges of objects that emerge towards the end of the first year of life, when infants give objects on request to adults and peers (Hay, Caplan, Castle, & Stimson, 1991; Rheingold et al., 1976). Adults' requests for objects are often incorporated into long, playful games of give-and-take, which may alert infants to other people's desires for objects. For example, 12-month-olds who played games of give-and-take with an unfamiliar adult were later more likely than other infants to offer toys and other objects in a novel environment to their mothers (Hay & Murray, 1982).

Very young children who imitate adults pay attention to the whole social situation in which acts are modelled; they attend not only to the behavioural features of modelled acts but the reactions of the persons to whom modelled acts are directed. Their imitation of the modelled acts then is sensitive to the preferences and desires of those recipients. In other words, imitation is more than motor mimicry and the social context of a young child's imitation provides evidence of that child's understanding of the wishes and pleasures of other people (Hay et al., 1990).

For example, 18-month-old children observed novel actions (unconventional symbolic uses of familiar toys, such as placing a paper party hat on a recipient's foot rather than head) that were directed to themselves or to an unfamiliar adult (Hay, Murray, Cecire, & Nash, 1985). These novel acts did not occur spontaneously. The majority of the children imitated at least one such act, but did so in accordance with the reactions of the original recipient. Toddlers who saw the acts directed to themselves directed their own imitation to themselves, particularly if they had reacted positively to the original modelling. In contrast, those who saw the novel acts directed to an unfamiliar adult directed their own imitation to that adult, who had seemed quite to enjoy wearing a hat on her foot or having her hair combed with a string of beads. This tendency persisted in a later trial, when new but similar objects were used as a means of interacting with that person. Thus, what the 18-month-olds learned from modelling was not just the motor movements involved in particular acts but how to interact with a new acquaintance, in accordance with her earlier positive reactions to these unconventional activities. In other words, they had an understanding of her desire for particular forms of interaction.

Brown and Dunn's (1991) longitudinal case study revealed that mothers talked about desires and feelings more in the context of didactic or disciplinary interactions than in other contexts. In those disciplinary encounters the mothers were primarily talking about the child's desires, rather than those of other people. In contrast, in other situations, when the mothers talked about other mental states such as knowledge or belief, they were usually talking about people other than the child. This finding suggests that young children's understanding of their own and other people's desires may be finely honed in situations where desires are in conflict, in the course of everyday disputes with parents, siblings, and peers.

The most common sort of conflict with peers in early childhood is indeed the quest for desired objects; the second most common reason why young peers engage in conflict concerns infringements on personal space (for reviews see Hay, 1984; Shantz, 1987). In general, conflict occurs when one person wants to do something and another person objects, and so a dispute is fundamentally a clash of desires (Hay, 1984). In the course of conflict, young children often make their desires known by reaching, pointing or grabbing onto their companions' possessions (Caplan, Vespo, Pedersen, & Hay, 1991; Hay & Ross, 1982; Vespo, Pedersen, & Hay, 1995). Two-year-olds are *less* likely than one-year-olds to acquiesce to their companions' desires by releasing a disputed object into a peer's possession (Hay et al., 1991). Spontaneous sharing with peers also declines somewhat over the second year of life (Eckerman, Davis, & Didow, 1989; Hay et al., 1991), and so the tendency to acquiesce to the desires of others may actually decline with age in early childhood. Very young children actually obey the commands of adults (i.e. the expressions of desire for particular objects or activities) with considerable good will and alacrity (Rheingold, Cook, & Kowlowitz, 1987).

Suppression and regulation of one's own desires

Children's understanding of the desires of others is possibly advanced by their growing abilities to control their own expressions of desire. Over the preschool years, children acquire some rudiments of manners, so that they may pursue their desires in socially acceptable fashions, for example, by saying "Please" and making polite requests, rather than grabbing what they want from their companions. At five years of age, girls are more likely than boys to report that they would use such socially acceptable tactics to pursue their self-interest (Hay, Zahn-Waxler, Cummings, & Iannotti, 1992).

Children's understanding of the nature of desire is also shown in studies where the children are asked to refrain from pursuing some very desirable end, for example, not touching an attractive telephone or not eating a packet of raisins; such tasks show that the ability to delay gratification of one's own desire increases between 18 and 30 months of age (Vaughn, Kopp, & Krakow, 1984). In many situations in childhood children must control their own behaviour—perhaps postpone gratification of their own desires—to comply with the requests and orders of adults, for example, by cleaning up their toys in response to an adult's request (e.g. Achermann, Dinneen, & Stevenson-Hinde, 1991). On some occasions, the children may anticipate such requests, which confirms their ability to guess what an adult might want in a given situation. In the second year of life, some children become distressed if things happen that conflict with what adults would want, for example, if toys break or buttons go missing (Cole, Barrett, & Zahn-Waxler, 1992; Kagan, 1984). Much of socialisation in early childhood consists of conflict and compromise between the desires of children and the desires of society, as often represented by their parents, and so it is hardly surprising that desire is a highly salient internal state at that point in development (Wellman, 1990).

Understanding of intention

Intention is an internal state that is closely related to desire (see Baron-Cohen, 1994). People do not simply want things; they try to pursue their aims and, in doing so, often signal their intentions. Important distinctions can, nonetheless, be made between desire and intention. For example, a person may want two incompatible things, but cannot intend to do both. Phillips (1993) gives the example of a person who wants to spend Christmas at home in England with her family and to spend it on a tropical beach; the two desires can exist simultaneously, but the person cannot intend to celebrate Christmas in both these ways.

   In addition, an understanding of a person's intention may be informed by information about that person's knowledge and beliefs. Thus, a child's understanding of intention may not be as easy as an appreciation of someone's desires expressed through conventional behavioural and emotional cues. In at least one sample, four-year-olds who could understand a person's false beliefs were unable to comprehend fortuitous, unintended positive outcomes (Phillips, 1993).

   Given that the understanding of intention is a complex achievement that may be refined throughout the preschool years, can the roots of this understanding be discerned in early life? There is evidence that infants can anticipate the actions of others, which eventually consolidates into an understanding that other people have intentions that they may try to carry out. For example, the infant who has just eaten a banana, feels sticky around the mouth, and now sees her mother coming toward her with a damp flannel may turn her head away to avoid being cleaned up. There are therefore signs that infants and toddlers are aware that acts may be intentional and they may sometimes make guesses about a companion's intent.

Understanding of intended vs. accidental acts

Frye (1993) has argued that, if infants are aware that their own actions are intentional, they should be able to direct their actions to a specific outcome and show awareness of the direct link between means and goal. He sought evidence for this awareness by studying infants' reactions to two different, surprising outcomes, one in which a familiar action had unusual effects and another where an odd action had to be used to produce a familiar effect (Frye, 1990). The infants were first presented with a standard "support task" (i.e. a toy resting on a cloth). Pulling the cloth towards themselves secured the toy. The task was then manipulated so that the toy was actually suspended slightly higher than the cloth. When the infant pulled the cloth, the toy shot off in the opposite direction. Infants as young as eight months of age showed surprise at this event, suggesting that they had expected the usual thing to happen when they pulled the cloth. In another version of the task, the toy would move towards the infant but only if the infant pulled a cloth that was 12 inches off to the side of the toy. The eight-month-olds did not show surprise at this mismatch between means and goal, and so Frye (1993) concluded that there is not sufficient evidence that their behaviour was intentional. Somewhat older toddlers at 16 and 24 months evinced surprise at both outcomes.

Anticipations of a companion's intent

Observations of very young children's conflicts with siblings and peers provide some evidence of anticipation of a companion's intents. As we noted earlier, toddlers often indicate their desires for an object by pointing to it, reaching for it, or simply naming the object in question. If such expressions of desire are shown, the possessor of an object is likely to pull the desired object out of the other child's reach, not waiting for a more concerted effort to get hold of the desired object (Hay & Ross, 1982; Caplan et al., 1991). Even a peer's approach from another part of the room may lead to possessors of objects taking steps to protect their possessions.

Sometimes, of course, the peer may have had no particular designs on the other child's possessions. As children grow older and spend time in preschool groups, the ability to assess peers' intentions accurately becomes critical. Aggressive children become increasingly disliked by their peers and, by the primary school years, actively rejected. Highly aggressive children often show particular deficits and biases in understanding the intentions of others; they are likely to assume that a peer who makes a neutral overture is actually intending to be aggressive (Dodge, Pettit, McClaskey, & Brown, 1986; Parker & Asher, 1987). By then making defensive, aggressive reactions to the misperceived intentions of the other child, aggressive children may escalate the encounters into disputes, and thus further confirm their reputations in the peer group. This association between misunderstanding of others' intentions and aggression may have long-term developmental consequences. In the primary school years, aggressive children who are rejected by their peers are more likely to associate with other generally antisocial children (Dishion, Patterson, Storlmiller, & Skinner, 1991), which in turn promotes eventual delinquency (Keenan, Loeber, Zhang, Stouthamer-Loeber, & Van Kammen, 1995; see also Farrington, Chapter 14 and Hartup, Chapter 6). It is important to learn more about very young children's understanding of their companions' intentions, in order to determine if these important individual differences emerge early in life and can be overcome.

THE "MACRO" LEVEL: INTERACTION, RELATIONSHIPS, AND THE GREATER SOCIAL ORDER

The foregoing review suggests that, by their third birthdays, children have come to understand a great deal about inner experience, their own, and other people's. Their understanding of the purely cognitive states of knowledge, belief and certainty is still incomplete (see Baron-Cohen, 1994), although they have achieved the ability to lie in some circumstances (e.g. Chandler, Fritz, & Hala, 1989). In general, it appears that the three-year-old has already learned a lot about what people are likely to want and how people are likely to feel in the course of immediate interaction. Children's own capacities for interaction have grown apace during this time. They share, help, co-operate, and resolve conflict with other people (Hay, 1984); they also have learned to argue their corners and pursue self-interest in socially acceptable, skilful ways (Dunn, 1988). What, then, could the three-year-old be said to understand about the social world in general? What have very young child's experiences with familiar companions taught them about the general properties of interaction, relationships, and society?

Understanding of interaction

Even in the first half of the first year of life, infants make significant contributions to interaction with their parents and other people (Reddy et al., 1997). The responsibility taken by infants to keep interaction progressing harmoniously is seen most clearly when they are paired with partners whose own capacities for interaction are immature or affected by circumstances, for example, when their mothers are depressed (e.g. Murray, 1992) or when they are interacting with other, equally unskilled infants (Hay, Nash, & Pedersen, 1983).

The capacity for interaction probably rests on the basically rhythmic nature of infants' own actions and vocalisations (see Kaye, 1977; Hay, 1985), but is soon bolstered by their growing awareness of social contingencies. Even very young infants can tell when they are dealing with a video representation of their mothers, taken out of real time and therefore showing behaviour that is not contingent on their actions (see Reddy et al., 1997). Sensitivity to contingency is also shown by the fact that the experience of noncontingent interaction not only disrupts infants' behaviour in the immediate situation but impedes their learning of other, nonsocial tasks (Dunham & Dunham, 1990).

Awareness of contingencies in social interaction of course can be discussed in terms of basic associative learning and thus would not qualify as a body of knowledge. Nonetheless, social understanding emerges gradually from the raw material of familiar associations and infants' growing appreciation of the patterns in their social experience. By the first birthday, infants can set the topics for interaction, by initiating as well as responding to familiar games (Gustafson, Green, & West, 1979; Ross & Goldman, 1977). At the most basic level, this implies that infants can associate particular interactive partners with particular themes for interaction.

Infants' understanding of what is required in a successful interaction can be discerned when the interaction breaks down. The co-operative games that infants characteristically play with adults and other children have several distinctive features: They entail mutual engagement, repetition of particular actions, and alternation of turns (Ross & Goldman, 1977). Infants themselves are sensitive to these critical features of co-operative interaction. In an experimental study, an experimenter engaged one-year-old infants in co-operative games with toys, and then failed to take her turn, instead merely sitting and smiling pleasantly at the infant (Ross & Kay, 1980). The infants responded to this interruption of the interaction by trying to get the adult to take her turn, gesturing and vocalising to her and sometimes demonstrating what precisely was needed to be done with the toys.

Just as children's understanding of syntax can be discerned in their overgeneralisation of grammatical rules, so their understanding about how to interact with a given partner can be revealed in overgeneralisation. For example, in an experimental study of 21-month-old children, pairs of children were observed together with their mothers on three consecutive days, in a playroom filled with toys (Hay & Ross, 1982). During their three days' acquaintance the pairs of children began to interact with each other in distinctive ways that persisted over the three days. One pair of

girls, whom we shall call Annie and Jenny, developed a particularly characteristic form of relating. Annie was extremely fond of playing with balls,
and was reported by her mother to own 36 balls at home. Each morning,
when they entered the playroom, she tried to get her hands on the ball. By
the second day, Jenny had noticed Annie's desire for the ball and inter-
fered with her goal, by running in, grabbing the ball, standing on a
cushion, and announcing "Jenny have ball!" This predictably led to even
more vociferous attempts on Annie's part to secure possession of the ball.
On the fourth day, half the pairs switched partners with another dyad who
had been following along the same procedures; the remaining dyads stayed
with the same partner. Jenny and Annie were in the group who switched
partners. On the fourth morning, Annie ran quickly to grab the ball and
held it close, away from the peer. Jenny, for her part, ran, grabbed the
ball, ran to the cushion, and made her speech. Both new partners seemed
completely uninterested in these proceedings. Both girls had generalised
from the specific interaction to a general way of interacting with peers,
which was now neither necessary nor successful.

Young children's understanding of the rules of interaction, including
turn-taking, and the strategies that can best be used to secure one's end in
interaction are perhaps most clear in their relationships with siblings
(Dunn, 1988, 1993). As children grow older, their understanding of interaction is revealed in their speech to their mothers and siblings, but it is also
shown in overtly emotional exchanges. For example, Dunn and
Slomkowski (1992, p. 74) quote a sequence in which a 36-month-old child
who has been kicking a football back and forth to the mother reacts when
the sibling gets in a kick:

> Child to sibling: No! It's Mummy's go again. No! It was Mummy's go again.
> Mother to child: Chrissie did it for me.
> Child: I'll put this ball away. I'm going to put it away if Chrissie's going to
> spoil it for Mummy.

With those words, the child indicates a clear awareness that actors take
turns in co-operative games, that nonparticipants should not necessarily
try to join in a game without agreement of all players, and that a game
might be spoiled if rules are not adhered to. At the same time, this is not
"cold cognition": The child ignores the fact that the mother has said she's
willing for the sibling to take her turn, and instead points out how the
game will be spoiled for the mother by the sibling's behaviour. This rather
manipulative interpretation of the incident reveals a keen understanding of
the relationships between the family members and perhaps the dynamics
of that family's life. Thus, children's growing understanding of the
features and rules of interaction probably takes place within the context

of their understanding of the important relationships in which they engage.

Understanding of relationships

By the end of the first year of life, infants have formed focused relationships with particular companions, notably their parents but also grandmothers, siblings, and other familiar persons (Schaffer & Emerson, 1964). Not all parent–infant relationships are alike. Qualitative features of particular parent–child relationships can be measured reliably in a mildly unpleasant laboratory procedure that might be deemed a "stress interview" for babies, Ainsworth's Strange Situation (Ainsworth & Wittig, 1969; for a review of studies using the procedure, see Belsky & Cassidy, 1994). Observations of children in the Strange Situation have revealed, for example, that an infant may be securely attached to the father yet insecurely attached to the mother, and vice versa (Main & Weston, 1981). Thus, even the one-year-old is accumulating experiences about qualitatively different relationships that will eventually underpin a more general understanding of the nature of and difficulties in interpersonal relationships.

The process of attachment is considered to be at least partly cognitive; Bowlby (1969) proposed that, by the end of the first three years of life, children have "working models" of relationships based on the specific features of their attachment relationships with their primary caregivers. Later writers in the attachment tradition have attempted to expand upon this concept of a working model in the light of more recent theories about children's social representations, scripts and world views (e.g. Bretherton, Ridgeway, & Cassidy, 1990). The Strange Situation is thought to provide behavioural evidence for the beginnings of a working model, but more elaborate, verbal representations of attachment relationships can then be tapped through projective tests and interview procedures in the preschool years (Belsky & Cassidy, 1994).

Bowlby (1969) believed that persons other than the biological mother could serve as attachment figures, but that human infants were biologically biased towards *monotropy*—a tendency to form one particularly salient relationship with a primary caregiver. This might suggest that children's concepts of relationships in general are particularly likely to be influenced by the quality of their relationship with their primary caregivers, who, in many societies, are often mothers. This hypothesis would of course be in line with Freud's (1938, p. 188) strong claim that the mother–child relationship was "unique, without parallel ... the template for all future love relationships". More recent attachment researchers have, however, pointed to the importance of the quality of the father–infant relationship as an influence on the child's approach to new relationships with nonfamily members (Bridges, Connell, & Belsky, 1988; Lamb, 1982). Still other theorists have argued for a multiple relationships approach, noting that children acquire their understanding of the social world from experiences with siblings, peers, and other adults, as well as their primary caregivers (Dunn, 1993; Nash & Hay, 1993). It is clear, however, that very aversive experiences with abusive caregivers can have particularly profound effects on children's understanding of relationships and their self-esteem (Cicchetti & Barnett, 1992). In particular, maltreatment impedes children's understanding of emotions (Camras et al., 1988) and intentions (Dodge, Bass, & Pettit, 1990).

There are certainly indications that one-year-olds are beginning to understand the distinctive features of particular relationships. They use conventional signs of affection with particular companions (Bretherton & Beeghley, 1982). They can enact the role of caregiver in their own symbolic play (Rheingold & Emery, 1986). The word "love" enters their vocabularies (Bretherton & Beeghley, 1982). Sometimes they appear to be distressed by events that encroach on their own attachment ties. For example, they may object to peers' interacting with their own mothers (Caplan et al., 1991; Hay & Ross, 1982). In an observational study of siblings, one toddler became greatly upset when the older sibling pretended to breast-feed a doll (Vespo et al., 1995).

Distinctive behavioural features of particular relationships are not limited to the realm of infant–caregiver attachment. Sibling relationships differ greatly in terms of their level of warmth, engagement, and conflict (Dunn, 1993). Behavioural preferences for individual peers can be discerned as early as the second year of life in day-care centres and play groups (Howes, 1988; Krawczyk, 1986). Children's emerging awareness of their own preferences and early friendships is attested to by the fact that parents are able, on the basis of conversation with their toddlers, to predict reliably the peers played with most in the preschool setting (Krawczyk, 1986). By the preschool years, children can name their friends and have strong preferences for peers who show prosocial as opposed to aggressive behaviour (Denham, McKinley, Couchoud, & Holt, 1990). Some early conceptions of friendship are surprisingly elaborate. Gottman (1983) cites an example of a pair of three-year-old children who maintained their friendship even after one child moved away. Although the parents were not close friends, the children insisted on keeping in touch and planned to marry when they reached the age of consent.

Social conventions and moral principles

We have seen that, in the first three years of life, children are gradually acquiring an understanding of a person's inner experiences, the structural features of social interaction, and the qualitative dimensions of particular interpersonal relationships. But are there any signs of a more general understanding of the greater social order—of the principles that regulate life in social groups? Classic theories of moral development have primarily charted important developments that take place around or after the age of six (Piaget, 1972; Kohlberg, 1964), and have paid little attention to developments in the first years of life. Nevertheless, there are indications that even toddlers can distinguish between moral issues and mere conventions (Smetana & Braeges, 1990), and observational studies of very young children's interactions with their parents, siblings, and peers have revealed some concern with general issues of social acceptability and justice (Dunn, 1988; Ross, Tesla, Kenyon, & Lollis, 1990).

In the first year of life, children seem to become aware of "standards" for their appearance and behaviour that have been set by the adult world; for example, they start becoming very concerned about broken toys, missing buttons, and the like (Cole et al., 1992; Kagan, 1984). Some children become distressed when adults use conventional objects in unconventional ways, for example, when an adult places a hat on a child's foot (Hay et al., 1985). This concern for "standards" is emerging at the same time that children are becoming better able to regulate their own behaviour, being able to wait patiently and refrain from touching attractive toys (Vaughn et al., 1984). At the same time, during the second and third years of life, relations with parents, siblings, and peers are becoming fraught with conflict over exactly such issues (Dunn, 1988; Hay, 1995).

Dunn (1988), Ross and her colleagues (1990) and Smetana (1989) have drawn attention to the fact that children's understanding of principles of justice emerges and becomes finely honed in these ordinary conflicts between peers and in the family circle. In conflict with their siblings, very young children defend their own positions and try to justify their actions (Dunn & Munn, 1986). They also begin to articulate principles of "fairness". Children's attempts to grapple with principles of justice in the context of conflict with siblings or peers are influenced by parents' reactions to such conflicts; parents themselves differ in the principles of justice they espouse (Ross et al., 1990).

Two concerns that bedevil social relations amongst adults and indeed nations—possession rights and justifications for aggression—are already salient matters for debate between toddlers and their companions. As we have seen, most disputes between young peers concern the possession and rightful use of particular objects (Hay, 1984; Ross & Conant, 1992), and many disputes between siblings also involve issues of possession (Dunn, 1988). Almost as soon as they can talk, toddlers claim rights to certain

objects: Assertions of possession—"Mine!", "Kenny have the phone!"—
are common features of toddlers' disputes with their peers (Caplan et al.,
1991; Hay & Ross, 1982). Conversely, even one-year-olds appear to
acknowledge the possession rights of others; young children who have had
prior possession of an object tend to win disputes over that object (for a
review of the evidence, see Ross & Conant, 1992). Right appears to make
might in the toddler years, a view that is upheld in interviews of five-year-
old children, who predict that the original owner of an object will indeed
win a dispute over its possession (Hay et al., 1992).

Interviews with preschoolers also indicate a belief that the use of
force may be justified if it is used to defend one's own possessions
(Ferguson & Rule, 1988; Hay et al., 1992). There are some indications
that this principle is adhered to in very young children's disputes with
peers and siblings. One- and two-year-olds rarely start their conflicts
with an act of force; rather, their designs on each others' possessions
are often expressed through gestures and speech, and nonforceful
reaching for or touching of the object in question. The use of force
becomes more likely as a conflict continues (Caplan et al., 1991; Hay
& Ross, 1982; Vespo et al., 1995).

Longitudinal observations of one- and two-year-olds at home with
familiar peers suggests that the tendency to use force whilst seeking objects
declines reliably over time (Hay, Castle & Davies, submitted). As children
acquire conversational powers, they are then able to justify their use of
retaliative aggression in particular situations (see Dunn, 1988, 1993).

In general, then, children's ordinary interactions with siblings and peers
provide many opportunities for the application of general moral principles,
and their understanding of both social conventions and justice emerges
gradually over the early years of life.

CONCLUSIONS: SELF AND SOCIETY

We began this exploration of the very early development of social understanding with reference to Baldwin's (1895) "dialectic of personal growth":
his notion that, as young humans learn about others, they come to understand themselves, and, as they learn about themselves, their understanding
of others is thereby increased. All the achievements that we have been
charting are paralleled by a growing emergence of a sense of self (see also
Moore, 1996). Towards the end of the second year of life, children come to
recognise themselves in mirrors (Lewis & Brooks-Gunn, 1979). They know
their names, use personal pronouns, and begin to make evaluative judgements about themselves and their own behaviour. During the first three
years of life we see burgeoning self-consciousness. Even infants may show
coy behaviour in interacting with adults (see Reddy et al., 1997); shyness

becomes more evident in the second year of life (Kagan, 1984). In the third years of life, children express both pride in their accomplishments and shame (Lewis, Stranger, & Sullivan, 1992). Even in the preschool years, some children report an excessive concern with responsibility for the problems of others and experience guilt (Zahn-Waxler & Robinson, in press). Understanding, and, perhaps more importantly, evaluation of the self is proceeding apace during the toddler and preschool years. Young children may be said to be constructing theories of mind; they are assuredly constructing models of themselves in relation to their social worlds.

In this chapter, as we tried to sketch out an organisational framework in which to consider young children's social understanding, we were impelled to consult many different sorts of studies, using quite different rules of evidence. It is not always easy nor indeed possible to integrate careful, parametric evaluations of children's performance in laboratory theory-of-mind tasks with the qualitative as well as quantitative evidence provided by less constrained interview studies or descriptions of children relating to familiar companions in familiar circumstances. We believe that the great variety of evidence on these matters needs to be sifted through with care. There are, however, some problems in doing so. Some important topics studied in past decades, such as children's very early relationships with siblings and peers, have almost disappeared from view in the 1990s. Only rarely are different methods used and different domains of social under-standing studied within the same sample, and so performance on standar-dised theory-of-mind tasks are only rarely seen in parallel with understanding-in-action in particular interpersonal relationships.

The recent focus on social understanding as an important dimension of development, and the particular fascination with children's potential as theorists of mind, has had a seminal impact on contemporary develop-mental and social psychology. Its influence on our thinking about social and cognitive development cannot be overemphasised. Nonetheless, it would be unfortunate indeed if the careful insights provided by the labora-tory paradigms became a hegemonic view of the social child that distracted critical attention away from all the many facets of social understanding. As humans, we are born as members of a social species, but there is a great deal about social life we only gradually come to understand.

REFERENCES

Achermann, J., Dinneen, E., & Stevenson-Hinde, J. (1991). Clearing up at 2.5 years. *British Journal of Developmental Psychology*, *9*, 365–375.

Ainsworth, M. D. S. & Wittig, B. A. (1969). Attachment and exploratory behavior of one-year-olds in a strange situation. In B. M. Foss (Ed.), *Determinants of infant behaviour* (Vol. 4, pp. 129–173). London: Methuen.

Astington, J. W., Harris, P. L., & Olson, D. R. (Eds.) (1988). *Developing theories of mind*. Cambridge, UK: Cambridge University Press.

Bakeman, R. & Adamson, L. B. (1984). Coordinating attention to people and objects in mother–infant and peer–infant interaction. *Child Development, 55*, 1278–1289.

Baldwin, J. M. (1895). *Mental development in the child and the race*. New York: Macmillan.

Baron-Cohen, S. (1994). Development of a theory of mind: Where would we be without the intentional stance? In M. Rutter & D. F. Hay (Eds.), *Development through life: A handbook for clinicians* (pp. 303–349). Oxford: Blackwell.

Baron-Cohen, S., Campbell, R., Karmiloff-Smith, A., Grant, J., & Walker, J. (1995). Are children with autism blind to the mentalistic significance of the eyes? *British Journal of Developmental Psychology, 13*, 379–398.

Belsky, J. & Cassidy, J. (1994). Attachment: Theory and evidence. In M. Rutter & D. F. Hay (Eds), *Development through life: A handbook for clinicians* (pp. 373–402). Oxford: Blackwell.

Bindra, D. (1974). A motivational view of learning, performance, and behavior modification. *Psychological Review, 81*, 1–26.

Bowlby, J. (1969). *Attachment and loss: Vol. 1. Attachment*. London: Hogarth Press.

Bretherton, I., Ridgeway, D., & Cassidy, J. (1990). The role of internal working models in the attachment relationship: Theoretical, empirical, and developmental considerations. In M. Greenberg, D. Cicchetti, & E. M. Cummings (Eds.), *Attachment in the preschool years* (pp. 273–320). Chicago, IL: University of Chicago Press.

Bretherton, I. & Beeghly, M. (1982). Talking about internal states: The acquisition of an explicit theory of mind. *Developmental Psychology, 18*, 906–921.

Bridges, K. (1932). Emotional development in early infancy. *Child Development, 3*, 324–341.

Bridges, L. J., Connell, J. P., & Belsky, J. (1988). Similarities and differences in infant–mother and infant–father interaction in the Strange Situation: A component process analysis. *Developmental Psychology, 24*, 92–100.

Brown, J. R. & Dunn, J. (1991). "You can cry, mum": The social and developmental implications of talk about internal states. *British Journal of Developmental Psychology, 9*, 237–255.

Butterworth, G. & Cochran, E. (1980). Towards a mechanism of joint visual attention in human infancy. *International Journal of Behavioural Development, 3*, 253–272.

Butterworth, G. & Jarrett, N. (1991). What minds have in common is space: Spatial mechanisms serving joint visual attention in infancy. *British Journal of Developmental Psychology, 9*, 55–72.

Campos, J. J. (1981). Human emotions: Their new importance and their role in social referencing. *Research and Clinical Center for Child Development Annual Report*, 1–7.

Campos, J. J. & Stenberg, C. (1981). Perception, appraisal, and emotion: The onset of social referencing. In M. E. Lamb & L. R. Sherrod (Eds), *Infant social cognition: Empirical and theoretical considerations* (pp. 273–314). Hillsdale, NJ: Lawrence Erlbaum Associates Inc.

Camras, L. A. Ribordy, S., Hill, J., Martino, S., Spaccarelli, S., & Stefani, R. (1988). Recognition and posing of emotional expressions by abused children and their mothers. *Developmental Psychology, 24*, 776–781.

Camras, L. A. & Sachs, V. B. (1991). Social referencing and caretaker expressive behavior in a day care setting. *Infant Behavior and Development, 14*, 27–36.

Caplan, M. Z. & Hay, D. F. (1989). Preschoolers' responses to peers' distress and beliefs about bystander intervention. *Journal of Child Psychology and Psychiatry, 30*, 231–242.

Caplan, M. Z., Vespo, J. E., Pedersen, J., & Hay, D. F. (1991). Conflict and its resolution in small groups of one- and two-year-olds. *Child Development, 62*, 1513–1524.

Chandler, M., Fritz, A. S., & Hala, S. (1989). Small scale deceit: Deception as a marker of two, three, and four-year-olds' early theories of mind. *Child Development, 60*, 1263–1277.

Charman, T., Swettenham, J., Baron-Cohen, S., Cox, A., Baird, G., & Drew, A. (1995).

Precursors to autism. Presentation to the Society for Research in Child Development, Indianapolis, IN.

Cicchetti, D. & Barnett, D. (1992). Attachment organization in maltreated preschoolers. *Development and Psychopathology*, *3*, 397–411.

Cohn, J. F. & Tronick, E. Z. (1983). Three-month-old infants' reaction to simulated maternal depression. *Child Development*, *54*, 185–193.

Cole, P. M., Barrett, K. C., & Zahn-Waxler, C. (1992). Emotion displays in two-year-olds during mishaps. *Child Development*, *63*, 314–324.

Cummings, E. M., Ballard, M., El-Sheikh, M., & Lake, M. (1991). Resolution and children's responses to interadult anger. *Developmental Psychology*, *27*, 462–470.

Cummings, E. M., Iannotti, R. J., & Zahn-Waxler, C. (1985). Influence of conflict between adults on the emotions and aggression of young children. *Developmental Psychology*, *21*, 495–507.

Cummings, E. M., Zahn-Waxler, C., & Radke-Yarrow, M. (1981). Young children's responses to expressions of anger and affection by others in the family. *Child Development*, *52*, 1274–1282.

Darley, J. M. & Latane, B. (1968). Bystander intervention in emergencies: Diffusion of responsibility. *Journal of Personality and Social Psychology*, *8*, 377–383.

Darwin, C. (1877). A biographical sketch of an infant. *Mind*, *2*, 285–294.

Demetriou, H. (in prep.) Children's reaction to the distress of their peers. Ph.D. thesis, University of London.

Denham, S. A., McKinley, M., Couchoud, E. A., & Holt, R. (1990). Emotional and behavioral predictors of preschool peer ratings. *Child Development*, *61*, 1145–1152.

Desrochers, S., Ricard, M., Decarie, T-G., & Allard, L. (1994). Developmental synchrony between social referencing and Piagetian sensorimotor causality. *Infant Behavior and Development*, *17*, 303–309.

Dishion, T. J., Patterson, G. R., Storlmiller, M., & Skinner, L. (1991). Family, school and behavioral antecedents to early adolescent involvement with antisocial peers. *Developmental Psychology*, *27*, 172–180.

Dodge, K. A., Bates, J. E., & Pettit, G. S. (1990). Mechanisms in the cycle of violence. *Science*, *250*, 1678–1683.

Dodge, K. A., Pettit, G. S., McClaskey, C. L., & Brown, M. M. (1986). Social competence in children. *Monographs of the Society for Research in Child Development*, *51* (Serial No. 213).

Dunham, P., & Dunham, F. (1990). Effects of mother–infant social interactions on infants' subsequent contingency task performance. *Child Development*, *61*, 785–793.

Dunn, J. (1988). *The beginnings of social understanding*. Cambridge, MA: Harvard University Press.

Dunn, J. (1993). *Young children's close relationships: Beyond attachment*. London: Sage.

Dunn, J. & Munn, P. (1986). Siblings and prosocial development. *International Journal of Behavioral Development*, *9*, 265–284.

Dunn, J. & Slomkowski, C. (1992). Conflict and the development of social understanding. In C. U. Shantz & W. W. Hartup (Eds.), *Conflict in child and adolescent development* (pp. 70–92). Cambridge, UK: Cambridge University Press.

Eckerman, C. O., Davis, C. C., & Didow, S. M. (1989). Toddlers' emerging ways of achieving coordination with a peer. *Child Development*, *60*, 440–453.

Farmer, J. A. M. & Frosch, D. L. (1996). L.A. stories: Aggression in preschoolers' narratives after the riots of 1992. *Child Development*, *67*, 19–32.

Feinman, S. & Lewis, M. (1983). Social referencing at ten months: A second-order effect on infants' responses to strangers. *Child Development*, *54*, 878–887.

Ferguson, T. J. & Rule, B. G. (1988). Children's attributions of retaliatory aggression. *Child Development*, *59*, 961–968.

Field, T. M., Healy, B., & Goldstein, S. (1988). Infants of depressed mothers show 'depressed' behaviour even with nondepressed adults. *Child Development, 59,* 1569–1579.

Field, T. M., Woodson, R., Greenberg, R., & Cohen, D. (1982). Discrimination and imitation of facial expressions by neonates. *Science, 146,* 668–670.

Freud, S. (1938). *An outline of psychoanalysis.* London: Hogarth Press.

Frye, D. (1990). The development of intention in infancy. In D. Frye & C. Moore (Eds.), *Children's theories of mind: Mental states and social understanding* (pp. 15–38). Hillsdale, NJ: Lawrence Erlbaum Associates Inc.

Frye, D. (1993). Causes and precursors of children's theories of mind. In D. F. Hay and A. Angold (Eds.), *Precursors and causes in development and psychopathology* (pp. 145–168). Chichester, UK: Wiley.

Gottman, J. M. (1983). How children become friends. *Monographs of the Society for Research in Child Development, 48* (Serial No. 201).

Gunnar, M. & Stone, C. (1984). The effects of positive maternal affect on infant responses to pleasant, ambiguous, and fear-provoking toys. *Child Development, 55,* 1231–1236.

Gustafson, G. E., Green, J. A., & West, M. J. (1979). The infant's changing role in mother–infant games: The growth of social skills. *Infant Behavior and Development, 2,* 301–308.

Haviland, J. M. & Lelwica, M. (1987). The induced affect response: 10-week-old infants' responses to three emotion expressions. *Developmental Psychology, 23,* 97–104.

Hay, D. F. (1984). Social conflict in early childhood. *Annals of Child Development, 1,* 1–44.

Hay, D. F. (1985). Learning to form relationships in infancy: Parallel attainments with parents and peers. *Developmental Review, 5,* 122–161.

Hay, D. F., Castle, J., & Davies, L. (submitted). Seeking precursors to serious aggression in very young girls and boys.

Hay, D. F., Caplan, M., Castle, J., & Stimson, C. A. (1991). Does sharing become increasingly "rational" in the second year of life? *Developmental Psychology, 27,* 987–993.

Hay, D. F. & Murray, P. (1982). Giving and requesting: Social facilitation of infants' offers to adults. *Infant Behavior and Development, 5,* 301–310.

Hay, D. F., Murray, P., Cecire, S., & Nash, A. (1985). Social learning of social behavior in early life. *Child Development, 56,* 43–57.

Hay, D. F., Nash, A., & Pedersen, J. (1981). Responses of six-month-olds to the distress of their peers. *Child Development, 52,* 1071–1075.

Hay, D. F., Nash, A., & Pedersen, J. (1983). Interaction between six-month-old peers. *Child Development, 54,* 557–562.

Hay, D. F. & Ross, H. S. (1982). The social nature of early conflict. *Child Development, 53,* 105–113.

Hay, D. F., Stimson, C. A., & Castle, J. (1990). Imitation and desire: A meeting of minds in infancy. In D. Frye & C. Moore (Eds.), *Children's theories of mind* (pp. 115–137). Hillsdale, NJ: Lawrence Erlbaum Associates Inc.

Hay, D. F., Zahn-Waxler, C., Cummings, E. M., & Iannotti, R. J. (1992). Young children's views about conflict with peers: A comparison of the daughters and sons of depressed and well women. *Journal of Child Psychology and Psychiatry, 33,* 669–683.

Hirshberg, L. M. & Svejda, M. (1990). When infants look to their parents: I. Infants' social referencing of mothers compared to fathers. *Child Development, 61,* 1175–1186.

Hobson, P. R. (1991). Against the theory of "theory of mind". *British Journal of Developmental Psychology, 9,* 33–51.

Hoffman, M. L. (1975). Developmental synthesis of affect and cognition and its implications for altruistic motivation. *Developmental Psychology, 11,* 607–622.

Hornik, R., Risenhoover, N., & Gunnar, M. (1987). The effects of maternal positive, neutral, and negative affective communications on infant responses to new toys. *Child Development,* *58,* 937–944.

Howes, C. (1988). Peer interaction of young children. *Monographs of the Society for Research in Child Development, 53* (Serial No. 217).

Izard, C. E., Fantauzzo, C. A., Castle, J. M., Haynes, O. M., Rayias, M. R., & Putnam, P. H. (1995). The ontogeny of infants' facial expressions in the first nine months of life. *Developmental Psychology, 31,* 997–1013.

Kagan, J. (1984). *The nature of the child.* New York: Basic.

Kaye, K. (1977). *The social and mental life of babies.* Brighton: Harvester.

Keenan, K., Loeber, R., Zhang, Q., Stouthamer-Loeber, M., & Van Kammen, W. B. (1995). The influence of deviant peers on the development of boys' disruptive and delinquent behavior: A temporal analysis. *Development and Psychopathology, 7,* 715–726.

Kohlberg, L. (1964). Development of moral character and moral ideology. In M. L. Hoffman & L. W. Hoffman (Eds.), *Review of child development research.* (Vol. 1, pp. 383–431). New York: Russell Sage.

Krawczyk, R. (1986). *Friendship in a toddler preschool.* Unpublished doctoral dissertation, State University of New York at Stony Brook.

Lamb, M. E. (1982). The father–child relationship: A synthesis of biological, evolutionary, and social perspectives. In L. W. Hoffman, R. Gandelman & H. R. Schoffman (Eds.), *Parenting: Its causes and consequences* (pp. 55–73). Hillsdale, NJ: Lawrence Erlbaum Associates Inc.

Leung, E. & Rheingold, H. L. (1981). Development of pointing as a social gesture. *Developmental Psychology, 17,* 215–220.

Lewis, M. & Brooks-Gunn, J. (1979). Self-knowledge and emotional development. In M. Lewis & L. A. Rosenblum (Eds.), *The development of affect* (pp. 205–226). New York: Plenum.

Lewis, M., Stranger, C., & Sullivan, M. W. (1992). Differences in shame and pride as a function of children's gender and task difficulty. *Child Development, 63,* 630–638.

Main, M. & Weston, D. (1981). The quality of the toddler's relationship to mother and father: Related to conflict behavior and readiness to establish new relationships. *Child Development, 52,* 932–940.

Moore, C. (1996). Theories of mind in infancy. *British Journal of Developmental Psychology, 14,* 19–40.

Murphy, L. B. (1937). *Social behavior and child personality: An exploratory study of the roots of sympathy.* New York: Columbia University Press.

Murray, L. (1992). The impact of postnatal depression on infant development. *Journal of Child Psychology and Psychiatry, 33,* 543–561.

Nash, A. (1988). *Mothers' and infants' behavior prior to separation and infants' subsequent encounters with new acquaintances.* Poster presented at the International Conference on Infant Studies, Washington, DC.

Nash, A. & Hay, D. F. (1993). Relationships in infancy as precursors and causes of later relationships and psychopathology. In D. F. Hay & A. Angold (Eds.), *Precursors and causes in development and psychopathology* (pp. 199–232). Chichester, UK: Wiley.

Parker, J. G. & Asher, S. R. (1987). Peer relations and later adjustment: Are low-accepted children "at risk"? *Psychological Bulletin, 102,* 357–389.

Phillips, W. (1993). *Understanding of intention and desire by children with autism.* Unpublished Ph.D. thesis, University of London.

Phillips, W., Baron-Cohen, S., & Rutter, M. (in press). To what extent can children with autism understand desire? *Development and Psychopathology.*

Piaget, J. (1972). *The moral judgement of the child.* London: Routledge & Kegan Paul. (Original work published 1951).

Preyer, W. (1889). *The mind of the child* (H. W. Brown, Trans.) New York: Appleton.

Radke-Yarrow, M. & Zahn-Waxler, C. (1984). Roots, motives, and patterning in children's prosocial behavior. In E. Staub, D. Bar-tal, J. Karylowski, & J. Reykowski (Eds.), *The development and maintenace of prosocial behavior: International perspectives on positive morality*. New York: Plenum.

Radke-Yarrow, M., Zahn-Waxler, C., Richardson, D. T., Susman, A., & Martinez, P. (1994). Caring behavior in children of clinically depressed and well mothers. *Child Development, 65*, 1405–1414.

Reddy, V., Hay, D. F., Murray, L., & Trevarthen, C. (1997). Communication in infancy: Mutual regulation of affect and attention. In G. Bremner, A. Slater, & G. Butterworth (Eds.), *Infant development: Recent advances* (pp. 247–273). Hove: Psychology Press.

Rheingold, H. L., Cook, K. V., & Kowlowitz, V. (1987). Commands activate the behavior and pleasure of 2-year-olds. *Developmental Psychology, 23*, 146–151.

Rheingold, H. L. & Eckerman, C. O. (1973). Fear of the stranger: A critical examination. In H. Reese (Ed.), *Advances in child development and behavior* (Vol. 8, pp. 186–222). New York: Academic Press.

Rheingold, H. L. & Emery, G. (1986). The nurturant acts of very young children. In D. Olweus, J. Block, & M. Radke-Yarrow (Eds.), *The development of antisocial and prosocial behavior: Research, theories, and issues* (pp. 75–96). New York: Academic Press.

Rheingold, H. L., Hay, D. F., & West, M. J. (1976). Sharing in the second year of life. *Child Development, 47*, 1148–1158.

Richters, J. E. & Martinez, P. E. (1993). The NIMH Community Violence Project: I. Children as victims of and witnesses to violence. *Psychiatry, 56*, 7–21.

Ross, H. S. & Conant, C. L. (1992). The social structure of early conflict: Interaction, relationships, and alliances. In C. U. Shantz & W. W. Hartup (Eds.), *Conflict in child and adolescent development* (pp. 153–185). Cambridge, UK: Cambridge University Press.

Ross, H. S. & Goldman, B. D. (1977). Infants' sociability toward strangers. *Child Development, 48*, 638–642.

Ross, H. S. & Kay, D. A. (1980). The origins of social games. *New Directions for Child Development, 9*, 17–31.

Ross, H. S., Tesla, C., Kenyon, B., & Lollis, S. (1990). Maternal intervention in toddler peer conflict: The socialization of principles of justice. *Developmental Psychology, 26*, 994–1003.

Sagi, A. & Hoffman, M. L. (1976). Empathic distress in the newborn. *Developmental Psychology, 10*, 175–176.

Schaffer, H. R. & Emerson, P. E. (1964). The development of social attachments in infancy. *Monographs of the Society for Research in Child Development, 29* (Serial No. 94).

Shantz, C. U. (1987). Conflicts between children. *Child Development, 58*, 283–305.

Sigman, M. D. & Mundy, P. (1993). Infant precursors of childhood intellectual and verbal abilities. In D. F. Hay & A. Angold (Eds.), *Precursors and causes in development and psychopathology* (pp. 123–144). Chichester, UK: Wiley.

Simner, M. L. (1971). Newborn's response to the cry of another infant. *Developmental Psychology, 5*, 135–150.

Smetana, J. G. (1989). Toddlers' social interactions in the context of moral and conventional transgressions in the home. *Developmental Psychology, 25*, 499–508.

Smetana, J. G. & Braeges, J. L. (1990). The development of toddlers' moral and conventional judgments. *Merrill-Palmer Quarterly, 36*, 329–346.

Sroufe, L. A. (1977). Wariness of strangers and the study of infant development. *Child Development, 48*, 731–746.

Stern, W. (1924). *Psychology of early childhood up to the sixth year of age* (A. Barwell, Trans.) New York: Holt.

Tronick, E. Z. & Weinberg, M. K. (1997). Depressed mothers and infants: Failure to form dyadic states of consciousness. In L. Murray & P. J. Cooper (Eds.) *Postpartum depression and child development* (pp. 54–81). London: Guilford Press.

Vaughn, B.E., Kopp, C. B., & Krakow, J. B. (1984). The emergence and consolidation of self-control from eighteen to thirty months of age: Normative trends and individual differences. *Child Development, 55*, 990–1004.

Vespo, J. E., Pedersen, J., & Hay, D. F. (1995). Young children's conflicts with peers and siblings. *Child Study Journal, 25*, 189–212.

Walden, T. A. & Ogan, T. A. (1988). The development of social referencing. *Child Development, 59*, 1230–1240.

Wellman, H. M. (1990). *The child's theory of mind.* Cambridge, MA: MIT Press.

Wellman, H. & Wooley, J. (1990). From simple desires to ordinary beliefs: The early development of everyday psychology. *Cognition, 35*, 245–275.

Zahn-Waxler, C., Radke-Yarrow, M., & King, R. (1979). Child rearing and children's prosocial initiations toward victims of distress. *Child Development, 50*, 319–330.

Zahn-Waxler, C., Radke-Yarrow, M., Wagner, E., & Chapman, M. (1992). Development of concern for others. *Developmental Psychology, 28*, 126–136.

Zahn-Waxler, C. & Robinson, J. (in press). Empathy and guilt: Early origins of feelings of responsibility. In J. P. Tangney & K. W. Fischer (Eds), *Self-conscious emotions: Shame, guilt, embarrassment, and pride.* New York: Guilford Press.

Zarbatany, L. & Lamb, M. E. (1985). Social referencing as a function of information source: Mothers versus strangers. *Infant Behavior and Development, 8*, 25–33.

10 Children's perspective on the emotional process

Mark Meerum Terwogt
Free University of Amsterdam, The Netherlands
Hedy Stegge
Free University of Amsterdam, The Netherlands

Both children and psychologists face essentially the same problem: How to understand human action? In line with the behaviourist tradition, children are initially inclined to explain human action exclusively in terms of situational determinants. However, they soon realise the limitations of their early theorising, and start to appreciate the need for the concept of an intermediate active mind. By then, children have taken the step from behaviourism to mentalism (Harris & Olthof, 1982) and develop a so-called "theory of mind" (e.g. Wellman, 1990).

In this chapter, we will focus on an important part of the child's general theory of mind—his or her understanding of emotion (see also Harris, 1989; Meerum Terwogt & Harris, 1993; Meerum Terwogt & Stegge, 1995a; Saarni & Harris, 1989). We will outline a general framework for a folk theory of emotion. We will then discuss some important aspects of the child's growing meta-emotional understanding: Their knowledge of the causes of emotion; and their understanding of the interpersonal consequences of emotional behaviour. First, it will be shown that with increasing age, children come to appreciate that the same eliciting condition can evoke different feelings both across and within individuals, depending on the perspective someone takes on the situation. Second, it will be shown that children come to understand that a particular feeling state may be expressed in different ways depending on the expected interpersonal consequences in a specific context. Finally, it will be shown how children's growing meta-emotional understanding offers the possibility of deliberate attempts to regulate their inner feeling states and influences the type of coping strategies that will be used.

THE CHILD'S NAÏVE "THEORY OF EMOTION"

It is common knowledge that people do not act on reality but on a mental representation of reality. And although there is presumably a useful similarity between the two, they will never be exactly the same. First, any representation implies the reduction of information. Attention is selective, so different people may react to different aspects of the same situation. Moreover, the meaning of the available information is not always obvious. It requires interpretation and completion and thus may have different implications. Suppose you think you are entering an empty house and you hear a noise in the adjacent room. It is conceivable that you immediately think of a burglar and become frightened. If, on the other hand, you have good reasons to assume that your partner has returned early from work, your reaction will be in accord with that hypothesis.

Do young children appreciate the difference between the real, physical world and one's mental representation of it? Piaget (1929) was quite sceptical about their abilities in this respect. He argued that young children's perception of mental entities (such as dreams) as external, palpable realities that are potentially visible to others, reflects an inability to discriminate between mental and physical phenomena. One can imagine that this "childhood realism", as Piaget called it, would make it virtually impossible to communicate with young children. And indeed, in the Rousseau–Piaget tradition, the child's consciousness was long considered primitive, irrational, and inaccessible (Koops, Meerum Terwogt, & Rieffe, in press). According to Wellman (1990), however, Piaget's claim of childhood realism is only valid with respect to epistemological questions that address the origin of phenomena. On the ontological level (i.e. when asked about the nature of mental vs. physical phenomena), children as young as three years of age seem to be able to make the relevant distinction: "You can touch the dog of your friend, but if you make a picture of that dog in your head, nobody can really touch that dog" (Wellman & Estes, 1986). They also realise that you need some physical strength to move objects (e.g. to open a pair of scissors) but if you want to open and close an imaginary pair of scissors, you "only need to think about it" (Estes, Wellman, & Woolley, 1989). Apparently, entities in different domains obey different rules, and three-year-olds already seem to have some basic knowledge of these rules (see Hay and Demetriou, Chapter 9).

Belief-desire reasoning

We have seen that young children can distinguish between physical and mental phenomena. However, this does not imply that they understand the possible relation between the two—the fact that our perception of reality is affected by what we *want* to see and what we *believe* we see. Young children seem to lack the conception of an active mind needed to appreciate such a relation. Wellman (1990) claims that before the age of 3 years, children consider the mind to be a kind of container: Mental entities, like thoughts or dreams, can enter and leave your head, but nothing happens with them in between. As a result of this early conceptualisation of the mind, young children explain their own and other peoples' actions in terms of desires only: "You do something because you want something". The adult folk psychology, in contrast, assumes the existence of two different kinds of psychological constructs: "desires" (wishes, needs, preferences, urges, hopes, ambitions and the like); and "beliefs" (opinions, convictions, expectations, assumptions, judgements, and the like)—"People do something because they *think* they can fulfil their desire by doing so".

The switch from a simple "desire theory" to a more complex "belief-desire theory" is usually demonstrated by studies within the so-called "false-belief paradigm". The basic assumption is that an adequate understanding of the constructive character of beliefs requires children to acknowledge that people may react differently in the same situation if they posses different information. In the original experiment conducted by Wimmer and Perner (1983), children saw the puppet Maxi putting away a bar of chocolate. After Maxi left the scene, his mother came in, found the chocolate and put it in a different place. The children were asked where Maxi would look for his candy when he returned. Whereas five-year-olds clearly succeeded on the task, three-year-olds mostly came up with the wrong answer. Apparently, they do not yet appreciate the fact that Maxi will act on the basis of his prior belief—information that they know to be false. Based on results of studies that used the false-belief paradigm, most "theory of mind" experimenters pinpoint the onset of an adult perspective on beliefs somewhere between the age of three and four. At the age of four, children seem to realise that people do act on the apparent rather than the real. They predict, for instance, that someone might even try to eat a stone if it looks like an egg (Flavell, Green, & Flavell, 1989).

Pretend play

The onset of belief-desire reasoning seems to be stimulated by an important learning experience—pretend play (Leslie, 1987). Usually, pretend play spontaneously emerges somewhere in the second year of life. A young girl acts as if her doll is a genuine person (Wolf, Rygh, & Altshuler, 1984). At first, the doll is nothing more than a passive recipient of the child's nursing. But later the young "mother" treats the doll as an independent person who will, for example, be reprimanded for actions the girl normally likes to do herself or be reassured and told not to be afraid of the girls's own loved pet dog. Although children may occasionally show confusion between pretence and reality (DiLalla & Watson, 1988), their experiences within the realm of pretend play are likely to improve the capacity for imaginative projection, by which mechanism different opinions and different feelings in others may be detected (Harris, 1989). This is particularly true when children are involved in joint pretend play and correct each other whenever the rules of the game are violated.

Empirical work has shown that children with siblings have a more precocious understanding of false-belief tasks than only children (Bowler & Norris, 1993), which suggests that engagement in conversation helps them to build a theory of mind. Experiences with siblings seem to be important not only because children are being taught by a more experienced person (for children with younger siblings seem to benefit as well) but also because it allows children to discover that not only their parents have thoughts and feelings different from their own, but also "people more like them" (i.e. their siblings). Whenever children experience a conflict of interest with their siblings, they need a model to explain the perspective of both parties in order to resolve the conflict (Bartsch & Wellman, 1995).

Ascribing emotions

Like any ability, belief-desire reasoning is initially used appropriately only within the simplest context. In a study on emotion, Harris et al. (1989) used the false-belief paradigm but lengthened the behavioural chain by asking for the protagonist's resulting emotional state. They showed children how Ellie the Elephant was tricked by the mischievous monkey, Mickey. Ellie planned to go for a walk. Before leaving, she had put a can of coke on the table, ready to drink when she later came home thirsty. The children were told explicitly that Ellie likes coke very much, but hates milk. After the elephant was gone, the children witnessed the monkey changing the content of the can for milk. They were then asked two different questions: When Ellie sees the can, how will she feel before see takes a sip? And how will see feel afterwards? The second question is a relatively simple one. To give the right answer, children only have to know that the fulfilment of a desire evokes a happy feeling, whereas an unhappy feeling is triggered if a desire is not satisfied. Both four- and six-year-olds were found to be quite able to apply this rule and predict the correct emotion. However, to answer the first question correctly, the same knowledge has to be applied within the context of false-belief reasoning: Ellie will be happy because she *thinks* that her wish (drinking coke) will be fulfilled. Less than 30 per cent of the four-year-olds (as opposed to 75 per cent of the 6-year-olds) were able to come up with the right answer under these more complicated conditions.

So the basis of young children's belief-desire reasoning is a rather shaky one. The slightest increase in complexity may cause them to abandon the newly acquired principle and return to the old model. Obviously, children still have a long way to go before the conception of an active, constructive mind is firmly established and widely applied.

In the Harris at al. (1989) experiment, children seem to understand the relation between desire and emotion. That is not to say, however, that they regard an emotion as an inner mental state under all circumstances. Six-year-olds still typically answer the identity question ("How do you know that you are happy/sad/etc.?") by referring either to the eliciting situation or to behavioural correlates; that is, to the observable components of the emotional process (Harris, Olthof, & Meerum Terwogt, 1981). They typically say "You are happy, when it is your birthday" or "You are happy when you are laughing and jumping up and down". Ten-year-olds, in contrast, behave more like adults and tend to answer with phrases like "I'm happy when I feel happy inside". Although it is an almost tautological response, it clearly shows that the internal state is now considered to be the central element of the emotional process. Not surprisingly, this switch from a "behaviouristic" to a "mentalistic theory" (Harris & Olthof, 1982) also has implications for children's beliefs regarding other aspects of emotion, such as the strategies they consider useful in regulating their inner emotional experience. Six-year-olds already acknowledge that a wilful attempt to improve your own mood state can be effective. When asked which strategies should be employed, they provide answers like: "Then you should go out and play with your friend". Thus, they suggest *doing* something that makes you happy. Four years later, however, children acknowledge that *thinking* of something fun can be just as effective (Harris et al., 1981). We will discuss this shift to a more mentalistic perspective on the process of emotion regulation at length in the section on coping with negative emotions (p. 261).

Before doing so, we would like to emphasise that the step from the first signs of a mentalistic conception of emotions to the strategic exploitation of the key notions of the model within the context of emotion regulation is quite a large one. Because an adaptive coping attempt involves almost everything there is to know about the emotional process, we will discuss first some other aspects of children's growing meta-emotional understanding, that is, their knowledge of the causes of emotion and their beliefs regarding the interpersonal consequences of emotional-expressive behaviour.

CHILDREN'S UNDERSTANDING OF THE CAUSES OF EMOTION

At about 2- to 2.5 years of age, children start to use simple emotion words like happy, sad, mad, and afraid to refer to their own inner states. Moreover, their causal use of these terms ("Grandma mad. I wrote on wall"; "Me fall down. Me cry") demonstrates an early understanding of the link between a particular emotion and the eliciting condition (Bretherton & Beeghly, 1982). Somewhat later, children spontaneously make inferences about the internal states of others in emotionally charged situations as well.

Additional evidence for an early understanding of the relation between situation and emotion comes from experimental work, in which the use of emotion words was elicited by presenting children with videotape recordings of affectively laden interactions, meant to evoke happiness, sadness, or anger (Smiley & Huttenlocher, 1989). About half of the 2- to 3-year-olds correctly applied the label "happy" and about a quarter appropriately used the labels "sad" and "mad". Studies with somewhat older children have convincingly shown that by the age of 3 to 5 years, children have a firm understanding of the causal link between several basic emotions (happiness, sadness, anger, and fear) and the common elicitors of these affective states (Borke, 1971; Harris, Olthof, Meerum Terwogt, & Hardman, 1987; Harter & Whitesell, 1989; Trabasso, Stein, & Johnson, 1981).

The empirical work discussed so far suggests that even very young children have an understanding of the common determinants of a set of basic emotions. Recent theoretical and empirical elaborations of these findings (Harris, 1989; Harris et al., 1989; Stein & Levine, 1989) shed some light on the question of how young children's knowledge about emotion is organised and exactly how emotions are differentiated from each other. It was shown that at the age of three years, children already combine goal-outcome information to both predict and explain a story character's emotional response: Getting something you want or avoiding something you don't want results in the positive emotion of happiness, whereas not being able to get something you do want or getting something you don't want elicits a negative emotion (sadness or anger). Even at a very young age, children seem to use one of the very same mental concepts as adults (i.e. the actor's goals or desires) to make sense of their own and other people's emotional lives.

However, that is not to say that children's emotional understanding does not change in important ways during the course of development. In the remaining part of this section, we will discuss how children's knowledge develops to include: (1) an understanding of the determinants of a broader array of more complex emotional reactions; (2) the capacity to analyse the antecedents of emotion into greater causal depth; and (3) a more sophisticated understanding of the subjective nature of the appraisal process, which results in an increased appreciation of the possible occurrence of simultaneous emotions and the significance of personal information.

Understanding complex emotions

Harris et al. (1987) presented children aged 5 to 14 with 20 common emotion terms and asked them to generate an appropriate eliciting condition for each emotion (to be judged as appropriate by a group of adults). Five-year-old children were found to mention situations that were distinctively associated with happiness, sadness, anger, fear, and shyness only. This list was rapidly extended to include pride, jealousy, worry, guilt, and gratitude at the age of 7, and disgust, relief, shame, surprise, curiosity, excitement, and disappointment at the ages of 10 to 14. Children thus quickly move from an understanding of basic emotions linked with a discrete facial expression (or posture as in the case of shyness) to an insight into more complex emotions for which proper identification critically requires the use of situational cues. Indeed, it has been shown that the significance of contextual information is increasingly appreciated as children grow older. Reichenbach and Masters (1983) presented 4- and 7-year-old children with stories in which conflicting emotional cues were offered (e.g. a sad facial expression, was paired with a happy event). The authors showed that the youngest age group tended to rely on the facial expression cues more often, whereas the older children used the situational information to a greater extent when predicting the protagonist's emotional reaction. Gnepp (1983) elaborated on this issue by studying in more detail *how* children of different ages tend to integrate the conflicting information provided by different emotional cues. When asked to tell a story about affectively equivocal situations, the percentages of cases in which a coherent story was provided increased from 46 per cent at the ages of 3 and 4, to 65 per cent at the ages of 6 and 7, to 80 per cent at the ages of 11 and 12. Moreover, it was shown that preschoolers most frequently attributed an idiosyncratic perspective to the story protagonist ("This boy likes getting a shot"), whereas older children were more likely to elaborate on the situation in an attempt to actually *explain* the actor's discrepant reaction in terms of his/her goals ("This girl is happy because the doctor is going to give her a shot and that'll relieve her pain").

Analysing affect-eliciting conditions

As already mentioned, preschoolers begin to understand simple emotions like happiness, sadness or anger in terms of private mental states, like the actor's goals or desires. For an adequate understanding of these simple, so-called outcome-dependent emotions, it suffices that the child analyses the affective situation in terms of goal-outcome structures: People are happy if they get what they want, but sad if they don't get what they want (Harris, 1989). However, in order to be able to understand more complex, so-called attribution-dependent emotions like guilt, shame, or pride, the child needs to move beyond a simple appraisal of the situation in terms of the outcome and has to engage in a more sophisticated appraisal process in which the causal conditions that evoke the emotion are analysed in greater detail. Thompson (1989) has found empirical evidence for a developmental transition from outcome-dependent to attribution-dependent emotional inferences in a sample of second-graders, fifth-graders, and college students. When questioned about achievement and moral issues, fifth-graders and adults were more likely to provide attribution-dependent emotional inferences, whereas second-graders most often made outcome-dependent emotional inferences. That is not to say that children younger than 8 years do not make attribution-dependent inferences at all. In fact, several studies show that they do but their usage of dimensions of causality is nondiscriminating. For example, they will profess to feel guilty not only in controllable situations (which adults claim as well), but also in uncontrollable situations (Graham, Doubleday, & Guarino, 1984; Stipek & De Cotis, 1988). It is only later in development that children's reports of emotion reflect a complex attribution-dependent structure (Ferguson, Olthof, Luiten, & Rule, 1984; Olthof, Ferguson, & Luiten, 1989; Thompson, 1989).

Understanding the simultaneity of emotions

In a lot of empirical work, it has been shown that young children do not understand that people can experience different emotional reactions simultaneously (e.g. Donaldson & Westerman, 1986; Harter, 1983; Meerum Terwogt, Koops, Oosterhoff, & Olthof, 1986; Olthof et al., 1989). A more systematic approach to the issue of simultaneity (Harter & Buddin, 1987; Harter & Whitesell, 1989) has resulted in a five-step developmental acquisition sequence governed by two dimensions; the valence of the two emotions and the number of targets toward which the emotions are directed. According to this model, 5-year-olds simply deny that two feelings can be experienced at the same time. At the age of 7, children acknowledge that two feelings can coexist if the emotions have the same valence and are directed to one target (e.g. You can be both sad and mad if your brother broke your toy). At 8 to 9 years of age, they understand that two same-valence emotions can be experienced that bear on different targets (e.g. You are mad that a friend hit you, and sad because she doesn't want to play with you anymore). At the age of 10, children appreciate the occurrence of two opposite valence feelings, but only if they are directed toward different targets (e.g. You are sad because you failed an important test in school, but happy because you are going to do something fun at the weekend). And finally, at the age of 11, children understand that two opposite-valence feelings can be evoked by the same target (You are sad because your dog is ill, but happy because he seems to be recovering quite well). This developmental sequence reflects children's growing understanding of the multiple or changing representations of emotion situations: They realise more and more that it is possible to look at the same situation or the same object from different perspectives.

The significance of personal information

As there are many events that elicit more or less the same emotion in different people, a person's affective reaction can often be predicted from a careful analysis of the prevailing situation. It has been shown, for example, that receiving presents on your birthday is associated with happiness, not only across different age groups but also across cultures (Lewis, 1989). Similarly, the loss of a pet generally elicits sadness, the presence of unpleasant food results in disgust, and an unexpected change in appearance (pink hair) evokes surprise. Children's understanding of these situation–emotion links can be understood in terms of a kind of two-part script based on experience (Lewis, 1989). Whenever they are provided with one part of the script, be it a specific emotion or a prototypical situation, children can easily come up with the other part of the knowledge structure.

However, some eliciting situations are more equivocal. Many events can trigger different emotions, because they can be evaluated in different ways depending on characteristics of the actors involved (Ferguson & Stegge, 1995). For example, failure on a task may elicit anger if someone else is thought to be responsible for it, but shame if it is attributed to a lack of personal competence. Likewise, a trip to the swimming pool at the weekend evokes happiness in someone who loves to swim, but anger, fear, or sadness in someone who hates swimming. In order to predict the actor's emotional reaction correctly under such circumstances, personal information needs to be taken into account that can explain individual differences in people's perspectives on the prevailing situation.

Gnepp (1989) has argued that children learn to recognise emotionally equivocal situations in the course of development. Moreover, they learn to use different types of personal information, as well as strategies to acquire information not yet available. We have already seen that even very young children (3 to 5 years of age) acknowledge the significance of personal goals for predicting another person's emotional reaction to a certain situation. In the Stein and Levine (1987) experiment, they referred back to the actor's desires when explaining his/her emotional reaction ("Tina is happy 'cause she likes puppies"). Similarly, they were found to predict correctly the protagonist's happiness or sadness on the basis of his/her personal goals and preferences, even if these are different from the child's own likings (Gnepp, Klayman, & Trabasso, 1982; Harris et al., 1989; Wellman, 1990). In these experiments, children were explicitly provided with the necessary information. However, in everyday experience, personal information that can explain an actor's individual perspective on a particular situation is not always that obvious and needs to be actively searched for. In a study by Gould (reported in Gnepp, 1989), it was shown that this is a particularly difficult task for children aged 5 and 6. Even if they acknowledged the necessity of gaining additional knowledge about the actor, they found it hard to ask the right questions to get to the information needed. With increasing age, children's abilities in this respect were shown to increase dramatically, which certainly helps them to make the correct emotional inferences not only in the laboratory but beyond it.

In the course of development, children not only learn to recognise emotionally equivocal situations, they also use different types of personal information more appropriately. Between the ages of 5 and 8, children learn to appreciate the influence of cultural stereotypes, like the actor's age or sex. They no longer need to be provided with the particular preferences of a specific actor, but are increasingly able to infer the actor's goals from a general knowledge base about preferences in particular social groups which may be different from their own. Thus, they can set aside their own perspective on the prevailing situation, and use a kind of cultural stereotype instead. However, it is only at a somewhat older age (8 to 12 years) that children learn to make personalised inferences about an actor's appraisals based on his/her previous behaviour, experiences or personality traits (Gnepp, 1989). They may come to realise, for example, that someone might be afraid even of a cute little dog, because this is a person that is easily frightened, or because he/she has had a bad experience involving a dog in the past.

In conclusion, we have seen that even very young children are endowed with a basic understanding of emotion, which rapidly develops into a more sophisticated knowledge base between the ages of 4 and 10, as children learn to combine different sources of information to predict which emotion will be felt by a particular person in a particular situation. Specifically, children acquire a more differentiated understanding of emotion as they begin to analyse the often multifaceted emotion-eliciting situations in greater detail. Moreover, they increasingly come to appreciate the subjective nature of the appraisal process by which an emotion is triggered, which results in their acknowledging not only that different people may experience different emotions because of different appraisals, but also that the same process may take place within individuals. That is, a person may adopt different perspectives on the same situation, which allows for the possibility of experiencing different emotions successively or simultaneously. In the section on coping (p. 261), we will see that this knowledge helps children to understand that someone can actually try to change a prevailing emotion by changing his or her appraisal of the eliciting event.

But first, we will discuss another important part of children's meta-emotional knowledge base, that is, their understanding of the interpersonal consequences of emotional behaviour.

UNDERSTANDING EMOTIONAL DISPLAY RULES

In recent publications, authors have stressed the critical role of the social context for studies on the development of emotional understanding (e.g. Gordon, 1989; Saarni, 1989). One aspect of the social context concerns the appraisal of meaning, which has been extensively discussed in the previous section. Children learn what a certain individual is likely to feel in a specific context not only as a result of cognitive maturation, but also through exposure to many different social situations that are emotionally relevant. As a result of verbal or nonverbal feedback provided by the social community, children may learn to conform to certain "feeling rules". They actually begin to feel what they think they *ought to feel* in a particular situation. In the present section, we will discuss another important aspect of children's meta-emotive understanding, one for which the social environment may be especially significant: Children's knowledge of the interpersonal consequences of their emotional-expressive behaviour.

Understanding the consequences of genuine expressions of emotion

Saarni (1987) conducted an interview study among 7- to 13-year-old children, in which she questioned them about the responses of both parents and peers to the expression of different emotions in different social situations. Although children's abilities were shown to improve with increasing age, even the youngest children proved to have some understanding of the conditions in which feelings should be genuinely expressed (i.e. when an empathic reaction or even tangible help was to be expected) and situations in which the emotion felt should be inhibited or modified (i.e.

when the self would be made even more vulnerable or when the feelings of others would be hurt). Apparently by the age of 7, children already start to appreciate that in order to control one's expressive behaviour appropriately (and thus behave adaptively in social situations), one needs to take into account the consequences of the genuine display of emotion for both the self and others—although in subsequent years their understanding was shown to improve in important ways (see also Saarni, 1979).

Saarni (1989) argues that there are three different features of the social context that increasingly influence children's expectations regarding the consequences of emotional-expressive behaviour. First, empirical work has shown that children believe that one is allowed to display the felt emotion even if negative interpersonal consequences are to be expected, in situations in which there is *limited control* (e.g. in the case of intense feelings, or when one is ill, or just a small child). Second, a perceived or expected *difference in status* between the self and the interaction partner is thought to be relevant (Saarni, 1989). Children who argued that they would not show their real feelings to adults justified their answers by referring to the risks of doing so in the presence of someone more powerful who might use it against them. Alternatively, children who refused to show their real feelings in the presence of peers expressed a fear of being ridiculed, which would obviously constitute a loss of status within the group. Third, it has been shown that children focus on the perceived *degree of affiliation* within the relationship (Saarni, 1989). They argued that feelings should be genuinely shown within the context of a trustworthy relationship only (e.g. in the presence of good friends rather than acquaintances or strangers). Thus, children learn to use complex, contextual information (regarding issues of control as well as the relationship with the interaction partner involved) to evaluate the consequences of their expressive behaviour, and become more and more able to do so with increasing age.

Appearance vs. reality

The actual display versus suppression (or modification) of an emotion might also change the inner experience. Someone who tries to hide his fear, might actually become less frightened. And someone who is smiling to prevent others from seeing her sadness, might in fact become a little less sad. However, it is also possible that one changes the outward expression only, while leaving the inner experience intact. This latter possibility implies that the distinction between outward expression (appearance) and the inner experience (reality) is an important one (Harris, 1989).

In several studies, it has been shown that children understand the difference between apparent and real emotion at about the age of 6 (Harris & Gross, 1988). The distinction is not yet appreciated by 4-year-olds, even though these younger children were shown to be able to actually try to hide their disappointment when receiving a disappointing gift in the presence of an experimentor (Cole, 1986). Apparently, children under the age of 6 have little conscious and explicit knowledge of the display rule they applied which, according to Harris, implies that they will not use such a rule in a deliberate attempt to mislead the interaction partner. They probably learned a local rule ("You need to be polite and smile whenever you get a present") without realising the impact of their (misleading) emotional reaction on the relationship partner. Once children come to appreciate that they can actually create a false impression in another person (leading the observer to believe that the apparent emotion reflects what the child actually feels), this possibility for emotional control increases in important ways. Children will discover that others need not necessarily know their inner feelings, which allows for privacy, and also that others will be tempted to act on their faked expression rather than the real emotion, which allows for deliberate attempts to emotionally manage the relationship (e.g. crying excessively in order make someone feel responsible for your misery or to get him/her to help you).

To conclude, the distinction between the outward expression and the inner experience is an important one, with implications for the strategies that people may adopt to regulate their emotional experiences. As already mentioned, a change in expression may not coincide with a change in actual experience. In the next section, therefore, we will discuss in more detail developmental changes in the strategies that children consider useful to modify the inner emotional experience.

COPING WITH NEGATIVE EMOTIONS

Even very early in life, deliberate attempts to cope with negative emotion can be observed (Thompson, 1990). Infants may ignore emotionally arousing stimuli or even cover their ears or eyes in order to blunt distressing sensory input. But for older children, simple denial or avoidance may not always be effective because it interferes with other important goals (that are frequently social in nature). Children have "to live up to their age". Violating social expectations by showing an inadequate coping response (e.g. one that is allowed for younger children only) may solve the child's immediate emotional needs, but also creates a new problem—disapproval by others. Such a dilemma makes coping a problem-solving activity, in which almost every piece of emotional knowledge discussed previously has to be applied in order to choose the "optimal" solution in the prevailing situation. Sometimes, merely a minor change of strategy will suffice and social experience may help the child to expand his/her coping repertoire in the expected way. Suppose a child encounters a fearful social situation. In this case, young children are likely to simply run from the scene, thereby clearly showing their fear to whoever is present. A few years later, children have learned that the expression of fear in the presence of peers has social repercussions (Saarni, 1979). They may then cover their retreat by claiming that "they have to be home in time", thereby adequately adapting the natural avoidance reaction to the social situation. Although such age-related changes are to be expected within a class of coping strategies, we would now like to discuss a remarkable age-related change in the perceived usefulness of different *types* of strategies.

Lazarus' and Rothbaum's classification of coping strategies

Lazarus and Folkman's (1984) "Ways of Coping" model distinguishes two types of coping strategies: "problem-focused" strategies (aimed at removing or diminishing the actual problems presented by the situation), and "emotion-focused" strategies (directly aimed at improving the resulting emotional state). Young children typically claim to use so-called "problem-focused" strategies for dealing with stressful situations, whereas older children increasingly profess to use "emotion-focused" strategies as well (e.g. Band & Weisz, 1988, Compas, Malcarne, & Fondacaro, 1988; Rossman, 1992). One of the reasons underlying this age-related shift in the perceived usefulness of different strategies might be that young children are less inclined to monitor their emotions (e.g. Selman, 1981). To the extent to which a problem is not considered to be an emotional one, a child will not seek a solution in the realm of emotion repair. However, this clearly is not the only reason for the observed age differ- ence. Long after children spontaneously acknowledge the emotional impact of situations, they still do not seem to be aware of the utility of emotion-focused strategies.

In an attempt to explain children's preferences in this respect more adequately, we will first discuss a closely related distinction in the coping literature, that is, between primary and secondary control (Rothbaum, Weisz, & Snyder, 1982). Primary control is directed at the external world, as it involves an attempt to change the actual conditions that gave rise to the emotional experience. Secondary control, on the other hand, requires a greater focus on the inner mental world in an attempt to maximise one's goodness-of-fit with conditions as they are. Although mood improvement is not mentioned explicitly as the goal in secondary control strategies, it is easy to see the correspondence with emotion focused strategies.

As might be expected, empirical work (Band & Weisz, 1988; Compas et al., 1988) has shown that children's beliefs regarding emotion regulation proceed from an early emphasis on the use of primary control (at the age of 6) to an increased acknowledgement of the usefulness of secondary control (at the age of 12). However, Rothbaum et al. (1982) argue that the distinction between primary and secondary control is not only relevant ontogenetically, but also in terms of micro-genesis; individuals, young and old alike, presumably always try to change the actual conditions first. Development should be understood then in terms of an increased appreciation that secondary control strategies are more useful under certain conditions. There are two obvious reasons for preferring the use of secondary coping. First, effective primary coping may not be possible. In cases of sickness and death, for instance, it is virtually impossible to change the actual conditions. In situations like this, which actually are or are perceived as being beyond control, secondary coping seems to be the more useful option. The same goes for situations in which the use of primary control is considered dangerous or at least unwise, for example, when new and possibly more serious problems are to be expected as a result of an attempt to change the actual circumstances. In this case, the costs outweigh the benefits and the use of secondary control will be preferred.

It is plausible to assume that young children are less inclined and also less able to envision the consequences of their actions. Therefore, they may opt for primary control in situations in which such a solution will be rejected by older children (i.e. when restrictions are experienced that prompt a search for another type of strategy). The finding that socially competent children make use of secondary coping strategies, such as cognitive avoidance, to a greater extent than socially incompetent children, should be interpreted within this context (Eisenberg et al., 1993; Kliewer, 1991).

It might also be that young children attempt to find another way out, before aiming directly at mood improvement. As these children are often restricted in the use of primary coping strategies by a relatively limited ability to change the actual course of events, they may first try to get the help of powerful others before deciding that a certain action simply will not bring about the desired change (Band & Weisz, 1988). They might even do so up to the point of illusionary thinking (Miller & Green, 1985). For example, they may simply choose to ignore the fact that death is an irrevocable phenomenon (even though they know better when asked directly about it, Carey, 1985) and try to deal with the death of their pet by asking daddy to "make it alive again". Denial, a primitive defensive mechanism that is frequently used by very young children (Glasberg & About, 1982), is probably related to this kind of illusionary thinking: If you do not acknowledge reality, it is simply not there. Strictly speaking, denial is a secondary control mechanism in the sense that it leaves the actual situation intact. The same goes for goal change or substitution in situations in which goal attainment fails. Stein and Trabasso (1989) found that even preschoolers used statements like: "I didn't want to play anyway" to cope with a situation in which they were not allowed to join their playmates. These findings suggest that at least some secondary control options are considered useful even by very young children.

Behavioural vs. mental strategies

We hesitate, however, to interpret the Stein and Trabasso (1989) findings as deliberate and direct attempts to improve one's emotional state. Such an explanation would be in conflict with young children's conception of emotions as autonomic responses to the situation, that can not be changed by mental manipulation (Harris et al. 1981). That is not to say that young children do not possess some local knowledge that suggests a contradictory view. For instance, they acknowledge that an earlier emotion can be revived by evoking memories of that experience (Harris, Guz, Lipian, & Man-shu, 1985) and that the dissipation of emotion can be promoted by "ceasing to think" about the emotionally charged event (Harris, 1983). However, as we have seen in the first section, these relatively isolated pieces of knowledge do not yet lead young children to conclude that an emotional state is linked not to the situation *per se*, but to our *mental representation* of that situation and, therefore, that it will co-vary with any change in that mental representation. Only if children's knowledge is firmly established in such a mentalistic theory is the strategic use of mental manipulations aimed directly at changing the prevailing emotional state to be expected.

To conclude, we would like to suggest that the developmental shift from a behavioural to a mentalistic conception of the emotional process is the critical prerequisite for an adequate understanding of the usefulness of emotion-focused strategies. Confirming this line of argument, we were recently able to demonstrate that the behavioural–mental distinction did a better job of explaining age differences in the perceived usefulness of different coping strategies than either of the two distinctions discussed previously (Meerum Terwogt & Stegge, 1995b). It was shown that 10-year-olds not only spontaneously produced more mental strategies, but also that they were better at predicting the specific effect of various mental manipulations. They generally agreed that people have to look for positive evaluations if they want to improve a negative feeling state. For example, thinking back to the good times spent with Blacky (a dead pet) diminishes sadness whereas "negative" thoughts like: "Now I can never play with Blacky again" will intensify the feelings of loss.

KNOWLEDGE AND BEHAVIOUR: A WORD OF CAUTION

In the present chapter, we focused on the development of children's conceptions of emotion. A question yet to be answered, however, concerns the issue of how children's emerging understanding is manifested in actual behaviour. The research described previously typically relies on verbal reports elicited by interviewing children about their emotional behaviour in hypothetical situations. And, of course, there is no guarantee that in reality children will act the way they say they will. In a sense, one would logically expect that knowledge lags behind behaviour—one has to be able to do something before one can know that one can do it. This seems to be a valid conclusion as long as we assume that knowledge originates from self-observation. However, next to this solipsistic source of input, two other sources of information are used; input based on the observation of other people's emotional behaviour and the (verbal) information provided by the social community (Harris & Olthof, 1982). As a consequence, children are sometimes provided with information that is quite general in nature ("I'm in a bad mood. So, don't bother me!") but also with complete strategies ("If you are angry, count to ten first"). But, like every other piece of information, emotional messages can only be handled effectively if their content does not deviate too much from the child's current knowledge base. Children must at least be able to detect the basic rules underlying the message. If not, they might be able to use the suggested strategy on that specific occasion, but will certainly fail to do so next time (Flavell, 1977). And even then, the strategy will probably only become part of their behavioural repertoire if they have acknowledged its effectiveness themselves.

Apparently, children's theoretical conceptions do not reflect unequivocally behavioural abilities. They may precede behaviour, but also lag behind. Anyway, they are significant because of their abstract nature which enables the child to apply old principles to "new" situations. Therefore, theories of emotion will not only extend children's behavioural repertoire but can also be expected to make it more flexible (Meerum Terwogt & Olthof, 1989).

REFERENCES

Band, E. B. & Weisz, J. R. (1988). How to feel better when it feels bad: Children's perspectives on coping with everyday stress. *Developmental Psychology, 24,* 247–253.

Bartsch, K. & Wellman, H. (1995). *Children talk about the mind.* Oxford: Oxford University Press.

Borke, H. (1971). Interpersonal perception of young children: egocentrism or empathy. *Developmental Psychology, 5,* 263–269.

Bowler, D. M. & Norris, M. (1993). *Predictors of success on false belief tasks in pre-school children*. Paper presented at the 6th European Conference on Developmental Psychology, Bonn, Germany.

Bretherton, I. & Beeghly, M. (1982). Talking about internal states of mind: The acquisition of an explicit theory of mind. *Developmental Psychology, 18*, 906–921.

Carey, S. (1985). *Conceptual change in childhood*. Cambridge, MA: MIT/Bradford.

Cole, P. M. (1986). Children's spontaneous control of facial expression. *Child Development, 57*, 1309–1321.

Compas, B. E., Malcarne, V. L., & Fondacaro, K. M. (1988). Coping with stressful events in older children and young adolescents. *Journal of Consulting and Clinical Psychology, 56*, 405–411.

DiLalla, L.F. & Watson, M. W. (1988). Differentiation of fantasy and reality: Preschoolers' reactions to interruptions in their play. *Developmental Psychology, 24*, 289–291.

Donaldson, S. K. & Westerman, W. A. (1986). Development of children's understanding of ambivalence and causal theories of emotion. *Developmental Psychology, 22*, 655–662.

Eisenberg, N., Fabes, R. A., Bernzweig, J., Karbo, M., Poulin, R., & Hanish, L. (1993). The relations of emotionality and regulation to preschoolers' social skills and sociometric status. *Child Development, 64*, 1418–1438.

Estes, D., Wellman, H. M., & Woolley, J. D. (1989). Children's understanding of mental phenomena. In H. Reese (Ed.), *Advances in child development and behavior* (pp. 41–87). New York: Academic Press.

Flavell, J. H. (1977). *Cognitive development*. Englewood Cliffs, NJ: Prentice Hall.

Flavell, J. H., Green, F. L., & Flavell, E. R. (1989). Development of knowledge about the appearance-reality distinction. *Monographs of the Society of Research in Child Development, 51* (Serial No. 212).

Ferguson, T. J., Olthof, T., Luiten, A., & Rule, B. G. (1984). Children's use of observed behavioral frequency vs. behavioral covariation in ascribing dispositions to others. *Child Development, 55*, 2094–2105.

Ferguson, T.J. & Stegge, H. (1995). Emotional states and traits in children: The case of guilt and shame. In J. P. Tangney & K. W. Fischer (Eds.), *Self-conscious emotions* (pp. 174–197). New York: Guilford Press.

Glasberg, R. & About, F. (1982). Keeping one's distance from sadness: Children's self-reports of emotional experience. *Developmental Psychology, 18*, 287–293.

Gnepp, J. (1983). Children's social sensitivity: Inferring emotions from conflicting cues. *Developmental Psychology, 19*, 805–814.

Gnepp, J. (1989). Children's use of personal information to understand other people's feelings. In C. Saarni & P. L. Harris (Eds.), *The child's understanding of emotion* (pp. 151–177). New York, Cambridge University Press.

Gnepp, J., Klayman, J., & Trabasso, T. (1982). A hierarchy of information sources for inferring emotional reactions. *Journal of Experimental Child Psychology, 33*, 111–123.

Gordon, S. L. (1989). The socialization of children's emotions: Emotional culture, competence, and exposure. In C. Saarni & P. L. Harris (Eds.), *The child's understanding of emotion* (pp. 319 –349). New York: Cambridge University Press.

Graham, S., Doubleday, C., & Guarino, P. A. (1984). The development of relations between perceived controllability and the emotions of pity, anger, and guilt. *Child Development, 55*, 561–565.

Harris, P. L. (1983). Children's understanding of the link between situation and emotion. *Journal of Experimental Child Psychology, 33*, 1–20.

Harris, P. L. (1989). *Children and emotion. The development of psychological understanding*. Oxford: Blackwell.

Harris, P. L. & Gross, D. (1988). Children's understanding of real and apparent emotion. In J. W. Astington, P. L. Harris, & D.R. Olson (Eds.), *Developing theories of mind* (pp. 295–314). New York: Cambridge University Press.

Harris, P. L., Guz, G. R., Lipian, M. S., & Man-shu, Z. (1985). Insight in the time-course of emotion among Western and Chinese children. *Child Development, 56*, 972–988.

Harris, P. L., Johnson, C. N., Hutton, D., Andrews, G., & Cooke, T. (1989). Young children's theory of mind and emotion. *Cognition and Emotion, 3*, 379–400.

Harris, P. L. & Olthof, T. (1982). The child's concept of emotion. In G. Butterworth & P. Light (Eds.), *Social cognition; Studies of the development of understanding* (pp. 188–209). Brighton, UK: Harvester.

Harris, P. L., Olthof, T., & Meerum Terwogt, M. (1981). Children's knowledge of emotion. *Journal of Child Psychology and Psychiatry, 22*, 247–261.

Harris, P. L., Olthof, T., Meerum Terwogt, M., & Hardman, C. E. (1987). Children's knowledge of situations that provoke emotion. *International Journal of Behavioral Development, 10*, 319–343.

Harter, S. (1983). Children's understanding of multiple emotions: A cognitive-developmental approach. In W. F. Overton (Ed.), *The relationship between social and cognitive development* (pp. 147–194). Hillsdale, NJ: Lawrence Erlbaum Associates Inc.

Harter, S. & Buddin, B. (1987). Children's understanding of the simultaneity of two emotions: A five-stage acquisition sequence. *Developmental Psychology, 23*, 388–399.

Harter, S. & Whitesell, N. (1989). Developmental changes in children's emotion concepts. In C. Saarni & P. L. Harris (Eds.), *The child's understanding of emotion* (pp. 81–116). New York: Cambridge University Press.

Kliewer, W. (1991). Coping in middle childhood: Relations to competence, Type A behavior, monitoring, blunting, and locus of control. *Developmental Psychology, 27*, 689–697.

Koops, W., Meerum Terwogt, M., & Rieffe, K. (in press). On the consciousness of children. *Consciousness and Cognition.*

Lazarus, R. S. & Folkman, S. (1984). *Stress, appraisal and coping.* New York: Springer.

Leslie, A. M. (1987). Pretense and representation: The origins of a "theory of mind". *Psychological Review, 94*, 412–426.

Lewis, M. (1989). Cultural differences in children's knowledge of emotion scripts. In C. Saarni & P. L. Harris (Eds.), *The child's understanding of emotion* (pp. 350–373). New York: Cambridge University Press.

Meerum Terwogt, M. & Harris, P. L. (1993). Understanding of emotion. In M. Bennett (Ed.), *The child as psychologist* (pp. 62–86). London: Harvester Wheatsheaf.

Meerum Terwogt, M., Koops, W., Oosterhoff, T., & Olthof, T. (1986). Development in processing of multiple emotional situations. *Journal of General Psychology, 113*, 109–119.

Meerum Terwogt, M. & Olthof, T. (1989). Awareness and self-regulation of emotion in young children. In C. Saarni & P. L. Harris (Eds.), *The child's understanding of emotion* (pp. 209–237). New York: Cambridge University Press.

Meerum Terwogt, M. & Stegge, H. (1995a). Emotional behaviour and emotional understanding: A developmental fugue. In I. M. Goodyer (Ed.), *The depressed child and adolescent; Developmental and clinical perspectives* (pp. 27–52). Cambridge, UK: Cambridge University Press.

Meerum Terwogt, M. & Stegge, H. (1995b). Strategic control of negative emotions. In J. A. Russell, J. Fernández-Dols, A. S. R. Manstead, & J. C. Wellenkamp (Eds.), *Everyday concepts of emotion: An Introduction to the psychology, anthropology and linguistics of emotion, NATO ASI Series* (pp. 373–390). Dordrecht: Kluwer.

Miller, S. M. & Green, M. L. (1985). Coping with stress and frustration; Origins, nature, and development. In M. Lewis & C. Saarni (Eds.), *The socialization of emotions* (pp. 263–314). New York: Plenum.

Olthof, T., Ferguson, T. J., & Luiten, A. (1989). Personal responsibility antecedents of anger and blame reactions in children. *Child Development, 60,* 1328–1366.

Piaget, J. (1929). *The child's conception of the world.* London: Routledge & Kegan Paul.

Reichenbach, L. & Masters, J. C. (1983). Children's use of expressive and contextual cues in judgements of emotion. *Child Development, 54,* 993–1004.

Rossman, B. B. R. (1992). School-age children's perceptions of coping with distress: Strategies for emotion regulation and the moderation of adjustment. *Journal of Child Psychology and Psychiatry, 33,* 1373–1397.

Rothbaum, F., Weisz, J. R., & Snyder, S. S. (1982). Changing the world and changing the self: A two-process model of perceived control. *Journal of Personality and Social Psychology, 42,* 5–37.

Saarni, C. (1979). Children's understanding of display rules for expressive behaviour. *Developmental Psychology, 15,* 424–429.

Saarni, C. (1987, April). *Children's beliefs about parental expectations for emotional-expressive behavior management.* Paper presented at the meeting in the Society for Research in Child Development, Baltimore, MD.

Saarni, C. (1989). Children's understanding of strategic control of emotional expression in social transactions. In C. Saarni & P. L. Harris (Eds.), *The child's understanding of emotion* (pp. 181–208). New York: Cambridge University Press.

Saarni, C. & Harris, P. L. (Eds.) (1989). *The child's understanding of emotion.* New York: Cambridge University Press.

Selman, R. L. (1981). What children understand of intrapsychic processes: The child as a budding personality theorist. In E. K. Shapiro & E. Weber (Eds.), *Cognitive and affective growth: Developmental interaction,* (pp. 46–73). Hillsdale, NJ: Lawrence Erlbaum Associates Inc.

Smiley, P. & Huttenlocher, J. (1989). Young children's acquisition of emotion concepts. In C. Saarni & P. L. Harris (Eds.), *The child's understanding of emotion* (pp. 27–49). New York: Cambridge University Press.

Stein, N. L. & Levine, L. J. (1987). Thinking about feelings: The development and organization of emotional knowledge. In R. E. Snow & M. Farr (Eds.), *Aptitude, learning, and instruction: Cognition, conation and affect* (Vol. 3, pp. 165–198). Hillsdale, NJ: Lawrence Erlbaum Associates Inc.

Stein, N. L. & Levine, L. J. (1989). The causal organisation of emotional knowledge: A developmental study. *Cognition and Emotion, 3,* 343–378.

Stein, N. L. & Trabasso, T. (1989). Children's understanding of changing emotional states. In C. Saarni & P. L. Harris (Eds.), *The child's understanding of emotion* (pp. 50–80). New York: Cambridge University press.

Stipek, D. J. & De Cotis, D. K. (1988). Children's understanding of the implications of causal attributions for emotional experiences. *Child Development, 59,* 1601–1616.

Thompson, R. A. (1989). Causal attributions and children'e emotional understanding. In C. Saarni & P. L. Harris (Eds.), *The child's understanding of emotion* (pp. 117–150). New York: Cambridge University press.

Thompson, R. A. (1990). Emotion and self-regulation. In R. A. Thompson (Ed.), *Socioemotional development, Nebraska symposium on motivation, 1988* (Vol. 36, pp. 367–467). Lincoln, NE: University of Nebraska Press.

Trabasso, T., Stein, N. L., & Johnson, L. R. (1981). Children's knowledge of events: A causal analysis of story structure. In G. Bower (Ed.), Learning and motivation (Vol. 15, pp. 254–276). New York: Academic Press.

Wellman, H. (1990). *The child's theory of mind.* Cambridge, MA: MIT Press.

Wellman, H. M. & Estes, D. (1986). Early understanding of mental entities: A reexamination of childhood realism. *Child Development, 57,* 910–923.

Wimmer, H., & Perner, J. (1983). Beliefs about beliefs: Representation and constraining function of wrong beliefs in young children's understanding of deception. *Cognition, 13,* 103–128.

Wolf, D. P. Rygh, J., & Altshuler, J. (1984). Agency and experience: Actions and states in play narratives. In I. Bretherton (Ed.), *Symbolic play* (pp. 134–147). Orlando, FL: Academic Press.

11

Agency and identity: A relational approach

John Shotter
University of New Hampshire, Durham, USA

> The very way we walk, gesture, speak is shaped from the earliest moments by our awareness that we appear before others, that we stand in public space, and that this space is potentially one of respect or contempt, of pride or shame. (Taylor, 1989, p. 15)

Although problems to do with the development of children's self-awareness (e.g. Lewis & Brooks-Gunn, 1979), with their self-concept or self-image (e.g. Damon, 1988) and with their existential "I" and their empirical "me" (e.g. Butterworth, 1990) have been at the centre of developmental psychologist's attention for some time, attention to the child's development of an *identity*—to its developing sense of how he or she stand in relation to the others around him or her—is a concern of a much more peripheral kind (Dunn, 1988; Kagan, 1981). Work of this kind ought, I think, to be of central importance. In this chapter, however, I want to argue that its importance cannot be properly understood if its results are seen as having relevance only within a cognitive approach to developmental research—with what I shall call its intellectu-alist-representational stance toward the phenomena it studies. For in this research tradition, processes of development are seen as taking place only in terms of supposed *mental states* in the head of the individual child, and are explained solely in terms of theories of the *information-processing mechanisms* it is said to contain. The development of children's unique identities, however, cannot be understood in this way. It introduces further concerns; concerns of a *relational* kind. More than events simply within the individual child, it can only be understood in terms of children's (to an extent moral and ethical) engagements with the others around them, with how at any one moment they are "positioned" and can "move" in relation to them, with the momentary effects their judgements of them can have on them, and so on. It is our knowledge of our selves as standing in some kind of peculiar, unique, *evaluative* relation to the others around us in this way, that connects us, as a source or locus of uncaused activity, with some of the important influences that can shape that activity; or, to put it another way, that connects the notion of the self as *agent* with people's need for a unique *identity*.

EVALUATIVE KNOWING FROM WITHIN A SITUATION

Thus, to have an identity, is to know where I stand in relation to the others around me within a particular "moral space" or "moral world" of possibilities. For, where I actually stand at a particular moment, allows me to gauge my possible next actions in terms of how those others are likely to react to them—for in such a "world", there are *rules* or *standards* as to what constitutes "proper" or "fitting" behaviour. Knowing how to relate to others in this evaluative way is to sense them also as occupying a certain kind of "position" in relation to ourselves (e.g. as our equals, as having some authority over us, as our rulers or as subordinates, as antagonists, as our friends, as strangers to us, as our parents, etc.). Thus, to lack an identity is to lack an evaluative orientation in a "moral world", to lack a grasp of what precisely my doings are *doing*, so to speak, in relation to my current social surroundings—whether, for instance, I am beginning to make the particular child development theorist currently reading me feel able to agree with me or whether I'm putting him/her in a difficult position; whether I'm making the mother I'm talking to about her child feel attacked over her attitudes to child care or whether I'm making her feel supported; and so on.

This kind of "practical-moral knowledge" (Bernstein, 1983) then, in being to do with relating oneself evaluatively to the others around one, is to do with learning how *to be* a person of this or that particular kind. As such, it cannot be a simple theoretical or propositional form of knowledge, a "knowing-that" something or other is the case in Ryle's (1949) terminology. For, in its primary form, it is not to do with individuals knowing *what* some "thing" or "object" *is*, with knowing true facts *about* it, but with knowing something of a much more particular and practical kind, to do with *doing* something uniquely appropriate to a circumstance. However, as such, it cannot be simply like the knowledge of skilful practice or a craft, a "knowing-how" possessed by an individual either:

For it is knowledge that only comes into existence momentarily, "in" one relating oneself to others. Indeed, in only making its appearance in the active, living, responsive interactions between us, it is quite unlike the other two forms of knowledge—it cannot exist within us as self-contained individuals. It is a third kind of knowledge, *sui generis*, which in being prior to the other two and in being linked both to people's social and personal identities, and to socially shared standards, determines their available forms, (i.e. those that we will experience as intelligible and legitimate). Indeed, in being knowledge of a *moral* kind, of socially sharable standards, depending on the (disputable) judgements of others as to whether one's use of it is appropriate or not, one cannot just have it or express it on one's own. In being the kind of knowledge one only has *from within* a momentary relational circumstance, in moments within a social situation or group, a social institution, or society, in line with Ryle's terminology above, we might call it a "knowing-from".

Elsewhere, I have discussed its strange nature extensively in relation to the concept of "joint action" (Shotter 1980, 1984, 1993a, b, 1995), but here I would like to connect it with Bakhtin's (1986) account of *dialogic* relations and with his claim (p. 142) that: "understanding is impossible without evaluation". For, in joint action or dialogic relations, first person speakers and actors not only orient toward second person listeners and recipients, but also toward, he claims (pp. 126–127): "an invisibly present third party who stands above all the participants in the dialogue ... [who] is a constitutive aspect of the whole utterance, [and] who, under deeper analysis, can be revealed in it". Rather than simply "in" the actions of first persons, or "in" the responses of second persons, "it" exists as an active, "third party" in the dialogue because "it" makes its appearance as a momentary "evaluative circumstance" only "in" the ongoing, dialogic *relations* between people's actions and responses. Your feeling that my claims here are (perhaps) "unjustified", say, belongs neither to your feelings alone, nor to my claims alone, but to the "momentary situation" in which your responses *are related to* my claims. Thus, this "third party" is "in" the same "momentary situation" that the participants are also "in", among the already happened and talked about "topics" or "common places" that they have already created between them, and "it" requires its say in the proceedings too. As Bakhtin (1986: p. 126) sees it, "it" exists as: "a higher *superaddressee* (third), whose absolutely just responsive understanding is presumed..." by all those participating in any (dialogic) activity. Thus, in this Bakhtinian view of things, it is not just simply our expectation of how the others immediately around us will respond to our actions that influences what we do, but how we sense ourselves as "placed" in a whole situation and how our actions will relate to that whole "situation". Thus, in a classroom, say, it is not just a student's sense of how his teacher will respond to him that makes him wary of what he might say, but it is his growing sense of the whole educational system and his place within *that* which makes him apprehensive of what, at any moment, he might do or say.

This is what makes this kind of ethico-relational knowledge so very special. In only coming into existence "in" the ongoing relations between people, it is what we might call an "active", "living", embodied, social, practical, relational kind of knowledge—where this distinction, between "active" or "living" kinds of knowledge and "passive" or "dead" forms will be crucial in what follows later. For "living" actions and utterances are actions and utterances done in the living, bodily presence of others, who thus cannot not *respond* to them in some way and, as a result, most importantly, give or afford[1] the original actors the opportunity to anticipate receiving such responses and to begin to shape their actions accordingly. The possibility of developing these forms of active, responsive, and anticipatory acting and understanding is crucial to Vygotsky's (1978, 1986), Volosinov's (1986), and Wittgenstein's (1953) stance toward language and interaction that I shall adopt in what follows below. For both our "active" understanding of people's actions in their doing of them and of their words in their speaking of them (as they body them forth) is of quite a different kind to our "passive", intellectual forms of understanding, in which we contemplate (disembodied) patterns of already completed acts or spoken words. Indeed, as we shall see in more detail later, the kind of passive understanding (Volosinov, 1986, p. 73): "that excludes active response in advance and on principle ... is not at all in fact the kind of understanding that applies in language-speech", nor in any of our other practical-moral understandings of others either. For, in our ongoing interactions with others, we are not so concerned with *what* in the end they actually "did" or "said"—the representational *content* or *meaning* of their actions or utterances—as with the way in which their ongoing, embodied "saying" and "doing" *moves* us, with how it "places" or "positions" us (evaluatively) in relation both to them and our circumstances, and with how we feel we must respond, moment by moment, to being so "positioned". That is, we are concerned with grasping the *relational* functions or roles of their activity—its links or connections with its surroundings. It is the development of this kind of ongoing, "living", ethico-relational way of knowing—to do *both*: (1) with children coming to know how they *should* understand the relation of their actions to their surrounding (cultural) situation at large, and being able to judge whether they fall short of it or not; *and* (2) with our use of such a way of knowing in our professional investigations of them—that is often ignored in studies focused on the other topics mentioned earlier.

OUR EMBODIED, SOCIALLY EMBEDDED BEING:
DEVELOPMENTAL SOCIAL PRACTICES

We can begin to see the nature of this living, ethico-relational knowing and its embodiment as a sensitivity to judgemental or evaluative situations in some examples drawn from Dunn (1988) see later. As she notes in studies of their everyday activities, even at 18 months infants "show" in their "way" of acting[2] that they anticipate their mother's responses to forbidden actions, and that they act into the situation in a teasing way or as a situation to be deliberately evaded:

Family B (Study 1). Child 18 months
Child heads for electric socket, forbidden twice during last 20 minutes of observation. Turns to look at observer, smiling. (p. 17)

Family H (Study 1). Child 18 months
Child has stitches in her forehead as the result of a fall the previous day. In the course of the observation she 'discovers' the stitches and begins to pull at them. M prohibits her and attempts to distract. After a few minutes the child feels for the stitches and is stopped again. Three minutes later she goes behind the settee and pulls at the stitches. (pp. 19–20)

To appreciate or to be sensitive to the social dynamics at work in such situations as these, in which infants "show" their momentary, evaluative relations to their circumstances in their actions, I want to suggest that an alternative stance to the intellectualist-representational stance of the cognitive approach—what we might call a dialogical[3], embodied-relational stance, associated with a social constructionist approach[4] to an understanding of human activities—is required. In other words, unless we as researchers "see" the meaning of such phenomena as these directly and unproblematically (and develop this shared ability further), we cannot discuss them between ourselves or formulate agreed ways of studying them and to do this, we need to change what we notice and are sensitive to (as well as what we care about and feel are the appropriate goals at which to aim in our studies). That is, instead of always ultimately seeking to explain the *underlying causes* of such actions as these, we should, I claim, seek their *connections or relations* with their larger social and cultural surroundings—and study further their possible meanings for those around the child who must respond to them. So, although in the examples cited earlier the mothers are likely to see their infants as, in one way or another, calling their authority into question or as exerting their own autonomy, we might go further and ask whether mothers *should* respond to such challenges harshly or gently, directly or indirectly, and so on.

Such a stance as this, although it may seem strange and peculiar to us as professional academics, is not so unusual at all to us as ordinary, everyday people. To an extent, it is nothing more than an attempt to adopt self-consciously and professionally the stance we already embody and adopt spontaneously in our daily activities (without, perhaps, noticing that we do so). For in our everyday lives together, in responding to what the others around us do, including our children, we are continually sensitive to and make use of many of the momentary and fleeting nuances occurring out in the spaces between them and ourselves. We respond evaluatively to their merest hesitations, their slight frowns and smiles, the tone of their voice, and so on. We do this, for the most part, immediately, unreflectively, and spontaneously, in how as embodied beings we react to them in our ongoing practices, in the continuous flow of the activity between us. For, in practice, we too "show" our understanding of the connections and relations between a person's action and its surroundings "in" how we respond to it, in how we "go on" with or "follow" the person concerned. Thus, the child's task in his/her social relations is not that of an already well-differentiated individual with the ability to control his/her own behaviour, simply learning more information about the objects around him/her. The child's initial task is of a much more complicated kind. It is: "To become a *person*—a member of that complex world [in which people communicate their moods and desires, their sense of absurdity and amusement, pride or shame]" as Dunn (1988) notes. And to do that (p. 5): "children must develop powers of recognizing and sharing emotional states, of interpreting and anticipating other's reactions, of understanding the relationships between others, of comprehending the sanctions, prohibitions, and accepted practices of their world".

Or, to put it in a slightly different way, in relational or social constructionist terms: *Our* joint task is to socially construct with our children a certain kind of *developmental practice*, such that from within it our children can develop from simple, unreflective, spontaneously acting, responsive beings (somewhat unself-aware as to how they are evaluatively placed in relation to their larger surroundings) into complex, reflective, self-controlled, deliberately acting persons, crucially aware of their relational position(s) in the larger, cultural schemes of things. Where, put relationally, this larger cultural scheme of things can include our ways of relating ourselves evaluatively to each other, to older and younger generations, to yet others (strangers, foreigners, etc.), to our past (history), to our future (and one's own death), to the earth, to the extraordinary, to the absolute, freedom, truth, human dignity, and so on—there being no end to the new evaluative relations with our surroundings we can create for ourselves and think of as important.[5] It is these ways of relating that we must transmit to our children from within the developmental practices we can construct or create with them.

As an example illustrating some small aspects of such a developmental practice, let me cite some early work of mine and Sue Gregory's (1976). We were interested in an incident in which a mother was "trying to show" her little girl Samantha, at the rather too early age of 11 months, how to fit some shapes on to[6] a form-board. In the incident in question, Samantha had succeeded in fitting one of the shapes on "by accident" and her mother had responded, as expected, by saying "Oh, clever girl". But what arrested our attention was that she then went on to say (after a brief pause) "... AREN'T YOU CLEVER!"[7] Why repeat herself? Why the emphasis? Why the pause? For what had she been waiting? Well, the trouble was (on examining the videotape record of this and other similar such incidents) that Samantha did not "reply" to her first exclamation as her mother expected (or required). She had wanted her infant to indicate to her that she had appreciated the social *value* of her act and only when Samantha stopped the continued flow of her activity on the board, turned to look at her, relaxed and smiled, was the mother satisfied that Samantha had a sense of "what" her doing had done, socially. This complex exchange was quite fleeting but nonetheless crucial to them both, and the mother was not going to proceed without it having occurred. Yet, of course, in one sense, she had acted unthinkingly and spontaneously, in response to immediate circumstances. And if she had been asked to articulate the character of her teaching "skills" here, abstractly, out of context, Samantha's mother would, no doubt, have been utterly nonplussed. For in what terms could they be best represented? Yet, in insisting that Samantha respond to her response, in insisting Samantha "show" that she appreciated the social value of her act before allowing her to continue, her mother was clearly spontaneously instituting a practice she felt to be conducive to Samantha's development. She "saw" in Samantha's failure to respond, something important, something connected with her future, with the kind of person her mother felt Samantha ought to become and in actively "expecting" Samantha's response a second time, her mother afforded[8] her again the developmental opportunity to become that kind of person—in treating her as already who she *should be*, she was helping her to develop as such.

And it is this kind of "presumptive" stance or sensibility, I want to suggest, that we need to develop as researchers ... except that in applying it, our task would be to go much further: That is, to repeat, it would not be to seek explanatory theories but to develop new social practices, new ways of participating in the "play of events" unfolding between us and those we study so that, like Samantha's mother, we could come to "see in" their unfolding, the relational opportunities they presented—that is, to "see" the many different relations and connections with their surroundings they made possible, thus to enable those involved in them to afford their children the appropriate development opportunities. Thus, in relation to such practices, rather than a passive, intellectual understanding of what something precisely "is" in theory, we would be seeking a much more active, embodied kind of understanding: An understanding of what might be connected or related to what, or what might follow from what, and so on, in practice. Among our tasks would be, to repeat, to understand the everyday conditions and circumstances structuring our current developmental practices, that is, the detailed and nuanced nature of the developmental opportunities involved in our children developing into this, that, or some other kind of person. For, rather than with their "theories", we are concerned with their development of this or that kind of sensibility, with their embodied ways of spontaneously relating to their surroundings. We want to know whether they will treat others with respect or contempt, whether they will show a concern with or disdain for the future, a fascination or boredom with history, literature, arcade games, e-mail, and so on.

TWO STANCES OR SENSIBILITIES: EMBODIED AND DISEMBODIED

Outlined earlier, then, is a very different kind of stance that we might adopt toward our understanding of the nature of our own mental activities: An embodied, practical, dialogical stance that can be contrasted with a disembodied, intellectualist stance. And I would now like to make more explicit how very, very different these two stances are. In adopting the intellectualist-representational stance associated with the cognitive approach, we ignore our living bodies and all our spontaneous, responsive activities relating us to our surroundings. Instead, we assume that all our activity, as such, originates in certain inner mental states, that such states are real and exist within our "minds", and further, that we find evidence of their nature in our talk "about" them to the others around us. On the other hand, the embodied-relational stance associated with the social constructionist approach that I am advocating here, suggests that, rather than stemming from anything hidden in our heads, we cannot not be in a living relation to those around us and that what some "inner thing" is for us is revealed, not in how we talk about "it" retrospectively, in reflection, after it has occurred but in how "it" necessarily "shapes" those of our everyday activities in which it is involved, in our ongoing, living, responsive practices. For example, as we have already seen in the incidents quoted from Dunn (1988) earlier, rather than in any of their reflective talk "about" their own or other people's activities *after* their occurrence, Dunn directly "sees" children as "showing" their anticipations of the "forbidding" responses of others "in" their "shaping" of their ongoing activity as teasing or as deceitful, *as it occurs*. These two stances are thus already very different indeed. We shall see how very different they are from each other, however, as the contrasts between them multiply.

Returning to the first of these stances, we can note that it is the stance adopted, for instance, in current research into children's "theory of mind" (see Meerum Terwogt and Stegge, Chapter 10 and Hay and Demetriou, Chapter 9). There, it is assumed that (Bartsch & Wellman, 1995, p. 6):

> ...perceptions, emotions, physiological states, and more—are a part of the web of psychological constructs used [by adults and children] to understand and explain action and mind... [and they] are centrally organized by consideration of the actor's thoughts and desires. These two sorts of generic mental states are, of course, internal and unobservable. But unobservable mental states can often be inferred...

And it is taken for granted that the everyday talk of adults "about" mental states is unproblematically definitive of our adult "commonsense conception of mind" (Bartsch & Wellman, 1995, p. 5). Thus, for example, when as adults we distinguish between, say, *desires* as implying a *subjective connection* to an external object without necessarily implying the possession of an *internal cognitive representation* of it, whereas *beliefs,* as such, always involve an inner representation, we always do so in terms of what we feel "can be said" *on the basis of* our own supposed common sense theory of mind. Given these assumptions in this tradition of research, records of children's everyday talk are studied inferentially for what they reveal "about" children's knowledge "about" such theoretical states—both in themselves and in others. A typical hypothesis under study is the suggestion that (Bartsch & Wellman, 1995, p. 14): "children go from understanding subjective connections to a later understanding of representational mental states"—as if a "proper" or "natural" set of developmental stages is already "there" awaiting discovery.

But in such research as this (to repeat the distinction made earlier), rather than "living" words in their speaking, what is studied are "dead" patterns of already spoken words. Rather than the voicing of utterances into a unique dialogical circumstance, the data considered are sentence forms, put into general contextual categories, with no interest in the subtleties of the interactive or responsive moments occurring, within or between them, in their uttering. Indeed, as the authors remark (Bartsch & Wellman, 1995, p. 11): "...our database is more than 200,000 child utterances[9] that yield almost 12,000 child conversations about mind using such everyday terms as *think, know, want* to talk about beliefs and desire". Thus, in the methodology employed here, children's utterances are first divorced both from who, as unique individuals, the children are (i.e. from their identities), and from the unique practical circumstances of their use. Then, in seeking an order or pattern in the "data" so constituted, researchers feel justified in going on to *theorising* about the development of certain supposed "inner mechanisms" of a general kind responsible for the supposed order "observed" on the basis of their own questionable theorising about the nature of adult talk. But in such a "methodology" as this, the ongoing processes in which children and those around them create certain kinds of "social worlds", containing certain kinds of "developmental practices" between them, is lost. So also are those fleeting moments of living uncertainty and indecision in which people, in the "gaps" between their spontaneous responses to each other, not only construct or establish their "positions" *in relation to* each other, but also (each other's) supposed *mental states*. For it is in such *relational moments* as these (if I can call them that), that the feelings—of Samantha's response as being "inadequate" or, in Dunn's examples, of the children's responses as being "deceitful" or "teasing"—arise. In these moments, a still-to-be-determined "situation" is created between the participants "into" which they feel they must direct their next actions. "It" invites or motivates or "calls out" from them certain kinds of "reply" and they spontaneously feel certain compulsions to respond, according to the momentary expectations created. Thus clearly, in such circumstances as these, if we turn to our second, more embodied, dialogical stance, we have a chance of "seeing" how those around the child have the power to shape the situation developmentally.

Middleton and Edwards (1990, pp. 38–39) provide us with an example. They discuss the following exchange occurring between a little boy, Paul (approximately five years old) and his mother, talking about some family photographs:

> *Mother*: Oh look/ there's when we went to the riding stables wasn't it?
> *Paul*: Yeh/ er er.
> *Mother*: You were trying to reach up and stroke that horse.
> *Paul*: Where? [laughs].
> *Mother*: Would you like to do that again.
> *Paul*: Yeh.
> *Mother*: You don't look very happy though.
> *Paul*: Because I thought I was going to fall off.
> *Mother*: You thought you were going to fall off did you?/ right misery/ daddy was holding on to you so that you didn't// did it FEEL very bumpy?
> *Paul*: Yeh.
> *Mother*: Did it make your legs ache? [Paul laughs] Rebecca enjoyed it.
> *Paul*: Yeh.
> *Mother*: She's a bit older wasn't she?/ you were a little boy then.

As Middleton and Edwards point out, we can "see" that most of the "work" done here is done by Paul's mother: She sets the scene, locates the picture in the context of past events and uses Paul's responses as opportunities to mark past events, as significant—by providing descriptions of them in terms of his past reactions and the relations such reactions created. Like Samantha's mother, she uses the everyday activity between the two of them also to create a developmental practice spontaneously, one specifically related to Paul's developing identity—"who" he "was" in relation to "who" he now is. For, as Middleton and Edwards (1990, p. 39) remark: "...children's identity and relationships change through time, and it is an important part of the developmental process that children come to see themselves as growing and changing, in specified, value-laden ways, within a culturally normative, moral world. This involves making sense of the past, of what one has been, and of the future, what one may become". Indeed as Wolf (1990) makes clear in her extensive studies, as early as their second year, in conversations of this kind, infants show an ability to speak in several different "voices" (i.e. as participants, as outsiders, as judges, as rememberers, as commentators, as themselves at different ages, and so on), thus to exhibit in brief-moment-by-brief-moment, different evaluative stances toward their circumstances.

In work of this kind then, the notion of us or our children as having an *identity*—our changing knowledge of who we are and how we are placed as a *person* in relation to all those around us—becomes of crucial importance to us. As I said earlier, it connects the idea of them as self-contained sources of their own actions, of them as *agents*, with the momentary social influences shaping their actions. For instead of seeing the organising centre of our children's actions as solely within them alone, in "inviting" them to direct what they do and say "into" a "situation" already, to an extent, "shaped" by *our* previous activity, we can "see" them as being shaped by *the relations* between them and us, by what we do, or do not, "call out" from them. It is in the relation between our identities that their behaviour is shaped, that is, by our evaluative "position" in relation to them—by what we can "refuse" them, "demand" of them, the different "opportunities" we can "afford" or "permit" them to make changes in the shared "situation" between us, and so on. Thus, as we have seen, we need to focus on those "relational moments", those "gaps" between people's spontaneous responses to each other, in which such "positions" are constructed and established. Observations of children's differential responding to their circumstances alone are insufficient for us to be able to grasp the nature of children's relational involvements. We cannot establish whether the children themselves have any knowledge of them, of *what* what they are doing *does* socially. It is not enough to attempt to characterise a child's activity on its own, as simply having this or that kind of pattern or form to it in itself. For children must show, in their actions, not just a consciousness or an awareness of their physical surroundings but a self-consciousness, an awareness of their evaluation of their relations to others, and how they might affect possible actions—actions not yet performed. Rather than merely behaving in ways *others* can recognise and evaluate as appropriate, children must come to be able to recognise "what" they are doing in the same way themselves and also ultimately, to *evaluate* their desire in doing "it", independently, as being indeed a desire of worth.[10] And this, as Middleton and Edwards point out, involves us and our children in being able to move back and forth in time, in both making sense of the past (of what one has been) and of the future (what one may become) in our evaluations of our own and others' actions.

THE METHOD: ATTENDING TO "FLEETING MOMENTS" WITHIN A PRACTICE

Like our children, we can only grasp the nature of these relational influences *from within* the ongoing activities in which they are created. From within such involvements, we can *directly observe* their nature "in" others' responses to our responses to their previous actions (or, if we are uninvolved observers, then they must be inferred from the *interrelational goings-on* between infants and their caretakers). But either way, instead of being hidden inside individuals, they are revealed, we might say, in the unfolding of a certain kind of dialogical or relational "movement" between those involved—a movement made up of "moments" in which the to-an-extent already specified "situation" between them is changed or specified further.

We have already seen the delicate sequence of events unfolding between Samantha and her mother, and the importance in that unfolding "movement" of the "moment" in which Samantha finally seems to acknowledge the social significance of her own actions and smiles at her mother. Kagan (1981) has studied similar such unfolding "movements" and "moments": For instance, he suggests that the subsequent distress shown by infants (over 15 months old) when failing to imitate an action modelled to them by an adult, implied an awareness of what a competent performance ought to have been. Similarly, he found that what he called "mastery smiles" followed either successful task completion or when adults complied with requests, and so on. Spitz (1957) also comments on infants approaching forbidden objects eagerly, while uttering the "No" they have undoubtedly heard from the others around them previously. In each case, the infants' actions "show" that they reflect on sequences of actions just performed and anticipate responses yet to come, doing both in a socially evaluative way. Indeed, Kagan (1981, p. 48) refers to a study by Charlotte Bühler (1935) in which one- and two-year-old children were forbidden to touch a toy by an adult. When the adult left the room briefly, many of the infants touched the toy. But when the adult returned (p. 67): "60 percent of the 1;4 and 100 percent of the 1;6 show the greatest embarrassment, blush, and turn to the adult with a frightened expression. From 1;9 on they attempt to make good what has happened by returning the toy quickly to its place". And what is brought out in all the studies mentioned so far—by Dunn; Shotter and Gregory; Middleton and Edwards; Wolf; Kagan; Spitz; and Bühler—are not supposed hidden mental states in the individual child responsible for his/her actions, but how his/her actions are related to, or intertwined with those of others, both preceding and following them. And in making sense of them, instead of referring to something supposedly hidden, existing behind appearances, inside the heads of individuals, we have referred instead to the emerging articulation of the appearances unfolding before our very eyes—to a detailed sequence of intertwined, or interrelated, fleeting responses occurring between people.

We can see in the aforementioned comparisons, two very different kinds of project: One centred in inferences, working from patterns or orders observable in already collected "data", about the nature of the intellectual activities supposedly occurring within individuals. The other "seeing" directly in the nuances and subtleties of the ongoing spontaneous activities between children and those around them, the workings of certain developmental practices between them. Dunn (1988), who to an extent spontaneously adopts what I have called an embodied, dialogical stance without explicitly stating it as such, notes in the first few lines of her book, the seeming *paradox* arising out of these two lines of research: That, on the one hand, in practice, children show all kinds of subtle differentiations in their responses to people in their first few months of life.[11] Whereas on the other hand, in research into children's talk *about* "minds" and "mental states", their conceptual knowledge of other people's psychology seems to develop only slowly.

There is only a paradox here though if one assumes, as Dunn does, that the same supposed "cognitive mechanisms" are at work in shaping both kinds of behaviours.[12] However, if we recognise the supportive and resourceful role played by the transient "social worlds" constituted between people in the fleeting "relational moments" between them, then we can see that, in these early activities, the influences "shaping" the child's activities are not and cannot be wholly within the child him/herself. Others, including the "situation", are at work "shaping" their activity also.

Indeed, we can go so far as to suggest that the developmental discrepancy Dunn notes between the abilities of older and younger children, is not so much an age-dependent as a *context-dependent* phenomenon. In other words, even persons of the same age will find it harder to talk "about" mental phenomena retrospectively, in reflecting on them after their occurrence, than in talking "of" them, during their ongoing occurrence in a practical context. And I think that Dunn "shows" her intuitive realisation of this—*and* of the loss of the context in which people establish their "positions" (and their identities) in relation to each other as I mentioned earlier—in her remarks that (Dunn, 1988, p. 5): "Our ignorance [of how we become *persons*] is in part the result of the way in which developmental psychology has grown and is practiced. Children have rarely been studied in the world in which these developments take place, or in a context in which we can be sensitive to the subtleties of the social understanding". To study these phenomena, we must study them from a position of involvement in them, in terms of our own embodied sense of their moment-by-moment fluctuations. We must show how their "mental movements", the "gestures" they "show" in their actions, can be made sense of in terms common to us all.

It is our involvement in these crucial, responsive, embodied-relational activities, that has remained for too long unnoticed and unacknowledged in the background to everything that we do. We have thus failed to notice how it works to connect or relate us, spontaneously and evaluatively, to our surroundings and we have also failed to notice how the others around us, in responding to us as if already a certain kind of person, help create the opportunities for us to become such. Thus I want to suggest, along with Vygotsky (1986), Bakhtin (1986), Volosinov (1986), and Wittgenstein (1953), that much of what we do individually and self-consciously—as we ourselves want, rather than our circumstances demand—depends on us being able to make use of possible ways of acting, of possible abilities, of resources first spontaneously "called out" from us by the others, or an Otherness, in our surroundings. For example, as we saw with Samantha earlier, what was at issue was not just Samantha acting in an instrumentally successful manner but that she also "showed" in her acting an awareness of how others would respond to her success or failure. And this is what her mother was determined to "call out" from her by her second, emphatic "... ARENT YOU CLEVER!" For without such "shows" of awareness, we tend to think of people as being unaware of what they are doing, as not being properly in control of their own actions. Indeed, as Vygotsky himself suggests (1986, p. 168): "Awareness and deliberate control appear only during a very advanced stage in the development of a mental function, after it has been used and practiced unconsciously and spontaneously. In order to subject a function to intellectual and volitional control we must first possess it".[13]

However, I want to go further and to suggest that, in the human sciences in general and developmental studies in particular, our cultural knowledge—our knowledge of our relations to our surroundings—develops by our continuing to involve ourselves in developmental processes very similar to those in which we involve our children. In other words, for us as well as for our children, many important first steps toward the growth of our cultural knowledge do not begin, as current myth has it, with us as uninvolved, disinterested individuals, testing new theories. Instead, they begin with an initial response "called out" from us by others or by an Otherness around us, *from within* our involvements with them or it. We start with something "fleeting" that "arrests" our attention, with a "sense of bewilderment and enthrallment". We notice something occurring momentarily out in our own or other people's spontaneous involvements with their surroundings "as if for the very first time". And the very activity of linguistically bringing the attention of others, similarly involved, also to see such (often fleeting) events as we see them, is a part of the very same process of us increasing our knowledge—not of the world, but of our relation to it, to ourselves, and to others as human agents, thus to be persons of this or that kind.

In other words, given the flow of embodied, spontaneous, responsive activity already going on between us, one *use* to which we are able to put our actions and utterances in "calling out" certain kinds of responses from the others around us, is to "point" or to "gesture" beyond our immediate circumstances, toward other affairs. In our research work at the moment however, we fail to notice the proper significance of these important, if fleeting, events—not simply because they are so fleeting and momentary, but because, as Wittgenstein (1953, no. 305) puts it, the very idea of our actions as having their origin in hidden, inner psychological states "stands in the way of our seeing" such events for what they are. Yet, in the "spaces" occurring between us, as Wittgenstein (1953, no. 435) again puts it, "nothing is hidden": "'How do sentences manage to represent'", he asks, "the answer might be: 'Don't you know? You certainly see it, when you use them'. For nothing is concealed". We grasp their *use* in the situation directly, in terms of their "place" or "role" in the whole scheme of things in which we are already involved.

Indeed to the extent that it is our grasp of the "role" of these fleeting, spontaneous, background activities occurring between us that makes our self-conscious theorising possible, they cannot themselves be understood theoretically. But what we can still do, as Wittgenstein (1953) realised, is to draw attention to them in our talk in such a way that their *use*—the practical part they play *in relation to* the rest of our affairs—becomes immediately clear and obvious to us. Thus as he says, a part of his "method" is to (no. 132): "constantly be giving prominence to distinctions which our ordinary forms of language easily make us overlook". His aim in doing this is to help us develop a shared ability to "see" the facts of our ordinary, everyday dealings with one another, directly and unproblematically: Thus, either to discuss them between ourselves or to go on to formulate agreed ways of studying them further. And as Vygotsky (1986,

p. 106) puts it: "it is a functional use of the word, or any other sign, as a means of focusing one's attention, selecting distinctive features and analyzing and synthesizing them, that plays a central role in concept formation". We say to each other and to our children such things as "Stop!", "Look!", "Listen!" and so on, and in doing so, draw their attention to something already in existence in their ongoing involvement with their surroundings to which they themselves had failed to attend. In so doing, we produce in the other that kind of understanding which, as Wittgenstein (1953, no. 122) puts it: "consists in 'seeing connections'". Thus, within such a process as this—in which an other draws to our attention events and occurrences that we ourselves have not noticed—we can come to a grasp of crucial features of our own activities from within our own very conduct of them, features that would otherwise escape our attention—even when an ultimate explanation of their underlying causes, their functioning in theory, is unavailable to us. In other words, between us, in practice, we can extend and transform our practices without it being necessary to make any excursions into the theoretical realm at all. Where, again as Vygotsky (1978, p. 57) puts it, the processes of development involved here are all ones in which: "an interpersonal function is transformed into an intrapersonal one... All the higher functions originate as actual relations between human individuals".

CONCLUSIONS

I have suggested that we cannot understand our children's development without taking their development of their unique identities into account. But to do this, we must make quite a number of changes both in ourselves and in our ways of studying the relevant phenomena: First, instead of studying retrospective "data" (i.e. records of already past and finished activities), we should begin our studies *from within* our own involvements in the activities in question. Second, from within those involvements, we should focus on the spontaneous and momentary, relational activities occurring between people. Third, we should begin our studies not by theorising but by making ourselves sensitive to their nature—using talk itself as a means for drawing our attention to possibly important "moments" and "movements". Fourth, in noticing the extent to which we are always, whether we like it or not, *responsively aware of* and *continuously spontaneously reacting to* the others around us, we must study how the very way we move, gesture (and eventually walk and speak) is shaped from the earliest moments by: (1) this awareness; (2) the responses others "call out" from us; and (3) the "spaces" they create for us to "act into"—an evaluative space that is always one of respect or contempt, of pride or shame (Taylor, 1989). This leads to a fifth and related shift, a shift away from age- and stage-related theories of supposed "normal" development to a greater attention to diverse, unique, age-independent events and processes, and to their place in development as a whole.[14] And finally, in not seeking explanatory theories, our task in all of this would be to help develop new developmental practices, new ways of participating in the "play of events" unfolding between us and those we study so that we could come to "see" events unfolding between children and their caretakers relationally: That is, to see them in terms of their possible relations and connections with their surroundings, in all their different aspects—with the goal of enabling all involved in them to afford children the appropriate development opportunities. Where among our tasks would be, to repeat, those to do with understanding the detailed and nuanced structure of the spontaneous, everyday, developmental practices in existence at the moment and the opportunities they offer for our children to develop into this, that, or some other kind of person—themselves also embodying certain kinds of sensibilities (or not, as the case may be) to do with their relations to their surroundings.

Running through all these shifts and changes is a common theme: The fact that, in all our current disciplinary practices in the human and behavioural sciences, the way in which our immediate reactions are *necessarily related* to our surroundings has remained *rationally invisible* to us. Mostly, as professionals, we have ignored our embodied embeddedness in this living flow of spontaneous responsive activity. Not only have we let it remain unnoticed in the background to everything that we do but we have ignored its importance *as* a sustaining, supportive, resourceful, ever-present background in all our ways of making sense in and of our lives. Indeed, in ignoring its nature, we have gone as far as to invent "hidden mechanisms" we suppose as serving some of these same functions: And this, of course, is the aim of the cognitive approach to developmental studies with its internalist, intellectualist-representational stance. By contrast, the externalist, embodied-relational stance that I have adopted suggests that in practice, everything of primary importance to development goes on outside us as individuals, in the "spaces" in between us. Thus, we should be wary of anything that seems to stand in the way of us seeing what occurs out there in that space in all its nuanced detail—especially theories about supposedly hidden processes occurring in the heads of individuals.

The assumption that this means that we must give up attempting to talk of the inner, psychic lives of individuals—about their feelings or experiences, about their thoughts and thinking, or about those inner moments when, all alone, we try to make sense of our own lives—would, however, be a great mistake. Indeed, there is even more to say than before, for our new stance opens up our inner psychic lives to forms of conversational investigation never before (because of their supposed hidden, inner nature) thought possible. For it suggests that what some inner thing "is" for us, is revealed not in how we talk *about* it when reflecting upon it but in how "it" necessarily "shapes" those of our everyday communicative activities in which it is involved, in practice. Furthermore, it suggests that as such, "it" has an emergent nature of a situated, socially constructed and thus incomplete, precarious, and contested kind—"it" has its being in the "movement" of our bodies and our voices as we speak our words and body forth our actions into the world. In short, the "things" supposedly in our "inner" lives are not to be found within us as individuals but "in" the momentary relational spaces occurring between ourselves and others or an Otherness in our surroundings. This gives rise to the strange consequence that (Volosinov, 1986, p. 25): "the processes that basically define the content of the psyche occur not inside but outside the individual organism, although they involve its participation". For it is only in their ongoing, relational involvements with others, that the influences important to children's development make their first appearance—their involvement being "called out" from them by those others around them.

REFERENCES

Bakhtin, M. M. (1986). *Speech genres and other late essays.* (Vern W. McGee, Trans.) Austin, TX: University of Texas Press.

Bartsch, K. & Wellman, H. W. (1995). *Children talk about the mind.* New York: Oxford University Press.

Berger, P. & Luckman, T. (1966). *The social construction of reality.* New York: Doubleday.

Bernstein, R. J. (1983). *Beyond objectivism and relativism.* Oxford: Blackwell.

Bühler, C. (1935). *From birth to maturity.* London: Kegan, Paul, Trench, & Trubner.

Butterworth, G. (1990). Self-perception in infancy. In D. Cicchetti & M. Beeghly (Eds.), *The self in transition: infancy to childhood.* Chicago/London: University of Chicago Press.

Clark, K. & Holquist, M. (1984). *Mikhail Bakhtin.* Cambridge, MA: Harvard University Press.

Coulter, J. (1979). *The social construction of mind.* London/Basingstoke: Macmillan.

Coulter, J. (1983). *Rethinking cognitive psychology.* London/Basingstoke: Macmillan.

Coulter, J. (1989). *Mind in action.* London/Basingstoke: Macmillan.

Damon, W. (1988). *Self understanding in childhood and adolescence.* Cambridge, UK: Cambridge University Press.

Dunn, J. (1988). *The beginnings of social understanding.* Cambridge, MA: Harvard University Press.

Gergen, K. J. (1985). The social constructionist movement in modern psychology. *American Psychologist, 40,* 266–275.

Gergen, K. J. (1991). *The saturated self: Dilemmas of identity in contemporary life.* New York: Basic Books.

Gergen, K.J. (1994). *Realities and relationships: Soundings in social construction.* Cambridge, MA: Harvard University Press.

Gibson, J. J. (1979). *The ecological approach to visual perception.* London: Houghton Mifflin.

Harré, R. (1983). *Personal being: A theory for individual psychology.* Oxford: Blackwell.

Harré, R. (1986). An outline of the social constructionist viewpoint. In R. Harré (Ed.), *The social construction of emotions* (pp. 2–14). Oxford: Blackwell.

Harré, R. & Gillet, G. (1994). *Discursive psychology*. London: Sage.

Kagan, J. (1981). *The second year: The emergence of self-awareness*. Cambridge, MA: Harvard University Press.

Lewis, M. & Brooks-Gunn, J. (1979). *Social cognition and the acquisition of self*. New York: Plenum.

Middleton, D. & Edwards, D. (1990). Conversational remembering: A social psychological approach. In D. Middleton & D. Edwards (Eds.), *Collective remembering* (pp. 23–45). London: Sage.

Ryle, G. (1949). *The concept of mind*. London: Methuen.

Shotter, J. (1975). *Images of man in psychological research*. London: Methuen.

Shotter, J. (1980). Action, joint action, and intentionality. In M. Brenner (Ed.), *The structure of action* (pp. 28–65). Oxford: Blackwell.

Shotter, J. (1984). *Social accountability and selfhood*. Oxford: Blackwell.

Shotter, J. (1993a). *Cultural politics of everyday life: Social constructionism, rhetoric, and knowing of the third kind*. Milton Keynes, UK: Open University Press.

Shotter, J. (1993). *Conversational realities: Constructing life through language*. London: Sage.

Shotter, J. (1995). Joint action, shared intentionality, and the ethics of conversation. *Theory and Psychology, 5*, 49–73.

Shotter, J. & Gregory, S. (1976). On first gaining the idea of oneself as a person. In R. Harré (Ed.), *Life sentences*. Chichester, UK: Wiley.

Spitz, R. (1957). *No and yes: On the genesis of human communication*. New York: International Universities Press.

Taylor, C. (1985). What is human agency? In C. Taylor (Ed.), *Human agency and language* (pp. 15–44). Cambridge, UK: Cambridge University Press.

Taylor, C. (1989). *Sources of the self: The making of the modern identity*. Cambridge, MA: Harvard University Press.

Trevarthan, C. (1977). Descriptive analysis of infant communicative behavior. In H. R. Schaffer (Ed.), *Studies in mother–infant interaction*. London: Academic Press.

Volosinov, V. N. (1986). *Marxism and the philosophy of language*. (L. Matejka & I. R. Titunik, Trans). Cambridge, MA: Harvard University Press.

Vygotsky, L. S. (1978). *Mind in society: The development of higher psychological processes*. Cambridge, MA: Harvard University Press.

Vygotsky, L. S. (1986). *Thought and language*. (Trans. revised by Alex Kozulin). Cambridge, MA: MIT Press.

Wittgenstein, L. (1953). *Philosophical investigations*. Oxford: Blackwell.

Wolf, D. P. (1990). Being in several minds: voices and versions of the self in early childhood. In D. Cicchetti & M. Beeghly (Eds.), *The self in transition* (pp. 183–212). Chicago/New York: University of Chicago Press.

NOTES

1. A resonance with Gibson's (1979) notion of "affordances" is intended here: We can act "into" the "invitations" offered us in such circumstances.
2. I put "show" and "way" in quotes to alert readers to the special resonances of these terms in my account. In Wittgenstein's (1953) work, the distinction between "saying" and "showing" is crucial: We "show" the relation between the said and the unsaid—the nature of our circumstances for us—"in" the "way" we body forth our speech into the world.

3. A *dialogical* approach can be contrasted with a *monological* one. A monological approach is one-sided, seeing all processes as centered in unitary entities, for example, seeing the organising centre of people's utterances as either in the individual (individualistic subjectivism) or the linguistic system (abstract objectivism) but not both. Dialogical approaches are two-sided. They see the "organising centre" of people's utterances as being in the relationship between speakers and listeners (Bakhtin 1986; Volosinov, 1986). In fact, as we shall see, a dialogical approach suggests that the influences at work in "shaping" a person's actions can be very diffusely distributed indeed.

4. The social constructionist approach is due: to Berger and Luckman (1966); Coulter (1979, 1983, 1989); Gergen (1985, 1991, 1994); Harré (1983, 1986); Harré and Gillet (1994); Shotter (1975, 1984, 1993a, b).

5. Indeed, as Taylor (1989, p. 28) remarks: "Talk about 'identity' in the modern sense would have been incomprehensible to our forebears of a couple of centuries ago... Underlying our modern talk of identity is the notion that questions of a moral orientation cannot all be solved in simply universal terms. And this is connected to our Postromantic understanding of individual differences as well as the importance we give to expression in each person's discovery of his or her moral horizon". In other words, it is the very increase in the relational complexity that we ourselves have introduced into our own lives, that has created the need for us to talk of ourselves as having an "identity".

6. The form-board was slightly unusual in that the shapes on it were raised, and the child had to fit brass "collars", so to speak, round them.

7. Her intonation here is, of course, of crucial importance, for, as Clark and Holquist (1984, p. 10) put it: "an utterance, spoken or written, is always expressed from a point of view ... utterance is an activity that enacts differences in values ... intonation is the sound that value makes". For, in always being bodily responsive to our circumstances, we express our evaluative relation to them in our intoning of our words: Thus here, Samantha's mother is offering Samantha an advantageous responsive position in relation to herself in her intoning of her words.

8. See note 1.

9. Unlike an utterance (Bakhtin, 1986, p. 74): "the sentence ... is not demarcated on either side by a change in speaking subjects; it has neither direct contact with reality (with an extraverbal situation) nor a direct relation to others' utterances; it does not have semantic fullness of value; and it has no capacity to determine directly the responsive position of the *other* speaker, that is, it cannot provoke a response". In short, rather than playing a "living", relational role in shaping the activity between people, the sentence appears as a "dead" form requiring interpretation.

10. Taylor (1985, 1989) points out that we human beings are not just concerned to evaluate our actions in relation to their outcomes; we also debate and evaluate the worth of desiring such outcomes. But we treat our desires, not as simply arbitrarily "chosen" desires, but as "articulations" of our identities, of who we are, of how we are "placed" in relation to those around us—a distinction, as Taylor calls it, between "first-" and "second-order desires"—(Taylor, 1985, p. 39): "So that a man may condemn himself by giving his sincerely held view on the nature of experience that he and others are living through, or on what is of importance to himself or what he sees as important to men in general". But can perhaps redeem himself, if he is open to fresh insights on the basis of evaluations of the others around him; or can perhaps show others connections between things they have failed to notice ... and so on.

11. Indeed, she notes that children "show" in their responses to others a sense of whether the other's activities "intertwine" in with their own, or not, as the case may be (Dunn, 1988, p. 1):—"At two months old, they distinguish a person who intends to communicate with them from one who speaks to someone else" (Trevarthan, 1977)."

12. Indeed, she goes as far as to say that (Dunn, 1988, p.11): "I should emphasize at the outset that focus on the children's emotions, motivation, and relationships does not imply a dismissal of cognitive mechanisms in the development of social understanding".

13. Wittgenstein (1980, p. 31) makes a similar point when he says: "The origin and the primitive form of the language game is a reaction; only from this can more complicated forms develop. Language—I want to say—is refinement, 'in the beginning was the deed' ".

14. Indeed, as Vygotsky (1978, p. 73) remarks: "Our concept of development implies a rejection of the frequently held view that cognitive development results from the gradual accumulation of separate changes. We believe that child development is a complex dialectical process characterized by periodicity, unevenness in the development of different functions, metamorphosis or qualitative transformation of one form into another, intertwining of external and internal factors, and adaptive processes which overcome impediments that the child encounters".

12 Sociomoral understanding

Nicholas Emler
University of Oxford, UK

> We are perpetually moralists, but we are geometricians only by chance. Our intercourse with intellectual nature is necessary; our speculations upon matter are voluntary and at leisure. (Samuel Johnson)

The average 15-year-old can articulate sophisticated and complex moral arguments about a wide range of issues including such matters as the degree of culpability or guilt of the perpetrators of harm to others, about what constitutes a fair punishment, an equitable distribution of rewards, a fair level of payment for work or a just allocation of burdens and responsibilities, about the purposes and desirability of different kinds of rules as well as proper procedures for their creation, revision and repeal. Children of this age have views about civil and other rights, the nature of contracts and promises, and the citizen's obligations in relation to laws. They can also demonstrate some understanding of principles underlying democracy, and those governing relations of commercial exchange, as well as insight into the legitimacy and proper uses of authority.

It is, of course, a little arbitrary to choose 15 years of age as a reference point for the development of sociomoral understanding. New and yet more sophisticated insights into the moral aspects of human relations and social institutions may well emerge later in life and indeed have been documented in various research programmes (e.g. Adelson, 1971; Kohlberg, 1984). On the other hand, 10-year-olds, 6-year-olds, and even 3-year-olds are by no means bereft of any capacity to render moral judgements or comprehend social arrangements (Dunn, 1988; Smetana, 1981). The point is that the acquisition of sociomoral understanding is a developmental process, which is to say it occurs over time, it is gradual and generally cumulative, and it is characterised by a certain order or sequence—straightforward insights generally precede those that are more profound, and simpler elements are combined to produce more general and complex notions.

It is the purpose of this chapter to set out some of what is now known and claimed about the development of sociomoral understanding, about its content and the order of its development, about the influences on its development and the processes by which development occurs, and about the uses to which such understanding may be put by the child, the adolescent, and the adult. The treatment has no pretence of being exhaustive; the literature on these subjects is now far too extensive to be covered adequately in a single chapter. Rather, the intention is to provide the reader who is relatively new to this subject with a flavour of the issues, a modest framework or "tourist guide" to help orient those who may wish to explore more deeply , and some indications as to where more comprehensive treatments of particular topics may be found. For the reader who already has some familiarity with this area of child development, I hope to be able to pose one or two new questions and offer some less familiar perspectives on a familiar terrain.

THEORIES OF MORAL DEVELOPMENT: A GLANCE TO THE PAST

Students attending a lecture or consulting a textbook on moral development in the mid 1960s would have learned first that a socialised adult is someone able to exercise self-control. This individual will be able to resist temptations to transgress or pressure from others to behave immorally to the degree that he/she has an internalised and autonomous commitment to moral standards. Students at this time would have learned next that there were two principal views about how this socialisation occurred, based respectively on the two major theoretical traditions of 20th-century psychology—psychoanalysis and behaviourism. Neither view, however, would have had much to say about the development of moral understanding, of concepts like justice, of moral judgements, reasoning, or insight.

For psychoanalysis, the interesting issues concerned the development of conscience, which was regarded as essentially a motivational and emotional disposition. The crucial research questions were about the effects of styles of parental discipline and of the quality of the parent–child relationship on strength of conscience, measured in terms of intensity of guilt (Allinsmith, 1960; Sears, Rau, & Alpert, 1966). If little attention was paid within this tradition to thought, reasoning, judgement, or insight it was because intellectual and rational processes were regarded as irrelevant to the childhood development of morality. Children did not become committed to moral standards through any process of rational choice or reflection but as an irrational emotional compulsion. Indeed, for Freud a well-developed conscience was more likely to distort the capacity to reason about moral questions and to do so in direct proportion to its strength.

For those working in the behaviourist tradition, intellectual processes were equally irrelevant to moral socialisation. But the important questions for the behaviourist were about the acquisition and persistence of moral habits (Bandura & Walters, 1963). Thus, children's moral judgements were not evidence of their capacity to think about issues of right and wrong. They were merely verbal habits, likely to be acquired, and modified, in the same way as any other behavioural regularity, through imitation of parents or other adults and as a result of reinforcement by these adults (Bandura & MacDonald, 1963).

There might have been some brief reference to the research of the Swiss psychologist Jean Piaget into children's moral ideas and possibly to the then very recently published ideas of the American, Lawrence Kohlberg, about moral reasoning. But, until the mid 1960s, outside the French-speaking world, Piaget's ideas had been of interest mainly to scholars in education; they had achieved little impact on the mainstreams of psychological thinking. Kohlberg's own Piagetian analysis of moral development was simply too recent to have made its mark.

Over the next few years the picture changed rapidly. Piaget's work on the stages of intellectual development and his constructivist theory became more widely known in North America, and as its significance was increasingly acknowledged so Kohlberg's analysis of moral reasoning, which employed the same constructivist framework of developmental stages, found an increasingly receptive audience. For a short period a kind of Balkanisation of the domain of moral development prevailed. The very different claims of psychoanalysis, behaviourism, and constructivism achieved a kind of coexistence by accepting that each referred to a different part of the developmental landscape—psychoanalysis to the development of moral emotions and therefore the affective domain, behaviourism to the domain of overt action and constructivism to cognition, the domain of ideas and judgements (see Brown & Herrenstein, 1975). But the contradictions of this solution were too obvious for it to survive. A theoretical choice had to be made and it was; the constructivists won the argument and seem to have gone on winning for thirty years.

So what is to be gained from this glance at the past? Constructivism, as a way of thinking about the process of moral socialisation, was adopted and elaborated by developmental psychologists as a self-conscious and explicit critique of psychoanalysis and behaviourism (see, for example, Kohlberg, 1964, 1971; also Gibbs & Schnell, 1985). It was, in other words, developed to contrast with the claims of these other theories. Once the argument was won, however, the claims which formed the heart of that argument became progressively part of the taken-for-granted framework within which constructivist research proceeded. Instead, other issues and debates took front stage. To understand, and more importantly to evaluate, the current position it is helpful to be clear about what it began as a criticism of.

In the following sections of this chapter I will discuss first the nature of the argument between the constructivists and the others and why the constructivists appeared to win it. I will then consider some of the substance of that view as it has evolved, particularly in the work of Piaget, Kohlberg, and Turiel. This will be followed by an alternative view of the developmental process which gives greater emphasis to social influences. Finally, I offer a reappraisal of the significance of sociomoral under-standing as it develops over childhood, in the process re-examining the assumptions that constructivism *shared* with psychoanalysis and behaviourism.

FROM SOCIALLY DETERMINED STANDARDS TO SELF-CONSTRUCTED INSIGHTS

Constructivism was first of all an attack on the moral relativism of psycho-analysis and behaviourism. These theories, and their counterparts in sociology and anthropology, took morality to be relative to culture. The authority of moral standards derived entirely from the fact that they were shared by the members of a society. Morals were customs and traditions passed from one generation to the next. In different cultures, different standards would be found. Hence, morals were not universally valid truths or rational principles for conducting social relations but local, historically or culturally relative, and essentially *arbitrary* prohibitions and require-ments. Which is to say there was no rational or absolute standard, independent of any one culture, to which one could appeal in deciding on the validity of the moral standards in a particular culture or which would allow one to say that the standards of that culture were morally superior to those of another.

To become morally socialised, therefore, was to absorb and accept these local standards. Psychoanalysis and behaviourism complemented anthro-pological and sociological theory by providing accounts of *how* these standards were transmitted across generations. Although the respective accounts differed in the detail of the mechanisms of socialisation, they coincided with the fundamental sociological assumption that beliefs and values are socially determined. If a person believes something is morally wrong it is not because he/she has independently arrived at an objective or rational conclusion but as a result of having been brought up to believe this. These were the elements attacked by the constructivists. They claimed instead that children independently and actively construct their own understanding of the social world and of the principles according to which social relations should be regulated. This was, in turn, linked to the claim that the understandings constructed by children and the principles they derive are nonrelative because social relations themselves contain objective and universal features.

I think the constructivists won this argument for two different reasons. The first is that moral relativism was becoming increasingly distasteful to scholars in the 1960s and a reason for this was undoubtedly the involvement of the United States in an unpopular war in Vietnam. The moral intuitions of those American citizens who opposed the war could find no support in other social science theories of morality. If all moral standards are relative what legitimate basis can individuals have for moral criticism of the actions of their government? Is it not more likely that such criticisms reflect the moral immaturity of the dissenters? This was precisely the view taken of anti-war protesters and draft resisters by some social scientists of the time who argued they were little different from delinquents. But a new generation of researchers who had grown up with the civil rights movement and gone to college during the protest era were attracted to a theory which gave scientific authority to their moral doubts.

The second reason was that the constructivists had better data. Their theoretical adversaries had never taken seriously the possibility that children could make moral judgements, that they might have ideas about moral questions, or think about moral obligations. For psychoanalysis, conscious thought was just too unreliable a guide to the process of moral control within the personality. For behaviourism, mental events were simply irrelevant. So neither tradition had seriously studied children's thoughts, judgements, or reasoning about moral matters; they had no evidence on these phenomena. When, in 1932, Piaget set out his agenda in the opening lines of *The moral judgment of the child,* as the investigation not of moral behaviour or sentiments but moral judgement, he may well have been aware that this was an open field, a phenomenon untouched by other theoretical traditions. And so it remained. When the argument came to a head thirty years later the constructivists had a huge advantage: They had built up a detailed account of children's moral thinking and its gradual evolution from the earliest years through to adulthood. So what had they learned? The story now requires a closer look at Piaget.

JEAN PIAGET AND THE DEVELOPMENT OF SOCIAL KNOWLEDGE

By the time Piaget published *The moral judgment of the child* he had already completed a number of studies of children's understanding of the natural world, of causality, and of logic. Over the course of those studies he had evolved the essence of his constructivist position, based on a view of humans as inherently active and inherently oriented towards adaptation. From the beginning of life these inherent tendencies are expressed in attempts to make sense of the surrounding environment and the continual repetition of such attempts results in a progressively more adequate and complete understanding of the nature of the material world and the effects of the child's own actions upon it. Thus, from infancy onwards each individual gradually and through a succession of modifications constructs his/her understanding of the nature of space and spatial relations, of physical properties such as mass, of concepts of number and causality, and ultimately an understanding of principles of logic. In effect, children progressively build for themselves and through their own actions and experiences an intelligent understanding of the world. This construction proceeds in an orderly sequence of reorganisations in thinking, which give to intellectual development a stage-like character. The development of intelligence is not, therefore, just a matter of accumulating an ever greater quantity of knowledge about the world; it involves qualitative changes in the way the child thinks—new *methods* of understanding and problem solving are developed.

This, then, was the general theoretical framework within which Piaget began his studies of children's moral ideas. These studies first examined children's views about the obligatory nature of rules, turned next to their understanding of those duties and expectations which seemed to derive directly from adults and which concerned such matters as not lying or damaging property, and finally examined their ideas about retributive and distributive justice. In each case, Piaget found that there was a point at which children's views appeared to undergo a qualitative change to a new level of insight, and in some areas of their thinking more than one such change.

In the first studies Piaget examined children's views about the rules of their own games, asking them where the rules came from, whether they could be changed, and if so how. He found that younger children, those up to about seven or eight years of age, could not imagine changing the rules which they regarded as fixed and eternal and possessing an authority which commanded respect by virtue of their external origin. Thereafter, a gradual change sets in. The idea that the rules of the game are eternal begins to recede and to be replaced by a recognition that changes are possible. But with this new recognition, from about 10 years onwards, comes a concern with the appropriate *procedures* for making changes and a realisation that the rules deserve respect precisely because of the procedures by which they have been made and modified. The appropriate procedures are those which allow an equal voice to all those to whom the rules apply and free consent to any changes. So, according to Piaget, by the beginning of adolescence the child has quite spontaneously become committed to democratic law making.

With respect to their understanding of duties concerning lying and property damage, the significant shift in children's views comes a little earlier. Young children, Piaget discovered, had an attitude of objective responsibility, regarding a lie as bad simply because it diverges from the truth and the larger the divergence the greater the offence. Similarly, causing damage is wicked in direct proportion to the amount of damage done. But eight- and nine-year-olds would almost invariably reject these conclusions, arguing that what matters above all is the intention of the actor. So the intention to deceive matters more than the size of the lie and a small amount of damage caused in the course of intentional disobedience is worse than a large amount of damage caused entirely by accident. Piaget described this as an attitude of subjective responsibility.

Piaget's studies next moved to children's views about just punishment. Here again he found age related changes in thinking with respect to the ideal qualities of punishment, although in this domain two distinct shifts were observed. The youngest children thought that punishment should ideally be severe and made no attempt to link it to the severity of the offence. This was then replaced with an attitude of reciprocity, a preference for an almost physical equivalence of punishment and offence. The oldest children, however, rejected this in favour of the view that punishment should ideally take a form likely to recompense the victim and reform the culprit. In the sphere of distributive justice, Piaget reported a parallel sequence of changes, beginning with the view that fair distributions are no more and no less than the distributions decided by adults, moving to the conviction that any resource should be shared according to strict equality and that adults and children alike should be bound by this requirement, and finally to a view that differences in merit or need should be recognised and that these should take precedence over rigid equality of treatment.

Piaget drew two more general conclusions from his studies. The first was that all the changes in their thinking that he had observed, with respect to rules, adult proscriptions, and justice, reflected the same underlying shift from a heteronomous view of morality to an autonomous view. In other words, there was an intellectual unity underlying the diverse specific changes. The second was that this more general change reflected a change in the focus of children's social relationships with increasing age. The lives of young children, Piaget argued, are dominated by relations of constraint. These are their relationships with adults which are inevitably unequal, intellectually as well as physically. Influence in such relationships is one-way, respect is one-sided or unilateral and the child's thinking about moral matters is "constrained" by adults' views. As children grow older, however, relationships with their peers assume increasing significance and these relationships are more equal. Constraint and unilateral respect are progressively replaced by the expectation of mutual respect and the method of co-operation. It is out of the equality, reciprocity, and co-operation of peer relations that children begin to understand that rules can also be products of agreements between equals, that intentions need to be considered in judging one another's actions, and that an equitable consideration of merit and need should govern the sharing of resources.

Following Piaget there have been four distinct lines of research within the constructivist tradition. The first is broadly a further elaboration of the same lines of inquiry (for reviews and more detailed discussion of this line of work see Kohlberg, 1964; Lickona, 1976; Turiel, 1983). Researchers have repeated Piaget's studies of the shift from objective to subjective responsibility many dozens of times and with largely the same result. It is true that the original conclusions have been refined and indeed significantly modified by this work. Thus, it seems that children much younger than the eight and nine year olds in Piaget's study have some appreciation of the relevance of intent in making moral judgements. It also seems that there is not one change but the accumulation of many small adjustments in thinking. Thus, some work has indicated that children consider intentions in judging actions involving harm to others and actions involving benefits to others at an earlier age than they do for actions involving material damage (Imamoglu, 1975; Constanzo, Coie, Grumet, & Farnhill, 1973). Children also take intentions into account before they consider the foreseeability of harm (e.g. Yuill & Perner, 1988). But the replications have also confirmed that the shift from objective to subjective responsibility was not a peculiarity in the views of children living in Neuchâtel and Geneva in the late 1920s. It has been found wherever it has been studied.

A similar picture has emerged from the less numerous replications of Piaget's studies of justice notions. Details of the conclusions have been adjusted in the light of these replications but the broad outline stands. Perhaps the most significant adjustments have come from the work of William Damon (1977) who found a different initial stage in children's notions of distributive justice; his American children first of all equated fairness with what they personally wanted and not, as had Piaget's Swiss children, with what adults decreed. Additionally, Damon identified a more differentiated sequence of changes; for example, the justice of need emerged as a distinct stage only after the recognition of relative merit and deservingness as relevant considerations. But Damon's conclusions reinforced the more general constructivist view that moral development is an aspect of intellectual development by linking changes in justice concepts directly to changes in logical concepts; the child's notions of justice are reflections of its more basic abilities to categorise, order, etc., in a logical fashion (Damon, 1975, see also Hook & Cook, 1979, who draw similarly direct parallels). Piaget's studies of rules received much less attention until, as we shall see, the question was reopened by Turiel (1975, 1983).

The second line of work extends well beyond the study of children's sociomoral understanding, and therefore beyond the proper scope of this chapter, so we cannot follow it far. Its interest for us lies primarily in its view of the child as problem solver and of the social world as an objective reality, the nature of which is progressively penetrated by the child's intelligence. Once Piaget had shown the stage-like nature of children's developing understanding of how the physical world works it was a natural progression for researchers to begin asking how the child understands the workings of the human and social world and whether this, too, follows a stage-like pattern of qualitative changes.

Research enquiries began modestly in the sense that the social environment was initially treated as no more than other people. Piaget had made his own contribution here, first of all with the concept of egocentrism—the idea that young children find it difficult distinguishing their own point of view from that of others—and then with studies of children's representations of spatial relations, which seemed to confirm the egocentrism of younger children—they could not reliably divorce their representation of those relations from the perspective of a particular observer, namely themselves (Piaget & Inhelder, 1956). The relevance to moral development of this and related work was that children's ability to treat others as moral agents, to consider their intentions, needs, and interests, appeared to be predicated on their capacity to recognise that other people can not only have a different point of view to the self, but also different knowledge, different intentions and different desires (see Selman, 1976, for a discussion of the relation between perspective-taking abilities and moral judgement development).

Gradually, the study of social cognition or social knowledge in childhood expanded to acknowledge the full complexity of the environment about which children might be trying to make sense. So it was recognised that social knowledge includes knowledge about types and categories of people, about social relationships such as friendship, about the social and organisational roles that people play such as teacher or policeman, about structured systems of exchange such as commercial exchange and therefore also the roles of shopkeepers and customers, about banking, money, and property, about occupations and their relation to income and therefore about wage-labour exchange systems, about social classes, and about institutions of law and government (for reviews of some of these areas see Adelson, 1971; Berti & Bombi, 1988; Furth, 1980; Jahoda, 1984; Leahy, 1983).

In each area of knowledge researchers have identified sequential changes in children's insight. The work assumes that the various elements of the social environment have an underlying logic which children eventually discover for themselves, the timing of these discoveries depending primarily on the complexity of the logic entailed. Finally, these insights are linked to changes in moral evaluations—inequalities in wealth, for example, are progressively understood and also come to be seen as equitable (Connell, 1977; Leahy, 1983).

LAWRENCE KOHLBERG AND THE PHILOSOPHER CHILD

Kohlberg initiated a third distinctive line of inquiry which began with a critique of Piaget. Its essence was that when it came to moral development Piaget had not been Piagetian enough. There were five problems with Piaget's work. The first was that some of his findings had not in fact been replicated and therefore probably did not represent true developmental changes (Kohlberg, 1964). The second was that Piaget's two broad kinds of moral thinking, heteronomy and autonomy, did not satisfy the criteria of true developmental stages and that Piaget had done little more than identify a set of disparate and only loosely connected changes in children's moral ideas. Kohlberg's aspiration was to remedy this by identifying general stages in the development of moral thinking.

The third was Piaget's proposal that developmental change in moral judgement resulted from a shift in the emphasis of social relations. This was dangerously close to a sociological explanation and Kohlberg argued that it was both inconsistent with the available evidence and unnecessary. A more authentically constructivist mechanism was at work producing developmental change, namely *equilibration*. What this meant in effect was that the potential for developmental change is inherent in thinking itself. The child's spontaneous inclination to think about and make sense of his/her experience is sufficient to precipitate successive reorganisations in the cognitive system as this system attempts to reconcile apparent contradictions both between expectation and experience and between successive reflections on the same problem. These are attempts to re-establish balance or "equilibrium" in the system and this can only be accomplished by elaborating greater complexity, in effect by developmental change. So, Kohlberg argued, the more frequently a child experiences moral problems and the more varied these experiences are the more likely is his/her moral thinking to develop. There is no special role of peer relations in this.

Fourth, Piaget had concentrated too much on children's conclusions and not enough on the reasoning underlying their conclusions. With this observation Kohlberg justified a shift of emphasis from moral *judgement* to moral *reasoning*. This allowed Kohlberg to introduce a new approach into the study of moral development. He argued that if one is to study the development of moral reasoning in childhood one must give children moral problems to reason about; this Piaget had not done. A moral problem involves a conflict of moral obligations or requirements, for example, an obligation to keep a promise to a friend may conflict with an obligation of obedience to one's father. For Kohlberg, moral reasoning is an intellectual and quasi-philosophical process necessitated by the fact that ends which we value, such as the right to life or to own property, respect for the truth, or the honouring of contracts and promises, can be in conflict with one another in particular situations. Deciding what one should do in these situations is therefore a problem of deciding how to reconcile the conflicting requirements that arise from these different values.

Kohlberg's research strategy was therefore to create hypothetical scenarios or "dilemmas" in which two or more values were in conflict and then interrogate children about what the protagonists in the dilemma should do and why. Perhaps the best known of these dilemmas is the "Heinz and the drug" problem, in which the value of life and the duty of care between husband and wife are in conflict with another's property rights and respect owed to the law. On the back of this strategy Kohlberg then produced research which pointed to the final fault in Piaget's analysis: the development of moral thought does not come to a conclusion at 10 or even 13 years of age.

Kohlberg (1963) initially identified six types of moral reasoning that he believed met the criteria for true developmental stages. That is, each type formed a generalised and structured whole; it was a complete, self-contained, and internally consistent system for thinking about moral problems. Furthermore, the six types taken together formed a chronological sequence. Different types would not be found coexisting within the reasoning of the same individual, except for the special case of transition between stages when two adjacent types in the sequence would temporarily coexist. The sequence was invariant—types always appeared in the same chronological order and no intermediate type was ever missed out—and the sequence was irreversible—there was never a return to an earlier type. Finally, the sequence was universal; developmental change always occurred in this particular sequence and no other, irrespective of culture, social background, or personal circumstances.

Kohlberg organised the six types of reasoning into three more general developmental "levels", which corresponded to different general strategies for thinking about moral dilemmas. At the first or preconventional level, problems are approached from the perspective of one of the particular characters involved and considered only in terms of this person's needs or fears. So at stage 1, people are assumed above all to fear punishment and the fact that an action is punishable itself makes the action wrong. At stage 2, however, punishment is just one potential outcome of the action to be considered along with its other costs and benefits; what is right is what is most beneficial or least costly to the actor. There is limited recognition at this stage that other parties to a conflict may want different things in which case they should strike a deal.

At the second or conventional level individual interests are no longer regarded as paramount. Instead, shared or collective standards of virtue are seen to lie behind and to determine the moral legitimacy of individual interests. Children at this level take the perspective of the community or of a member of society, not of an isolated individual. Stage 3 is a matter of defining the moral solution to a dilemma in terms of the extent to which individual claims are consistent with collective notions of what is nice or decent. This means that, when the claims of different individuals conflict, those of the person whose intentions or motives are closest to this informal stereotype of virtue are given greatest weight. At stage 4, the relevant standards derive their legitimacy from a social system that is more general than any particular set of relations between individuals. Moral action is defined in terms of upholding the law of the land or the duty of the good citizen, primarily a duty to defend and maintain the system against anarchy or personal interests; good intentions are not enough.

The third level sees another qualitative shift in perspective. Moral dilemmas are considered from a standpoint outside the conventions of any particular society. In effect, the individual asks from this "prior to society" perspective: "What should the rules of a good or just society ideally be?" Stage 5, the first attempt to define nonrelative principles, involves reasoning in terms of individual rights, contract, social utility, and such rules of thumb as the greatest good of the greatest number. Stage 6 is reasoning in terms of universally valid ethical principles.

Change from one stage to the next occurs, Kohlberg argued, because the internal coherence of each system of thought is incomplete. Either the same reasoning can lead to different and mutually incompatible conclusions or there are problems it cannot satisfactorily resolve. So, for example, stage 2 does not tell you whose interests you should consider and can justify more than one of the alternatives in a dilemma, depending on which character's interests you identify with. The limits of stage 3 reasoning are reached when all parties to a conflict are acting with stereotypically virtuous intentions. Stage 4 leaves open the question of obligations to those who are not members of your own society and provides no guidelines for the creation of laws from first principles. And so on. Given sufficient experience of moral problems that test the limits of any particular stage of reasoning, developmental progression to the next stage in the sequence is likely, and each successive stage is a little more complete and satisfactory than the one it replaces.

Initially, much of this argument was speculation. Kohlberg (1963) had studied the moral reasoning of 10-, 13- and 16-year-old boys and had indeed found that his lower stages were more commonly used by the younger boys, whereas the higher stages were most likely to be found in the responses of the oldest subjects. But in the years that followed, Kohlberg and his colleagues began to accumulate the evidence that would support these speculations and in particular the claim that these six types of reasoning were indeed true developmental stages (Kohlberg, 1984). In this enterprise, four kinds of evidence were to carry particular weight. The first kind came from longitudinal studies which provided more decisive confirmation that the types did indeed form an invariant and irreversible sequence (e.g. Colby & Kohlberg, 1987). The second came from experimental studies that confirmed that change in moral reasoning could be induced artificially but only towards the next adjacent stage in the developmental sequence (e.g. Turiel, 1966), a further confirmation of the progressive and sequential nature of the types of reasoning. The third consisted of correlational evidence that showed that stage of moral reasoning was related to other measures of intellectual sophistication, such as IQ. Perhaps of more significance were demonstrations that certain levels of cognitive functioning or role-taking ability were necessary conditions for a particular type of moral reasoning (e.g. Selman, 1971; Kuhn, Langer, Kohlberg, & Haan, 1977). Their importance lay in the confirmation they provided for Kohlberg's claim that moral reasoning is both an aspect and an outcome of intellectual development. Fourth and finally, cross-cultural studies provided essential tests of the claim that the types formed a universal sequence, independent of culture (Snarey, 1985).

The cumulative impact of this research programme was not merely to verify Kohlberg's claims. The research evidence also produced significant modifications in the original conception. These included extensive refinements in the definitions of the different types of reasoning. The descriptions of the types given earlier were necessarily brief. The coding manual (Colby et al., 1987), which is effectively a definitive description of each type, runs to a few hundred pages. The successive redefinitions of stages led to reclassification of much of the moral reasoning elicited in previous studies so that in the longer run it has been accepted that reasoning at the third level, stages 5 and 6, does not emerge until at the earliest the beginning of adulthood. Indeed, it was concluded that even in adult samples there were few people who had reached stage 5 and Kohlberg conceded eventually that no case of stage 6 had been found in a research sample (Kohlberg, Levine, & Hewer, 1983). This does raise a question about where the stage definitions originally came from, and it now seems this sixth type of moral reasoning was from the beginning more of a hypothesis, an assumption about where moral development ought logically to be heading, rather than a conclusion from evidence. Apart from this, however, the picture that emerged was of the development of moral insight as an open-ended process, not one completed in childhood or even adolescence, in many and perhaps most lifetimes unfinished and maybe unfinishable, and in a significant proportion of cases a process that has ground to a halt at some quite early stage in the sequence. Stage mixture also turned out to be commonplace (see Colby et al., 1987) and if individuals can so frequently and for so long be comfortable reasoning with what is supposedly a mixture of types this must cast some doubt on the claim that each type is a structured whole with its own equilibrium. If this were so the coexistence of two types would be inherently unstable and the instability would be resolved by moving to the higher stage.

Since its first appearance, Kohlberg's theory has been the subject of an immense amount of critical scrutiny and a great deal has been written both for and against virtually every detail from the specifics of individual stage definitions to the ideological and philosophical stance of the theory's author (see Emler, 1983; Gilligan, 1982; Simpson, 1974; Sullivan, 1977). The substance of the various debates has created a confusing picture of claims and counter-claims, much of it only marginally relevant for our purposes. Let me pick out just two points here.

The first concerns the post-conventional or principled level of moral reasoning. Because it is only found in adult samples it is of no practical significance for childhood sociomoral insight. It has always possessed, however, considerable symbolic significance. For Kohlberg (1971) the existence of this level directly refutes the claim that morality must be relative to culture. Research also appeared to indicate that American civil rights and anti-war protesters in the 1960s were not morally immature but actually reasoned about moral issues in principled terms (Haan, Smith, & Block 1968; Sampson, 1971). The developmental status of principled or post-conventional reasoning therefore validated political and moral dissent.

The second point is that the notion of general stages, and Kohlberg's broad-band assessment procedure have not proved especially useful in studying children's moral reasoning and the method has rarely been employed with children younger than ten years of age. The more Piagetian style of focus on specific areas of insight and specific changes in these has continued to be more productive. The child as moral philosopher has proved elusive.

ELIOT TURIEL AND THE FUNDAMENTAL DOMAINS
OF SOCIAL KNOWLEDGE

Beginning in the 1970s, Eliot Turiel initiated an important critique of existing ideas about moral development (Turiel, 1975, 1983). He first pointed out that many of the examples of rules, prohibitions, and their violation that researchers had used to study moral development did not really involve moral questions at all. This was true of much of the behaviourist and psychoanalytically inspired work but also of some of Piaget's studies. The rules of a game, for example, whether of marbles or tennis, are not moral rules. They are conventions, argued Turiel. The defining features of moral rules is that they concern actions that have consequences for others' welfare or rights; therefore, they cannot legitimately be abolished or suspended by any group or authority. Conventions, on the other hand, are arbitrary requirements for various aspects of social interaction and include such matters as rules of address, tables manners, dress codes, and so on. Unlike moral rules, they can legitimately be changed and do vary from community to community; such changes and variations have no consequences for others' welfare or rights.

For Turiel, this distinction was important in two respects. The first, was that in Kohlberg's stage model of the development of moral reasoning a clear understanding of the distinction between morality and convention appeared to be a relatively late developmental achievement (the post-conventional level). Moreover, it had previously been supposed that much earlier in development children would regard all social rules as alike and all such rules as stemming from adult authority and deserving respect for this reason. Piaget's observation that older children come to regard rules as agreements which can also be modified by mutual consent actually only applied, Turiel argued, to their understanding of conventions and game rules and even young children may understand that rules of these kinds can be modified by the appropriate authorities. Moreover, children are likely to understand the basics of the distinction between moral rules and conventions long before they attain let alone pass beyond Kohlberg's "conventional" level of moral reasoning.

The second reason the distinction is important is because it goes to the heart of the debate between constructivist and socialisation accounts of moral development. In effect, advocates of the latter were right that there are customs, traditions, and mores that are relative to culture, that their content is somewhat arbitrary, and that children must learn them from adults precisely because their content cannot be rationally deduced. The mistake was to confuse them with moral rules that are not relative to culture, not arbitrary, and not learned in this way.

Turiel and his colleagues devised various tests of children's ability to distinguish morality and convention. Among the most useful of these have turned out to be the tests of *rule contingency* (would the act still be wrong if there was no rule prohibiting it?), *authority jurisdiction* (would the act still be wrong even if a teacher/your parents said you could do it?), and *generalisability* (would it be all right to do this in a different school/country etc.?). Other tests, such as relative seriousness, are correlated with the distinction but are less discriminating. In a representative study (Smetana, 1981) young children were asked such questions about prototypical moral transgressions (hitting or shoving another child, throwing water at another child, not sharing, taking another child's apple), and about transgression of a nursery's school's conventions (not participating in show and tell, not putting toys or belongings away in the correct places, not saying grace before snack, etc.). What seems remarkable in the light of previous conclusions about the development of moral insight is that children as young as two and a half distinguished consistently between the two kinds of rules according to such tests as rule contingency and generalisability, as well as tests of seriousness. A later study by Smetana and Braeges (1990) did reveal more variation in degree of understanding of the morality-convention distinction between 26- and 42-month-old children. The youngest children did not distinguish between moral and conventional transgressions. At 34 months, a distinction was made in terms of the criterion of generalisability, but the rule contingency and authority jurisdiction criteria were only interpreted appropriately by the oldest group.

Another method for examining children's understanding of these different domains has been to explore the justifications they give for their responses to the rule contingency and other criterion judgement questions. Davidson, Turiel, and Black (1983) asked 6-, 8-, and 10-year-olds why transgressions of various kinds of rules would be wrong. The reasons given for condemning transgressions differed in accordance with the authors' own *a priori* division of transgressions into moral and conventional. As might be expected, given the defining characteristics of the moral domain, justifications here referred to adverse effects on others' welfare or to unfairness. However, whereas the younger children almost exclusively offered the former justification, older children were likely in addition to invoke the issue of fairness. With respect to conventions, the justifications were quite different; here, the appeals were to authority, to the existence of the rule, or the need to avoid punishment or getting into trouble.

Later research showed that children also distinguish a domain of prudential rules, those rules designed to protect the self from harm or loss (e.g. Tisak & Turiel, 1984). The hazards examined have been physical threats to comfort, safety, or health and thus are not obviously relevant to the development of sociomoral understanding. However, many of the hazards of childhood reside in children's social environments, such as hazards of being victimised by bullies, exploited by cheats, duped by scoundrels and, as is now believed with varying degrees of justification, sexually abused by adults and older children, induced into substance abuse by drug pushers, or assaulted or even murdered by strangers. It would be interesting to know more about what children understand of the moral failings of others, the risks these pose for themselves, and the precautions they can take against these risks.

But to return to moral and conventional rules, how do children develop knowledge of these? Turiel argues these relate to categorically distinct types of experience. Moral rules can be inferred directly from the effects of actions, most obviously the pain or suffering of a victim. In contrast children learn about the nature of conventions from their experience of adult reactions and from noticing that these are context-bound; an action in one setting (e.g. the classroom), elicits an adult's condemnation but not in another setting (e.g. the home). This claim has been supported by observational evidence that children as well as adults respond to moral transgressions and their responses typically refer to the effects on the victim whereas usually only adults respond to conventional transgressions and their responses emphasise the disorder created by the transgression (Smetana, 1993).

The Turiel programme argues for a radical reappraisal of Piaget's conclusions about children's understanding of social rules. It also, nonetheless, represents a constructivist interpretation of the development of sociomoral understanding, claiming that children spontaneously and directly construct an understanding of different kinds of social rules on the basis of their own experience, that their understanding reflects objectively and categorically distinct kinds of experience, and that their understanding is not relative to culture or a product of social influence. The next section offers an alternative view of the way in which children's social knowledge is constructed.

SOCIOMORAL UNDERSTANDING: SELF-CONSTRUCTION OR SOCIAL CONSTRUCTION?

Perhaps surprisingly, a theory of society has remained largely implicit in research on children's sociomoral understanding. The more explicit model of society proposed here draws on open systems theory (Katz & Kahn, 1978). It proposes that human societies are social organisations which is to say they are structures of rules, roles, and procedures that are combined to achieve a variety of objectives. These objectives always include but are not limited to the survival of a viable society itself. The ways in which this and other objectives can be achieved are numerous and subject to continual revision, and so rules, roles, and procedures are likely to vary between times and places. As social organisations, human societies contain a number of control mechanisms to produce compliance with their rules and procedures. These control mechanisms include collections of interpretations, justifications, and explanations for the procedures, practices, and arrangements which define the organisation of society. The operation of the control mechanisms depends to a degree, therefore, on the members' possession of some familiarity with these justifications for the rules and arrangements. This does not mean that we as members of social systems are bound to think in socially predetermined patterns, or that they are characterised by a harmonious consensus. On the contrary, as MacIntyre (1981, p. 222) observes:

> when an institution—a university say, or a farm or hospital—is the bearer of a tradition of practice or practices, its common life will be partly but in a centrally important way, constituted by a continuous argument as to what a university is or ought to be or what good farming is or what good medicine is.

It is precisely for these reasons that social systems are *open*, which is to say susceptible to continual modification and evolution.

Where do children stand in relation to these practices and arguments about practices? I would suggest that they do not have to work out for themselves how to conduct social relations or what principles might underlie the social practices they encounter. Instead, they are initiated into the practices, familiarised with their justifications, and provided with guidelines for the conduct of social relations through mechanisms of social influence. The construction of this knowledge in the child is therefore a social process. By this, I mean in particular that knowledge is *transmitted* to children and derives from the social groups, cultures, and communities of which they are members. What social knowledge is assembled in the mind of any individual child will depend on the society to which that child belongs, and the position occupied by that child within it.

If this alternative analysis has any virtue, it must, on the one hand, be able to accommodate the available evidence on the childhood development of sociomoral insight and, on the other, answer the criticisms that constructivism has traditionally made of socialisation theories. There are five criticisms to answer, about the active versus passive role of the child, the existence of developmental sequence, the arbitrary versus nonarbitrary nature of social knowledge, the child's spontaneous and independent discovery of (objective, rational) moral principles, and the (lack of) differences in the direction or content of sociocognitive development between societies or social groups.

The issues of activity–passivity and developmental sequence are linked. Contemporary theory and research on social influence argues very clearly that influence attempts have a greater impact when the target actively processes the content of a persuasive message (Doise & Mugny, 1984; Moscovici, 1976; Petty & Cacioppo, 1986). This is because influence involves cognitive change and not merely overt verbal agreement. This in turn suggests why, if children's sociomoral ideas are products of social influence, these develop according to a sequence. Research with adult subjects shows that their cognitive systems provide all kinds of resistance to influence and there is no reason to expect children to be any different, except perhaps in degree. The resistance stems from the fact that neither adults nor children are cognitively empty in advance of any influence attempt, and the impact of influence depends upon the initial cognitive state of the target. Children who give more weight to consequences than to intentions in judging culpability may be influenced to reverse the relative importance of these considerations, because this only involves a small modification in their reasoning but cannot equally readily be influenced to consider the foreseeability of harm because this involves a larger change. Interestingly, also, children who give greater weight to intentions than to consequences cannot be influenced in the other direction. It would also be expected, from what is known about conditions for effective social influence (Moscovici, 1976), that influence is more likely to flow from adult to child than the reverse, given that adults have more extensive cognitive resources and therefore more capacity to generate distinctive and consistent arguments.

The third objection, that children's social knowledge is nonarbitrary, and could not therefore have been acquired as a result of social influence, can be dealt with quite briefly. It is entirely possible for children to acquire more objective representations of the material world or more logically coherent patterns of reasoning through a process of social transmission, and this has now been demonstrated experimentally many times (Botvin & Murray, 1975; Russell, 1981). If logic and knowledge about the material environment can be acquired in this way it is surely no less likely to be the case for social or moral knowledge.

The Turiel research programme on children's differentiation of the moral and conventional domains would appear to offer a compelling demonstration of the spontaneous and independent discovery by children of objective truths about social relations. In fact, what the research shows is that children are likely to encounter different reactions on the part of others, depending on the nature of the transgression and the context. In other words, it shows that children are exposed to messages from others about their own and others' actions. Why should these reactions not be recognised as potential social influence attempts, and why should we not conclude that the distinctions children make among different kinds of social rules are precisely the result of these influence attempts and the information they convey?

Let us take this a little further. Why should children's experience of others' reactions to moral and conventional transgressions respectively be different or to put it another way why do other children react critically to moral but not conventional transgressions and why do adults justify their criticisms of these two kinds of transgression in different ways? The contrast between moral and conventional transgressions is also a contrast between actions with immediate, obvious, certain, and noncontingent negative effects and actions the damaging effects of which, taken individually, may well be remote, obscure, uncertain, and contingent. In the former case the damage is clear to child victims and adults alike, easily communicated and easily understood. One way to minimise avoidable injury and suffering is to outlaw violent attacks with fists or sharp instruments on innocent victims, and it is difficult to imagine any social or environmental conditions under which such a prohibition would not have this effect. But many other measures could have similar effects, such as making handguns less widely available to private citizens. It should, however, also be acknowledged that even adults do not uniformly enforce such prohibitions by invoking the welfare or suffering of potential victims (cf. Hoffman, 1977).

In the case of what Turiel and others have called "conventional" transgressions the connection between action and effect cannot so readily be communicated and may not even be understood by those with a responsibility for enforcing the rules. So there should be no surprise that adults justify the rules with other kinds of argument whereas child onlookers, failing to see a connection between action and damaging effect and certainly no obvious injury to their own interests, fail to respond at all. How could the connection between a prohibition on eating pig meat or slaughtering cattle and the viability of an entire way of life (cf. Harris 1975) be readily communicated to young children?

Nor should we accept that conventions are arbitrary. They may take several different forms and still contribute to the same end, just as Piaget's older informants understood that their games could have alternative rules while retaining the spirit of the game (Piaget, 1932, pp. 68–69). There are, for example, many different ways in which water supplies and waste water disposal can be organised to protect the health of a community by reducing the risk of contaminated supply, but there is nothing arbitrary about the content of these alternatives. I am arguing here that we need to see social rules as lying along a continuum (or perhaps even a number of continua) rather than as belonging to categorically distinct domains of experience. Selecting examples from opposite extremes of these continua, which the Turiel programme has tended to do, only creates the illusion that they are categorically distinct.

A particularly persuasive feature of the constructivist case against any role for social influence in the development of social knowledge has been that variations in children's sociomoral understanding appear to be related to age but never to social group membership. If sociomoral knowledge is transmitted to children, research should surely have revealed variations in such knowlege between children growing up in different cultures. But is it really the case that researchers have failed to find obvious differences of this kind? The picture looks so consistent on this point because researchers have not been especially interested in looking for social influences on sociomoral knowledge or for differences between social groups, have used methods which were unlikely to detect them, have reinterpreted them as other kinds of difference or have simply failed to notice them (Emler & Ohana, 1993; Emler & Dickinson, 1993).

One difficulty is that developmental research has often lacked sufficient historical perspective. Consequently, widespread beliefs are mistaken for human universals and the social processes which generated them become invisible. Hygiene rules provide an example. Children will spontaneously remark on a connection between lack of cleanliness and risk of illness and there is indeed an objective, nonarbitrary connection between the two. But it is not a self-evident connection which children could have verified for themselves. It is a relatively recent discovery in human history and quite possibly it required social conditions peculiar to 18th- and 19th-century Europe for medical science to produce the germ theory of disease (Horton, 1967). If children now almost universally voice a version of this theory it is because the theory has been disseminated within the cultures to which they belong and not because they have each individually and spontaneously discovered the connection for themselves.

To take another example, Gold, Darley, Hilton, and Zanna (1984, p. 1758) write: "one is struck by the degree to which the pattern of children's moral judgments approximates what one would intuitively regard as a sensible, mature pattern of judgments about procedural justice" (see also Demetriou & Charitides, 1986). But our intuitions about what is sensible or mature in this regard are historically relative. In other periods of history very dissimilar procedures have seemed equally defensible and reasonable. Armed combat was once regarded as a proper way to resolve disputes because it submitted the argument to the judgement of God. In another century, witchcraft trials were held to be equally reasonable and just procedures for settling questions of guilt and innocence.

Occasionally, documented social group differences have simply been ignored. Piaget's (1932) own data on retributive justice, for example, show that a form of reciprocity becomes a more common response with increasing age. That is, older children recommend retaliation by victims against aggressors. But more striking was a sex difference; most of the oldest boys questioned, 11- and 12-year-olds, recommended returning at least blow for blow if not giving back more than they received whereas the great majority of girls recommended giving back less. Working in America, Durkin (1961) found no sex differences but reported that children of a similar age to those in Piaget's study had abandoned retaliation in favour of forgiveness or reconciliation. No mention was made of the possibility that these divergent results reflected divergent cultural influences on moral judgement (see Jahoda, Chapter 4). Yet, such cultural influences are easy enough to find if one looks and is prepared to notice them (for examples and further discussion, see Emler, 1987; Emler & Ohana, 1993; Nisan, 1987).

Occasionally, research methods are unsuited to detecting group differences. This is particularly true of cross-cultural research on Kohlberg's theory. Moral reasoning is classified, using a coding manual, according to the stage to which it most closely corresponds. If any sample of reasoning cannot be matched with a category in the manual, it risks being discarded as unanalysable noise. This method of doing research means that, almost by definition, forms of thinking or arguing which have not already been defined in the coding scheme cannot be detected, and the hypothesised stages are virtually immune to falsification. It is therefore all the more remarkable that evidence of cultural influences has emerged from this research programme (see Snarey, 1985).

It would be wrong to say that constructivism allows no possibility of social or cultural influences on sociomoral development. On the contrary, it anticipates such influences but assumes that these are entirely influences on the *rate* of development, not on its substance or direction. Children belonging to different social classes or growing up in different cultures are expected to develop the same insights but at different rates in so far as their different environments present them with experiences differing in variety, richness, or density. The consequence is that group differences are acknowledged when they can be interpreted in terms of the anticipated direction of such influences. If cultures can be seen as pre-literate or pre-industrial and therefore less informationally rich then children are expected and found to develop moral insights less rapidly than children growing up in literate, industrialised cultures. For similar reasons middle class children are expected and discovered to advance faster and further in moral understanding than their working class peers (Kohlberg, 1971, p. 160; Enright, Manheim, & Harris, 1980; Leahy, 1983).

In studies of children's representations of social inequalities we have asked middle and working class children about the earnings of people in different occupations and the fairness of the income differentials they perceived (Emler & Dickinson, 1985). Most children agreed that the differentials were fair and this response was unrelated to their own social class background. We also asked whether it would be preferable to make incomes more equal and this produced both age and class differences. The proposal was more likely to be rejected by older children (the age range was 6–12) and by the middle class children. A constructivist view of these results would be that working class children lag behind their middle class peers in their appreciation of the principle of equity. Our interpretation is rather different. Equity is part of a powerful social myth in Western cultures. Studies by Nisan (1984) and Mann, Radford, and Kanagawa (1985) reveal a lesser emphasis on equity as a distributive principle in other cultures. In the West it provides an explanation and justification for inequalities. And among the middle class, more likely to be the beneficiaries of equity, this myth is more extensively developed and middle class adults and their children are more fully committed to it. Consistent with this interpretation, middle class children gave more explanations and justifications for inequalities of income and had a more realistic representation of their scale and their consequences.

This leads to one final observation for this section. Not all differences between communities or social groups will take the form of possessing one kind of knowledge rather than another. Sometimes the differences will be of degree, for knowledge, like wealth, is unequally distributed in society. Knowledge about the socioeconomic structure of society is distributed among people, adults and children, in terms of their own social class positions.

THINKING OR ARGUING: SELF-CONTROL OR SOCIAL CONTROL?

We need finally to consider the relation between sociomoral understanding and behaviour. In one quite fundamental sense the agenda of constructivism has been no different from the theories of moral development it has criticised: It aspires to be a theory of the nature of internalised and autonomous controls over conduct and of the manner of their acquisition. Whereas psychoanalysis proposed that internalised control requires an internalised representation of the parents, and some learning theorists equated it with conditioned anxiety, for constructivism it depends on the sophistication with which the individual can reason about moral obligations. In other words, thought controls action, and the level to which the capacity for moral reasoning has been developed should be linearly related to the inclination to uphold moral standards in one's behaviour (Kohlberg & Candee, 1984).

Does the evidence support this expectation? There are scattered findings of a relationship between children's and adolescents' moral reasoning about justice and consideration for others and their tendency to show generosity to others or to treat them equitably (Blasi, 1980). But as Light (1987) observed, research on correlations between various indices of children's social insight and measures of their behaviour towards others has not consistently revealed strong relationships between such cognitive abilities and social behaviour. Claims for a clear association between moral reasoning level and delinquency, or the inclination to violate rules relating to property and injury to others, have been rather more confident (Jennings, Kilkenny, & Kohlberg, 1983; Smetana, 1990). Smetana, for example, reviewed 35 studies of the link between antisocial conduct and moral reasoning. In most of these cases a Kohlbergian measure of moral reasoning level was used and in a majority the predicted inverse relationship was found: Greater involvement in antisocial behaviour was associated with a lower level of moral reasoning. More specifically, delinquents were more likely than nondelinquents to reason in stage 2 terms.

This evidence is, however, less persuasive than it first appears. In all of the cases in which conduct was found to be related to moral reasoning, conduct was assessed indirectly. A court conviction, police record, psychiatric diagnosis, counselling staff classification, or institutional placement was used as a proxy for conduct (see Farrington, Chapter 14). In one of the very few studies to use an alternative, more direct assessment of conduct, Emler, Heather, and Winton (1978) found no relationship between moral reasoning and conduct, which suggests that the indirect measures used in other research are potentially confounded with other effects. So, for example, the institutionalisation of young offenders may itself retard moral development. Additionally, clinical diagnoses and court decisions may be influenced by the moral reasoning of those assessed by clinicians and court officials as much as by their actual conduct.

It has to be said that at present the evidence for a direct causal link between sociomoral understanding and behaviour is not strong, unambiguous, and persuasive. This confronts us with various possibilities. One is that the hypothesised link still awaits an adequate empirical test, and I think there is some merit in this view. Another is that we have seriously overestimated the significance of sociomoral understanding in moral development generally and in the control over behaviour in particular. But intuitively it seems unlikely that such sophisticated skills would be developed if they serve no identifiable purpose. I therefore favour a third possibility, that we have misunderstood the significance of sociomoral understanding in the life of children and indeed of adults.

The essence of my argument here is that, on the one hand, conduct is subject to extensive social control compared to which self-control is of more limited significance whereas on the other hand, sociomoral understanding plays a significant role in social control—which is to say *other*-control. There is an implicit if not an explicit theory of society underlying 20th-century moral psychology and it is one which constructivism seems to share with psychoanalysis and behaviourism. The roots of this theory lie in analyses at the beginning of this century and before on the effects of the industrial revolution. It was widely supposed among social theorists that this economic revolution had also produced a social revolution, in the following sense. It had replaced small-scale rural communities of mutually acquainted individuals, often linked by kinship, with large-scale concentrations of populations around centres of industrial production. The predominant quality of social life under these new conditions was supposedly anonymity; people would dwell among strangers, their relations with others would be primarily formal and impersonal, and often limited to single transactions. The social control mechanisms of small-scale communities would not work under these new conditions; social control would have to be replaced by self-control. Moral psychology in its various forms offered accounts of the nature of such controls and the way in which they would be acquired.

It has turned out that this vision of mass society greatly overestimated the degree of anonymity that prevails in contemporary social relationships. Even in large cities, people continue to inhabit social worlds populated primarily by family, friends, and other acquaintances. Under these conditions they remain chronically identifiable and their conduct remains chronically visible and therefore open to social control (Emler & Reicher, 1995). This being so, we do not need to assume that conduct can only be moral to the degree that the individual has acquired internalised and autonomous controls, although we do need to ask why social controls sometimes fail.

Let us now consider the problems facing the child and how their solution might turn children into agents of social control. First, children are people too, and like other people they have problems to solve in their relations with others, even if to some degree their specific problems reflect their age, size, and lack of power, or decision-making discretion. It is, however, reasonable to assume that children, like other people will be motivated to avoid trouble and distress and to get what they want.

Given these aims the following kinds of abilities help. It is useful to be able to predict how others will behave, and for this some knowledge of context-specific rules, roles, and scripts is useful as is insight into others' intentions, desires, emotions, and personalities. Thus, part of the function of sociomoral understanding is to increase the predictability of the social environment. It also helps to be able to explain oneself to others, particularly if those others—one's parents, siblings, or playmates—might otherwise conclude that one's actions merited a punitive or retaliatory response. In this, powers of moral reasoning would allow the child to generate moral excuses and justifications for its own actions. Just one illustration of the benefits of being able to do this will have to suffice here. Blumstein (1974) found that explanations given by actors for their actions had a more powerful impact on audiences' evaluations of these actions than the content of the actions themselves.

A third way in which children can increase their control over their fate is by persuading other people to modify *their* behaviour. At this point it is worth observing that we already have a great deal of evidence about the childhood development of such powers of persuasion. The clue is in the opening sentence of this chapter. Piaget, Kohlberg, Turiel and others have revealed in considerable detail children's developing ability to *articulate* moral arguments. These powers might have been appreciated more readily had not these researchers treated the judgements, reasons, and arguments children expressed to them as no more than clues to the structure of internal mental processes. I would submit that moral reasoning is not primarily a tool of thought but a social instrument, used to influence and modify the behaviour of others, and that we should treat the moral judgement research literature as a rich source of evidence about the development and use of this social instrument.

Averill (1983) has shown that feelings of anger are typically mediated by a moral judgement that the object of one's anger has acted unfairly, inconsiderately, or unreasonable, in effect, that there has been a moral transgression of which one is the victim. Averill's research also revealed that expressions of anger are typically directed at the offender, are likely to be accompanied by moral criticism, and are reported as more often than not having positive side effects (e.g. the other is persuaded to modify his/her future behaviour). This is but one example of the ways in which powers of moral argument play a role in social control. Future research could profitably give more attention to the ways in which children use moral arguments both to influence the adults around them (see Dunn, 1988, for examples of such use by very young children), and to exercise control over one another. One intriguing question which research of this kind might also address is what makes moral arguments persuasive and why certain kinds of moral argument are more persuasive than others.

CONCLUSIONS

For some thirty years the study of moral development has been dominated by a particular point of view. This point of view has not only defined the questions worth asking—these have been taken to be questions about what children understand about moral principles, in what order their understanding develops, and how they come by what they understand—but has also accepted that only certain kinds of answer are plausible. Children develop an understanding of the principles according to which social life is and should be regulated through their own direct experience of the world and their own spontaneous reflections upon this experience. In effect, each child independently constructs an understanding of social life and moral principles. The substance of this understanding turns out to be the same in every child, for two reasons. First, social life contains a number of invariant and universal features. Second, the intellectual system of the individual child has an inherent tendency towards internal consistency and external adaptation. It will, therefore, construct a representation that progressively approximates the principles according to which social life is actually organised. It will also construct progressively more adequate procedures for solving the problems that social life throws up.

This constructivist point of view has not eliminated all argument about the development of sociomoral understanding. On the contrary, new ideas, new questions, and new possibilities continue to emerge and have done ever since Piaget introduced this way of thinking about child development. Some of this evolution has been summarised in this chapter. What has been little questioned, however, is the "how" of development. In the latter part of this chapter I have argued that it is time for a reappraisal of our assumptions about the developmental process. The dominance of a constructivist point of view has rested on a caricature of any theoretical alternative that accords a role to social influence in sociomoral development. Nonetheless, there is ample evidence for the effects of such influence and it is perhaps now time for researchers to turn their attention to the manner in which social influence operates. But future research will also need to be rooted in a more explicit theory of society and social life.

I have argued, finally, that it may also have been inappropriate to regard sociomoral understanding as primarily a mechanism of behavioural self-control. Instead, we should consider the other roles that cognitive developments in this area may play in the child's adaptation to a social world. These are likely to include a role in making the social world more predictable, a role in managing self-presentation and identity in relations with others through the provision of explanations and justifications for actions, and thirdly a role in controlling relations with the social environment by influencing the actions of others. In this, we should recognise that the cognitive changes equip children with the means to be competent agents of social control and do so by providing a capacity to generate persuasive arguments.

REFERENCES

Adelson, J. (1971). The political imagination of the young adolescent. *Daedalus, 100,* 1013–1050.

Allinsmith, W. (1960). The learning of moral standards. In D. R. Miller & G. E. Swanson (Eds.), *Inner conflict and defence* (pp. 141–176). New York: Holt, Rinehart, & Winston.

Averill, J. R. (1983). Studies on anger and aggression: Implications for theories of emotion. *American Psychologist, 38,* 1145–1160.

Bandura, A. & Walters, R. (1963). *Social learning and personality development.* New York: Holt, Rinehart, & Winston.

Bandura, A. & MacDonald, F. J. (1963). The influence of social reinforcement and the behavior of models in shaping children's moral judgments. *Journal of Abnormal and Social Psychology, 67,* 274–281.

Berti, A. E. & Bombi, A. S. (1988). *The child's construction of economics.* Cambridge, UK: Cambridge University Press.

Blasi, A. (1980). Bridging moral cognition and action: A critical review of the literature. *Psychological Bulletin, 88,* 1–45.

Blumstein, P. W. (1974). The honoring of accounts. *American Sociological Review, 39,* 551–556.

Botvin, G. J. & Murray, F. B. (1975). The efficacy of peer modelling and social conflict in the acquisition of conservation. *Child Development, 46,* 796–799.

Brown, R. & Herrenstein, R. (1975). *Psychology.* Boston: Little, Brown.

Colby, A., & Kohlberg, L. (1987). *The measurement of moral judgment: Vol 1. Theoretical foundations and research validation.* Cambridge, UK: Cambridge University Press.

Colby, A., Kohlberg, L., Speicher, B., Hewer, A., Candee, D., Gibbs, J., & Power, C. (1987). *The measurement of moral judgment* (Vol. 2). Cambridge, UK: Cambridge University Press.

Connell, R. W. (1977). *Ruling class, ruling culture.* Cambridge, UK: Cambridge University Press.

Constanzo, P., Coie, J., Grumet, J., & Farnill, D. (1973). A reexamination of the effects of intent and consequences on children's moral judgments. *Child Development, 45,* 799–802.

Damon, W. (1975). Early conceptions of positive justice as related to the development of logical operations. *Child Development, 46,* 301–312.

Damon, W. (1977). *The social world of the child.* San Fransisco: Jossey-Bass.

Davidson, P., Turiel, E., & Black, A. (1983). The effect of stimulus familiarity on the use of criteria and justifications in children's social reasoning. *British Journal of Developmental Psychology, 1,* 49–65.

Demetriou, A. & Charitides, L. (1986). The adolescent's construction of procedural justice as a function of age, formal thought and sex. *International Journal of Psychology, 21,* 333–353.

Doise, W. & Mugny, G. (1984). *The social development of the intellect.* Oxford: Pergamon.

Dunn, J. (1988). *The beginnings of social understanding.* Oxford: Blackwell.

Durkin, D. (1961). The specificity of children's moral judgments. *Journal of Genetic Psychology, 98,* 3–14.

Emler, N. (1983). Morality and politics: The ideological dimension in the theory of moral development. In H. Weinreich-Haste & D. Locke (Eds.), *Morality in the making* (pp. 47–71). Chichester, UK: Wiley.

Emler, N. (1987). Socio-moral development from the perspective of social representations. *Journal for the Theory of Social Behaviour, 17*, 371–388.

Emler, N. & Dickinson, J. (1985). Children's representations of economic inequalities: The effects of social class. *British Journal of Developmental Psychology, 3*, 191–198.

Emler, N. & Dickinson, J. (1993). The child as sociologist. In M. Bennett (Ed.), *The child as psychologist* (pp. 168–190). Hemel Hempstead, UK: Harvester.

Emler, N., Heather, N., & Winton, M. (1978). Delinquency and the development of moral reasoning. *British Journal of Social and Clinical Psychology, 17*, 325–331.

Emler, N. & Ohana, J. (1993). Studying social representations in children: Just old wine in new bottles? In G. M. Breakwell & D. V. Canter (Eds), *Empirical approaches to social representations* (pp. 63–89). Oxford: Oxford University Press.

Emler, N. & Reicher, S. (1995). *Adolescence and delinquency: The collective management of reputation.* Oxford: Blackwell.

Enright, R., Enright, W., Manheim, L., & Harris, B. E. (1980). Distributive justice development and social class. *Developmental Psychology, 16*, 555–563.

Furth, H. G. (1980). *The world of grown-ups.* New York: Elsevier.

Gibbs, J. C. & Schnell, S. (1985). Moral development 'versus' socialization: A critique. *American Psychologist, 40*, 1071–1080.

Gilligan, C. (1982). *In a different voice: Psychological theory and women's development.* Cambridge, MA: Harvard University Press.

Gold, L. J., Darley, J. M., Hilton, J. L., & Zanna, M. P. (1984). Children's perceptions of procedural justice. *Child Development, 55*, 1752–1759.

Haan, N., Smith, B., & Block, J. (1968). The moral reasoning of young adults: Political-social behavior, family background and personality correlates. *Journal of Personality and Social Psychology, 10*, 183–201.

Harris, M. (1975). *Cows, pigs, wars and witches: The riddles of culture.* London: Hutchinson.

Hoffman, M. (1977). Moral internalization: Current theory and research. In L. Berkowitz (Ed.), *Advances in experimental social psychology* (Vol. 10) (pp. 85–139). New York: Academic Press.

Horton, J. (1967). African traditional thought and Western science. In M. F. D. Young (Ed.), *Knowledge and control.* London: Collier-MacMillan.

Hook, J. & Cook, T. (1979). Equity theory and the cognitive ability of children. *Psychological Bulletin, 86*, 429–445.

Imamoglu, E. O. (1975). Children's awareness and usage of intention cues. *Child Development, 46*, 39–45.

Jahoda, G. (1984). The development of thinking about socio-economic systems. In H. Tajfel (Ed.), *The social dimension: European developments in social psychology* (Vol. 1). Cambridge, UK: Cambridge University Press.

Jennings, W. S., Kilkenny, R., & Kohlberg, L. (1983). Moral development theory and practice for youthful and adult offenders. In W. S. Laufer & J. M. Day (Eds.). *Personality theory, moral development and criminal behavior* (pp. 281–355). Lexington, MA: Lexington Books/Heath.

Katz, D. & Kahn, R. L. (1978). *The social psychology of organisations* (2nd edn). New York: Wiley.

Kohlberg, L. (1963). The development of children's orientations toward a moral order: I. Sequence in the development of human thought. *Vita Humana, 6*, 11–33.

Kohlberg, L. (1964). The development of moral character and ideology. In M. Hoffman & L. Hoffman (Eds.), *Review of child development research* (Vol. 1) (pp. 1–113). New York: Russell Sage.

Kohlberg, L. (1971). From is to ought. How to commit the naturalistic fallacy and get away with it in the study of moral development. In T. Mischel (Ed.), *Cognitive development and epistemology* (pp. 151–235). New York: Academic Press.

Kohlberg, L. (1984). *The psychology of moral development: Vol. 2. Essays on moral development*. New York: Harper & Row.

Kohlberg, L. & Candee, D. (1984). The relation of moral judgment to moral action. In L. Kohlberg (Ed.), *The psychology of moral development: Vol. 2. Essays on moral development* (pp. 498–581). New York: Harper & Row.

Kohlberg, L., Levine, C., & Hewer, A. (1983). *Moral stages: A current formulation and a response critique*. Basel: Karger.

Kuhn, D., Langer, J., Kohlberg, L., & Haan, N. (1977). The development of formal operations in logical and moral judgment. *Genetic Psychology Monographs, 95*, 97–188.

Leahy, R. L. (1983). The development of the conception of social class. In R. L. Leahy (Ed.), *The child's construction of social inequality*. New York: Academic Press.

Lickona, T. (1976). Research on Piaget's theory of moral development. In T. Lickona (Ed.). *Moral development and behavior: Theory, research and social issues*. New York: Holt, Rinehart & Winston.

Light, P. (1987). Taking roles. In J. Bruner and H. Haste (Eds.), *Making sense* (pp. 219–240). London: Methuen.

MacIntyre, A. (1981). *After virtue: A study in moral theory*. London: Duckworth.

Mann, L., Radford, M., & Kanagawa, C. (1985). Cross-cultural differences in children's use of decision rules: A comparison between Japan and Australia. *Journal of Personality and Social Psychology, 49*, 1557–1564.

Moscovici, S. (1976). *Social influence and social change*. London: Academic Press.

Nisan, M. (1984). Distributive justice and social norms. *Child Development, 55*, 1020–1029.

Nisan, M. (1987). Moral norms and social conventions: A cross-cultural comparison. *Developmental Psychology, 25*, 719–725.

Petty, J. & Cacioppo, J. T. (1986). *Communication and persuasion: Central and peripheral routes to attitude change*. New York: Springer.

Piaget, J. (1932). *The moral judgment of the child*. London: Routledge & Kegan Paul.

Piaget, J. & Inhelder, B. (1956). *The child's conception of space*. London: Routledge & Kegan Paul.

Russell, J. (1981). Dyadic interaction in a test requiring class inclusion ability. *Child Development, 55*, 1020–1029.

Sampson, E. E. (1971). *Social psychology and contemporary society*. New York: Wiley.

Sears, R. R., Rau, L., & Alpert, R. (1966). *Identification and child rearing*. London: Tavistock.

Selman, R. (1971). The relation of role taking to the development of moral judgment in children. *Child Development, 42*, 79–91.

Selman, R. (1976). Social-cognitive understanding: A guide to educational and clinical practice. In T. Lickona (Ed.), *Moral behavior and development: Theory, research and social issues* (pp. 219–316). New York: Holt, Rinehart, & Winston.

Simpson, E. L. (1974). Moral development research. *Human Development, 17*, 81–106.

Smetana, J. G. (1981). Pre-school children's conceptions of moral and social rules. *Child Development, 52*, 1333–1336.

Smetana, J. G. (1990). Morality and conduct disorders. In M. Lewis and S. M. Miller (Eds.), *Handbook of developmental psychopathology* (pp. 157–179). New York: Plenum.

Smetana, J. (1993). Understanding of social rules. In M. Bennett (Ed.), *The child as psychologist* (pp. 111–141). Hemel Hempstead, UK: Harvester.

Smetana, J. G. & Braeges, J. L. (1990). The development of toddlers' moral and conventional judgments. *Merrill-Palmer Quarterly, 36*, 329–346.

Snarey, J. (1985). Cross cultural universality of socio-moral development: A critical review of Kohlbergian research. *Psychological Bulletin, 97,* 202–232.

Sullivan, E. V. (1977). A study of Kohlberg's structural theory of moral development: A critique of liberal social science ideology. *Human Development, 20,* 353–376.

Tisak, M. S. & Turiel, E. (1984). Children's conceptions of moral and prudential rules. *Child Development, 55,* 1030–1039.

Turiel, E. (1966). An experimental test of the sequentiality of developmental stages in the child's moral judgments. *Journal of Personality and Social Psychology, 3,* 611–618.

Turiel, E. (1975). The development of social concepts: Mores, customs and conventions. In D. J. De Palma & J.M. Foley (Eds.), *Moral development: Current theory and research* (pp. 7–37). Hillsdale, NJ: Lawrence Erlbaum Associates Inc.

Turiel, E. (1983). *The development of social knowledge.* Cambridge, UK: Cambridge University Press.

Yuill, N. & Perner, J. (1988). Intentionality and knowledge in children's judgments of actor's responsibility and recipient's emotional reaction. *Developmental Psychology, 24,* 358–365.

13 Gender and the development of interpersonal orientation

Anne Campbell
Durham University, Durham, UK

There is no shortage of theoretical perspectives on sex differences in social behaviour—the last twenty years have see an explosion of interest in gender from academics in many disciplines including sociology, anthropology, psychology, linguistics, neuroanatomy, and biology. Within psychology alone, hormonal, genetic, cognitive, structural, cultural, and constructionist explanations vie with one another. Recent years have seen a growing interest in evolutionary theory as a potent means of uniting these approaches stressing as it does the functional roots of sex differences, their genetic basis and biological mediation, their particular instantiation in diverse cultures, and their capacity for facultative adaptation to changing environmental circumstances (see Barkow, Cosmides, & Tooby, 1992). In this chapter I will outline such an approach to the development of sex differences based on established empirical findings. I will begin by describing the principal social dimensions on which adults and children show sex differences. I will then consider critically explanations that focus on the internalisation of parental and cultural expectations before examining a cognitive developmental approach that accords more importance to the child as a force in his/her own development of gendered behaviour. I will then suggest that sex differences in children's behaviour predate cognitive awareness of their own sex and outline an epigenetic approach in which genes and environment simultaneously set the child on a sex-typed trajectory of development which is enhanced by later cognitive processes.

HOW AND WHY DO THE SEXES DIFFER?

Adult men and women differ with respect to two dimensions; agency and communion (Bakan, 1966). Agency refers to the condition of being a differentiated individual and is manifest in strivings for mastery and power which enhance and protect that differentiation. Communion refers to the condition of being part of a larger social or spiritual entity and is manifest in strivings for intimacy, union, and solidarity with that larger unit. Two contemporaneous but independent empirical projects (Bem, 1974; Spence, Helmreich, & Stapp, 1974) took adjectives that are stereotypically associated with males (dominant, forceful, individualistic) and females (warm, sympathetic, compassionate) and asked men and women to rate themselves on them. The two resulting dimensions were called masculinity and femininity although their content corresponds very closely to agency and communion. Spence (1985) later rejected the idea that these were measures of masculinity and femininity because they do not show the expected correlations with individuals' self-ratings of their own masculinity or femininity nor with measures of sex role identification (e.g. housewife). Instead, she refers to them as measures of instrumentality (agency) and expressivity (communion) which she takes to be dimensions of interpersonal style which differentiate men and women. This is an important point and one worth emphasising here: I take people's self descriptions to represent their estimation of the extent to which various traits and behaviours characterise them. They do not show (nor would I expect them to) high correlations with attitudes to women or with other attitudinal variables (Archer, 1989) any more than we would expect extraversion or neuroticism to predict political opinion. In this chapter I will refer to these dimensions as agency and communion. To say that men and women differ on them is to say that the between-sex difference exceeds the within-sex difference but, of course, there is much overlap in the distributions. In addition, it is important to remember that these are two orthogonal dimensions (rather than a single bipolar one) and consequently an individual may score high or low on both or either of them.

There are three strands of evidence that suggest that these dimensions are of considerable importance in understanding adult sex differences. The first is the wide use of self-rating adjective inventories. As indicated earlier, dozens of studies have now confirmed sex differences on the Bem Sex Role Inventory and the Personal Attributes Questionnaire that employ Likert scales of adjectives measuring agency and communion (see K. B. Hoyenga & K. T. Hoyenga, 1993). Furthermore, the use of Wiggin's (1982) circumplex model of personality which employs the related dimensions of dominance and nurturance has produced strong corroboration of such sex differences (Paulhus, 1984; Wiggins & Holzmuller, 1978, 1981). Williams and Best (1990), using subjects from 14 different countries, found that men rated themselves higher on adjectives such as ambitious, dominant, and hostile whereas women rated themselves higher on sensitive, sympathetic, and kind. Second, the use of standard psychometric personality inventories to construct national norms affords a wealth of supporting data. In a recent series of meta-analyses, Feingold (1994) reports that women exceed men on anxiety, trust, tender-mindedness, and gregariousness whereas men exceed women on assertiveness. These differences are invariant across ages, educational levels, and nations. Third, meta-analyses have been used to examine between-sex effect sizes on a number of experimental behavioural variables. Eagly (1987) reports that men exceed women on aggression (d = 0.29) and restlessness (d = 0.72). They are more likely to emerge as group leaders (d = 0.49) and make a greater task contribution in small groups (d = 0.59). Women make greater socio-emotional contributions in small groups (d = 0.59) and are more easily influenced than are men (d = 0.26). Women exceed men on a variety of measures of nonverbal sensitivity (see Hall, 1984) including facial expressiveness (d = 1.01), decoding skill (d = 0.43), gazing (d = 0.68), smiling (d = 0.63), and bodily expressiveness (d = 0.58). Women also experience emotions (love, joy, sadness, and fear) more intensely and more frequently than do men, whether measured by self-report or physiological measures (Grossman & Wood, 1993). Taken together these data suggest that the agency-communion dimensions can effectively organise a variety of data on sex differences measured by self-assessment, formal personality tests, and behaviour.

One argument concerning the functions and causes of this cross-cultural pattern of sex differences has come from evolutionary theory (see MacDonald, Chapter 2). This approach begins with the assumption that where sex differences are consistent and ubiquitous, they have likely arisen from the benefits that they conferred on males and females who possessed such traits. (Note that this does not necessarily require the invocation of any genetic basis. Cultural transmission operating in parallel or interacting with genetic transmission may also favour these traits and cause societies everywhere to selectively foster them in boys and girls, see Durham, 1991. However, for this exposition, we will pursue an argument based on genetic transmission.) Evolution depends upon the inclusive fitness benefits of a given behaviour pattern in the environment of evolutionary adaptedness occurring in the Pleistocene. The question is not what advantages these traits confer in our present society, but what benefits they conferred at that time. The answer is thought to lie with sex differences in parental investment (Trivers, 1972). Females make a dispro-portionately large investment in reproduction—from the costly produc-tion of an ovum through to gestation, birth, and lactation. Males, by contrast, produce their gametes cheaply and plentifully. In species where these differences are large, we typically find that males compete for reproductive access to the female (either by conspicuous display or combat or both) whereas the female's strategy is one of discriminating passivity. (In species where sex differences in parental investment are reversed, there is a corresponding reversal of mating strategy with females competing with one another.) For a male, qualities that are likely to increase inclusive fitness are those which give him dominance over male competitors and which appeal to women. Competitiveness (which brings with it the possibility of social dominance) is clearly an important consideration for the first of these. This serves to not only gain access to females but to guard her from rival males and thus ensure his paternity of any offspring. Females chiefly require protection and resources from their mates and these are likely to require physical agility and strength in the first instance and social dominance in the second. Male dominance has been found to be associated with number of offspring in many pre-industrial societies (Fisher, 1992).

For a female, other qualities are likely to increase her fitness. Chief amongst these are the capacity to form a strong and enduring bond with her offspring in order to provide for and protect them until they are independent. Because of the cost and time involved in reproduction, even the most fecund woman would have produced fewer offspring in her lifetime than the most dominant male and this meant that she invested heavily in ensuring their survival. From this high investment, we can suggest two routes leading to the enhancement of traits of communion in women. According to the first, the formation of dominance hierarchies would have been too costly for women given the high probability of injury and the uncertain benefits. Whereas males benefit in terms of reproductive success by the multiple matings associated with dominance, females compete with each other not for sex but for the resources necessary to raise their offspring to maturity. Although status in a female dominance hierarchy might increase access to food and shelter, the costs associated with agonistic encounters (orphaned infants' chances of survival are far lower when a mother rather than a father dies) mean that females would do better to fission and seek new territories rather than risk their lives (and those of their actual and unborn children) in a fight for status. Under this scenario, female communion is the result of an absence of concern with dominance. A second scenario accords a more positive role to female communion. Prior to agriculture and animal husbandry, which brought with it control over a stable food supply and the beginnings of patriarchy, it is likely that women collected their own food (Smuts, 1995). Given their limited range of movements with young infants, women likely co-operated with one another in infant care, food gathering, and food preparation.

Clearly, qualities of nurturance, interpersonal sensitivity, and co-operation would be paramount.

The sex differences I have described are something of a caricature of the real state of affairs. Humans produce few offspring in their lifetimes and must invest heavily in all of them. The long period of infant dependency—which followed increases in brain size and the necessary early birth of babies—meant that women had to rely on males for assistance and this meant that males also would have benefited from communal qualities. Men needed such qualities also to support group living and to form tactical alliances with other males. By the same token, a woman devoid of any agentic qualities would be a poor protector of her offspring and a weak competitor in any struggle for scant resources. Both qualities are needed by both sexes but not with equal weighting. As a species we are only mildly polygynous (with males forming pair bonds but seeking more pre- and extra-pair sexual opportunities than women) and to that extent should show many overlapping traits (Buss & Schmitt, 1993).

Is there evidence that in childhood we can see the beginnings of adult sex differences in agency and communion? Because psychometric tests, self-ratings, and laboratory studies are less commonly used among young children, the relevant data come principally from observational studies of children's social worlds. Such studies (Archer, 1992; Maccoby & Jacklin, 1987; Maltz & Borker, 1982) provide a very clear view of the distinctive cultures of boys' and girls' peer groups. Boys tend to play in larger groups involving rough-and-tumble play and zero-sum team games (Lever, 1978). When disputes occur, boys try to resolve them by reference to the application of rules. Boys enjoy games that involve pretence of driving vehicles, fighting, and killing. When given a choice, boys choose to compete more than to co-operate whereas girls show the opposite pattern (Ahlgren, 1983; Boehnke, Silbereisen, Eisenberg, Teykowski, & Palmmari, 1989; Moely, Skarin, & Weil, 1979). In groups, boys more often use speech to command, threaten, boast, refuse to comply, give information, heckle, tell jokes or stories, and top someone else's story. According to Maltz and Borker (1982), these acts function to attract and maintain an audience, to assert a position of dominance, and to interject oneself when others have the floor. Influence attempts by boys involve giving direct commands whereas girls are more likely to use polite suggestion. This challenging and competitive interpersonal style is manifest in the dominance hierarchies which boys develop (Maccoby, 1988, 1990; Omark & Edelman, 1975; Savin-Williams, 1977). Because these dominance hierarchies can show significant stability over ten-year periods, childhood status within them has long-term implications (Weisfeld, Omark, & Cronin, 1980). Among young children status is a function of toughness and athletic ability. Even among college students, male dominance is associated with physical size (Crosbie,

1979). The dominance hierarchy once established means that aggression largely occurs between boys who are adjacent to one another in the pecking order.

Girls often play in dyads or small cliques, spend more time talking to one another and their games are indirectly competitive, involving turn-taking so that the winner is decided by highest score rather than by direct competition (see the references cited earlier). When disputes occur, the game is more likely to break up and attempts at resolution involve appeals to others' feelings and fairness. Girls often choose domestic themes for play which allow for the elaboration of family relationships especially parenting. Girls' friendships are more intimate with more self-disclosure and more distress when the friendship breaks up. Girls' friends are more matched for personal characteristics and values than are boys. Dominance plays a less obvious part in girls' groups and attempts to assert superiority over others can result in social rejection. Girls use speech to create and maintain relationships of intimacy and equality, to criticise others in accep-table ways, and to interpret accurately the speech of others. They show less interruption, more often express agreement, and more often acknowledge what another girl has said before beginning to speak. It appears that adult differences in agency and communion can be seen in the typical forms of girls' and boys' early peer group interactions.

Nonetheless, it is important to note that among both adults and children there is considerable fluctuation in the manifestation of these traits as a function of situation. Among adults, Deaux and Major (1987) have pointed to the importance of situational expectancies in regulating the manifestation of sex-typed behaviour. Nurturance, for example, may be appropriate in a home situation but not in a job interview. Among children, Laosa and Brophy (1972) found that same-sex play was ten times more frequent than cross-sex play, yet Maccoby and Jacklin (1987) found little individual stability in same- versus opposite-sex playmate choice. Different individuals on different days may be found engaged in cross-sex play. Sex differences in agency and communion emerge as a function of aggregation over settings and both personality theory and evolutionary psychology would lead us to expect such short-term fluctuation, termed by the former "situational variability" and by the latter "facultative adapta-tion".

THE EMPTY CHILD: SOCIALISATION THEORIES

In searching for the origins of these sex differences, a number of theorists have turned to examination of the child's environment. This approach is often termed the standard social science model (see Tooby & Cosmides, 1992). These theories proceed from the assumption of a "tabula rasa child" who in the course of socialisation acquires and internalises society's expectations about appropriate male and female behaviour. The central mechanisms of that internalisation have been suggested to be differential reinforcement and the acquisition of gender stereotypes.

Early learning theorists such as Mischel (1966) suggested that parents respond differently to the same behaviour in boys and girls and, through a process of shaping, the child learns to associate sex-appropriate behaviour with reinforcement. An oft-cited study (Seavey, Katz, & Zalk, 1975) showed that adults, when presented with a baby of unknown sex dressed as a boy or a girl, respond differently offering a doll only to the little "girl". For many years this was offered as evidence for differential parental treatment but it has recently come under challenge. A meta-analysis of 23 studies of the impact of infant gender labels concluded that (Stern & Karraker, 1989, p. 501): "knowledge of an infant's gender is not a consistent determinant of adults' reactions". Maccoby and Jacklin (1974) in an early narrative review suggested that there were few consistent differences in how parents responded to sons and daughters, except in the provision of sex-typed toys. More recently, Lytton and Romney (1991) performed a meta-analysis of 172 studies from a variety of countries conducted between 1952 and 1987 which reported quantitative data on the treatment of sons and daughters by mothers or fathers or both. They examined eight socialisation areas (amount of interaction, encouragement of achievement, warmth, encouragement of dependency, restrictiveness, disciplinary strictness, clarity of communication/use of reasoning, and encouragement of sex-typed activities) composed of 13 subsidiary measures. The only significant effects were found for encouragement of sex-typed activities (and a tendency restricted to non-North American studies for boys to receive more physical punishment). However, the authors note that giving children different toys and chores might arise because parents accurately perceive their children's sex-typed preferences. In fact, Caldera, Huston, and O'Brien (1989) demonstrated that children show greater involvement in sex-appropriate toys even when their parents do not overtly and preferentially promote play with them. Furthermore, sex-typed toy preference occurs very early in life (at about 14 to 18 months of age) before children can correctly label the sex-typing of a toy (Blakemore, LaRue, & Olejnik, 1979; Perry, White, & Perry, 1984). More generally, there is little consistency between child-rearing practices and adult outcomes (Maccoby & Martin, 1983; McCrae & Costa, 1988a, b) and parents' attitudes about sex stereotypes are poor predictors of their children's sex-typed behaviours (see Huston, 1983).

Gender stereotypes play a central role in the theories of Eagly (1987) and S. Bem (1981). Eagly's social role theory proposes that sex differences result from conformity to the gender role stereotypes of agency and

communion derived from the division of labour in society. Gender stereotypes embody belief in the appropriateness of expected characteristics, a
high degree of consensual agreement about these expectations and
awareness that such consensus exists. "Expectancy confirming behaviour
should be especially common when expectancies are broadly shared in a
society, as is the case for expectancies about women and men" (Eagly,
1987, p. 15). These stereotypes are internalised resulting in men's higher
self-ratings on agency and women's on communion. S. Bem (1981) argues
that boys and girls develop schema about the world based on distinctions
that are accorded salience by adults. The dimension that pervades adults'
thinking is gender and so the child begins to schematise the world in these
terms. Ultimately, the child's own self-concept is incorporated into this
schema resulting in sex-typed behaviour. According to both these theories,
the child's knowledge of gender stereotypes acts on an initially sex-neutral
infant, ultimately causing the child to conform to them. Hence, differences
in self-ratings of agency and communion in adults and in their analogous
behaviour in children are the result, rather than the cause, of sex stereotypes. There is abundant evidence that ratings of gender stereotypic
qualities and men's and women's own self-ratings are very similar
(Williams & Best, 1990) but the real question concerns the direction of
causality.

Gender stereotypes are robust over cultures (Williams & Best, 1982),
show little change over time (Helmreich, Spence, & Gibson, 1982;
Lueptow, 1985; Lewin & Tragos, 1987) and are reasonably accurate
pictures of empirically measured effect sizes (Swim, 1994). The robust,
universal, and temporally stable nature of these differences themselves
constitute a problem for the theories offered earlier. From Eagly's perspective, common stereotypes suggest universal division of labour. Indeed, in
most human societies men hunt, fish, make weapons, and do metalwork
whereas women cook, do housework, and are primary caretakers of
children (D'Andrade, 1966; Ember, 1981). One obvious reason for this
could be that men and women show a clear evolutionary-based preference
for these activities, yet Eagly's exclusive focus on Western societies
obscures consideration of this possibility. S. Bem's emphasis on the
arbitrariness of categorising the world according to sex (rather than height
or eye colour) begs the question of why acknowledgement of the different
natures of men and women is so universal (Brown, 1991) and why gender
stereotypes are so similar in content.

The impact of gender stereotypes however can most directly be
addressed by examining their impact on children's development. Children
acquire gender stereotypes at quite a young age (see K. B. Hoyenga & K.
T. Hoyenga, 1993). At age three, children believe that boys, but not girls,
like to build things, play with cars and say "I can hit you". By five, they

believe that boys are more aggressive, assertive, dominant, independent, and ambitious than girls. At age three, children believe that girls, but not boys, like to play with dolls, like to cook and clean and say "I need some help". By five, girls are believed to be more sentimental, dependent, emotional, submissive, and talkative than are boys. However, evidence for impact of knowledge of gender stereotypes on sex-typed behaviours in the children is weak. Huston (1983, p. 409) concludes: "...the literature does not support the proposition that concepts about gender (gender stereotypes) precede preferences or behavioural enactment". Eight years later, Martin's (1993, pp. 191–192) review reaches similar conclusions: "seldom are individual differences in behaviour and thinking explained by differing levels of gender stereotype knowledge".

THE THINKING CHILD: COGNITIVE-DEVELOPMENTAL THEORIES

Both social learning theorists (Mischel, 1966) and cognitive developmental theory (Kohlberg, 1966) suggest that children preferentially imitate their own sex and so acquire sex-typed behaviours from observing adults. Kohlberg's theory was, from the start, an explicitly cognitive one. Social learning theorists came to accept the need for cognitive mediation much later. Kohlberg saw sex-typed behaviour as driven by age-related changes in cognition which, following Piaget, he believed to be stage-like and to result from the child's desire for competence. By age three, children have acquired gender identity and can correctly label the sex of adults and peers. In boys especially, this is later accompanied by a sense of prestige and the child asserts that his/her sex is superior and preferable to the opposite sex. Sex-typing in behaviour now acquires moral force and the child believes it is wrong to behave in opposite-sex ways. Selective modelling of same-sex adults begins at around the age of five and gender knowledge is reinforced at about the age of six to seven when the child acquires gender constancy (analogous to conservation)—an understanding that superficial changes in hair length or clothing cannot alter one's gender. For Kohlberg, the developmental path begins with gender identity, results in high evaluation of sex-appropriate behaviours, and leads to selective imitation. Learning theorists such as Bandura (1977) initially emphasised the joint impact of reinforcement and modelling. Children were thought to preferentially imitate adults of their own sex and a number of early studies were devoted to demonstrating this. In general, results were disappointing, as Huston (1983, p. 424) concludes: "There is little support for the prediction that children attend differentially to same sex models, even when gender cues are apparent". Bandura (1986) later asserted that behaviour change could only occur to the extent that conscious thoughts were changed and thus seemed to move closer to a cognitive position. Nonetheless, in his trajectory, children are reinforced for sex-appropriate behaviour and model same-sex adults resulting in a recognition of gender identity through self-observation.

Both views agree that children imitate same-sex parents and we would expect to see a significant correlation between the degree of agency/ communion of a mother and that of her daughter. However, Maccoby and Jacklin (1987) have noted that there is little correspondence between measures of parental sex-typing and that of their children, suggesting that children are not slavishly imitating same-sex parents. However, imitation on the basis of the sex appropriateness of behaviour rather than the sex of model has been shown in six-year-olds (Barklay, Ullman, Otto, & Brecht, 1977). In an ingenious study, Perry and Bussey (1979) showed how children establish which models are particularly useful guides to sex-appropriate behaviour. Children viewed tapes of eight adults (four of each sex) who made a choice from 16 pairs of sex-neutral objects. For each sex of adult, one of the four models made a choice that was sex incongruent (i.e. matched the choice made by the majority of opposite-sex models). In the next part of the study, children viewed a same-sex model or an opposite-sex model making choices among 16 pairs of objects. Half of the children saw a sex-appropriate model (as established in the first part of the study) and half saw a sex-inappropriate model (who had previously made sex-incongruent choices). Control subjects saw only the second tape or no tape at all. The dependent measure was the number of choices that matched the model on the second tape. Boys significantly and preferentially copied the male who had made sex-appropriate choices and girls did the same with the female model. There was no differential same-sex modelling in the control group who had no prior information on the appropriateness of the model—indicating that children do not preferentially imitate their own sex except where they have prior information on the sex appropriateness of the model. (In this study, for obvious reasons, the models' choices were from neutral objects so that the children had no preconceptions about their sex appropriateness. A study by Barklay et al., 1977, raises the possibility that, in the real world, children already possess preferences for imitating sex-appropriate behaviours regardless of who models them. We shall shortly consider the possibility that this may arise directly through epigenetic processes that cause girls and boys to find different behaviours appealing.)

This form of learning differs in important respects from the simple internalising of prevailing adult stereotypes. First, it is able to explain why children do not mimic in a parrot-like way the behaviour of their parents or of television characters. Although they may see their fathers cooking or a female film star gunning down baddies, they are also aware that such activities are not typical of most men and women that they see. Second, such discriminating construction of prototypes allows the child to acquire behaviour that is appropriate for his/her own ecological niche. In an inner city area where men establish status by fighting prowess, this is the prototype that boys will develop while in a more affluent neighbourhood a boy may learn that money or profession are the keys to men's status. Third, the child can establish prototypes that are age appropriate and specific from observing his/her peers in comparison with adults.

Gender identity is critical to arguments that depend on child-driven cognitive mediation. Although Kohlberg emphasised the importance of gender constancy for sex typing, it is clear that children begin to show differences in social behaviour before the age of five—which is the earliest time at which children unambiguously understand the immutability of gender. A number of authors have concluded that gender constancy fails to consistently predict either sex-typed behaviour or knowledge (Huston, 1983; Martin, 1993). Instead, it is widely accepted that gender identity is, in principle, sufficient to support sex-typed learning. What impact does the recognition of gender identity have upon the acquisition of sex-typed behaviour? Fagot, Leinbach, & Hagan (1986) demonstrated that, at 26 months, children with gender identity (the ability to sort pictures accurately by sex) show increased preference for same-sex playmates and that the acquisition of gender identity for girls, but not boys, is associated with a decrease in aggression. Fagot and Leinbach (1989) in a longitudinal study, observed children at 18 months (before they had gender identity) and again at 27 months (when half of them had achieved gender identity). At 27 months, children of both sexes with gender identity played with sex-appropriate toys significantly more than the other groups. Girls with gender identity showed a drop in aggression and an increase in communication with adults relative to the other three groups.

The evidence suggests that the children's formal understanding of their gender has important consequences for their social development. From a cognitive-behavioural perspective, its importance is threefold. Formally measured knowledge of one's own gender follows the ability to discriminate male and female peers (Fagot, 1985a) and together these two abilities allow the child to select preferentially same-sex peers. In the next section I shall discuss why children do this and why it may be an important step in social development. Second, gender identity forms the basis for the establishment of locally sensitive prototypes of male and female behaviour and allows the child to form a working model of sex-typical forms of social behaviour. This is important because peers are ruthlessly sensitive to departures from sex-appropriate behaviours. Recall that data reviewed earlier suggest that parents do not show patterns of differential reinforcement as a function of their child's sex. In this regard, they are startlingly different from children. Children unlike adults react differently to infants on the basis of their sex (Stern & Karraker, 1989). Furthermore, peers tend to reward sex-typical behaviour and punish sex-atypical behaviour (Fagot, 1977, 1984; Langlois & Downes, 1980; McCandless, Bush, & Carden, 1976; Lamb & Roopnarine, 1979). Third, gender identity allows for differential sensitivity to reactions from same-sex peers. Girls' responses change the behaviour of other girls whereas boys' responses affect the behaviour of boys but the sexes seem to pay little attention to reactions from the opposite sex (Fagot, 1984, 1985b; Maccoby, 1990). Same-sex reactions seem to serve as reinforcers and punishers although they may not always look like them to an observer. For example, boys attend to other boys' aggression and often they respond quite negatively to it. Yet the impact of this attention (regardless of its positive or negative social content) is to increase boys' levels of aggression. Girls often ignore the aggression of other girls and this has the more predictable effect of decreasing girls' aggression. From a cognitive perspective, gender identity sensitises the child to members of its own sex which results in selective frequency-dependent modelling and sensitivity to same-sex reinforcement.

THE ADAPTED CHILD: AN EPIGENETIC APPROACH

An alternative point of view, while acknowledging the enhancing and accelerating effects of gender identity, places the origins of sex differences at a much earlier point in time when formal cognitive operations play little part. Before describing this epigenetic viewpoint in detail, let us pause to examine some problems with an exclusively cognitively mediated account of sex typing. In the studies described earlier, gender identity is measured by a sorting task. Children are given pictures of adults and children and asked to place them into piles according to their sex. Clearly, such a task cannot be given before the child is mature enough to understand the instructions and to carry them out. This may account for why gender identity, when measured in this way, is not usually apparent until the age of three years. There are, however, *a priori* reasons to suspect that children may have gender awareness well before this time. As Maccoby and Jacklin (1987) note, many lower species of animals respond differentially to same- versus opposite-sex others and we have no reason to suppose that they possess the elaborate cognitive mechanisms of gender identity. Human infants respond more negatively to men than to women in stranger approach studies (Greenberg, Hillman, & Grice, 1977). Children as young as 15 months will use the term "Daddy" to refer generically to males but not to females (Brooks-Gunn & Lewis, 1979; Thomas & Chapman, 1977).

Studies have demonstrated that 1.7-day-old infants, when presented with two face-like stimuli, prefer the one with the amplitude and phase spectrum of the human face (Kleiner, 1987). It has been proposed that infants arrive in the world with structural information about the general characteristics of faces which does not require specific exposure to them (Johnson & Morton, 1991). This subcortical mechanism orients the infant to faces allowing for increasing cortical processing of information which informs differentiation. Differentiation by sex-of-face may be innate (in the Gibsonian sense of a specific attunement) or may be acquired in the first few months of life. Infants at 7 months of age react differently to male and female faces suggesting that they are capable of discriminating them (Fagan & Singer, 1979). Lewis and Brooks (1975) showed 10-month-old infants pairs of slides of similarly aged infants and found a significant same-sex preference. It seems that infants can discriminate the sex of another infant and this is particularly remarkable because adults fail at such a task. This finding was replicated by Bower (1989). He extended the original study by also showing slides of cross-sex dressed infants playing with cross-sex toys (a drum vs. a doll). He found that the infant subjects now gazed most at opposite-sex children who were cross-dressed to appear same-sex. He concluded that infants must have already acquired knowledge of culturally preferred styles of dress by 12 months. However, and to anticipate my later argument, it may be the case that what attracted the children's attention was the toy that was being played with. If toy preference, with its very early (and certainly preverbal) onset, has an innate basis then we would expect infants to attend to sex-typical toys. In another study, Aitken (1977) used moving film of cross-dressed boys and girls and found that movement cues could override the effects of cross dressing. In other words, at 12 months children are responsive to the locomotion differences between the sexes and use this to guide their choice. More recently, Kujawski and Bower (1993) found that 10- to 14-month-old infants showed a significant first fixation length difference when presented with patch light displays which effectively remove all visual cues to sex except movement. How do infants do it?

Viewed from a strictly cognitive perspective, the task requires that the child can do three things: (1) identify others as belonging to one of two mutually exclusive classes of person; (2) identify themselves in the same way; and (3) relate these two pieces of information to allow for matching. Stranger approach studies show that infants can certainly discriminate gender (although we can only speculate as to whether they understand concepts of binary categorisation and exclusivity) and this capacity to abstract a set of perceptual features from a series of stimuli has been demonstrated in studies with artificial stimuli (Younger, 1985). But do infants know to which sex they belong? Lewis and Brooks (1975) presented infants with photos of same-age peers. Their own face was included in one of the presentations. They found that infants up to the age of 18 months do not discriminate (in terms of fixation duration) between photographs of themselves and photographs of same-sex babies given on other trials. Lewis and Brooks conclude that this demonstrates that infants recognise their own shared categorical membership. However, given the infants' same-sex preference, the same results would be found if infants did not recognise themselves but did recognise a same-sex baby. Indeed Amsterdam (1972) examined infants' reactions to mirrors and found that up to the age of 18 months, infants treated the image as another baby, smiling and vocalising to the image. Lewis and Brooks (1975) applied rouge to the noses of infants aged 9 to 24 months. None of the infants aged less than one year and only 25 per cent of the 15- to 18-month-old infants touched their own noses when presented with a mirror image of themselves. This suggests that infants are unlikely to know their own sex until at least 18 months of age. Even if they did, they would have to be able to match knowledge about self with corresponding knowledge about others. This is doubtful because cross-modal integration (voice and face) of the sex of another person is not mastered until well into the second year of life (Poulin-Dubois, Serbin, Kenyon, & Derbyshire, 1994). Even if infants could do all this, we are left with the question of where this same-sex preference came from and without some concept of attunement or readiness, it is hard to account for its universal and ubiquitous nature.

If infants arrive in the world with a preference for attending to their own sex (and a few other preferences that I will describe later) then the need for sophisticated concepts of self and sex-of-self are redundant. The infant need not know to which sex he/she belongs. He/she needs only find the appearance and behaviour of members his/her own sex more intrinsically interesting than that of the opposite sex. Although this sounds quite radical, recent research has revealed a startling array of predispositions that children bring to the world and which serve to speed development in the first few years of life. For example, they seem to have expectations about cause and effect, trajectories of motion and number, as well as a capacity to identify nouns, verbs, and phrases in sentences they have never heard before (see Pinker, 1994). It would seem odd indeed if evolution had not generated an ability to orient preferentially to one's sex and thus open the way for the expression and cultural elaboration of agency and communion that are critical to the survival of the species. But how would such a mechanism operate?

The epigentic process I will now describe is presented graphically in Fig. 13.1. The term "epigenesis" is used to describe how the genes and environment acting together determine the structure and function of the brain cells and thus the behaviour of the individual. Which genes are turned on in each cell of the body are a product of the surrounding cells and the external environment. The majority of genetic information we inherit orchestrates species-typical attributes and behaviours, resulting in the fact

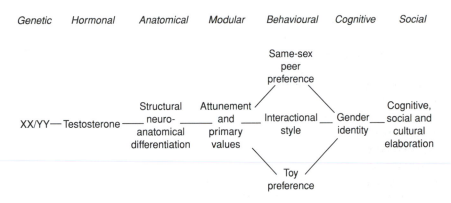

FIG. 13.1 A proposed developmental sequence of sex differences.

that we all (barring genetic or environmental accident) have two eyes, one brain, two kidneys, and so on. But male and female represent distinctive morphs or forms of our species and information carried on chromosome 23 causes the formation of male or female gonads at around six weeks after conception. Although some have insisted that the only difference between the sexes resides in their reproductive organs which have no effect on nonsexual behaviour (e.g. S. Bem, 1993), there is a wealth of evidence that this is not true. Fetal testes begin production of testosterone which in turn crosses the blood–brain barrier and affects the development of the brain. (Ovarian hormones have been less well studied but also have affects on development, see Fitch & Denenberg, 1995.) For example, the bed nucleus of the stria terminalis and the preoptic area of the hypothalamus—which control reproductive cycles and sexual and aggressive behaviour—is more than twice as large in males as in females (Zhou, Hofman, Gooren, & Swaab, 1995). Males and females as distinct morphs are embarked prior to birth on different developmental trajectories. Just as evolution has affected our universal readiness to acquire and employ language, to sort the colour spectrum into similar categories, and to respond preferentially to faces rather than scrambled features (see Lumsden, 1988), I propose it has also affected boys' and girls' readiness to attend to sex-appropriate features of the world. Male and female development is canalised into different pathways.

The mechanisms for how this takes place are still in question. Although some researchers seek a direct casual pathway from hormones to brain anatomy and neurochemistry and thence to behaviour, there are at least two other candidates that offer a more flexible and less clearly deterministic route. One way to conceive of these differences is in terms of ecological psychology (Valenti & Good, 1991). This approach originally grew from studies of depth perception when Gibson (1979) argued for a direct (rather than a computational) process whereby depth is "given" via the texture gradient of the scene. Babies demonstrate depth perception from a very young age and this suggests that complex learned computations are not required. Instead, he argued that humans are attuned to relevant information in the environment in much the same way that a radio receiver is set to detect certain pre-set frequencies. Extending these ideas into the domain of social behaviour, the term "affordances" has been used to describe the possibilities for action and learning offered by features of the environment (McArthur & Baron, 1983). Using this terminology, we could conceive of boys and girls as attuned to different stimuli that afford them the opportunity to express and elaborate sex-typed skills. Girls are attuned to dolls because they afford the possibility of expressing nurturance, and boys are attuned to weapons because they offer the possibility of expressing competition and aggression.

Another mechanism that might give rise to pre-cognitive sex differences is differential activation of dopaminergic reward systems. Within co-evolutionary theory, the term "primary value" has been used to describe the intrinsic aversions and approach tendencies that have evolved through evolution (Durham, 1991). (These largely correspond to primary reinforcers and punishers, in psychologists' terminology.) For example, many people are phobic about heights, snakes, or spiders and such an aversion makes good evolutionary sense. Most people find sex, food, and pleasant ambient temperatures intrinsically satisfying and seek them out, for equally good evolutionary reasons. These universal and cross-historical preferences appear to be innate and are often quite resistant to change. Differences in primary values between the sexes provide a mechanism for different developmental choices and preferences. Although boys find direct competition exciting and interesting, girls find it much less so. A combination of these approaches suggests that boys and girls are attuned to different activities that afford different elaborative routes and which are pursued because of differences in primary values.

Evolutionary psychology has argued for domain-specific mechanisms rather than a general all-purpose learning mechanism (see MacDonald, Chapter 2). Problems associated with successful reproduction are different from problems associated with detecting valuable foodstuffs and require different evaluative mechanisms. If this is true, then we might expect that the domains of what we now call sex-typed behaviours would be diverse indeed. In evolutionary terms, some differences between men and women were connected with gaining mating opportunities, others with within-sex co-operation and competition, and others with parenting. Although we can conveniently refer to them as communion and agency, we must recognise that they represent the solution to different problems posed to inclusive fitness. For this reason, it seems probable that not one but several mechanisms or modules are involved, of which I will consider three.

Maccoby and Jacklin's (1987) extensive investigation of the universal and early preference for same-sex peers has established that it is not the result of direct adult pressure, temperamental similarity of same-sex children, toy preference, or sex typing in children. Preference for same-sex peers is not a stable individual difference variable on which children differ—rather, it is a property of maleness and femaleness considered in aggregate. Boys in general prefer other boys, and girls other girls despite the fact that on occasion individuals will play with members of the opposite sex. This strongly suggests the presence of some underlying canalisation of development which on average predisposes children to choose members of their own sex to play with.

But why should such a predisposition have evolved? That children respond differentially to social feedback from their own sex suggests that same-sex peer groups act as socialisers to their members, almost always in sex-stereotypic ways. Learning from one's peers through both reinforcement and imitation allows for fast adjustment to ecological conditions so that levels of aggression or nurturance can be adjusted to the prevailing conditions and demands of the local situation. Another explanation, mentioned but not elaborated by Maccoby and Jacklin (1987), is based on a well-known evolutionary concept, the Westermarck effect. This describes the tendency of males and females to avoid marriage or copulation with individuals whom they have known since infancy. Its purpose is to reduce incest by ensuring that siblings experience no romantic interest in one another. (One of the side-effects, unforeseen by evolution, is that kibbutzim children do not intermarry.) In an evolutionary environment where the choice of potential mates was smaller than it is today, it would make good sense for opposite-sex children to avoid close contact in childhood and so to remain eligible mates in adulthood. Interestingly, Maccoby and Jacklin (1987, p. 244) note that among children: "cross-sex contact often seems to have overtones of romantic interest ... children know that members of the opposite sex are their future romantic partners, but also know that they are not ready for dating". D. Bem (1996) has recently proposed a theory of sexual orientation which similarly emphasises the same-sex peer group as a factor in later sexual attraction. He suggests that familiarity, caused by frequent and intense same-sex interactions, is responsible for the later attractiveness of the opposite sex, or as he elegantly puts it: "The exotic becomes erotic". I differ with him only in the role he accords to biological factors. The exclusive starting point of his linear model is biological variables (including genes and prenatal hormones). All other sequentially implicated variables (biological factors

→ childhood temperament → sex typical peer and activity preferences → feelings of similarity/dissimilarity → arousal → erotic attraction) flow from it. It is therefore surprising that he asserts that his model provides a "culturally based alternative" to biological accounts of gender. This sleight of hand is achieved by suggesting, in the text of the article, that same-sex peer groups are a result of a (p. 13): "gender polarising culture like ours in which most individuals come to be familiar with one sex while simultaneously being estranged from the other". He goes on to surmise that if cultures ceased to force such same-sex groupings on children, we might escape our heterosexuality and assess our partners on the basis of their personality not their sex. What Bem fails to acknowledge is the universal and adult-resistant nature of children's sex segregation. Although Bem has provided an elegant account of the possible functions of sex segregation in childhood, I do not accept his textual assertion that "our culture" forces sex segregation on children. His diagrammatic model where biological forces influence temperament and consequent peer choice fits very much more persuasively with the empirical evidence.

Another clear area of difference between boys and girls is their play styles. Although boys prefer a cut-and-thrust approach to interaction, girls follow a share-and-care model. Again, Maccoby and Jacklin (1987) were unable to account for this in terms of temperamental differences. Boys' activity level was found to be no higher than girls, and boys with higher activity levels were not the ones who most preferred play with same-sex peers. With regard to timidity, they found that timid girls were no more likely than others to select same-sex playmates and timid boys tended to associate slightly more with other boys than with girls. However, Maccoby and Jacklin suggest that different play styles may be related to same-sex preference at a group, rather than at an individual level. They argue that boys' groups dominate those of girls in cross-sex interaction and this motivates girls to avoid boys. They also note that such an explanation is unable to explain why boys should avoid girls—from whom they have nothing to fear in terms of dominance. I suggest that an explanation in terms of attainment, affordances, and primary values may be more parsimonious. At nine months of age, boys already show more assertiveness in reaching for toys and facing challenges for its possession, rather than moving away (DeBoer, 1984). Boys seek out and enjoy rough and tumble games and competition whereas girls seek out opportunities to create and maintain affiliative relationships. Because of this, cross-sex play is not particularly satisfying to either sex.

Sex differences in toy preference have been documented as early as 14 months of age (Caldera et al., 1989; O'Brien & Huston, 1985), well before children can label the sex-typing of toys (Perry et al., 1984). I consider toy preference as a distinct module because Maccoby and Jacklin (1987) found that toy preference was unrelated to same-sex peer reference and that in same-sex groups girls and boys do not necessarily or even typically engage in play with dolls or guns. Rehearsing the common wisdom, K. B. Hoyenga and H. T. Hoyenga (1993, p. 308) conclude that: "Girls seem to be encouraged to be nurturant by their toys and boys are encouraged to compete". The curiously active role accorded to toys completely obscures the fact that they are chosen by children rather than the reverse. If girls choose dolls, they do so because they like them. I suggest they like them because dolls afford the possibility of expressing behaviours and experiencing emotions that are more pleasurable to girls than to boys.

The idea that such modules may be relatively discrete helps to explain the typically low correlations that are found between them. A girl who likes climbing trees or playing football is no more or less likely to prefer same-sex friends than one who enjoys playing at being a nurse. Furthermore, it is important to bear in mind that both sexes are characterised by variability as much as consistency. Although sex differences are consistent, individual differences are not. Although children on average prefer their own sex and their own sex's style of play, they also cross boundaries quite frequently in each of these modules. Occasionally, girls will play football with each other and, from time to time, a boy will agree to act as father in a family role-playing game.

Thus far, I have spoken of morphological differences between males and females in their canalised epigenetic development. Genes, as well as directing the growth of species- and sex-typical patterns, also give rise to individual differences in personality. Some theorists believe that these individual differences represent little more than random noise of little evolutionary significance (Tooby & Cosmides, 1990), others have argued that frequency-dependent selection would have maintained variability in personality in the face of unpredictable and fast-changing ecological conditions. Whatever their function, behavioural genetic studies (see Rowe, Chapter 3) leave little room for doubt that such differences within the population have a strong heritable component accounting for as much as 50 per cent of the population variance (Loehlin, 1992). As well as genes that specify species- and sex-typical attributes, each of us has our own unique configuration of traits which are in part heritable. Although some of these traits appear to show sex differences, many do not. For example, on the "big five" dimensions, extroversion and openness show no differences between men and women despite a high degree of heritability (MacDonald, 1995). These individual differences interact with sex-typical attributes to form unique individuals. An extroverted boy may be attracted to sports that afford the possibility of being the centre of a crowd's acclaim and attention, whereas an introverted boy might fulfil his agentic strivings by becoming a chess master. A girl high in openness might be interested in female politicians although another might confine her same-sex interest to her mother or her neighbours. Personality doubtless modulates the expression of sex-typical attainments and interests.

If epigenetic processes play an early role in orienting the child to sex-appropriate activities, toys, and peers, there can be no doubt that this is accelerated and elaborated by the acquisition of formal gender identity. Speculatively, I would suggest that the understanding of oneself as a boy or a girl follows rapidly on the appearance of intersubjective understanding. In recognising both that other people are the object of the child's attention and also that the child is the object of their attention, we see the beginning of objective self-awareness. This would seem to be critical for a basic conception of self as a social agent and object. Gender is likely to form a fundamental part of such a conception of self. Indeed, Spence (1985, p. 80) has noted: "Gender identity is thus a primitive, unarticulated concept of self, initially laid down at an essentially preverbal stage of development and maintained at an unverbalised level. As such, a person's sense of masculinity and femininity is ineffable—incapable of being put into words". Although we cannot articulate what it is to be or to know that we are male and female, we can certainly apply the label "boy" or "girl" by the age of three and often well before then. This ability, together with a natural tendency to associate with one's own sex, lays the groundwork for Maccoby and Jacklin's (1987) emphasis on the impact of group processes. Hogg and Abrams (1988) have documented how mere classification into a group is sufficient to set in motion inter-group competition. This involves twin processes of social categorisation and social comparison. To the extent that one's social identity is bound up in group membership, as in the case of sex, there are strong motives to make favourable evaluations of one's own group relative to the outgroup. Group membership also has the effect of maximising perceived differences between the two groups. Hence, a child's knowledge that she is "one of the girls" is likely to result in a clear distinction between boys and girls and a devaluation of boys' activities and interests (see also Abrams, 1989, for a discussion of social identity theory in relation to power relations between boys and girls).

Harris (1995) has also pointed to the peer group as the effective agent in children's socialisation, in response to behavioural genetic studies which demonstrate the negligible impact of shared parental treatment (see Muncer and Campbell, Chapter 15). Harris suggests that the appropriate place to search for shared environmental effects is not at a shared "postal address" as is done in traditional behavioural genetic studies but at shared peer groups. She continues to endorse shared socialisation effects but argues that they are realised via the peer group rather than the parents. Group processes are central to her conceptualisation: Assimilation into the group creates similarity among members in the face of out-groups and differentiation within the group (e.g. status and social comparisons) increase variability. With regard to gender, she suggests that self-categorisation into two dichotomous groups causes sex differences to widen and that modal sex differences will be maximised where there are enough same-sex peers to allow formation of sex-segregated groups. Although I agree with much of her conceptualisation, there are two important differences in emphasis between us. First, Harris accords a relatively minor role to biological differences between the sexes, placing greater weight on the importance of sex segregation as the active force. She suggests that a major variable in accounting for this is simply availability of a sufficient number of same-sex peers (see also Jahoda, Chapter 4). Although this is certainly a pre-condition for sex segregation, she fails to underscore that, given this condition is fulfilled, children spontaneously form such groups—they do so universally and the groupings are resistant to adults' attempts to dissolve them. This implicates a biological basis to which she accords scant attention. Second, the model effectively places the peer group *in loco parentis* with regard to the direction of influence in the transmission of behavioural preferences and patterns (Harris, 1995, p. 482): "According to the theory presented here, *children learn how to behave* outside the home by becoming members of and identifying with a social group". This leaves unaddressed the problem of where the values, attitudes, and behavioural preferences came from unless we invoke indeterminate forces such as "emergent norms". In doing so, we would expect that peer groups even within the same culture would differ radically from each other. With no firm biological emphasis, Harris' position suggests that although girls' and boys' groups will differ (as a function of group contrast effects), there is no way to predict what form this difference will take. Hence, we should expect to find societies where girls' groups are significantly more aggressive than boys' groups who share the same ecological niche. Studies to date do not support such a view. Harris (1995, p. 483) also states: "Children usually turn out all right because the environment that does have important and lasting effects is found with little variation in every society: the children's play group". Again, this begs the question of the origin of such reassuring invariance. With regard to sex differences, I believe it derives from primary values held by boys and girls which themselves have a biological basis. In short, I view the peer group as a manifestation as much as a cause of sex differences. I do not doubt that these behavioural differences are modulated and elaborated by local social and material resources—in short, by facultative adaptation. Cultural patterns also affect the form in which they are expressed (in the sense that boys' aggression in our century is expressed through gun play rather than sword play and that available cultural heroes are Hollywood stars rather than local highwaymen). Similarly, the memes that are culturally available to characterise and explain sex differences may affect the way such behavioural differences are interpreted and expressed. A series of studies has demonstrated that men and women differ in the way they understand their own aggression (Campbell, 1994; Campbell & Muncer, 1987, 1994; Campbell, Muncer, & Gorman, 1993). Men more than women view it as a means of controlling others and so enhancing self-esteem, whereas women more than men view it as a loss of self-control and a source of guilt. This difference has also been documented in eight-year-old children (Archer & Parker, 1994). It is likely that ways of representing aggression have changed through history and these instrumental and expressive aggression "allomemes" reflect those that are current in contemporary society. Such culturally supplied memes most likely enhance as well as reflect patterns of behavioural sex differences.

Social identity research has been conducted for the most part on adults but the processes of in-group favouritism and out-group disparagement are likely to be even stronger in children. Kohlberg (1966) described developmental components of gendered values and behaviour of which two are especially relevant here: (1) the tendency to make value judgements consistent with self-identity (including the tendency for prestige, competence, or goodness to be associated with one's own sex); and (2) the tendency to view nonconformity to sex-appropriate behaviour as morally wrong. The first of these is a result of the child's cognitive egocentricity which peaks at the age of six and decreases with increasing decentration. Prior to this, children's own preferences are taken to be natural and universal so that, for example, a child who dislikes pizza will announce that "Pizza is horrible" without consideration of individual differences in people and their tastes. Abrams (1989, p. 65) provides a nice illustration of how boys and girls view themselves and each other. His sample of girls aged five said:

> 'boys scratch, fight and wear trousers', 'boys are naughty', 'they're horrid', 'girls are better than boys, girls can skip and boys can't', 'girls are gooder than boys', 'girls wear pretty clothes and bumble bee dresses'.

Boys' views were somewhat different:

> 'boys can run faster, they have shorter hair, they're much stronger than girls', 'boys are better than girls I think. Girls have got dollies and boys haven't', 'I don't think girls are strong enough'; 'girls are sometimes a bit bossy'.

The second component—sex-role rigidity—results from the child's early inability to distinguish between conventional social expectation and moral duty. This rigidity of sex-typical behaviour and attitudes increases from age five to eight, after which the child begins to recognise the distinction between convention and morality. This rule rigidity can be seen in other domains. Linguists have observed that once children have discovered the rule that "-s" is added to nouns to make a plural, they tend to overgeneralise producing incorrect plurals like "sheeps". Young children also view conventional rules in games as immutable and non-negotiable. The child seeks a rigid structure to support generalisation in a social world where exceptions and special cases cause cognitive confusion. Turiel (1983) has studied children's understanding of conventions in some detail and has identified three stages of development. Up to age eight conventions reflect the natural order of things and violating conventions amounts to unnatural behaviour, as in this extract (Damon, 1977, p. 255):

Interviewer: Can George play with Barbie dolls if he wants to?
Michael (aged 5 years 11 months): No Sir!
Interviewer: How come?
Michael: If he doesn't want to play dolls then he's right, but if he does want to play with dolls then he's double wrong.
Interviewer: Why is he double wrong?
Michael: All the time he's playing with girls stuff.

Later, children reject the need for social conventions but by late childhood they recognise that, although conventions may be arbitrary, they have a legitimate role in the regulation of social life. However, at preschool and early school age the tendency to favour one's own group is likely to be augmented by egocentricity and by confusion between convention and morality. This goes some way to explaining the profoundly conservative nature of young children's reactions to sex-atypical behaviour.

SUMMARY

I have argued that infants arrive in the world with an attunement to a variety of sex-appropriate stimuli including peers, toys, styles of play, and interaction. These attunements are proposed to correspond to discrete psychological modules and hence there are low correlations between behavioural measures of them. These stimuli afford the possibility of expressing behaviours that in the course of evolution have had fitness consequences for males and females and these fitness consequences are mediated by sex differences in primary values. Hence, sex-typed peer interaction is the expression of already existing differences (active gene-environment correlations) as much as the cause of them (shared environment). By the age of three (and likely well before then) children develop objective self-awareness and a formal knowledge of their own and others' gender. This ability to form a binary categorisation of self and peers allows for the formation of initially rigid prototypes of sex-appropriate behaviour in the peer group, a marked in-group preference, an increase in sex-typed behaviour, strong sanctioning of departures from sex-appropriate behaviour, and selective responding to same-sex feedback. With increasing cognitive sophistication children are able to abandon this rigidity and question the utility of social conventions about sex-appropriate behaviour. In adulthood, it is this capacity for reflection combined with a desire for social justice that can fuel movements for change and generate a society where sex differences are not coterminous with personal or institutionalised superiority or inferiority.

REFERENCES

Abrams, D. (1989). Differential association: Social developments in gender identity and inter-group relations during adolescence. In S. Skevington & D. Baker (Eds.), *Social identity of women* (pp. 59–83). London: Sage.

Ahlgren, A. (1983). Sex differences in the correlates of co-operative and competitive school attitudes. *Developmental Psychology, 19*, 881–888.

Aitken, S. (1977). *Psychological sex differentiation as related to the emergence of a self-concept in infancy.* Unpublished MA thesis, University of Edinburgh.

Amsterdam, B. (1972). Mirror self image reactions before age two. *Developmental Psycho-biology, 5*, 297–305.

Archer, J. (1989). The relationship between gender role measures: A review. *British Journal of Social Psychology, 28*, 173–184.

Archer, J. (1992). Childhood gender roles: Social context and organisation. In H. McGurk (Ed.), *Childhood social development: contemporary perspectives* (pp. 31–61). Hillsdale, NJ: Lawrence Erlbaum Associates Inc.

Archer, J. & Parker, S. (1994). Social representations of aggression in children. *Aggressive Behaviour, 20*, 101–114.

Bakan, D. (1966). *The duality of human existence. Isolation and communion in Western man.* Boston: Beacon.

Bandura, A. (1977). *Social learning theory.* Englewood Cliffs, NJ: Prentice Hall.

Bandura, A. (1986). *Social foundations of thought and action.* Englewood Cliffs, NJ: Prentice Hall.

Barkow, J., Cosmides, L., & Tooby, J. (Eds.) (1992). *The adapted mind: Evolutionary psychology and the generation of culture.* Oxford: Oxford University Press.

Barklay, R., Ullman, D., Otto, L., & Brecht, J. (1977). The effects of sex typing and sex appropriateness of modelled behaviour on children's imitation. *Child Development, 48*, 721–725.

Bem, D. (1996). Exotic becomes erotic: A developmental theory of sexual orientation. *Psychological Review, 103*, 320–335.

Bem, S. (1974). The measurement of psychological androgyny. *Journal of Consulting and Clinical Psychology, 42*, 153–162.

Bem, S. (1981). Gender schema theory: A cognitive account of sex typing. *Psychological Review, 88*, 354–364.

Bem, S. (1993). *The lenses of gender: Transforming the debate on sexual inequality*. New Haven, CT: Yale University Press.

Blakemore, J., LaRue, A., & Olejnik, A. (1979). Sex-appropriate toy preference and the ability to conceptualise toys as sex role related. *Developmental Psychology. 15*, 339–340.

Boehnke, K., Silbereisen, R., Eisenberg, N., Teykowski, J., & Palmonari, A. (1989). Developmental pattern of prosocial motivation: A cross-national study. *Journal of Cross Cultural Psychology, 20*, 219–243.

Bower, T. (1989). *The rational infant: Learning in infancy*. New York: Freeman.

Brooks-Gunn, J. & Lewis, M. (1979). "Why mama and papa?" The development of social labels. *Child Development, 50*, 1203–1206.

Brown, D. (1991). *Human universals*. New York: Basic Books.

Buss, D. & Schmitt, D. (1993). Sexual strategies theory: An evolutionary perspective on human mating. *Psychological Review, 100*, 204–232.

Caldera, Y., Huston, A., & O'Brien, M. (1989). Social interaction and play patterns of parents and toddlers with feminine, masculine and neutral toys. *Child Development, 60*, 70–76.

Campbell, A. (1994). *Men, women and aggression*. New York: Basic Books.

Campbell, A. & Muncer, S. J. (1987). Models of anger and aggression in the social talk of women and men. *Journal for the Theory of Social Behaviour, 17*, 489–512.

Campbell, A. & Muncer, S. J. (1994). Sex differences in aggression: Social roles and social representations. *British Journal of Social Psychology, 33*, 233–240.

Campbell A., Muncer, S., & Gorman, B. (1993). Sex and social representations of aggression: A communal-agentic analysis. *Aggressive Behaviour, 19*, 125–135.

Carter, D. (1989). The role of peers in sex role socialisation. In D. Carter (Ed.), *Current conceptions of sex roles and sex typing*. New York: Praeger.

Crosbie, P. (1979). The effects of sex and size on status ranking. *Social Psychology Quarterly, 2*, 340–354.

Damon, W. (1977). *The social world of the child*. San Francisco, CA: Jossey-Bass.

D'Andrade, R. (1966). Sex differences in cultural institutions. In E. Maccoby (Ed.). *The development of sex differences* (pp. 173–204). Stanford, CA: Stanford University Press.

Deaux, K. & Major, B. (1987). Putting gender into context: An interactive model of gender-related behaviour. *Psychological Review, 94*, 369–389.

DeBoer, M. (1984). *Competition for toys in 9-12 month old twins and triplets*. Paper presented to the Fourth International Conference on Infant Studies. New York.

Durham, W. (1991). *Coevolution: Genes culture and human diversity*. Stanford, CA: Stanford University Press.

Eagly, A. (1987). *Sex differences in social behaviour: A social role interpretation*. Hillsdale, NJ: Lawrence Erlbaum Associates Inc.

Ember, C. (1981). A cross-cultural perspective on sex differences. In R. H. Monroe, R. L. Monroe, & B.Whiting (Eds.), *Handbook of cross-cultural human development* (pp. 531–580) New York: Garland.

Fagan, J. & Shepherd, P. (1981). Theoretical issues in the early development of visual perception. In M. Lewis & L. Taft (Eds.), *Developmental disabilities: Theory, assessment and intervention*. New York: Spectrum.

Fagan, J. & Singer, L. (1979). The role of simple feature differences in infant's recognition of faces. *Infant Behaviour and Development, 2*, 39–45.

Fagot, B. (1977). Consequences of moderate cross-gender behaviour in pre-school children. *Child Development, 48*, 902–907.

Fagot, B. (1984). Teacher and peer reactions to boys and girls play styles. *Sex Roles, 11*, 691–702.

Fagot, B. (1985a). Changes in thinking about early sex role development. *Developmental Review, 5*, 83–98.

Fagot, B. (1985b). Beyond the reinforcement principle: Another step toward understanding sex role development. *Developmental Psychology, 21*, 471–476.

Fagot, B. & Leinbach, M. (1989). The young child's gender schema: Environmental input, internal organisation. *Child Development, 60*, 663–672.

Fagot, B., Leinbach, M., & Hagan, R. (1986). Gender labelling and the adoption of sex-typed behaviours. *Developmental Psychology, 22*, 440–443.

Feingold, A. (1994). Gender differences in personality: A meta-analysis. *Psychological Bulletin, 116*, 429–456.

Fisher H. (1992). *The anatomy of love*. New York: Touchstone.

Fitch, R. & Denenberg, V. (1995). A role for ovarian hormones in sexual differentiation of the brain. *Psycholoquy, 95.6.05.*

Gibson, J. (1979). *The ecological approach to visual perception*. Boston: Houghton Mifflin.

Greenberg, D., Hillman, D., & Grice, D. (1977). Infant and stranger variables related to stranger anxiety in the first year of life. *Developmental Psychology, 9*, 207–212.

Grossman, M. & Wood, W. (1993). Sex differences in intensity of emotional experience: A social role interpretation. *Journal of Personality and Social Psychology, 65*, 1010–1022.

Hall, J. (1984). *Nonverbal sex differences: Communication accuracy and expressive style*. Baltimore, MA: Johns Hopkins University Press.

Harris, J. R. (1995). Where is the child's environment? A group socialization theory of development. *Psychological Review, 102*, 458–489.

Helmreich, R., Spence, J., & Gibson, R. (1982). Sex role attitudes 1972–1980. *Personality and Social Psychology Bulletin, 8*, 656–663.

Hogg, M. & Abrams, D. (1988). *Social identification*. London: Routledge.

Hoyenga, K. B. & Hoyenga, K. T. (1993). *Gender related differences*. Boston: Allyn & Bacon.

Huston, A. (1983). Sex typing. In P. Mussen & M. Hetherington (Eds.), *Handbook of child psychology: Vol. 4. Socialisation. Personality and social behaviour* (pp. 387–467). New York: Wiley.

Johnson, M. & Morton, J. (1991). *Biology and cognitive development: The case of face recognition*. Oxford: Blackwell.

Kleiner, K. (1987). Amplitude and phase spectra as indices of infant's pattern preferences. *Infant Behaviour and Development, 10*, 45–59.

Kohlberg, L. (1966). A cognitive-developmental analysis of children's sex role concepts and attitudes. In E. Maccoby (Ed.), *The development of sex differences* (pp. 82–170). Stanford, CA: Stanford University Press.

Kujawski, J. & Bower, T. (1993). Same-sex preferential looking during infancy as a function of abstract representation. *British Journal of Developmental Psychology, 11*, 201–209.

Lamb, M. & Roopnarine, J. (1979). Peer influences on sex-role development in pre-schoolers. *Child Development, 50*, 1219–1222.

Langlois, J. & Downes, A. (1980). Mothers, fathers and peers as socialisation agents of sex-typed play in young children. *Child Development, 51*, 1217–1247.

Laosa, L. & Brophy, J. (1972). Effects of sex and birth order on sex-role development and intelligence among kindergarten children. *Developmental Psychology, 6*, 409–415.

Lever, J. (1978). Sex differences in the games children play. *Social Problems, 23*, 478–487.

Lewin, M. & Tragos, L. (1987). Has the feminist movement influenced adolescent sex role attitudes? A reassessment after a quarter century. *Sex Roles, 16*, 125–135.

Lewis, M. & Brooks, J. (1975). Infants' social perception: A constructivist view. In L. Cohen & P. Salaptek (Eds.), *Infant perception: From sensation to cognition: Vol. 2. Perception of space, speech and sound* (pp. 101–148). New York: Academic Press.

Loehlin, J. (1992). *Genes and environment in personality development*. Newbury Park, CA: Sage.

Lueptow, L. (1985). Concepts of masculinity and femininity: 1974–1983. *Psychological Reports*, *57*, 859–862.

Lumsden, C. (1988). Psychological development: Epigenetic rules and gene-culture coevolution. In K. Macdonald (Ed.). *Sociobiological perspectives on human development* (pp. 234–265). New York: Springer.

Lytton, H. & Romney, D. (1991). Parents' differential socialisation of boys and girls: A meta-analysis. *Psychological Bulletin*, *109*, 267–296.

Maccoby, E. (1988). Gender as a social category. *Developmental Psychology*, *24*, 755–765.

Maccoby, E. (1990). Gender and relationships: A developmental account. *American Psychologist*, *5*, 513–520.

Maccoby, E. & Jacklin, C. (1974). *The psychology of sex differences*. Stanford, CA: Stanford University Press.

Maccoby, E. & Jacklin, C. (1987). Gender segregation in childhood. In H. Reese (Ed.), *Advances in child development* (Vol. 20) (pp. 239–286). New York: Academic Press.

Maccoby, E. & Martin, C. (1983). Socialisation in the context of the family: Parent child interaction. In E. Hetherington & P. Mussen (Eds), *Handbook of child psychology: Vol. 4. Socialisation. Personality and social development* (pp. 1–30). New York: Wiley.

MacDonald, D. (1995). Evolution, the five factor model and levels of personality. *Journal of Personality*, *63*, 525–567.

Maltz, D. & Borker, R. (1982). A cultural approach to male–female miscommunication. In J. Gumperz (Ed.), *Language and social identity* (pp. 196–216). New York: Cambridge University Press.

Martin, C. (1993). New directions for investigating children's gender knowledge. *Developmental Review*, *13*, 184–204.

McArthur, L. & Baron, R. (1983). Toward an ecological theory of social perception. *Psychological Review*, *90*, 215–238.

McCandless, B., Bush, C., & Carden, A. (1976). Reinforcing contingencies for sex role behaviours in pre-school children. *Contemporary Educational Psychology*, *1*, 241–246.

McCrae, R. & Costa, P. (1988a). Recalled parent–child relationships and adult personality. *Journal of Personality*, *56*, 417–436.

McCrae, R. & Costa, P. (1988b). Do parental influences matter? A reply to Halverson. *Journal of Personality*, *56*, 445–449.

Mischel, W. (1966). A social learning view of sex differences in behaviour. In E. Maccoby (Ed.), *The development of sex differences* (pp. 56–82). Stanford, CA: Stanford University Press.

Moely, B., Skarin, K., & Weil, S. (1979). Sex differences in competition–co-operation behaviour of children at two age levels. *Sex Roles*, *5*, 329–342.

Mussen, P. (1987). Longitudinal study of the life span. In N. Eisenberg (Ed.), *Contemporary topics in developmental psychology*. New York: Wiley.

O'Brien, M. & Huston, A. (1985). Development of sex-typed play behaviour in toddlers. *Developmental Psychology*, *21*, 866–871.

Omark, D. & Edelman, M. (1975). A comparison of status hierarchies in young children: An ethological approach. *Social Science Information*, *14*, 87–107.

Paulhus, D. (1984). Two component models of socially desirable responding. *Journal of Personality and Social Psychology*, *46*, 598–609.

Perry, D. & Bussey, K. (1979). The social learning theory of sex differences: Imitation is alive and well. *Journal of Personality and Social Psychology*, *37*, 1699–1712.

Perry, D., White, A., & Perry, L. (1984). Does early sex typing result from children's attempts to match their behaviour to sex role stereotypes? *Child Development*, *55*, 2114–2121.

Pinker, S. (1994). *The language instinct*. London: Penguin.

Poulin-Dubois, D., Serbin, L., Kenyon, B., & Derbyshire, A. (1994). Infants' intermodal knowledge about gender. *Developmental Psychology*, *30*, 436–442.

Savin-Williams, R. (1977). Dominance in a human adolescent group. *Animal Behaviour*, *25*, 400–406.

Seavey, C., Katz, P., & Zalk, S. (1975). Baby X: The effect of gender labels on adult responses to infants. *Sex Roles*, *1*, 103–110.

Smuts, B. (1995). The evolutionary origins of patriarchy. *Human Nature*, *6*, 1–32.

Spence, J. (1985). Gender identity and its implications for the concepts of masculinity and femininity. In T. Sonderegger (Ed.), *Nebraska symposium on motivation, 1984: Vol. 32. Psychology and gender* (pp. 59–95). Lincoln, NE: University of Nebraska Press.

Spence, J., Helmreich, R., & Stapp, J. (1974). The Personality Attributes Questionnaire: A measure of sex role stereotypes and masculinity–femininity. *Journal Supplement Abstract Service Catalog of Selected Documents in Psychology*, *4*, 42 (No. 617).

Stern, M. & Karraker, K. (1989). Sex stereotyping of infants: A review of gender labelling studies. *Sex Roles*, *20*, 501–522.

Swim, J. (1994). Perceived versus meta-analytic effect sizes: An assessment of the accuracy of gender stereotypes. *Journal of Personality and Social Psychology*, *66*, 21–36.

Thomas, J. & Chapman, R. (1977). Who is 'daddy' revisited: The status of two-year-olds' over-extended words in use and comprehension. *Journal of Child Language*, *4*, 359–375.

Tooby, J. & Cosmides, L. (1990). On the universality of human nature and the uniqueness of the individual: The role of genetics and adaptation. *Journal of Personality*, *58*, 17–67.

Tooby, J. & Cosmides, L. (1992). Psychological foundations of culture. In J. Barkow, L. Cosmides, & J. Tooby (Eds.), *The adapted mind: Evolutionary psychology and the generation of culture* (pp. 19–135). New York: Oxford University Press.

Trivers, R. (1972). Parental investment and sexual selection. In B. Campbell (Ed.), *Sexual selection and the descent of man* (pp. 136–179). Chicago, IL: Aldine Atherton.

Turiel, E. (1983). *The development of social knowledge*. Cambridge: Cambridge University Press.

Valenti S. & Good, J. (1991). Social affordances and interaction: 1. Introduction. *Ecological Psychology*, *3*, 77–98.

Weisfeld, G., Omark, D. R., & Cronin, C. (1980). A longitudinal and cross-sectional study of dominance in boys. In D. R. Omark, F. Strayer, & D. Freedman (Eds.), *An ethological view of human conflict and social interaction*. New York: Garland.

Wiggins, J. (1982). Circumplex models of interpersonal behaviour in clinical psychology. In P. Kendall & J. Butcher (Eds.), *Handbook of research methods in clinical psychology* (pp. 183–221). New York: Wiley.

Wiggins, J. & Holzmuller, A. (1978). Psychological androgyny and interpersonal behaviour. *Journal of Consulting and Clinical Psychology*, *46*, 40–52.

Wiggins, J. & Holzmuller, A. (1981). Further evidence on androgyny and interpersonal flexibility. *Journal of Research in Personality*, *15*, 67–80.

Williams, J. & Best, D. (1982). *Measuring sex stereotypes: A thirty nation study*. Beverly Hills, CA: Sage.

Williams, J. & Best, D. (1990). *Sex and the psyche: Gender roles and self concepts viewed cross culturally*. Beverly Hills, CA: Sage.

Younger, B. (1985). The segregation of items into categories by ten-month-old infants. *Child Development*, *56*, 1574–1583.

Zhou, J-N., Hofman, M. A., Gooren, L. J., & Swaab, D. F. (1995). A sex difference in the human bairn and its relation to transsexuality. *Nature*, *378*, 68–70.

14 Youth crime and antisocial behaviour

David P. Farrington
Cambridge University, UK

The major aim of this chapter is to review evidence about youth crime and antisocial behaviour. The main focus is on research in Great Britain and North America. I will review the natural history of offending and antisocial behaviour, the most crucial risk factors, and a plausible theory that explains many of the most important results.

Fortunately or unfortunately, there is no shortage of factors that are significantly correlated with youth crime and antisocial behaviour; indeed, literally thousands of variables differentiate significantly between official offenders and nonoffenders and correlate significantly with reports of antisocial behaviour by teenagers, peers, parents, and teachers. In this chapter, it is only possible to review briefly some of the most important risk factors for offending and antisocial behaviour: Individual difference factors such as impulsivity and intelligence, family features such as parental supervision and discipline, socioeconomic deprivation, peer and school influences. I will discuss the various kinds of influences one by one, neglecting the problem of how they might add, interact, or have sequential effects on antisocial behaviour. There is insufficient space to review biological, community, or situational influences on crime.

Offending is a type of behaviour, similar in many respects to other types of antisocial or deviant behaviour. Hence, the theories, methods, and knowledge of other types of antisocial behaviour can be applied to the study of youth crime. It is plausible to suggest that, like other types of behaviour, criminal behaviour results from the interaction between a person (with a certain degree of criminal potential or antisocial tendency) and the environment (which provides criminal opportunities). Some people will be consistently more likely to commit offences than others in different environments, and conversely the same person will be more likely to commit offences in some environments than in others.

A major problem in criminological theories is to explain the development of individual differences in criminal potential. It is often assumed that offences and other types of antisocial acts are behavioural manifestations of an underlying theoretical construct such as antisocial personality. In particular, there will be different antisocial manifestations at different ages from birth to adulthood. For example, the antisocial child may be troublesome and disruptive in school, the antisocial teenager may steal cars and burgle houses, and the antisocial adult male may beat up his wife and neglect his children. The variation in antisocial behaviour with age is one of the key issues that any theory needs to explain.

This chapter has a developmental focus. In order to understand the causes of offending, it is important to study influences on developmental processes such as onset, persistence, escalation, and desistance. The focus is not only on offending when it is in full flow in the teenage years, but also the childhood precursors and adult sequelae. Because of the chapter's focus on human development, unchanging variables such as gender and ethnicity are not reviewed. Most criminological research has concentrated on offending by males, since this is generally more frequent and serious than offending by females (e.g. Farrington, 1987a). Hence, this chapter is primarily concerned with male offending.

In this short chapter, it is obviously impossible to review everything that is known about predictors and possible causes of delinquency (for more detailed reviews of risk factors, see Blackburn, 1993; Rutter & Giller, 1983; Wilson & Herrnstein, 1985). I will be very selective in focusing on some of the more important and replicable findings obtained in some of the more methodologically adequate studies: Especially prospective longitudinal follow-up studies of large community samples, with information from several data sources (e.g. the child, the parent, the teacher, official records) to maximise validity. I will refer especially to knowledge gained in the Cambridge Study in Delinquent Development, which is a prospective longitudinal survey of over 400 London males from age 8 to age 32 (e.g. Farrington & West, 1990; Farrington, 1995). Fortunately, results obtained in British longitudinal surveys of delinquency (e.g. Kolvin, Miller, Scott, Gatzanis, & Fleeting, 1990; Wadsworth, 1979) are highly concordant with those obtained in comparable surveys in North America (e.g. McCord, 1979; Robins, 1979), the Scandinavian countries (e.g. Pulkkinen, 1988; Wikström, 1987) and New Zealand (e.g. Fergusson, Horwood, & Lynskey, 1993; Moffitt & Silva, 1988a), and indeed with results obtained in British cross-sectional surveys (e.g. Boswell, 1995; Graham & Bowling, 1995; Hagell & Newburn, 1994).

THE NATURE AND EXTENT OF YOUTH CRIME

Definition and measurement

Antisocial behaviour covers a multitude of sins. It includes acts prohibited by the criminal law, such as theft, burglary, robbery, violence, vandalism, and drug use; the definition of youth crime in this chapter focuses on these types of acts. It also includes other clearly deviant acts, such as bullying, reckless driving, heavy drinking, and sexual promiscuity, and more marginally or arguably deviant acts, such as heavy smoking, heavy gambling, employment instability, and conflict with parents. All of these acts tend to be interrelated, in the sense that people who commit any one of them have a considerably increased risk of committing any of the others (West & Farrington, 1977).

Certain types of antisocial behaviour are used as diagnostic criteria for the psychiatric category of "conduct disorder" in the International Classification of Diseases of the World Health Organisation and in the Diagnostic and Statistical Manual of the American Psychiatric Association (see, for example, Robins, 1991). The major types are stealing, running away from home, lying, arson, truancy, burglary, vandalism, forced sex, fighting, robbery, and cruelty to people and animals. Conduct disorder is diagnosed when the disturbed behaviour includes at least two or three of the specified symptoms displayed in the previous year. Although this is usually termed "childhood conduct disorder", the diagnosis can be made up to age 17, and hence often reflects teenage antisocial behaviour.

Offending is commonly measured using either official records of arrests or convictions or self-reports of offending. The advantages and disadvantages of official records and self-reports are to some extent complementary. In general, official records include the worst offenders and the worst offences, whereas self-reports include more of the normal range of delinquent activity. Self-reports have the advantage of including undetected offences, but the disadvantages of concealment and forgetting. The key issue is whether the same results are obtained with both methods. For example, if official records and self-reports both show a link between parental supervision and delinquency, it is likely that supervision is related to delinquent behaviour (rather than to any biases in measurement). This chapter focuses on such replicable results.

In reviewing knowledge about youth crime in England and Wales, the focus is on the more serious "indictable" offences rather than the less serious "summary" offences (Barclay, 1995). The most important indictable offences are theft, burglary, robbery, violence, vandalism, fraud, and drug use, while the most important summary offences are motoring and drunkenness. Since 1 October 1992, youth crime in England and Wales (dealt with in the Youth Court) covers the years 10 to 17 inclusive; prior to that date, the maximum age for Juvenile Court processing was 16. Officially recorded juvenile offenders are either found guilty in court or cautioned. Although the minimum age of criminal responsibility is 10, few offenders under the age of 14 are found guilty in the Youth Court. In the United States, the focus is on arrests of juveniles (in most states, those under 18) for the "index" offences of homicide, rape, robbery, aggravated assault, burglary, motor vehicle theft, larceny, and arson.

Self-reports of offending reveal many more offences than official records, but not necessarily many more offenders. In the Cambridge Study, only 13 per cent of burglaries committed between ages 15 and 18 led to convictions, and only 6 per cent of vehicle thefts. However, 62 per cent of burglars were convicted of burglary at least once, and 38 per cent of vehicle thieves were convicted of this offence (West & Farrington, 1977, p. 28). Between ages 15 and 18, 11 per cent of the boys admitted burglary and 7 per cent were convicted of burglary, and 15 per cent admitted vehicle theft and 6 per cent were convicted of this offence. Hence, although self-reports revealed many more offences than official records of convictions, self-reports and official records agreed fairly well in estimating the prevalence of serious offenders.

Self-reports and official records agreed less well in estimating the prevalence of less serious offenders. In the Cambridge Study, 39 per cent of the boys admitted shoplifting between ages 10 and 14 and 16 per cent between ages 15 and 18, but the corresponding proportions convicted of shoplifting were 3 per cent and 2 per cent, respectively (Farrington, 1989b; this was before the widespread use of police cautioning in London). As many as 89 per cent of the boys admitted at least one indictable offence between ages 10 and 14, and 67 per cent between ages 15 and 18; but the corresponding proportions convicted were 11 per cent and 20 per cent, respectively. Generally, minor offending is very common, serious offending (such as burglary) is uncommon, and the most frequent and serious offenders are the ones who tend to get convicted (Farrington, 1973). To a considerable extent, the convicted boys are the worst self-reported offenders, and conclusions about characteristics of offenders based on convictions are very similar to those based on self-reports of offending (Farrington, 1992c).

Changes in youth crime over time

Recorded male juvenile offending has decreased markedly in England and Wales in the last 15 years. The number of boys per 100 aged 10 to 13 found guilty or cautioned decreased by 42 per cent between 1983 and 1993, and the decrease for 14- to 17-year-olds was 15 per cent. The number of girls per 100 aged 10 to 13 found guilty or cautioned decreased by 34 per cent, but the number aged 14 to 17 increased by 25 per cent (Home Office, 1994, table 5.24). The biggest decreases in recorded juvenile offenders were between 1985 and 1989. During these years, 10- to 13-year-old boys decreased by 40 per cent, 14- to 16-year-old boys by 31 per cent, 10- to 13-year-old girls by 60 per cent, and 14- to 16-year-old girls by 36 per cent (Home Office, 1990, table 5.22). Combining all 10- to 16-year-olds (the juvenile ages at that time), there was a 32 per cent decrease in recorded male juvenile offenders and a 44 per cent decrease in recorded female juvenile offenders between 1985 and 1989; remarkable decreases in a very short time period (Farrington, 1992d).

In the United States in the last 15 years, recorded juvenile violent crimes have increased, but recorded juvenile property crimes have not (Snyder & Sickmund, 1995; Snyder, Sickmund, & Poe-Yamagata, 1996). The biggest increase in violence was between 1988 and 1991, when there was a 38 per cent increase in the arrest rate. The juvenile arrest rate for homicide increased by an amazing 84 per cent between 1987 and 1991, but then remained constant up to 1994. In contrast, the juvenile arrest rate for burglary (like the number of recorded burglaries in the United States) has steadily decreased (e.g. by 44 per cent between 1975 and 1992).

Did the decrease in recorded juvenile offenders in England and Wales reflect a real decrease in juvenile offending? This seems highly unlikely. For example, burglary and vehicle theft are crimes typically committed by young people. Between 1981 and 1991, the rate of domestic burglary per household in England and Wales increased by 66 per cent according to the British Crime Survey (BCS) and by 63 per cent according to police-recorded offences (Farrington, Langan, & Wikstrom, 1994). The corresponding increases for the rate of vehicle theft were 65 per cent according to the BCS and 70 per cent according to the police. And yet, recorded juvenile offending (findings of guilt and cautions per 100 population) decreased by 22 per cent between 1981 and 1991 (Home Office, 1993, table 5.22). As another example, between 1985 and 1989, the number of recorded juvenile shoplifters decreased by 59 per cent, but the number of juvenile shoplifters apprehended by major stores and reported to the police did not change significantly (Farrington & Burrows, 1993).

In the light of the large increases in crimes reported by victims and crimes recorded by the police, it seems likely that the true prevalence of youth crime in England and Wales has increased in the last 15 years. Why, then, has there been a decrease in recorded juvenile offenders? Since 1985, police forces have increasingly begun to use informal (unrecorded) warnings and to take no further action with apprehended juveniles whom they believe to be guilty (Barclay, 1990), thereby eliminating them from the official records. Also, the introduction in 1986 of the Police and Criminal Evidence Act 1984, which provided increased safeguards for accused persons, caused a marked decrease in the number of detected offenders (Irving & MacKenzie, 1989).

The introduction in 1985 of the Crown Prosecution Service, which transferred responsibility for the prosecution of offenders from the police to lawyers, caused a decrease in the number of persons prosecuted; the number of discontinued or withdrawn cases increased from 21,300 in 1981 to 108,300 in 1991 (Home Office, 1993, table 6.2). The Criminal Justice Act 1988 downgraded the offence of unauthorised taking of a motor vehicle from the indictable to the summary category, thereby eliminating about 25,000 (mostly young) offenders from the statistics of recorded offenders. Consequently, the decrease in recorded juvenile offenders between 1985 and 1989 is attributable to procedural changes and is almost certainly illusory.

The Home Affairs Committee of the House of Commons (1993) tried to reconcile the increase in recorded crime with the decrease in recorded juvenile offenders by suggesting that there was an increasing number of persistent juvenile offenders. However, there is little hard evidence either about true changes in juvenile delinquency in England and Wales or about the most likely explanations for any such changes. In order to advance knowledge in the future, repeated surveys of nationally representative samples of juveniles are needed, which measure both self-reported offending and possible causal influences on offending. Repeated surveys of this kind have been carried out in the United States. For example, in the "Monitoring the Future" project, a nationally representative sample of American high school students is interviewed each year and asked about their delinquency and drug use (Johnson, O'Malley, & Bachman, 1987).

Setting aside a few questions in the British Crime Survey (Mayhew & Elliott, 1990), the first large-scale national self-reported delinquency survey was completed in England in 1993 (Bowling, Graham, & Ross, 1994). The first large-scale drugs survey was carried out in four areas: Bradford, Glasgow, Lewisham (London), and Nottingham, in 1992 (Leitner, Shapland, & Wiles, 1993). These kinds of surveys need to be repeated at intervals. It is very important that validity checks on the accuracy of the self-report data are carried out (e.g. by comparing them with official records of offending by the same people).

Natural history of offending

The prevalence of offending increases to a peak in the teenage years and then decreases in the twenties. This pattern is seen both cross-sectionally and longitudinally (Farrington, 1986a). The peak age of official offending (convictions plus cautions) for English males was 15 until 1987, but it increased to 18 in 1988 as a result of the decrease in detected juvenile shoplifting offenders (Barclay, 1990) and it remained at 18 until 1994 (Home Office, 1995). The peak age for females is 14. In England and Wales in 1994, the rate of findings of guilt or cautions of males for indictable offences increased from 0.5 per 100 at age 10 to 6.2 at age 15 and a peak of 8.9 at age 18, then decreased to 7.0 at age 20 and 1.6 at age 30–40 (Home Office, 1995, table 5.25). The corresponding figures for females were 0.1 per 100 at age 10, a peak of 2.1 at age 14, 1.6 at age 18, 1.2 at age 20, and 0.4 at age 30–40.

The cumulative or lifetime prevalence of convictions is much greater than most people realise. On the basis of 1977 figures, it was estimated that 44 per cent of males and 15 per cent of females in England and Wales would be convicted of "standard list" (nontraffic) offences during their lifetimes (Farrington, 1981). These estimates were later verified by a longitudinal follow-up of a 1953 birth cohort in official records (Home Office Statistical Bulletin, 1995); 34 per cent of males and 9 per cent of females were convicted of nontraffic offences up to age 39. Because of the decrease in conviction rates during the 1980s, the conviction figures for later cohorts would be somewhat lower, although cumulative prevalence would be greater if cautions were included.

In the Cambridge Study, the rate of convictions increased to a peak at age 17 and then declined (Farrington, 1992a). It was 1.7 per 100 males at age 10, 6.8 at age 13, 16.8 at age 17, 10.1 at age 22, and 4.2 at age 30. The median age for most types of offences (burglary, robbery, theft of and from vehicles, shoplifting) was 17, whereas it was 20 for violence and 21 for fraud. Using national data, Tarling (1993) found that peak ages varied from 14 for shoplifting to 17 for burglary, robbery and vehicle theft, 18 for violence and 20 for drugs and fraud.

Although the cumulative prevalence of convictions in the Cambridge Study was high (37 per cent up to age 32), it was nevertheless true that only 6 per cent of the sample—the chronic offenders—accounted for nearly half of all the convictions (Farrington & West, 1993). Similarly, chronic offenders were disproportionally likely to commit other types of antisocial behaviour. In numerous other projects, such as the Philadelphia cohort study of Wolfgang, Thornberry, and Figlio (1987) and the Finnish research of Pulkkinen (1988), there was a similar concentration of offending in a small proportion of the sample.

Self-report studies also show that the most common types of offending decline from the teens to the twenties. In the Cambridge Study, the prevalence of burglary, shoplifting, theft of and from vehicles, theft from slot machines, and vandalism all decreased from the teens to the twenties, but the same decreases were not seen for theft from work, assault, drug abuse, and fraud (Farrington, 1989b).

Many theories have been proposed to explain why offending peaks in the teenage years (see Farrington, 1986a). For example, offending has been linked to testosterone levels in males, which increase during adolescence and early adulthood and decrease thereafter, and to changes in physical abilities or opportunities for crime. The most popular explanation focuses on social influence. From birth, children are under the influence of their parents, who generally discourage offending. However, during their teenage years, young people gradually break away from the control of their parents and become influenced by their peers, who may encourage offending in many cases. After age 20, offending declines again as peer influence gives way to a new set of family influences hostile to offending, originating in spouses and cohabitees.

In the Cambridge Study, the peak age of onset (the first conviction) was at 14 (Farrington, 1992a). An early age of onset foreshadows a long criminal career and many offences (Home Office Statistical Bulletin, 1987). The males first convicted at the earliest ages (10–13) in the Cambridge Study tended to become the most persistent offenders, committing an average of 8.1 offences leading to convictions in an average criminal career lasting almost exactly 10 years up to age 32 (Farrington, 1992a). Those first convicted at age 10–11 had an average career length of 11.5 years. Over a quarter of all convicted males had criminal careers lasting longer than 10 years. The average duration of criminal careers declined precipitously from onset at age 16 (7.9 years) to onset at age 17 (2.9 years), suggesting that those males first convicted as juveniles were much more persistent offenders than those first convicted as adults. These results agree with Moffitt's (1993) theory suggesting that offenders can be divided into "life-course-persistent" ones with an early onset and a long criminal career and "adolescence-limited" ones with a later onset and a short criminal career.

Co-offending and motives for crime

Juveniles tend to commit their offences with others. In the Cambridge Study, about half of all offences were committed with (usually one or two) others, and the prevalence of co-offending decreased steadily from age 10 to age 32 (Reiss & Farrington, 1991). This was not because co-offenders had short criminal careers but because the boys changed from co-offending in their teenage years to lone offending in their twenties. Boys who committed their first offence with others tended to have a longer criminal career than those who committed their first offence alone.

Burglary, robbery, and theft from vehicles were especially likely to involve co-offenders. Generally, co-offenders were similar in age, gender, and ethnicity, and lived close to each other and to the locations of offences. Co-offending relationships tended not to persist for very long; rarely more than one year. About one-third of the most persistent offenders continually offended with less criminally experienced co-offenders, and hence appeared to be repeatedly recruiting others into a life of crime. Recruiting was especially common for burglary offences.

In the Cambridge Study, the most common motives given for property offences (46 per cent of self-reported offences, 43 per cent of offences leading to convictions) were utilitarian, rational, or economic ones: Offences were committed for material gain. This is concordant with the rational decision-making theory of Cornish and Clarke (1986). The next most common motives (31 per cent of self-reported offences, 22% of conviction offences) might be termed "hedonistic": offences were committed for excitement, for enjoyment, or to relieve boredom (West & Farrington, 1977). In general, utilitarian motives predominated for most types of property offences, such as burglary and theft, except that vandalism and motor vehicle theft were committed predominantly for hedonistic reasons, and shoplifting was partly utilitarian and partly hedonistic. Offences at younger ages (under 17) were relatively more likely to be committed for hedonistic reasons, whereas offences at older ages (17 or older) were relatively more likely to be committed for utilitarian reasons.

With regard to physical violence, the key dimension was whether the boy fought alone or in a group (Farrington, Berkowitz, & West, 1982). In individual fights, the boy was usually provoked, became angry, and hit out in order to hurt his opponent and to discharge his own internal feelings of tension. In group fights, the boy often said that he became involved in order to help a friend or because he was attacked, and rarely said that he was angry. The group fights were more serious, occurring in pubs or streets, and they were more likely to involve weapons, produce injuries, and lead to police intervention. Fights often occurred when minor incidents escalated, because both sides wanted to demonstrate their toughness and masculinity and were unwilling to react to perceived challenges in a conciliatory way.

Juvenile delinquency and antisocial behaviour

Juvenile delinquents are predominantly versatile rather than specialised in their offending (e.g. Klein, 1984; Farrington, Snyder, & Finnegan, 1988). In other words, people who commit one type of offence have a significant tendency also to commit other types. For example, 86 per cent of convicted violent offenders in the Cambridge Study also had convictions for nonviolent offences (Farrington, 1991b).

Just as young offenders tend to be versatile in their types of offending, they also tend to be versatile in their antisocial behaviour generally. The Cambridge Study shows that delinquency is only one element of a much larger syndrome of antisocial behaviour that tends to persist over time. For example, the boys who were convicted up to age 18 (most commonly for offences of dishonesty, such as burglary and theft) were significantly more deviant than the nondelinquents on almost every factor that we investigated at that age (West and Farrington, 1977). The convicted delinquents drank more beer, they got drunk more often, and they were more likely to say that drink made them violent. They smoked more cigarettes, they had started smoking at an earlier age, and they were more likely to be heavy gamblers. They were more likely to have been convicted for minor motoring offences, to have driven after drinking at least 10 units of alcohol (e.g. five pints of beer), and to have been injured in road accidents. The delinquents were more likely to have taken prohibited drugs, such as marijuana or LSD, although few of them had convictions for drug offences. Also, they were more likely to have had sexual intercourse, especially with a variety of different girls, and especially beginning at an early age, but they were less likely to use contraceptives.

The convicted delinquents at age 18 tended to hold relatively well-paid but low-status (unskilled manual) jobs, and they were more likely to have erratic work histories including periods of unemployment. They were more likely to be living away from home, and they tended not to get on well with their parents. They were more likely to be tattooed, possibly reflecting their "machismo" orientation. The delinquents were more likely to go out in the evenings, and were especially likely to spend time hanging about on the street. They tended to go around in groups of four or more, and were more likely to be involved in group violence or vandalism. They were much more likely to have been involved in fights, to have started fights, to have carried weapons, and to have used weapons in fights. They were also more likely to express aggressive and anti-establishment attitudes on a questionnaire (negative to police, school, rich people, and civil servants).

The convicted delinquents were also deviant in their schools. At age 8–10, before anyone was convicted, the future delinquents were more likely than nondelinquents to be rated as troublesome and dishonest in their primary schools; 45 per cent of troublesome boys at age 8–10 were convicted as juveniles, compared with 14 per cent of the remainder (Farrington, 1995). At age 14, when they were in their last year of compulsory schooling, the delinquents were rated by their teachers as aggressive and frequent liars, and they tended to admit bullying. Interestingly, the bullies at age 14 tended still to be bullies at age 32 and to report that their children were bullies (Farrington, 1993c).

Delinquents also tended to be truants, in both their primary and secondary schools (Farrington, 1996). Troublesome boys in the primary school tended to become truants in the secondary school. Generally, truants and delinquents were similar in childhood, adolescent, and adult features, but the most important difference was that truants, unlike delinquents, tended to be nervous. This suggested that, for some children, truancy was a behavioural symptom of a nervous–withdrawn temperament rather than of an antisocial personality, in agreement with the distinction between truancy and school refusal (Bools, Foster, Brown, & Berg, 1990).

These results are consistent with findings obtained in numerous other studies. For example, in a St. Louis survey, Robins and Ratcliff (1980) reported that juvenile delinquency tended to be associated with truancy, precocious sex, drinking, and drug use. In two American studies separated by 13 years, Donovan, Jessor, and Costa (1988) concluded that a single common factor accounted for the positive correlations among a number of adolescent antisocial behaviours, including problem drinking, marijuana use, precocious sexual intercourse, and delinquent behaviour. Hence, as R. Jessor and S. L. Jessor (1977) argued, there is a syndrome of problem behaviour in adolescence.

Continuity in offending

Despite the changes in prevalence with age, there is significant continuity between offending in one age range and offending in another. In the Cambridge Study, nearly three-quarters (73 per cent) of those convicted as juveniles at age 10–16 were reconvicted at age 17–24, in comparison with only 16 per cent of those not convicted as juveniles (Farrington, 1992a). Nearly half (45 per cent) of those convicted as juveniles were reconvicted at age 25–32, in comparison with only 8 per cent of those not convicted as juveniles. Furthermore, this continuity over time did not merely reflect continuity in police reaction to crime. Farrington (1989b) showed that, for 10 specified offences, the significant continuity between offending in one age range and offending in a later age range held for self-reports as well as official convictions.

Other studies (e.g. McCord, 1991) show similar continuity. For example, in Sweden, Stattin and Magnusson (1991) reported that nearly 70 per cent of males registered for crime before age 15 were registered again between ages 15 and 20, and nearly 60 per cent were registered between ages 21 and 29. Also, the number of juvenile offences is an effective predictor of the number of adult offences (Wolfgang et al., 1987). Farrington and Wikstrom (1994) showed that there was considerable continuity in offending between ages 10 and 25 in both London and Stockholm.

It is not always realised that relative continuity is quite compatible with absolute change. In other words, the relative ordering of people on some underlying construct such as criminal potential can remain significantly stable over time, even though the absolute level of criminal potential declines on average for everyone. For example, in the Cambridge Study, the prevalence of self-reported offending declined significantly between ages 18 and 32, but there was a significant tendency for the worst offenders at 18 also to be the worst offenders at 32 (Farrington, 1990a).

These results are in agreement with the idea that there tends to be persistence of an underlying "antisocial personality" from childhood to the teenage years and into adulthood. Robins (e.g. 1986) has consistently shown how a constellation of indicators of childhood antisocial behaviour predicts a constellation of indicators of adult antisocial behaviour. In several longitudinal studies, the number of different childhood symptoms predicted the number of different adult symptoms, rather than there being a linkage between any specific childhood and adult symptoms (Robins & Ratcliff, 1978, 1980; Robins & Wish, 1977). Numerous other studies also show that childhood conduct problems predict later offending and antisocial behaviour (e.g. Loeber & LeBlanc, 1990). For example, Spivack, Marcus, and Swift (1986) in Philadelphia discovered that troublesome behaviour in Kindergarten (age 3–4) predicted later police contacts; and Ensminger, Kellam, and Rubin (1983) in Chicago and Tremblay, Le Blanc, and Schwartzman (1988) in Montreal showed that ratings of aggressiveness by teachers and peers in the first grade (age 6–7) predicted self-reported offending at age 14–15.

Similarly, in the Cambridge Study there was evidence of continuity in antisocial behaviour from childhood to the teenage years. An antisocial personality scale at age 10 correlated 0.50 with the corresponding scale at age 14 and 0.38 with the scale at age 18 (Farrington, 1991a). The second best predictor of the antisocial tendency scale at age 18 was childhood troublesomeness (getting into trouble at school, e.g. for bad behaviour or laziness) at age 8–10, rated by peers and teachers (Farrington, 1993a); the best predictor was having a convicted parent by age 10. With regard to specific types of antisocial behaviour, troublesomeness was the only factor measured at age 8–10 that significantly predicted bullying at both ages 14 and 18 (Farrington, 1993c). Again, troublesomeness at age 8–10 was the best predictor of both truancy and aggression at age 12–14 in secondary schools (Farrington, 1980, 1989a).

There is also continuity in antisocial behaviour at younger ages. For example, Rose, Rose, and Feldman (1989) in New York City found that externalising scores on the Achenbach Child Behaviour Checklist (reflecting a broad-band antisocial syndrome; see Achenbach & Edelbrock, 1983), were significantly correlated ($r = 0.57$) between ages 2 and 5. Furthermore, a mother's ratings of her boy's difficult temperament at age 6 months significantly predicted his externalising scores at age 8 in the Bloomington longitudinal survey (Bates, Bayles, Bennett, Ridge, & Brown, 1991). It might possibly be argued that these kinds of relationships reflected the stability of the parent's personality rather than of the child's behaviour, but similar results are obtained even with different data sources (parents at an earlier age and teachers later). In Outer London, Richman, Stevenson, and Graham (1985) reported that behaviour problems tended to persist between ages 3 and 8, and in New Zealand White, Moffitt, Earls, Robins, and Silva (1990) showed that externalising scores and being difficult to manage at age 3 predicted antisocial behaviour at age 11. The fact that antisocial behaviour in the first few years of life predicts later antisocial behaviour and delinquency is a strong argument for concentrating prevention efforts around the time of the child's birth.

Developmental sequences

In studying development, it is important to investigate developmental sequences over time, for example, where one behaviour facilitates or acts as a kind of stepping stone to another. It is desirable to identify noncriminal behaviours that lead to criminal behaviours, and long-term developmental sequences including types of offending. For example, hyperactivity at age 2 may lead to cruelty to animals at 6, shoplifting at 10, burglary at 15, robbery at 20, and eventually spouse assault, child abuse and neglect, alcohol abuse, and employment and accommodation problems later on in life. Typically, a career of childhood antisocial behaviour leads to a criminal career, which often coincides with a career of teenage antisocial behaviour and leads to a career of adult antisocial behaviour. The criminal career is a legally defined subset of a longer-term and more wide-ranging antisocial career. A deeper understanding of the development of the criminal career requires a deeper understanding of the wider antisocial career.

It is important to investigate developmental sequences in antisocial and criminal careers. In a study of Montreal delinquents, LeBlanc and Frechette (1989) discovered that shoplifting and vandalism tended to occur before adolescence (average age of onset 11), burglary and motor vehicle theft in adolescence (average onset 14–15), and sex offences and drug trafficking in the later teenage years (average onset 17–19). With regard to other types of antisocial behaviour, Loeber, Green, Lahey, Christ, and Frick (1992), on the basis of retrospective reports by parents of clinic-referred boys, found that rule-breaking at home tended to occur at a median age of onset of 4.5 years, then cruelty to animals (5.0), bullying (5.5), lying, stealing, fighting (6.0), vandalism (6.5), and eventually burglary (10.0).

Loeber et al. (1993) proposed that there were three different developmental pathways for antisocial behaviour, which they labelled "overt, covert, and authority conflict". The overt pathway specified an escalation from minor aggression to fighting and violence, the covert pathway specified an escalation from lying to theft and burglary, and the authority conflict pathway specified an escalation from stubbornness to disobedience and truancy. The frequency of occurrence of any particular behaviour predicted the likelihood of transition to a more serious level. Three types of behavioural sequences can be distinguished (see Farrington et al., 1990a). First of all, different acts following each other may be different behavioural manifestations of the same underlying construct (e.g. antisocial personality) at different ages. Second, different acts may be different behavioural manifestations of the same or similar underlying constructs at different ages and also part of a developmental sequence, where one act is a stepping stone to or facilitates another (e.g. where smoking cigarettes leads to marijuana use). Third, different acts may be indicators of different constructs and part of a causal sequence, where changes in an indicator of one construct cause changes in an indicator of a different construct (e.g. where school failure leads to truancy).

MODIFIABLE RISK FACTORS FOR YOUTH CRIME

A great deal is known about risk factors for youth crime. In contrast, less is known about protective factors, which cannot be reviewed here because of lack of space. Loeber reviewed extensively risk factors for male offending (Loeber & Dishion, 1983; Loeber & Stouthamer-Loeber, 1987), and found that the most important predictors were poor parental child management techniques, childhood antisocial behaviour, offending by parents and siblings, low intelligence and low educational attainment, and separation from parents. In contrast, low socioeconomic status was a rather weak predictor. All these factors will be reviewed here, focusing especially on results obtained in prospective longitudinal surveys.

Prospective longitudinal surveys are needed because of the retrospective bias in cross-sectional surveys. For example, if parents of delinquents are asked about the methods of child rearing that they used, their recollections will be biased by the knowledge that their child has become a delinquent. In contrast, in prospective longitudinal surveys, methods of child rearing are measured contemporaneously, before anyone becomes a delinquent. Also, in cross-sectional surveys it is impossible to establish what came first, and what caused what. For example, it is hard to know whether poor parental supervision caused childhood conduct problems, or whether parents gave up trying to supervise in the face of the child's troublesome behaviour.

Also, although cross-sectional surveys can (and do) demonstrate that delinquents disproportionally come from deprived backgrounds, they cannot specify what proportion of children from deprived backgrounds did not become delinquents, or what protective factors might have prevented the development of delinquency. In addition, repeated contacts over time in longitudinal surveys can help to maximise validity, because mistaken assessments in one interview might be detected in a later interview.

It is often difficult to decide if any given risk factor is a cause of delinquency or an indicator (symptom) of the same underlying antisocial tendency. For example, do heavy drinking, truancy, unemployment, and divorce measure antisocial tendency, or do they cause (an increase in) it? It is not unreasonable to argue that some factors may be both symptomatic and causal. For example, long-term variations *between* individuals in antisocial tendency may be reflected in variations in alcohol consumption, just as short-term variations *within* individuals in alcohol consumption may cause more antisocial behaviour during the heavier drinking periods. My review of risk factors is restricted to those that are not indicators of antisocial behaviour, and hence to those that may have causal effects on youth crime.

Prenatal and perinatal factors

At least in Western industrialised countries, early child bearing, or teenage pregnancy, predicts many undesirable outcomes for the children, including low school attainment, antisocial school behaviour, substance use, and early sexual intercourse (Furstenberg, Brooks-Gunn, & Morgan, 1987a, b). The children of teenage mothers are also more likely to become offenders. For example, Morash and Rucker (1989) analysed results from four surveys in the United States and England (including the Cambridge Study) and found that teenage mothers were associated with low income families, welfare support and absent biological fathers, that they used poor child-rearing methods, and that their children were characterised by low school attainment and delinquency. However, the presence of the biological father mitigated many of these adverse factors and generally had a protective effect. In the Newcastle Thousand Family Study, Kolvin, Miller, Scott, Gatzanis, and Fleeting (1990) reported that mothers who married as teenagers (a factor strongly related to teenage child bearing) were twice as likely as others to have sons who became offenders by age 32 (49 per cent as opposed to 23 per cent).

Substance use (smoking, drinking, and drug use) in pregnancy is also associated with the later undesirable development of children. For example, Streissguth (1986) showed that smoking in pregnancy was associated with low birth weight, small height, and low school attainment of children. Steinhausen, Willms, and Spohr (1993) found that excessive alcohol consumption in pregnancy predicted hyperactivity, low intelligence, and speech disorders of children. Trad (1993) reported that infants of cocaine-abusing mothers tended to have low birth weight and small head circumference, and to be small for their gestational age. Of course, none of these results necessarily prove causal effects; for example, smoking and low school attainment could both be caused by a deprived background.

A low birth weight, a relatively small baby, and perinatal complications (such as forceps delivery, asphyxia, a long duration of labour, or toxaemia in pregnancy) also predict later conduct problems and delinquency of children, although the low prevalence of such complications in representative community samples makes it difficult to establish their effects. Also the effects of perinatal complications depend on other factors such as the quality of the home environment. For example, Kolvin et al. (1990) in Newcastle-upon-Tyne found that neonatal injuries significantly predicted offending up to age 32 only for boys who were in deprived families (low income or disrupted) at age 5. In Dunedin (New Zealand), McGee, Silva, and Williams (1984) reported that children who were small at birth for their gestational age significantly tended to be badly behaved at age 7, especially if they were also exposed to family adversities.

Hyperactivity and impulsivity

These are among the most important individual difference factors that predict later delinquency. Hyperactivity usually begins before age 5 and often before age 2, and it tends to persist into adolescence (Taylor, 1986). It is associated with restlessness, impulsivity, and a short attention span, and for that reason has been termed the "hyperactivity–impulsivity–attention deficit" or HIA syndrome (Loeber, 1987). Related concepts include a poor ability to defer gratification (Mischel, Shoda, & Rodriguez, 1989) and a short future time perspective (Stein, Sarbin, & Kulik, 1968).

Many investigators have reported a link between hyperactivity or impulsivity and offending. For example, in a Swedish longitudinal survey, Klinteberg, Andersson, Magnusson, and Stattin (1993) found that hyperactivity at 13 (rated by teachers) predicted violent offending up to age 26. Satterfield (1987) tracked hyperactive and matched control boys in Los Angeles between ages 9 and 17, and showed that six times as many of the hyperactive boys were arrested for serious offences. In the most extensive study using 11 different impulsivity measures in the Pittsburgh Youth

Study, White et al. (1994) found that behavioural impulsivity (e.g. restlessness) was more strongly related to delinquency than was cognitive impulsivity (e.g. poor planning), which was more closely linked to intelligence.

In the Cambridge Study, a combined measure of HIA was developed at age 8–10, and it significantly predicted juvenile convictions independently of conduct problems at age 8–10 (Farrington, Loeber, & Van Kammen, 1990b). Hence, HIA is not merely another measure of antisocial personality, but it is a possible cause, or an earlier stage in a developmental sequence leading to delinquency. For example, in Outer London, Richman et al. (1985) found that restlessness at age 3 predicted conduct disorder at age 8. Similar constructs to hyperactivity, such as sensation seeking, are also related to delinquency (Farley & Sewell, 1976; White, Labouvie, & Bates, 1985). In the Cambridge Study, the extent to which the boy was daring or took risks at age 8–10, as rated by parents and peers, significantly predicted his convictions up to age 32 independently of all other factors (Farrington, 1990b, 1993a); 57 per cent of daring boys were later convicted. Also, poor concentration or restlessness was the most important predictor of convictions for violence (Farrington, 1994a). It has been suggested that HIA might be a behavioural consequence of a low level of physiological arousal. Offenders have a low level of arousal according to their low alpha (brain) waves on the electroencephalogram (EEG), or according to autonomic nervous system indicators such as heart rate, blood pressure, or skin conductance, or they show low autonomic reactivity (e.g. Venables & Raine, 1987). Heart rate was measured in the Cambridge Study at age 18. In agreement with the low arousal theory, a low heart rate correlated significantly with convictions for violence (Farrington, 1987b), although it was not significantly related to convictions in general.

Gottfredson and Hirschi's (1990) theory emphasises impulsivity. Their key individual difference factor is low self-control, which refers to the extent to which individuals are vulnerable to the temptations of the moment. People with low self-control are impulsive, take risks, have low cognitive and academic skills, are egocentric, have low empathy, and have short time horizons. Hence, they find it hard to defer gratification and their decisions to offend are insufficiently influenced by the possible future painful consequences of offending.

Intelligence and attainment

Low intelligence is an important predictor of offending, and it can be measured very early in life. For example, in a prospective longitudinal survey of about 120 Stockholm males, low intelligence measured at age 3 significantly predicted officially recorded offending up to age 30 (Stattin &

Klackenberg-Larsson, 1993). Frequent offenders (with four or more offences) had an average IQ of 88 at age 3, whereas nonoffenders had an average IQ of 101. All these results held up after controlling for social class. Also, in the Perry preschool project in Michigan, low intelligence at age 4 significantly predicted the number of arrests up to age 27 (Schweinhart, Barnes, & Weikart, 1993).

In the Cambridge Study, twice as many of the boys scoring 90 or less on a nonverbal intelligence test (Raven's Progressive Matrices) at age 8–10 were convicted as juveniles as of the remainder (West & Farrington, 1973). However, it was difficult to disentangle low intelligence and low school attainment. Low nonverbal intelligence was highly correlated with low verbal intelligence (vocabulary, word comprehension, verbal reasoning) and with low school attainment, and all of these measures predicted juvenile convictions to much the same extent. In addition to their poor school performance, delinquents tended to leave school at the earliest possible age (which was then 15) and to take no school examinations.

Low nonverbal intelligence was especially characteristic of the juvenile recidivists and those first convicted at the earliest ages (10–13). Furthermore, low nonverbal intelligence predicted juvenile self-reported offending to almost exactly the same degree as juvenile convictions (Farrington, 1992c), suggesting that the link between low intelligence and delinquency was not caused by the less intelligent boys having a greater probability of being caught. Also, measures of intelligence and attainment predicted measures of offending independently of other variables, such as family income and family size; 53 per cent of boys with low nonverbal intelligence (90 or less) at age 8–10 were convicted up to age 32 (Farrington, 1990b). Similar results have been obtained in other projects (Lynam, Moffitt, & Southamer-Loeber, 1993; Moffitt & Silva, 1988a; Wilson & Herrnstein, 1985). Delinquents often do better on nonverbal performance tests, such as object assembly and block design, than on verbal tests (Walsh, Petee, & Beyer, 1987), suggesting that they find it easier to deal with concrete objects than with abstract concepts.

Intelligence may lead to delinquency through the intervening factor of school failure, as Hirschi and Hindelang (1977) suggested. The association between school failure and offending has been demonstrated consistently in longitudinal surveys (Maguin & Loeber, 1996; Polk et al., 1981; Wolfgang, Figlio, & Sellin, 1972). However, a more plausible explanatory factor underlying the link between intelligence and offending is the ability to manipulate abstract concepts. People who are poor at this tend to do badly in intelligence tests, such as the Matrices, and in school attainment, and they also tend to commit offences, mainly because of their poor ability to foresee the consequences of their offending and to appreciate the feelings of victims (i.e. their low empathy). Wilson and Herrnstein's (1985) theory suggested that criminal behaviour depended on the extent to which people were influenced by immediate as opposed to delayed consequences, and related this to intelligence and the ability to think about or plan for the future.

Modern research is studying not just intelligence but also detailed patterns of cognitive and neuropsychological deficit. For example, in a New Zealand longitudinal study of over 1000 children from birth to age 15, Moffitt and Silva (1988b) found that self-reported offending was related to verbal, memory, and visual–motor integration deficits, independently of low social class and family adversity. Neuropsychological research might lead to important advances in knowledge about the link between brain functioning and delinquency. For example, the "executive functions" of the brain, located in the frontal lobes, include sustaining attention and concentration, abstract reasoning and concept formation, anticipation and planning, self-monitoring of behaviour, and inhibition of inappropriate or impulsive behaviour (Moffitt, 1990). Deficits in these executive functions are conducive to low measured intelligence and to offending. Moffitt and Henry (1989) found deficits in these executive functions especially for delinquents who were both antisocial and hyperactive.

Parental supervision, discipline, and attitude

Many studies report a link between delinquency and parental supervision, discipline and attitude. In a Birmingham survey, Wilson (1980) followed up nearly 400 boys in 120 large intact families, and concluded that the most important correlate of convictions, cautions, and self-reported delinquency was lax parental supervision at age 10. In their English national survey of juveniles aged 14–15 and their mothers, Riley and Shaw (1985) found that poor parental supervision was the most important correlate of self-reported delinquency for girls, and that it was the second most important for boys (after delinquent friends). Also, in their follow-up of nearly 700 Nottingham children in intact families, J. Newson and E. Newson (1989) reported that physical punishment by parents at ages 7 and 11 predicted later convictions.

In the Cambridge Study, harsh or erratic parental discipline; cruel, passive, or neglecting parental attitude; poor supervision; and parental conflict; all measured at age 8, all predicted later juvenile convictions (West & Farrington, 1973). Generally, the presence of any of these adverse family background features doubled the risk of a later juvenile conviction. Furthermore, poor parental child-rearing behaviour (a combination of discipline, attitude, and conflict) and poor parental supervision both predicted juvenile self-reported as well as official offending (Farrington, 1979). Poor parental child-rearing behaviour was related to early rather than later offending, and it predicted early convictions between ages 10 and 13 independently of all other factors (Farrington, 1984, 1986b). However, it was not characteristic of those first convicted as adults (West & Farrington, 1977). In contrast, poor parental supervision predicted both juvenile and adult convictions (Farrington, 1992b); 55 per cent of boys who were poorly supervised at age 8 were convicted up to age 32 (Farrington, 1990b).

There seems to be significant intergenerational transmission of aggressive and violent behaviour from parents to children, as Widom (1989) found in a retrospective study of over 900 abused children in Indianapolis. Children who were physically abused up to age 11 were significantly likely to become violent offenders in the next 15 years. Similarly, harsh discipline and attitude of parents when the boys were aged 8 predicted later violent as opposed to nonviolent offenders up to age 21 in the Cambridge Study (Farrington, 1978). More recent research (Farrington, 1991b) showed that harsh discipline and attitude predicted both violent and persistent offending up to age 32. The extensive review by Malinosky-Rummell and Hansen (1993) confirms that being physically abused as a child predicts later violent and nonviolent offending.

Parental criminality

Criminal, antisocial and alcoholic parents tend to have delinquent sons, as Robins (1979) showed. Robins, West, and Herjanic (1975) followed up over 200 males in St. Louis and found that arrested parents tended to have arrested children, and that the juvenile records of the parents and children had similar rates and types of offences. McCord (1977) in her 30-year follow-up of about 250 treated boys in the Cambridge–Somerville study, also reported that convicted fathers tended to have convicted sons. Whether there is a specific relationship in her study between types of convictions of parents and children is not clear. McCord found that 29 per cent of fathers convicted for violence had sons convicted for violence, in comparison with 12 per cent of other fathers, but this may reflect the general tendency for convicted fathers to have convicted sons rather than any specific tendency for violent fathers to have violent sons. Wilson (1987) in Birmingham also showed that convictions of parents predicted convictions and cautions of sons; more than twice as many sons of convicted parents were themselves convicted.

In the Cambridge Study, the concentration of offending in a small number of families was remarkable. Less than 6 per cent of the families were responsible for half of the criminal convictions of all members (fathers, mothers, sons, and daughters) of all 400 families (Farrington, Barnes, & Lambert, 1996). Having a convicted mother, father, brother or sister significantly predicted a boy's own convictions. Furthermore, convicted parents and delinquent siblings were related to self-reported as well as to official offending (Farrington, 1979).

Unlike most early precursors, a convicted parent was related less to offending of early onset (age 10–13) than to later offending (Farrington, 1986b). Also, a convicted parent predicted which juvenile offenders went on to become adult criminals and which recidivists at age 19 continued offending rather than desisted (West & Farrington, 1977), and predicted convictions up to age 32 independently of all other factors (Farrington, 1990b, 1993a). As many as 59 per cent of boys with a convicted parent were themselves convicted up to age 32 (Farrington, 1990b).

It is not entirely clear why criminal parents tend to have delinquent children. In the Cambridge Study, there was no evidence that criminal parents directly encouraged their children to commit crimes or taught them criminal techniques. On the contrary, criminal parents were highly critical of their children's offending; for example, 89 per cent of convicted men at age 32 disagreed with the statement that: "I would not mind if my son/daughter committed a criminal offence". Also, it was extremely rare for a parent and a child to be convicted for an offence committed together (Reiss & Farrington, 1991).

There was some evidence that having a convicted parent increased a boy's likelihood of being convicted, over and above his actual level of misbehaviour (West & Farrington, 1977). However, the fact that a convicted parent predicted self-reported offending as well as convictions shows that the labelling of children from known criminal families was not the only reason for the intergenerational transmission of criminality. The main link in the chain between criminal parents and delinquent children that was discovered in the Cambridge Study was the markedly poor supervision by criminal parents.

These results are concordant with the theory (e.g. Trasler, 1962) that antisocial behaviour develops when the normal social learning process, based on rewards and punishments from parents, is disrupted by erratic discipline, poor supervision, parental disharmony, and unsuitable (antisocial or criminal) parental models. Hirschi's (1969) theory is somewhat similar, focusing on the importance of attachment to conventional parents and parent–child relations in building up a strong bond to society. However, some part of the link between antisocial parents and antisocial children may reflect genetic transmission (Mednick, Gabrielli, & Hutchings, 1983).

Broken homes and separations

Most studies of broken homes have focused on the loss of the father rather than the mother, simply because the loss of a father is much more common. McCord (1982) in Boston carried out an interesting study of the relationship between homes broken by loss of the natural father and later serious offending of the children. She found that the prevalence of offending was high for boys reared in broken homes without affectionate mothers (62 per cent) and for those reared in united homes characterised by parental conflict (52 per cent), irrespective of whether they had affectionate mothers. The prevalence of offending was low for those reared in united homes without conflict (26 per cent) and—importantly—equally low for boys from broken homes with affectionate mothers (22 per cent). These results suggest that it is not so much the broken home that is criminogenic as the parental conflict which often causes it, and that a loving mother might in some sense be able to compensate for the loss of a father.

In the Newcastle Thousand Family Study, Kolvin, Miller, Fleeting, and Kolvin (1988) reported that marital disruption (divorce or separation) in a boy's first five years predicted his later convictions up to age 32. Similarly, in the Dunedin study in New Zealand, Henry, Moffitt, Robins, Earls, and Silva (1993) found that children who were exposed to parental discord and many changes of the primary caretaker tended to become antisocial and delinquent.

The cause of the broken home is emphasised in the English national longitudinal survey of over 5000 children born in one week of 1946 (Wadsworth, 1979). Illegitimate children were excluded from this survey, so all the children began life with two married parents. Boys from homes broken by divorce or separation had an increased likelihood of being convicted or officially cautioned up to age 21, in comparison with those from homes broken by death or from unbroken homes. Homes broken when the boy was between birth and age 4 especially predicted delinquency, while homes broken when the boy was between age 11 and age 15 were not particularly criminogenic. Remarriage (which happened more often after divorce or separation than after death) was also associated with an increased risk of delinquency, suggesting a possible negative effect of step-parents. The meta-analysis by Wells and Rankin (1991) also shows that broken homes are more strongly related to delinquency when they are caused by parental separation or divorce rather than by death.

In the Cambridge Study, both permanent and temporary separations before age 10 (usually from the father) predicted convictions and self-reported delinquency, providing that they were not caused by death or hospitalisation (Farrington, 1992c). However, homes broken at an early age (under age 5) were not unusually criminogenic (West & Farrington, 1973). Separation before age 10 predicted both juvenile and adult convictions (Farrington, 1992b) and predicted convictions up to age 32 independently of all other factors, such as low family income or poor school attainment (Farrington, 1990b, 1993a); 56 per cent of separated boys were convicted.

In a survey of over 1000 adults carried out for the *Sunday Times* (14 November 1993), the majority (63 per cent) thought that it was vital for a child to grow up with both a mother and a father. Indeed, growing up in a single-parent, female-headed household is an important predictor of offending in American research (e.g. Ensminger et al., 1983). In Canada, the large-scale Ontario Child Health Study of 3300 children aged 4–16 reported that single-parent families tended to have conduct-disordered and substance-abusing children (Boyle & Offord, 1986; Blum, Boyle, & Offord, 1988). However, the researchers found it difficult to disentangle the effects of single-parent families from the effects of low income families, because most single-parent families were living in poverty. The analyses of Morash and Rucker (1989) suggest that women who have children as teenagers and then become lone mothers are particularly likely to have delinquent children.

Large family size

Many studies show that large families predict delinquency (Fischer, 1984). For example, in the National Survey of Health and Development, Wadsworth (1979) found that the percentage of boys who were officially delinquent increased from 9 per cent for families containing one child to 24 per cent for families containing four or more children. The Newsons in their Nottingham study also concluded that large family size was one of the most important predictors of offending (Newson et al., 1993).

In the Cambridge Study, if a boy had four or more siblings by his tenth birthday, this doubled his risk of being convicted as a juvenile (West & Farrington, 1973). Large family size predicted self-reported delinquency as well as convictions (Farrington, 1979), and adult as well as juvenile convictions (Farrington, 1992b). Large family size was the most important independent predictor of convictions up to age 32 in a logistic regression analysis (Farrington, 1993a); 58 per cent of boys from large families were convicted up to this age.

There are many possible reasons why a large number of siblings might increase the risk of delinquency. Generally, as the number of children in a family increases, the amount of parental attention that can be given to each child decreases. Also, as the number of children increases, the household will tend to become overcrowded, possibly leading to increases in frustration, irritation, and conflict. In the Cambridge Study, large family size did not predict delinquency for boys living in the least crowded conditions, with two or more rooms than there were children (West & Farrington, 1973). More than 20 years earlier, Ferguson (1952) drew a similar conclusion in his study of over 1300 Glasgow boys, suggesting that an overcrowded household might be an important intervening factor between large family size and delinquency. Another possible reason is that delinquent siblings are more likely to act as deviant models in large families (Brownfield & Sorenson, 1994), and in the Cambridge Study a boy's delinquency was more closely related to having delinquent older siblings than delinquent younger ones (Farrington et al., 1996).

Socioeconomic deprivation

Most delinquency theories assume that offenders disproportionally come from lower class social backgrounds, and aim to explain why this is so. For example, Cohen (1955) proposed that lower class boys found it hard to succeed according to the middle class standards of the school, partly because lower class parents tended not to teach their children to delay immediate gratification in favour of long-term goals. Consequently, lower class boys joined delinquent subcultures by whose standards they could succeed. Cloward and Ohlin (1960) argued that lower class children could not achieve universal goals of status and material wealth by legitimate means and consequently had to resort to illegitimate means.

Generally, the social class or socioeconomic status (SES) of a family has been measured primarily according to rankings of the occupational prestige of the family breadwinner. Persons with professional or managerial jobs are ranked in the highest class, whereas those with unskilled manual jobs are ranked in the lowest. However, these occupational prestige scales may not correlate very highly with real differences between families in socioeconomic circumstances. The scales often date from many years ago, when it was more common for the father to be the family breadwinner and for the mother to be a housewife. Because of this, it may be difficult to derive a realistic measure of SES for a family with a single parent or with two working parents (Mueller and Parcel, 1981).

Beginning with the pioneering self-report research of Short and Nye (1957), it was common in the United States to argue that low SES was related to official offending but not to self-reported offending, and hence that the official processing of offenders by police and courts was biased against lower class youth. However, British studies have reported more consistent links between low social class and offending. In the English National Survey, Douglas, Ross, Hammond, and Mulligan (1966) showed that the prevalence of official juvenile delinquency of boys varied considerably according to the occupational prestige and educational background of their parents, from 3 per cent in the highest category to 19 per cent in the lowest.

Numerous indicators of SES were measured in the Cambridge Study, both for the Study boy's family of origin and for the boy himself as an adult, including occupational prestige, family income, housing, and employment instability. Most of the measures of occupational prestige (based on the Registrar General's scale) were not significantly related to offending. However, in a reversal of the American results, low SES of the family when the boy was aged 8–10 significantly predicted his later self-reported but not his official delinquency. More consistently, low family income and poor housing predicted official and self-reported, juvenile and adult, offending (Farrington, 1992b, c).

Socioeconomic deprivation of parents is usually compared with offending by children. However, when the children grow up, their own socioeconomic deprivation can be related to their own offending. In the Cambridge Study, official and self-reported delinquents tended to have unskilled manual jobs and an unstable job record at age 18. Between ages 15 and 18, the Study boys were convicted at a higher rate when they were unemployed than when they were employed (Farrington, Gallagher, Morley, St Ledger, & West, 1986), suggesting that unemployment in some way causes crime, and conversely that employment may lead to desistance from offending. Because crimes involving material gain (e.g. theft, burglary, robbery) especially increased during periods of unemployment, it seems likely that financial need is an important link in the causal chain between unemployment and crime.

It was interesting that the peak age of offending, at 17–18, coincided with the peak age of affluence for many convicted males. In the Cambridge Study, convicted males tended to come from low income families at age 8 and later tended to have low incomes themselves at age 32. However, at age 18, they were relatively well paid in comparison with nondelinquents. Whereas convicted delinquents might be working as unskilled labourers on building sites and getting the full adult wage for this job, nondelinquents might be in poorly paid jobs with prospects, such as bank clerks, or might still be students. These results show that the link between income and offending is quite complex.

Peer influences

The reviews by Zimring (1981) and Reiss (1988) show that delinquent acts tend to be committed in small groups (of two or three people, usually) rather than alone. Large gangs are comparatively unusual. The major problem of interpretation is whether young people are more likely to commit offences while they are in groups than while they are alone, or whether the high prevalence of co-offending merely reflects the fact that, whenever young people go out, they tend to go out in groups. Do peers tend to encourage and facilitate offending, or is it just that most kinds of activities out of the home (both delinquent and nondelinquent) tend to be committed in groups? Another possibility is that the commission of offences encourages association with other delinquents, perhaps because "birds of a feather flock together" or because of the stigmatising and isolating effects of court appearances and institutionalisation.

It is surprisingly difficult to decide among the various possibilities, although most researchers argue that peer influence is an important factor. In the Rochester Youth Development Study, Thornberry, Lizotte, Krohn, Farnworth, and Jang (1994) concluded that associating with delinquent peers led to an increase in delinquency and also that engaging in delinquency led to an increased association with delinquent peers. Similar conclusions were drawn by Elliott and Menard (1996) in the US National Youth Survey, although they found that the influence of delinquent peers on delinquency was stronger than the reverse effect. Peer (and family) influences are emphasised in Sutherland and Cressey's (1974) theory, which suggests that a child's delinquency depends on the number of persons in the immediate social environment with norms and attitudes favouring delinquency.

There is clearly a close relationship between the delinquent activities of a boy and those of his friends. Both in the United States (Hirschi, 1969) and in the United Kingdom (West & Farrington, 1973), it has been found that a boy's reports of his own offending are significantly related to his reports of his friends' delinquency. In the National Youth Survey, having delinquent peers was the best independent predictor of self-reported offending in a multivariate analysis (Elliott, Huizinga, & Ageton, 1985). However, it is unclear how far this association reflects co-offending. In the same survey, Warr (1993) found that the importance of delinquent friends was lessened or eliminated by spending time with family members.

In the Cambridge Study, association with delinquent friends at age 14 was an important independent predictor of convictions at the young adult ages (Farrington, 1986b). Also, the recidivists at age 19 who ceased offending differed from those who persisted, in that the desisters were more likely to have stopped going round in a group of male friends. Furthermore, spontaneous comments by the youths indicated that withdrawal from the delinquent peer group was seen as an important influence on ceasing to offend (West & Farrington, 1977). Therefore, continuing to associate with delinquent friends may be a key factor in determining whether juvenile delinquents persist in offending as young adults or desist.

Delinquent peers are likely to be most influential where they have high status within the peer group and are popular. However, studies both in the United States (Roff & Wirt, 1984) and in the United Kingdom (West & Farrington, 1973) show that delinquents are usually unpopular with their peers. It seems paradoxical for offending to be a group phenomenon facilitated by peer influence, and yet for offenders to be largely rejected by other adolescents (Parker & Asher, 1987). However, it may be that offenders are popular in antisocial groups and unpopular in prosocial groups, or that rejected children band together to form adolescent delinquent groups (Cairns, Cairns, Neckerman, Gest, & Gariepy, 1988).

School influences

It is clear that the prevalence of offending varies dramatically between different secondary schools, as Power et al. (1967) showed many years ago in London. Characteristics of high delinquency-rate schools are well known (Graham, 1988). For example, such schools have high levels of distrust between teachers and students, low commitment to school by students, and unclear and inconsistently enforced rules. However, what is far less clear is how much of the variation between schools should be attributed to differences in school organisation, climate, and practices, and how much to differences in the composition of the student body.

In the Cambridge Study, the effects of secondary schools on offending were investigated by following boys from their primary schools to their secondary schools (Farrington, 1972). The best primary school predictor of juvenile offending was the rating of the boy's troublesomeness at age 8–10 by peers and teachers, showing the continuity in antisocial behaviour. The secondary schools differed dramatically in their official offending rates, from one school with 21 court appearances per 100 boys per year to another where the corresponding figure was only 0.3. Moreover, going to a high delinquency-rate secondary school was a significant predictor of later convictions (Farrington, 1993a).

It was, however, very noticeable that the most troublesome boys tended to go to the high delinquency-rate schools whereas the least troublesome boys tended to go to the low delinquency-rate schools. Furthermore, it was clear that most of the variation between schools in their delinquency rates could be explained by differences in their intakes of troublesome boys. The secondary schools themselves had only a very small effect on the boys' offending.

The most famous study of school effects on offending was also carried out in London, by Rutter, Maughan, Mortimore, and Ouston (1979). They studied 12 comprehensive schools, and again found big differences in official delinquency rates between them. High delinquency-rate schools tended to have high truancy rates, low ability pupils, and low social class parents. However, the differences between the schools in delinquency rates could not be entirely explained by differences in the social class and verbal reasoning scores of the pupils at intake (age 11). Therefore, they must have been caused by some aspect of the schools themselves or by other, unmeasured factors.

In trying to discover which aspects of schools might be encouraging or inhibiting offending, Rutter et al. (1979) developed a measure of "school process" based on school structure, organisation, and functioning. This was related to children's misbehaviour in school, academic achievement and truancy independently of intake factors. However, it was not significantly related to delinquency independently of intake factors. The main school factors that were associated with delinquency were a high amount of punishment and a low amount of praise given by teachers in class. Unfortunately, it is difficult to know whether much punishment and little praise are causes or consequences of antisocial school behaviour, which in turn is probably linked to offending outside school. Therefore, it is not clear what school factors are conducive to delinquency.

EXPLAINING THE DEVELOPMENT OF OFFENDING

In explaining the development of offending, a major problem is that most risk factors tend to coincide and tend to be interrelated. For example, adolescents living in physically deteriorated and socially disorganised neighbourhoods disproportionally tend also to come from families with poor parental supervision and erratic parental discipline and tend also to have high impulsivity and low intelligence. The concentration and co-occurrence of these kinds of adversities makes it difficult to establish their independent, interactive, and sequential influences on offending and antisocial behaviour.

A first step is to establish which factors predict offending independently of other factors. In the Cambridge Study, it was generally true that each of six categories of variables (impulsivity, intelligence, parenting, antisocial family, socioeconomic deprivation, child antisocial behaviour) predicted offending independently of each other category (Farrington, 1990b; 1993a). Any theory needs to give priority to explaining these results.

The modern trend (e.g. Catalano & Hawkins, 1996; Elliott et al., 1985; Pearson & Weiner, 1985) is to try to achieve increased explanatory power by integrating propositions derived from several earlier theories. My own theory of offending and antisocial behaviour (Farrington, 1986b, 1992c, 1993b) is also integrative. It contains elements of Cohen's (1955) status frustration–delinquent subculture theory, Cloward and Ohlin's (1960) opportunity–strain theory, Trasler's (1962) social learning theory, Hirschi's

(1969) control–social bonding theory, Sutherland and Cressey's (1974) differential association theory, Wilson and Herrnstein's (1985) discounting future consequences theory, Cornish and Clarke's (1986) situational decision-making theory, and Gottfredson and Hirschi's (1990) self-control theory. It distinguishes explicitly between the development of antisocial tendency and the occurrence of antisocial acts. The theory suggests that offending is the end result of a four-stage process: energising, directing, inhibiting, and decision making.

The main long-term energising factors that ultimately lead to variations in antisocial tendency are desires for material goods, status among intimates, and excitement. The main short-term energising factors that lead to variations in antisocial tendency are boredom, frustration, anger, and alcohol consumption. The desire for excitement may be greater among children from poorer families, perhaps because excitement is more highly valued by lower class people than by middle class ones, because poorer children think they lead more boring lives, or because poorer children are less able to postpone immediate gratification in favour of long-term goals (which could be linked to the emphasis in lower class culture on the concrete and present as opposed to the abstract and future).

In the directing stage, these motivations produce antisocial tendency if socially disapproved methods of satisfying them are habitually chosen. The methods chosen depend on maturation and behavioural skills (e.g. a 5-year-old would have difficulty stealing a car). Some people (e.g. children from poorer families) are less able to satisfy their desires for material goods, excitement, and social status by legal or socially approved methods, and so tend to choose illegal or socially disapproved methods. The relative inability of poorer children to achieve goals by legitimate methods could be because they tend to fail in school and tend to have erratic, low status employment histories. School failure in turn may often be a consequence of the unstimulating intellectual environment that lower class parents tend to provide for their children, and their lack of emphasis on abstract concepts.

In the inhibiting stage, antisocial tendencies can be inhibited by internalised beliefs and attitudes that have been built up in a social learning process as a result of a history of rewards and punishments. The belief that offending is wrong, or a strong conscience, tends to be built up if parents are in favour of legal norms, if they exercise close supervision over their children, and if they punish socially disapproved behaviour using love-oriented discipline. Antisocial tendency can also be inhibited by empathy, which may develop as a result of parental warmth and loving relationships. The belief that offending is legitimate, and anti-establishment attitudes generally, tend to be built up if children have been exposed to attitudes and behaviour favouring offending (e.g. in a modelling process), especially by members of their family, by their friends, and in their communities.

In the decision-making stage, which specifies the interaction between the individual and the environment, whether a person with a certain degree of antisocial tendency commits an antisocial act in a given situation depends on opportunities, costs and benefits, and on the subjective probabilities of the different outcomes. The costs and benefits include immediate situational factors such as the material goods that can be stolen and the likelihood and consequences of being caught by the police, as perceived by the individual. They also include social factors, such as likely disapproval by parents or spouses, and encouragement or reinforcement from peers. In general, people tend to make rational decisions. However, more impulsive people are less likely to consider the possible consequences of their actions, especially consequences that are likely to be long delayed.

Applying the theory to explain some of the results reviewed here, children from poorer families are likely to offend because they are less able to achieve their goals legally and because they value some goals (e.g. excitement) especially highly. Children with low intelligence are more likely to offend because they tend to fail in school and hence cannot achieve their goals legally. Impulsive children, and those with a poor ability to manipulate abstract concepts, are more likely to offend because they do not give sufficient consideration and weight to the possible consequences of offending. Children who are exposed to poor parental child-rearing behaviour, disharmony, or separation are likely to offend because they do not build up internal controls over socially disapproved behaviour, whereas children from criminal families and those with delinquent friends tend to build up anti-establishment attitudes and the belief that offending is justifiable. The whole process is self-perpetuating, in that poverty, low intelligence, and early school failure lead to truancy and a lack of educational qualifications, which in turn lead to low status jobs and periods of unemployment, both of which make it harder to achieve goals legitimately.

The onset of offending might be caused by increasing long-term motivation (an increasing need for material goods, status, and excitement), an increasing likelihood of choosing socially disapproved methods (possibly linked to a change in dominant social influences from parents to peers), increasing facilitating influences from peers, increasing opportunities (because of increasing freedom from parental control and increasing time spent with peers), or an increasing expected utility of offending (because of the greater importance of peer approval and lesser importance of parental disapproval). Desistance from offending could be linked to an increasing ability to satisfy desires by legal means (e.g. obtaining material goods through employment, obtaining sexual gratification through marriage), increasing inhibiting influences from spouses and cohabitees, decreasing opportunities (because of decreasing time spent with peers), and a decreasing expected utility of offending (because of the lesser importance of peer approval and the greater importance of disapproval from spouses and cohabitees).

The prevalence of offending may increase to a peak between ages 14 and 20 because boys (especially lower class school failures) have high impulsivity, high desires for excitement, material goods and social status between these ages, little chance of achieving their desires legally, and little to lose (because legal penalties are lenient and their intimates—male peers—often approve of offending). In contrast, after age 20, desires become attenuated or more realistic, there is more possibility of achieving these more limited goals legally, and the costs of offending are greater (because legal penalties are harsher and their intimates—wives or girlfriends—disapprove of offending).

CONCLUSIONS

A great deal has been learned in the last 20 years, particularly from longitudinal surveys, about risk factors for youth crime and other types of antisocial behaviour. The most important individual factors in offending are high impulsivity and low intelligence. Both of these may be linked to a poor ability to manipulate abstract concepts, which may also be related to other individual factors, such as egocentricity and low empathy. The most important family factors are poor parental supervision, harsh and erratic parental discipline, cold and rejecting parental attitude, separation from a parent, large family size, and having a criminal parent. These features are present before, during, and after criminal careers.

Most theories assume that there are consistent individual differences in an underlying construct such as criminal potential or antisocial personality. Most assume that hedonism or the pursuit of pleasure is the main energising factor. Most assume that there is internal inhibition of offending through the conscience or the strength of the bond to society, and that methods of child rearing used by parents are crucial in developing this in a socialisation process. However, where parents provide antisocial models, there can also be learning of antisocial behaviour. Most theories assume that the commission of offences in any situation essentially involves a rational decision in which the likely costs are weighed against the likely benefits. And most assume that impulsivity, or a poor ability to take account of and be influenced by the possible future consequence of offending, is an important factor.

Criminological theories should address developmental processes. The theory proposed here suggested that offending depended on energising, directing, inhibiting, and decision-making processes. In addition to explaining between-individual differences in the prevalence or frequency of offending, theories should explain within-individual changes: why people start offending, why they continue or escalate their offending, and why they stop offending. Because most is known about risk factors for prevalence and onset, research is needed on risk factors for escalation, duration, and desistance. Although the precise causal chains that link these factors with antisocial behaviour, and the ways in which these factors have independent, interactive, or sequential effects, are not known, it is clear that individuals at risk can be identified with reasonable accuracy.

Offending is one element of a larger syndrome of antisocial behaviour that arises in childhood and tends to persist into adulthood, with numerous different behavioural manifestations. However, although there is continuity over time in antisocial behaviour, changes are also occurring. It is commonly found that about half of a sample of antisocial children go on to become antisocial teenagers, and about half of antisocial teenagers go on to become antisocial adults. More research is needed on factors that vary within individuals and that predict these changes over time. Research is especially needed on changing behavioural manifestations and developmental sequences at different ages. More efforts should especially be made to identify factors that protect vulnerable children from developing into antisocial teenagers.

The stability of antisocial behaviour from childhood to adulthood suggests that delinquency prevention efforts should be implemented as early in a child's life as possible. Teenage pregnancy, substance use in pregnancy, and perinatal complications (including low birth weight), especially in conjunction with poverty, tend to be followed by a variety of undesirable outcomes, including low intelligence and attainment, hyperactivity and impulsivity, and child conduct problems, aggression, and delinquency. It is important to mount delinquency prevention programmes targeting these various risk factors, and to follow up the children into adolescence and adulthood to establish the long-term effects on delinquency and crime (Farrington, 1994b).

Because of the link between offending and numerous other social problems, any measure that succeeds in reducing crime will have benefits that go far beyond this. Any measure that reduces crime will probably also reduce alcohol abuse, drunk driving, drug abuse, sexual promiscuity, family violence, truancy, school failure, unemployment, marital disharmony, and divorce. It is clear that problem children tend to grow up into problem adults, and that problem adults tend to produce more problem children. Major efforts to tackle the roots of crime are urgently needed, especially those focusing on early childhood development.

REFERENCES

Achenbach, T. M. & Edelbrock, C. S. (1983). *Manual of the child behaviour checklist and revised child behaviour profile*. Burlington, VT: Department of Psychiatry, University of Vermont.

Barclay, G. C. (1990). The peak age of known offending by males. *Home Office Research Bulletin, 28*, 20–23.

Barclay, G. C. (1995). *The criminal justice system in England and Wales* (3rd edn). London: Home Office.

Bates, J. E., Bayles, K., Bennett, D. S., Ridge, B., & Brown, M. M. (1991). Origins of externalizing behaviour problems at 8 years of age. In D. J. Pepler & K. H. Rubin (Eds.), *The development and treatment of childhood aggression* (pp. 93–120). Hillsdale, NJ: Lawrence Erlbaum Associates Inc.

Blackburn, R. (1993). *The psychology of criminal conduct*. Chichester, UK: Wiley.

Blum, H. M., Boyle, M. H., & Offord, D. R. (1988). Single-parent families: Child psychiatric disorder and school performance. *Journal of the American Academy of Child and Adolescent Psychiatry, 27*, 214–219.

Bools, C., Foster, J., Brown, I., & Berg, I. (1990). The identification of psychiatric disorders in children who fail to attend school: A cluster analysis of a non-clinical population. *Psychological Medicine, 20*, 171–181.

Boswell, G. (1995). *Violent victims: The prevalence of abuse and loss in the lives of Section 53 offenders*. London: The Prince's Trust.

Bowling, B., Graham, J., & Ross, A. (1994). Self-reported offending among young people in England and Wales. In J. Junger-Tas, G-J. Terlouw, & M. W. Klein (Eds.), *Delinquent behaviour among young people in the western world* (pp. 42–64). Amsterdam: Kugler.

Boyle, M. H. & Offord, D. R. (1986). Smoking, drinking and use of illicit drugs among adolescents in Ontario: Prevalence, patterns of use and socio-demographic correlates. *Canadian Medical Association Journal, 135*, 1113–1121.

Brownfield, D. & Sorenson, A. M. (1994). Sibship size and sibling delinquency. *Deviant Behaviour, 15*, 45–61.

Cairns, R. B., Cairns, B. D., Neckerman, H. J., Gest, S., & Gariepy, J. L. (1988). Social networks and aggressive behaviour: Peer support or peer rejection? *Developmental Psychology, 24*, 815–823.

Catalano, R. F. & Hawkins, J. D. (1996). The social development model: A theory of antisocial behaviour. In J. D. Hawkins (Ed.), *Delinquency and crime: Current theories* (pp. 149–197). Cambridge, UK: Cambridge University Press.

Cloward, R. A. & Ohlin, L. E. (1960). *Delinquency and opportunity*. New York: Free Press.

Cohen, A. K. (1955). *Delinquent boys*. Glencoe, IL: Free Press.

Cornish, D. B. & Clarke, R. V. (Eds.) (1986). *The reasoning criminal*. New York: Springer.

Donovan, J. E., Jessor, R., & Costa, F. M. (1988). Syndrome of problem behaviour in adolescence: A replication. *Journal of Consulting and Clinical Psychology, 56*, 762–765.

Douglas, J. W. B., Ross, J. M., Hammond, W. A., & Mulligan, D. G. (1966). Delinquency and social class. *British Journal of Criminology, 6*, 294–302.

Elliott, D. S., Huizinga, D., & Ageton, S. S. (1985). *Explaining delinquency and drug use*. Beverly Hills, CA: Sage.

Elliott, D. S. & Menard, S. (1996). Delinquent friends and delinquent behaviour: Temporal and developmental patterns. In J. D. Hawkins (Ed.), *Delinquency and crime: Current theories* (pp. 28–67). Cambridge, UK: Cambridge University Press.

Ensminger, M. E., Kellam, S. G., & Rubin, B. R. (1983). School and family origins of delinquency. In K. T. Van Dusen & S. A. Mednick (Eds.), *Prospective studies of crime and delinquency* (pp. 73–97). Boston: Kluwer-Nijhoff.

Farley, F. H. & Sewell, T. (1976). Test of an arousal theory of delinquency: Stimulation-seeking in delinquent and non-delinquent black adolescents. *Criminal Justice and Behaviour, 3*, 315–320.

Farrington, D. P. (1972). Delinquency begins at home. *New Society, 21*, 495–497.

Farrington, D. P. (1973). Self-reports of deviant behaviour: Predictive and stable? *Journal of Criminal Law and Criminology, 64*, 99–110.

Farrington, D. P. (1978). The family backgrounds of aggressive youths. In L. Hersov, M. Berger, & D. Shaffer (Eds.), *Aggression and antisocial behaviour in childhood and adolescence* (pp. 73–93). Oxford: Pergamon.

Farrington, D. P. (1979). Environmental stress, delinquent behaviour, and convictions. In I. G. Sarason & C. D. Spielberger (Eds.), *Stress and anxiety* (Vol. 6, pp. 93–107). Washington, DC: Hemisphere.

Farrington, D. P. (1980). Truancy, delinquency, the home and the school. In L. Hersov & I. Berg (Eds.), *Out of school: Modern perspectives in truancy and school refusal* (pp. 49–63). Chichester, UK: Wiley.

Farrington, D. P. (1981). The prevalence of convictions. *British Journal of Criminology, 21*, 173–175.

Farrington, D. P. (1984). Measuring the natural history of delinquency and crime. In R. A. Glow (Ed.), *Advances in the behavioural measurement of children* (Vol. 1, pp. 217–263). Greenwich, CT: JAI Press.

Farrington, D. P. (1986a). Age and crime. In M. Tonry & N. Morris (Eds.), *Crime and justice* (Vol. 7, pp. 189–250). Chicago, IL: University of Chicago Press.

Farrington, D. P. (1986b). Stepping stones to adult criminal careers. In D. Olweus, J. Block, & M. R. Yarrow (Eds.), *Development of antisocial and prosocial behaviour* (pp. 359–384). New York: Academic Press.

Farrington, D. P. (1987a). Epidemiology. In H. C. Quay (Ed.), *Handbook of juvenile delinquency* (pp. 33–61). New York, Wiley.

Farrington, D. P. (1987b). Implications of biological findings for criminological research. In S. A. Mednick, T. E. Moffitt, & S. A. Stack (Eds.), *The causes of crime: New biological approaches* (pp. 42–64). Cambridge, UK: Cambridge University Press.

Farrington, D. P. (1989a). Early predictors of adolescent aggression and adult violence. *Violence and Victims, 4*, 79–100.

Farrington, D. P. (1989b). Self-reported and official offending from adolescence to adulthood. In M. W. Klein (Ed.), *Cross-national research in self-reported crime and delinquency* (pp. 399–423). Dordrecht, Netherlands: Kluwer.

Farrington, D. P. (1990a). Age, period, cohort, and offending. In D. M. Gottfredson & R. V. Clarke (Eds.), *Policy and theory in criminal justice: Contributions in honour of Leslie T. Wilkins* (pp. 51–75). Aldershot, UK: Avebury.

Farrington, D. P. (1990b). Implications of criminal career research for the prevention of offending. *Journal of Adolescence, 13*, 93–113.

Farrington, D. P. (1991a). Antisocial personality from childhood to adulthood. *The Psychologist, 4*, 389–394.

Farrington, D. P. (1991b). Childhood aggression and adult violence: Early precursors and later life outcomes. In D. J. Pepler & K. H. Rubin (Eds.) *The development and treatment of childhood aggression* (pp. 5–29). Hillsdale, NJ: Lawrence Erlbaum Associates Inc.

Farrington, D. P. (1992a). Criminal career research in the United Kingdom. *British Journal of Criminology, 32*, 521–536.

Farrington, D. P. (1992b). Explaining the beginning, progress and ending of antisocial behaviour from birth to adulthood. In J. McCord (Ed.), *Facts, frameworks and forecasts: Advances in criminological theory* (Vol. 3, pp. 253–286). New Brunswick, NJ: Transaction.

Farrington, D. P. (1992c). Juvenile delinquency. In J. C. Coleman (Ed.), *The school years* (2nd ed.) (pp. 123–163). London: Routledge.

Farrington, D. P. (1992d). Trends in English juvenile delinquency and their explanation. *International Journal of Comparative and Applied Criminal Justice, 16*, 151–163.

Farrington, D. P. (1993a). Childhood origins of teenage antisocial behaviour and adult social dysfunction. *Journal of the Royal Society of Medicine, 86*, 13–17.

Farrington, D. P. (1993b). Motivations for conduct disorder and delinquency. *Development and Psychopathology, 5*, 225–241.

Farrington, D. P. (1993c). Understanding and preventing bullying. In M. Tonry & N. Morris (Eds.), *Crime and justice* (Vol. 17, pp. 381–458). Chicago, IL: University of Chicago Press.

Farrington, D. P. (1994a). Childhood, adolescent and adult features of violent males. In L. R. Huesmann (Ed.), *Aggressive behaviour: Current perspectives* (pp. 215–240). New York: Plenum.

Farrington, D. P. (1994b). Early developmental prevention of juvenile delinquency. *Criminal Behaviour and Mental Health, 4*, 209–227.

Farrington, D. P. (1995). The development of offending and antisocial behaviour from childhood: Key findings from the Cambridge Study in Delinquent Development. *Journal of Child Psychology and Psychiatry, 36*, 929–964.

Farrington, D. P. (1996). Later life outcomes of truants in the Cambridge Study. In I. Berg & J. Nursten (Eds.), *Unwillingly to school* (4th ed.) (pp. 96–118). London: Gaskell.

Farrington, D. P., Barnes, G., & Lambert, S. (1996). The concentration of offending in families. *Legal and Criminological Psychology, 1*, 47–63.

Farrington, D. P., Berkowitz, L., & West, D. J. (1982). Differences between individual and group fights. *British Journal of Social Psychology, 21*, 323–333.

Farrington, D. P. & Burrows, J. N. (1993). Did shoplifting really decrease? *British Journal of Criminology, 33*, 57–69.

Farrington, D. P., Gallagher, B., Morley, L., St Ledger, R. J., & West, D. J. (1986). Unemployment, school leaving, and crime. *British Journal of Criminology, 26*, 335–356.

Farrington, D. P., Langan, P. A., & Wikstrom, P-O. H. (1994). Changes in crime and punishment in America, England and Sweden between the 1980s and the 1990s. *Studies in Crime and Crime Prevention, 3*, 104–131.

Farrington, D. P., Loeber, R., Elliott, D. S., Hawkins, J. D., Kandel, D. B., Klein, M. W., McCord, J., Rowe, D. C., & Tremblay, R. E. (1990a). Advancing knowledge about the onset of delinquency and crime. In B. B. Lahey & A. E. Kazdin (Eds.), *Advances in clinical child psychology* (Vol. 13, pp. 283–342). New York: Plenum.

Farrington, D. P., Loeber, R., & Van Kammen, W. B. (1990b). Long-term criminal outcomes of hyperactivity–impulsivity–attention deficit and conduct problems in childhood. In L. N. Robins & M. Rutter (Eds.) *Straight and devious pathways from childhood to adulthood* (pp. 62–81). Cambridge, UK: Cambridge University Press.

Farrington, D. P., Snyder, H. N., & Finnegan, T. A. (1988). Specialization in juvenile court careers. *Criminology, 26*, 461–487.

Farrington, D. P. & West, D. J. (1990). The Cambridge study in delinquent development: A long-term follow-up of 411 London males. In H. J. Kerner & G. Kaiser (Eds.), *Criminality: Personality, behaviour, life history* (pp. 115–138). Berlin: Springer.

Farrington, D. P. & West, D. J. (1993). Criminal, penal and life histories of chronic offenders: Risk and protective factors and early identification. *Criminal Behaviour and Mental Health, 3*, 492–523.

Farrington, D. P. & Wikstrom, P-O. H. (1994). Criminal careers in London and Stockholm: A cross-national comparative study. In E. G. M. Weitekamp & H. J. Kerner (Eds.), *Cross-national longitudinal research on human development and criminal behaviour* (pp. 65–89). Dordrecht, Netherlands: Kluwer.

Ferguson, T. (1952). *The young delinquent in his social setting*. London: Oxford University Press.

Fergusson, D. M., Horwood, L. J., & Lynskey, M. T. (1993). The effects of conduct disorder and attention deficit in middle childhood on offending and scholastic ability at age 13. *Journal of Child Psychology and Psychiatry, 34*, 899–916.

Fischer, D. G. (1984). Family size and delinquency. *Perceptual and Motor Skills, 58*, 527–534.

Furstenberg, F. F., Brooks-Gunn, J., & Morgan, S. P. (1987a). Adolescent mothers and their children in later life. *Family Planning Perspectives, 19*, 142–151.

Furstenberg, F. F., Brooks-Gunn, J., & Morgan, S. P. (1987b). *Adolescent mothers in later life*. Cambridge, UK: Cambridge University Press.

Gottfredson, M. & Hirschi, T. (1990). *A general theory of crime*. Stanford, CA: Stanford University Press.

Graham, J. (1988). *Schools, disruptive behaviour and delinquency*. London: Her Majesty's Stationery Office.

Graham, J. & Bowling, B. (1995). *Young people and crime*. London: Her Majesty's Stationery Office.

Hagell, A. & Newburn, T. (1994). *Persistent young offenders*. London: Policy Studies Institute.

Henry, B., Moffitt, T., Robins, L., Earls, F., & Silva, P. (1993). Early family predictors of child and adolescent antisocial behaviour: Who are the mothers of delinquents? *Criminal Behaviour and Mental Health, 3*, 97–118.

Hirschi, T. (1969). *Causes of delinquency*. Berkeley, CA: University of California Press.

Hirschi, T. & Hindelang, M. J. (1977). Intelligence and delinquency: A revisionist review. *American Sociological Review, 42*, 571–587.

Home Office (1990). *Criminal statistics, England and Wales, 1989*. London: HMSO.

Home Office (1993). *Criminal statistics, England and Wales, 1991*. London: HMSO.

Home Office (1994). *Criminal statistics, England and Wales, 1993*. London: HMSO.

Home Office (1995). *Criminal statistics, England and Wales, 1994*. London: HMSO.

Home Office Statistical Bulletin (1987). *Criminal careers of those born in 1953: Persistent offenders and desistance*. London: Home Office.

Home Office Statistical Bulletin (1995). *Criminal careers of those born between 1953 and 1973*. London: Home Office.

House of Commons, Home Affairs Committee (1993). *Juvenile offenders*. London: HMSO.

Irving, B. L. & MacKenzie, I. K. (1989). *Police interrogation*. London: Police Foundation.

Jessor, R. & Jessor, S. L. (1977). *Problem behaviour and psychosocial development*. New York: Academic Press.

Johnson, L. D., O'Malley, P. M., & Bachman, J. G. (1987). *National trends in drug use and related factors among American high school students and young adults, 1975–1986*. Rockville, MD: National Institute of Drug Abuse.

Klein, M. W. (1984). Offence specialization and versatility among juveniles. *British Journal of Criminology, 24*, 185–194.

Klinteberg, B. A., Andersson, T., Magnusson, D., & Stattin, H. (1993). Hyperactive behaviour in childhood as related to subsequent alcohol problems and violent offending: A longitudinal study of male subjects. *Personality and Individual Differences, 15*, 381–388.

Kolvin, I., Miller, F. J. W., Fleeting, M., & Kolvin, P. A. (1988). Social and parenting factors affecting criminal-offence rates: Findings from the Newcastle Thousand Family Study (1947–1980). *British Journal of Psychiatry, 152*, 80–90.

Kolvin, I., Miller, F. J. W., Scott, D. M., Gatzanis, S. R. M., & Fleeting, M. (1990). *Continuities of deprivation?* Aldershot, UK: Avebury.

LeBlanc, M. & Frenchette, M. (1989). *Male criminal activity from childhood through youth*. New York: Springer.

Leitner, M., Shapland, J., & Wiles, P. (1993). *Drug usage and drugs prevention*. London: HMSO.

Loeber, R. (1987). Behavioural precursors and accelerators of delinquency. In W. Buikhuisen & S. A. Mednick (Eds.), *Explaining criminal behaviour* (pp. 51–67). Leiden, Netherlands: Brill.

Loeber, R. & Dishion, T. (1983). Early predictors of male delinquency: A review. *Psychological Bulletin, 94*, 68–99.

Loeber, R., Green, S. M., Lahey, B. B., Christ, M. A. G., & Frick, P. J. (1992). Developmental sequences in the age of onset of disruptive child behaviours. *Journal of Child and Family Studies, 1*, 21–41.

Loeber, R. & LeBlanc, M. (1990). Toward a developmental criminology. In M. Tonry & N. Morris (Eds.), *Crime and justice* (Vol. 12, pp. 375–473). Chicago, IL: University of Chicago Press.

Loeber, R. & Stouthamer-Loeber, M. (1987). Prediction. In H. C. Quay (Ed.), *Handbook of juvenile delinquency* (pp. 325–382). New York: Wiley.

Loeber, R., Wung, P., Keenan, K., Giroux, B., Stouthamer-Loeber, M., & Van Kammen, W. B. (1993). Developmental pathways in disruptive child behaviour. *Development and Psychopathology, 5*, 101–132.

Lynam, D., Moffitt, T., & Stouthamer-Loeber, M. (1993). Explaining the relation between IQ and delinquency: Class, race, test motivation, school failure or self-control? *Journal of Abnormal Psychology, 102*, 187–196.

Maguin, E. & Loeber, R. (1996). Academic performance and delinquency. In M. Tonry (Ed.), *Crime and justice* (Vol. 20, pp. 145–264). Chicago, IL: University of Chicago Press.

Malinosky-Rummell, R. & Hansen, D. J. (1993). Long-term consequences of childhood physical abuse. *Psychological Bulletin, 114*, 68–79.

Mayhew, P. & Elliott, D. (1990). Self-reported offending, victimization, and the British Crime Survey. *Violence and Victims, 5*, 83–96.

McCord, J. (1977). A comparative study of two generations of native Americans. In R. F. Meier (Ed.), *Theory in criminology* (pp. 83–92). Beverly Hills, CA: Sage.

McCord, J. (1979). Some child-rearing antecedents of criminal behaviour in adult men. *Journal of Personality and Social Psychology, 37*, 1477–1486.

McCord, J. (1982). A longitudinal view of the relationship between paternal absence and crime. In J. Gunn & D. P. Farrington (Eds.), *Abnormal offenders, delinquency, and the criminal justice system* (pp. 113–128). Chichester, UK: Wiley.

McCord, J. (1991). Family relationships, juvenile delinquency, and adult criminality. *Criminology, 29*, 397–417.

McGee, R., Silva, P. A., & Williams, S. (1984). Perinatal, neurological, environmental and developmental characteristics of seven-year-old children with stable behaviour problems. *Journal of Child Psychology and Psychiatry, 25*, 573–586.

Mednick, S. A., Gabrielli, W. F., & Hutchings, B. (1983). Genetic influences on criminal behaviour: Evidence from an adoption cohort. In K. T. Van Dusen & S. A. Mednick (Eds.), *Prospective studies of crime and delinquency* (pp. 39–56). Boston, MA: Kluwer-Nijhoff.

Mischel, W., Shoda, Y., & Rodriguez, M. L. (1989). Delay of gratification in children. *Science, 244*, 933–938.

Moffitt, T. E. (1990). The neuropsychology of juvenile delinquency: A critical review. In M. Tonry & N. Morris (Eds.), *Crime and justice* (Vol. 12, pp. 99–169). Chicago, IL: University of Chicago Press.

Moffitt, T. E. (1993). Adolescence-limited and life-course-persistent antisocial behaviour: A developmental taxonomy. *Psychological Review, 100,* 674–701.

Moffitt, T. E. & Henry, B. (1989). Neuropsychological assessment of executive functions in self-reported delinquents. *Development and Psychopathology, 1,* 105–118.

Moffitt, T. E. & Silva, P. A. (1988a). IQ and delinquency: A direct test of the differential detection hypothesis. *Journal of Abnormal Psychology, 97,* 330–333.

Moffitt, T. E. & Silva, P. A. (1988b). Neuropsychological deficit and self-reported delinquency in an unselected birth cohort. *Journal of the American Academy of Child and Adolescent Psychiatry, 27,* 233–240.

Morash, M. & Rucker, L. (1989). An exploratory study of the connection of mother's age at childbearing to her children's delinquency in four data sets. *Crime and Delinquency, 35,* 45–93.

Mueller, C. W. & Parcel, T. L. (1981). Measures of socio-economic status: Alternatives and recommendations. *Child Development, 52,* 13–30.

Newson, J. & Newson, E. (1989). *The extent of parental physical punishment in the UK.* London: Approach.

Newson, J., Newson, E., & Adams, M. (1993). The social origins of delinquency. *Criminal Behaviour and Mental Health, 3,* 19–29.

Parker, J. G. & Asher, S. R. (1987). Peer relations and later personal adjustment: Are low accepted children at risk? *Psychological Bulletin, 102,* 357–389.

Pearson, F. S. & Weiner, N. A. (1985). Toward an integration of criminological theories. *Journal of Criminal Law and Criminology, 76,* 116–150.

Polk, K., Alder, C., Bazemore, G., Blake, G., Cordray, S., Coventry, G., Galvin, J., & Temple, M. (1981). *Becoming adult.* Final Report to the National Institute of Mental Health, Washington, DC.

Power, M. J., Alderson, M. R., Phillipson, C. M., Shoenberg, E., & Morris, J. N. (1967). Delinquent schools? *New Society, 10,* 542–543.

Pulkkinen, L. (1988). Delinquent development: Theoretical and empirical considerations. In M. Rutter (Ed.), *Studies of psychosocial risk* (pp. 184–199). Cambridge, UK: Cambridge University Press.

Reiss, A. J. (1988). Co-offending and criminal careers. In M. Tonry & N. Morris (Eds.), *Crime and justice* (Vol. 10, pp. 117–170). Chicago, IL: University of Chicago Press.

Reiss, A. J. & Farrington, D. P. (1991). Advancing knowledge about co-offending: Results from a prospective longitudinal survey of London males. *Journal of Criminal Law and Criminology, 82,* 360–395.

Richman, N., Stevenson, J., & Graham, P. (1985). Sex differences in the outcome of preschool behaviour problems. In A. R. Nicol (Ed.), *Longitudinal studies in child psychology and psychiatry* (pp. 75–89). Chichester, UK: Wiley.

Riley, D. & Shaw, M. (1985). *Parental supervision and juvenile delinquency.* London: HMSO.

Robins, L. N. (1979). Sturdy childhood predictors of adult outcomes: Replications from longitudinal studies. In J. E. Barrett, R. M. Rose, & G. L. Klerman (Eds.), *Stress and mental disorder* (pp. 219–235). New York: Raven.

Robins, L. N. (1986). Changes in conduct disorder over time. In D. C. Farran & J. D. McKinney (Eds.), *Risk in intellectual and psychosocial development* (pp. 227–259). New York: Academic Press.

Robins, L. N. (1991). Conduct disorder. *Journal of Child Psychology and Psychiatry, 32,* 193–212.

Robins, L. N. & Ratcliff, K. S. (1978). Risk factors in the continuation of childhood antisocial behaviour into adulthood. *International Journal of Mental Health 7,* 96–116.

Robins, L. N. & Ratcliff, K. S. (1980). Childhood conduct disorders and later arrest. In L. N. Robins, P. J. Clayton, & J. K. Wing (Eds.), *The social consequences of psychiatric illness* (pp. 248–263). New York: Brunner/Mazel.

Robins, L. N. West, P. J., & Herjanic, B. L. (1975). Arrests and delinquency in two generations: A study of black urban families and their children. *Journal of Child Psychology and Psychiatry*, *16*, 125–140.

Robins, L. N. & Wish, E. (1977). Childhood deviance as a developmental process: A study of 223 urban black men from birth to 18. *Social Forces*, *56*, 448–473.

Roff, J. D. & Wirt, R. D. (1984). Childhood aggression and social adjustment as antecedents of delinquency. *Journal of Abnormal Child Psychology*, *12*, 111–126.

Rose, S. L., Rose, S. A., & Feldman, J. F. (1989). Stability of behaviour problems in very young children. *Development and Psychopathology*, *1*, 5–19.

Rutter, M. & Giller, H. (1983). *Juvenile delinquency*. Harmondsworth, UK: Penguin.

Rutter, M., Maughan, B., Mortimore, P., & Ouston, J. (1979). *Fifteen thousand hours*. London: OpenBooks.

Satterfield, J. H. (1987). Childhood diagnostic and neurophysiological predictors of teenage arrest rates: An 8-year prospective study. In S. A. Mednick, T. E. Moffitt, & S. A. Stack (Eds.), *The causes of crime: New biological approaches* (pp. 146–167). Cambridge, UK: Cambridge University Press.

Schweinhart, L. J., Barnes, H. V., & Weikart, D. P. (1993). *Significant benefits*. Ypsilanti, MI: High/Scope.

Short, J. F. & Nye, F. I. (1957). Reported behaviour as a criterion of deviant behaviour. *Social Problems*, *5*, 207–213.

Snyder, H. N. & Sickmund, M. (1995). *Juvenile offenders and victims: A national report*. Washington, DC: Office of Juvenile Justice and Delinquency Prevention.

Snyder, H. N., Sickmund, M., & Poe-Yamagata, E. (1996). *Juvenile offenders and victims: 1996 update on violence*. Washington, DC: Office of Juvenile Justice and Delinquency Prevention.

Spivack, G., Marcus, J., & Swift, M. (1986). Early classroom behaviours and later misconduct. *Developmental Psychology*, *22*, 124–131.

Stattin, H. & Klackenberg-Larsson, I. (1993). Early language and intelligence development and their relationship to future criminal behaviour. *Journal of Abnormal Psychology*, *102*, 369–378.

Stattin, H. & Magnusson, D. (1991). Stability and change in criminal behaviour up to age 30. *British Journal of Criminology*, *31*, 327–346.

Stein, K. B., Sarbin, T. R., & Kulik, J. A. (1968). Future time perspective: Its relation to the socialization process and the delinquent role. *Journal of Consulting and Clinical Psychology*, *32*, 257–264.

Steinhausen, H-C., Willms, J., & Spohr, H-L. (1993). Long-term psychopathological and cognitive outcome of children with fetal alcohol syndrome. *Journal of the American Academy of Child and Adolescent Psychiatry*, *32*, 990–994.

Streissguth, A. P. (1986). Smoking and drinking during pregnancy and offspring learning disabilities: A review of the literature and development of a research strategy. In M. Lewis (Ed.), *Learning disabilities and prenatal risk* (pp. 28–67). Urbana, IL: University of Illinois Press.

Tarling, R. (1993). *Analysing offending*. London: HMSO.

Taylor, E. A. (1986). Childhood hyperactivity. *British Journal of Psychiatry*, *149*, 562–573.

Thornberry, T. P., Lizotte, A. J., Krohn, M. D., Farnworth, M., & Jang, S. J. (1994). Delinquent peers, beliefs and delinquent behaviour: A longitudinal test of interactional theory. *Criminology*, *32*, 47–83.

Trad, P. V. (1993). Substance abuse in adolescent mothers: Strategies for diagnosis, treatment and prevention. *Journal of Substance Abuse Treatment, 10*, 421–431.

Trasler, G. B. (1962). *The explanation of criminality*. London: Routledge & Kegan Paul.

Tremblay, R. E., LeBlanc, M., & Schwartzman, A. E. (1988). The predictive power of first-grade peer and teacher ratings of behaviour: Sex differences in antisocial behaviour and personality at adolescence. *Journal of Abnormal Child Psychology, 16*, 571–583.

Venables, P. H. & Raine, A. (1987). Biological theory. In B. J. McGurk, D. M. Thornton, & M. Williams (Eds.), *Applying psychology to imprisonment* (pp. 3–27). London: HMSO.

Wadsworth, M. (1979). *Roots of delinquency*. London: Martin Robertson.

Walsh, A., Petee, T. A., & Beyer, J. A. (1987). Intellectual imbalance and delinquency: Comparing high verbal and high performance IQ delinquents. *Criminal Justice and Behaviour, 14*, 370–379.

Warr, M. (1993). Parents, peers and delinquency. *Social Forces, 72*, 247–264.

Wells, L. E. & Rankin, J. H. (1991). Families and delinquency: A meta-analysis of the impact of broken homes. *Social Problems, 38*, 71–93.

West, D. J. & Farrington, D. P. (1973). *Who becomes delinquent?* London: Heinemann.

West, D. J. & Farrington, D. P. (1977). *The delinquent way of life*. London: Heinemann.

White, H. R., Labouvie, E. W. & Bates, M. E. (1985). The relationship between sensation seeking and delinquency: A longitudinal analysis. *Journal of Research in Crime and Delinquency, 22*, 197–211.

White, J. L., Moffitt, T. E., Caspi, A., Bartusch, D. J., Needles, D. J. & Stouthamer-Loeber, M. (1994). Measuring impulsivity and examining its relationship to delinquency. *Journal of Abnormal Psychology, 103*, 192–205.

White, J. L., Moffitt, T. E., Earls, F., Robins, L. N., & Silva, P. A. (1990). How early can we tell? Predictors of child conduct disorder and adolescent delinquency. *Criminology, 28*, 507–533.

Widom, C. S. (1989). The cycle of violence. *Science, 244*, 160–166.

Wikström, P. O. (1987). *Patterns of crime in a birth cohort*. Stockholm: Department of Sociology, University of Stockholm.

Wilson, H. (1980). Parental supervision: A neglected aspect of delinquency. *British Journal of Criminology, 20*, 203–235.

Wilson, H. (1987). Parental supervision re-examined. *British Journal of Criminology, 27*, 275–301.

Wilson, J. Q. & Herrnstein, R. J. (1985). *Crime and human nature*. New York: Simon & Schuster.

Wolfgang, M. E., Figlio, R. M., & Sellin, T. (1972). *Delinquency in a birth cohort*. Chicago, IL: University of Chicago Press.

Wolfgang, M. E., Thornberry, T. P., & Figlio, R. M. (1987). *From boy to man, from delinquency to crime*. Chicago, IL: University of Chicago Press.

Zimring, F. E. (1981). Kids, groups and crime: Some implications of a well-known secret. *Journal of Criminal Law and Criminology, 72*, 867–885.

15 Concluding remarks

Steven Muncer
University of Teesside, Middlesbrough, UK
Anne Campbell
University of Durham, Durham, UK

In writing this final chapter we are aware of the importance of tying together the previous chapters but equally aware of the difficulty of doing so. Rowe's chapter (and to some extent MacDonald's and Campbell's) with its nativist position stands in marked opposition to those who argue for the importance of environment. Perhaps the clearest and starkest statement of that dichotomy is presented by Jahoda when he argues that most cross-cultural psychologists would agree with Vernon (1969, p. 251) that genetic effects on intelligence: "are probably small and we have no means of proving them". Although we would be delighted to reconcile these two different views we feel that any attempt to do so would require serious distortion of the two arguments.

THE QUESTION OF CULTURE

We find ourselves sceptical of the importance of cross-cultural differences in development for the following reasons. First, in Jahoda's fascinating account of various child-rearing practices around the world, we were struck by the many similarities in techniques rather than differences. To give one example from the Punan Bah society:

> [A small boy had] prematurely assumed that he had the rights of an adult man. Note that no one lectured him about this in so many words ("You are still a small boy", as we probably would have done). Instead, the grandfather

treated him as though he were an important personage, which was obviously absurd, and the boy reacted with shame and fury at being humiliated by laughter, a powerful sanction in this culture.

This strikes us as a fairly commonplace use of sarcasm by a child rearer, perhaps not recommended by child-centred parenting manuals, but frequently used in the West.

Jahoda also criticises mainstream accounts of intelligence for failing to attend to cross-cultural differences. Here again we find ourselves struck by cross-cultural similarity rather than difference. For example, the Kpelle tribespeople when asked to classify objects do so according to use rather than by size, shape, or common taxonomic membership such as fruit or instrument (Cole, Gay, Glick, & Sharp, 1971). They sort fruit and knife together because a knife would be required to cut fruit. This is taken to mean that intelligence is indexed by different sorting methods in different cultures. Surely the more striking fact is that in all cultures classification is a critical component of intelligent thought and action. It is true that lay people perceive their own sorting criterion to be superior (as when the Kpelle are asked how a stupid person would sort these objects, they do it by Western criteria). But the superior value attached by members of a community to their own patterns of behaviour should not blind psychologists to the over-arching commonality of categories as a fundamental aspect of intelligent thought.

Second, as Rowe points out some cross-cultural differences may be caused by genetic factors as evidenced by Kagan et al.'s (1994) demonstration of differences in behavioural reactivity between Asian and Caucasian infants as young as four months old. Similarly, Tu and Israel (1995) show that a genetic inability to breakdown alcohol (common among Japanese) can have a dramatic effect on the likelihood of drinking. Here we have clear examples of racially variable genes constraining culture. More common, however, is the case of species-typical genes constraining universal culture. This position has been argued forcibly by Lumsden and Wilson (1981) in their famous dictum "genes hold culture on a leash" and by Durham (1991) who suggests that a cultural practice that did not accord with universal primary values (themselves a product of biological imperatives for survival and reproduction) would be doomed to extinction. The challenge to cross-cultural psychology posed by a co-evolutionary approach is to locate both human universals and their unique expression in a particular ecological niche. Marriage or raising children may both be universal but their form may vary as a function of local ecological or economic pressures. The attraction of discovering cultural differences has perhaps been too strong. The inferential leap from such differences to a denial of underlying universality and an assertion of culture as the sole causal agent has been made too easily.

We conceive of culture as socially transmitted knowledge (as distinct from knowledge gained by individual trial-and-error learning or "off-line" thought experiments). This knowledge may be technological (how to irrigate a field, how to use a personal computer), social (who is feuding with whom), interpretative (what a given action means in a particular culture) or evaluative (whether specific forms of behaviour are honoured or punished). Knowledge which remains in the culture pool is knowledge that has brought with it advantages to the knower (or at least has not conferred significant disadvantages) in the ecological niche in which it exists. We do not deny the importance of this view of culture, but we query whether culture is free to operate independently of its members' best interests. These best interests are generally related to survival and reproductive concerns that are by nature universal.

Third, although cross-cultural research may provide a useful descriptive function of the "how unlike the life of our own dear Queen" type, it does not presently offer unambiguous evidence of the importance of socialisation. To show, for example, that two cultures treat their children differently is not to show that their children's behaviour is shaped or even altered by the practice. For example, in no recorded society is female crime rate as high as that of males. Because this is true everywhere, it cannot be the case that differences between cultures in the way they socialise sons and daughters have an impact on criminality between the sexes. We need much better evidence of two things: first, that parental socialisation is reliably correlated with child outcome; and second, that there is a unique effect of socialisation practice independent of parents' and children's shared genes.

THE QUESTION OF SHARED ENVIRONMENT

Historical changes in rates of various social indicators pose an equally serious challenge for geneticists. Divorce has increased (and some of its effects are noted by McGurk and Soriano), crime rates change (see Farrington's chapter), and there have been technological advances that change the way in which we spend our leisure time (see Crook's chapter). Such developments can hardly be explained by changes in the genetic base of the population, but are likely to have a significant effect on the way in which children are socialised. An examination of societal and cultural changes over time and their effect on both the socialisation of the child and adult would be of great importance.

In this respect, Rowe again offers an impressive challenge with his explanation of divorce. He acknowledges that the rise in divorce rate has no genetic cause but argues that the easier availability of divorce means that more of those with the predisposing inherited characteristics (low agreeableness and high impulsivity; Loehlin, 1992) will be inclined to divorce.

(It is important to note here that McGue and Lykken, 1992, estimate the heritability of divorce to be about 0.5 with almost no effect of shared environment and also to remember that the divorce rate in America is approaching 50%.) Rowe also argues that the divorce itself will have little effect on any children of the marriage, and cites Cherlin et al.'s (1991) research which shows that children's behaviour problems often precede by several years the actual divorce. This latter argument accords with Rowe's central thesis that shared environmental effects or the impact of parent's on children's later development is minimal. It is this view that we will now attempt to challenge.

It should not be surprising that children's behaviour problems precede divorce as it would be usual for parents to show some higher levels of conflict before divorce. McGurk and Soriano provide a detailed account of the effects of divorce on both parents and children. They note that a longitudinal study by Kurtz and Derevensky (1994) identified three consistent findings. First, that children invariably experience short-term adverse effects; second, that age, gender, and a number of other factors influence post-divorce adjustment; and third, that childhood depression, conduct, and behavioural disorders are the most frequent diagnoses five years after divorce. This evidence suggests that divorce does have immediate and also some longer-lasting consequences, suggesting that there is an impact on family environment.

Twin studies have, however, suggested that within a normal range of child rearing, parents have little impact on children *over the longer term*. It is the time scale used by behavioural geneticists that we query. We would argue that parental treatment has important immediate effects. They may last only three minutes or three months but the fact remains that parents are usually more preoccupied with effecting an immediate change in the child's behaviour ("Any more screaming and you go straight to bed") than in engineering an enduring change in personality. To take an example, let us suppose that a father teaches his child how to ride a bike. This has effects (short-term probably) on a child's physical confidence, ability to get to friends' houses, and consequently on form and frequency of play. Admittedly, bike riding at age eight is unlikely to make him more or less neurotic, extroverted, agreeable, open, conscientious, or intelligent at age 30, but it will affect the child's behaviour in the short term. What we are emphasising is that the motivation for and impact of child rearing is in the "here and now", not in the future—a suggestion also made in rather different ways by Shotter and Emler in this volume. Shotter suggests that the static and retrospective study of children's behaviour should be replaced by a focus on moment-to-moment dynamics and Emler suggests that the importance of moral reasoning as a social instrument used in the day-to-day interactions between children should be investigated.

Let us pass over the extended time frame of behaviour genetic studies and ignore for a moment some worries about methodology (Wachs, 1983). Instead, let us examine the logic and consequences of the argument for the differential impact of unshared and shared environment because it seems to us to posit some very unlikely things. The child envisaged by behaviour geneticists is almost impervious to learning from experience. Recall Rowe's anecdote about the twins—although one was reared by a sloppy mother and the other a meticulous mother they both in adulthood manifested similar levels of obsessive neatness. Now it is true that we have no way of knowing the extent to which the two mothers attempted to alter the child's behaviour and perhaps they did not—leaving the child free to express her neat disposition. But a lack of flexibility of response to reward and punishment implied by many behavioural geneticists would be a grossly maladaptive pattern of behaviour.

Furthermore, how can we align this inflexibility with the fact that children's behaviour can be altered in the short term? For example, Kutnick and Manson describe how using a variant of social skills training they were able to modify the behaviour of some children making them less antisocial. Presumably, behavioural geneticists would argue that although short-term changes in a closed environment may be possible, the changes will be eroded by genetically driven "niche picking" when the child is free to choose his/her own environments and behaviours. Nonetheless, if children's behaviour can be altered where reinforcement contingencies are artificially maintained in the classroom, it is unclear why similar effects should not occur in the home. The evidence from twin studies is very compelling yet seems to fly in the face of common sense. One might be tempted to view behaviour genetic results in the same way as the mathematical proof that hummingbirds cannot fly, were it not for the fact that few studies of any type have found significant effects of parental behaviour on the later development of children (Maccoby & Martin, 1983).

Twin studies tell us of the negligible effect of shared environment (experiences which are common to children in the same household including shared parental treatment) and the powerful impact of unshared environment (experiences that are unique to one child including particular relationships unshared by their siblings). Now let us apply this to a particular child. We are told that only unshared environment will shape her future personality whereas shared environment will have no effect. Hence, a pattern of constant friction with her mother will have an affect on her—provided that her mother does not show a similar irritability with her sister. Or to use an example from Rowe, an "inspired teacher" may have an impact on her but an equally inspired parent with whom a child spends considerably more time will not—if her siblings also benefit from the parent's charisma. For this to occur, children must have some way of discriminating which forces to attend to in the environment. But the experience of the child is seamless. The people with whom she interacts do not come ready labelled as agents of shared or unshared environment nor are the interactions conveniently compartmentalised as formative or trivial.

Rowe cites Harris (1995) as offering a possible solution with her emphasis on the role of the peer group (see also Campbell's chapter). Harris (1995) accepts the lack of effect of parental influence on children's later behaviour and, instead, argues that we have searched in the wrong place for the child's shared environment. What makes children similar is their shared peer group which is the principle form of socialisation and cultural transmission. As she puts it: "What group socialisation theory implies is that children would develop onto the same sort of adults if we left them in their homes, their schools, their neighbourhoods and their cultural or subcultural groups but switched all the parents around". Between group processes (in-group favouritism and out-group hostility) pull members closer together while pushing groups apart, and within group processes (status and social comparison) create differences between individuals (see Hartup and MacDonald's chapters for a more detailed discussion of the impact of friends and peers). Thus, the source of similarities and differences among children is not in the home but among the child's peers. Although same-sex monozygotic twins and siblings share the same fraction of genes, the latter are more alike because, being the same age, they are more likely to share the same peer group. A group socialisation explanation of child development also makes sense from an evolutionary perspective as it is clearly important that the child's behaviour is modified by the cohort that will represent their allies, rivals, and mates in future years.

Harris uses her theory to offer an explanation for the effect of divorce on children. After divorce, 38 per cent of custodial mothers move to a new residence, usually in a poorer neighbourhood (McLanahan & Booth, 1989), and thus the child loses his peer group. A study of the effect of family relocation found that children whose families had moved frequently were 77 per cent more likely to have multiple behavioural problems (Wood, Haflon, Scarlatta, Newacheck, & Nessim, 1993). Hence, the problems of children after divorce may well be caused by a disruption in their peer environment rather than their home environment.

THE QUESTION OF FOCUS

Perhaps the most transcending distinction between the various approaches outlined in this book lies in the conceptualisation of what is to be explained. Behaviour geneticists, evolutionary psychologists, and constructivists as well as differing in their selection of causal variables also differ in the form of behaviour they want to explain.

Behaviour geneticists have focused the vast majority of their research effort in explaining *personality traits* and to a lesser extent social attitudes. They have often assumed an unproblematic isomorphism of questionnaire scores and overt behaviour. It is apparently taken for granted that two people who have the same extroversion score will behave identically. The conceptual and vocabulary shift from "personality" to "behaviour" is largely unexamined. Yet the correlation between personality variables and behaviour is scarcely above 0.3 (Hartshorne & May, 1928; Mischel, 1968). If we take personality to consist of the "Big Five" which appear to show substantial heritability and suggest that overall they have a heritability of 0.7 (which would be a generous estimate), this would still mean that 0.7 × 0.3, or 21% of any given behaviour was attributable to genetic factors. Some, like Epstein (1979) have argued that higher correlations between personality and behaviour can be achieved by item aggregation—that multiple measures of both personality and behaviour can reveal stronger relationships. This effect is achieved by increasing the reliability of the measurement by summing over (and so eliminating) situational differences (Campbell, Bibel, & Muncer, 1985; Campbell, Muncer, & Bibel, 1987; Ross & Nisbett, 1991). However, when measurement reliability is increased by other means there is still evidence for substantial cross-situational variability (Bukowski, Ferber-Goff, & Newcomb, 1990). It is precisely such situational differences that are at the heart of many developmental psychologists' interests. The same argument applies with equal force to social attitudes that have shown the same pattern of weak associations with behaviour. It is important to remember that if we accept the heritability estimates that have been given, the ability to predict behaviour in a given situation will be quite low.

Evolutionary psychologists are frequently concerned with adaptive *behavioural strategies*. Life presents us with problems which must be solved but rather than inventing solutions *de novo* in each situation, humans capitalise on evolved dispositions that guide their behaviour in ways that were (and in many cases still are) adaptive. Much of children's development is driven by such evolved processes that economise on time-consuming and costly trial-and-error learning (such as language acquisition devices and attachment). In another example, preference for same-sex peers is not taught to children by adults but appears spontaneously and brings with it both ecologically sensitive sex-role learning and a later romantic attraction to the opposite sex (Bem, 1995). Too often, however, evolutionary psychologists have been content simply to document behavioural patterns and identify their putative adaptive function. Two key elements are missing from such an analysis. First, by what psychological mechanisms are these behaviours mediated? If they are to avoid invoking mysterious "whisperings within" they must consider how adaptive behaviours may be linked to dopaminergic reward systems, to emotions, to genetically specified neurogenesis, or to specific modular architecture (such as theory of mind). They must also exercise caution about the distinction between adapted and adaptive. Where we see evidence of universality, it is reasonable to look for evolutionary function and associated psychological mechanisms. When a behaviour goes to fixation and is present in every child, it is likely that it reflects a past evolutionary advantage to its possessors. However, it is a far cry from this hypothesis to the assertion that it is currently adaptive. We cannot say whether current patterns of behaviour are adaptive or not because we are not in a position to know the consequences in terms of reproductive success for the bearers (nor shall we be for several thousand years). We should tread even more carefully where behaviours have not gone to fixation. The presence of variance in social behavioural traits may indicate that such variance is a useful hedge against an unknown future but it may equally argue that individual differences are unrelated to inclusive fitness—that they are truly epiphenomenal.

Mainstream social developmentalists have been principally concerned with the description of social *competencies* and their consequences. In this volume both Meerum Terwogt and Stegge and Hay and Demetriou chart the developmental sequence along which children move in their appreciation of their own and others' mental states. The emphasis is firmly on the time course of development, on children's capabilities, and on the implications for social interaction. Hartup emphasises the reciprocal nature of friendship and social abilities which inform and enhance one another. Shotter also highlights the social competence of the child as it is expressed in the everyday management of interactions. As all these contributors note, a narrow focus on competence is not without dangers. It threatens to turn the study of social development into an obsession with method—the invention of new and more sensitive measures of what children are able to do. It also threatens to draw us away from the child as an intrinsically social being in favour of a view of the child as a detached social problem-solver. Theory of mind research, springing as it did from a desire to explain the peculiarly asocial world of the autistic, has perhaps in its methods and theorising given inadequate attention to the spontaneously social nature of our species. What children do in the real world may be far in advance of what they can do under laboratory conditions where experimental control of extraneous variables robs the child of sources of information that would normally shape his/her response.

In addition, competence studies often become preoccupied with smaller scale cause-and-effect relations (e.g. Does empathy lead to more prosocial behaviour?), but shying away from any grand causal explanation of the sequence in its entirety. Hence, less attention is accorded to the possible epigenetic or cultural foundations of such capabilities. One notable exception is the debate on theory of mind as a modular evolutionary adaptation. It is not hard to see that, in a social species, the ability to understand that human action is driven by others' mental representations of the world might confer a significant advantage in understanding, controlling, and predicting other people's behaviour. Debate currently focuses on whether such an ability is a distinctively specified module unfolding in response to social stimuli (Leslie, 1987), whether the innate component is a more general ability to create theories from evidence (Gopnik & Wellman, 1994), or whether children's privileged access to their own mental states is employed as a model for understanding other minds (Harris, 1994).

The areas we have discussed—cross-cultural psychology, evolutionary psychology, behaviour genetics, and mainstream developmental psychology—identify different forms of behaviour or knowledge that are deemed to require explanation, employ different explanatory variables, differ in their understanding of causality, and look to different time scales (ranging from minutes to thousands of years). The question that seems too big to ask but which must be answered is: What is the relationship between evolutionarily adapted problem-solving strategies, genetic predisposition, cultural and social practices, and developmentally sequenced competencies? Some tentative links can be identified. Evolutionary psychology can identify species-typical competencies or behaviours and consider the adaptive problems they may have solved (e.g. *Boys exhibit more competitive aggression than girls because dominance is more central to male reproductive success*). These competencies unfold in a particular cultural context in which ecological constraints may affect how they are valued and consequently regulated or enhanced (e.g. *Where boys are denied access to culturally approved ways of achieving status, they will employ aggression and develop counter-cultural values supporting it*). Individual differences may still have to be explained both in terms of function and in terms of their source (e.g. *Aggression is variable and has a substantial heritable component but its form may yet be affected by peer group membership*). The interrelation of these various competencies as they unfold ontogenetically may still be the major preoccupation of developmentalists (e.g. *Between sex similarity of competitiveness in infancy, gives way to sex differences via a reduction in girls' levels of overt aggression*). Rather than seeking to subsume one explanation under another, the first task is to find a common language in which to communicate. To achieve this goal we need to encourage more than we do at present, and aim for a truly broad understanding and appreciation of developmental influences.

REFERENCES

Bem, D. (1995). Exotic becomes erotic: A developmental theory of sexual orientation. *Psychological Review, 103*, 320–335.

Bukowski, W. M., Ferber-Goff, J., & Newcomb, A. F. (1990). The stability and coherence of single-item measures of antisocial behaviour. *British Journal of Social Psychology, 29*, 171–180.

Campbell, A., Bibel, D., & Muncer, S. J. (1985). Predicting our own aggression: Person, subculture or situation? *British Journal of Social Psychology, 24*, 169–180.

Campbell, A., Muncer, S. J., & Bibel, D. (1987). For disaggregation: A reply to Rushton and Erdle. *British Journal of Social Psychology, 26*, 90–92.

Cherlin, A. J., Furstenberg, F. F., Chase-Lansdale, P. L., Kiernan, K. E., Robins, P. K., Morrison, D. R., & Teitler, J. O. (1991). Longitudinal studies of effects of divorce on children in Great Britain and the United States. *Science, 252*, 1386–1389.

Cole, M., Gay, J., Glick, J., & Sharp, D. W. (1971). *The cultural context of learning and thinking*. New York: Basic Books.

Durham, W. (1991). *Coevolutionary theory*. Stanford, CA: Stanford University Press.

Epstein, S. (1979). The stability of behavior: 1. On predicting most of the people much of the time. *Journal of Personality and Social Psychology, 37*, 1097–1126.

Gopnik, A. & Wellman, H. M. (1994). The theory theory. In L. A. Hirschfield and S. A. Gelman (Eds.), *Mapping the mind* (pp. 257–294). Cambridge, UK: Cambridge University Press.

Harris, J. R. (1995). Where is the child's environment? A group socialization theory of development. *Psychological Review, 102*, 458–489.

Harris, P. L. (1994). Thinking by children and scientists: False analogies and neglected similarities. In L. A. Hirschfield and S. A. Gelman (Eds.), *Mapping the mind* (pp. 294–316). Cambridge, UK: Cambridge University Press.

Hartshorne, H. & May, A. (1928). *Studies in the nature of character: Vol. 1. Studies in deceit*. New York: Macmillan.

Kagan, J., Arcus, D., Snidman, N., Feng, W. Y., Hendler, J., & Greene, S. (1994). Reactivity in infants: A cross-national comparison. *Developmental Psychology, 30*, 342–345.

Kurtz, L. & Derevensky, J. (1994). Family configuration and maternal employment: Effects on family environment and children's outcomes. *Journal of Divorce and Remarriage, 22*, 137–154.

Leslie, A. M. (1987). Pretense and representation: The origins of "theory of mind". *Psychological Review, 94*, 412–426.

Loehlin, J. C. (1992). *Genes and environment in personality development*. Newbury Park, CA: Sage.

Lumsden, C. J. & Wilson, E. O. (1981). *Genes, mind and culture*. Cambridge, MA: Harvard University Press.

Maccoby, E. E. & Martin, J. A. (1983). Socialization in the context of the family: Parent–child interaction. In P. H. Mussen (Series Ed.) and E. M. Hetherington (Vol. Ed.), *Handbook of child psychology: Vol. 4. Socialisation. Personality and social development* (4th ed., pp. 1–101). New York: Wiley.

McGue, M. & Lykken, D. T. (1992). Genetic influence on risk of divorce. *Psychological Science, 3*, 368–373.

McLanahan, S. & Booth, K. (1989). Mother-only families: Problems, prospects and politics. *Journal of Marriage and the Family, 51*, 557–608.

Mischel, W. (1968). *Personality and assessment*. New York: Wiley.

Ross, L. & Nisbett, R. E. (1991). *The person and the situation: Perspectives of social psychology*. New York: McGraw Hill.

Tu, G., & Israel, Y. (1995). Alcohol consumption by Orientals in North America is predicted largely by a single gene. *Behavior Genetics, 25*, 59–65.

Vernon, P. (1969). *Intelligence and cultural environment*. London: Methuen.

Wachs, T. D. (1983). The use and abuse of environment in genetic research. *Child Development, 54*, 416–423.

Wood, D., Haflon, N., Scarlatta, D., Newacheck, P., & Nessim, S. (1993). Impact of family relocation on children's growth, development, school function, and behaviour. *Journal of the American Medical Association, 270*, 1334–1338.

Author Index

Subject Index